INTRODUCTION TO ENGINEERING PROGRAMMING

Solving Problems with Algorithms

INTRODUCTION TO ENGINEERING PROGRAMMING

Solving Problems with Algorithms

JAMES PAUL HOLLOWAY

University of Michigan

John Wiley & Sons, Inc.

ACQUISITIONS EDITOR	Joseph Hayton
SENIOR MARKETING MANAGER	Katherine Hepburn
SENIOR PRODUCTION EDITOR	Ken Santor
SENIOR DESIGNER	Kevin Murphy
ILLUSTRATION EDITOR	Sigmund Malinowski
COVER IMAGE	Courtesy Motawi Tileworks, Ann Arbor, MI

This book was set in Times Roman by Publication Services and printed and bound by R.R. Donnelley Crawfordsville. The cover was printed by Phoenix Color Corporation.

This book is printed on acid-free paper. ∞

This document was composed using vim and emacs, and typeset using LATEX 2_ε. LATEX sources were first preprocessed with cmarktex to extract C++ code for testing and compilation, and to provide cross references between C++ code and the text. Cmarktex is written in Eiffel, and was compiled with the SmallEiffel compiler. All named C++ code was originally compiled and tested under Linux using the Gnu-based C++ compiler, g++ 2.96, distributed by RedHat and by Mandrake; most of the code was also compiled with the Sun Workshop 6 C++ compiler, version 5.2, under Solaris. The code was later compiled under Windows 2000 and Linux using the Gnu g++ compiler version 3.1.

ISBN-0-471-20215-0

Printed in the United States of America

10 9 8 7 6 5 4 3 2 1

For J. and P. J.

PREFACE

It is clear that the concept of the algorithm fully deserves its place among the supreme accomplishments of human thought. There, in its rightful place with such ideas as calculus and quantum mechanics, the algorithm can be celebrated for its continuing contribution to the advancement of humanity. Although the idea of the algorithm is old, the twentieth-century development of extremely fast electronic algorithm execution machines has catapulted algorithms into the center of our technological culture. The Internet, digital communications, video games, and physical simulation—all are founded on algorithms, and I believe that all educated women and men should be familiar with the basic ideas of algorithmic thought.

Engineers and scientists have long recognized the potential of algorithms to model the physical universe, and thus also to model and even control technological artifacts. With algorithms we can determine the details of the fluid flow about the bow of a ship, or the distribution of neutrons within a nuclear reactor. We can determine the stress on each beam in a bridge, and we can control the performance of a car engine. The algorithms to do such things can be developed without computers, but actually carrying out the detailed computations to execute these algorithms is mind-numbing and, in the end, far beyond human endurance. But the mid-twentieth century invention of electronic algorithm execution machines—now simply called computers—provided us with an escape from the trap of tedium, and then algorithms became an immensely powerful analysis tool.

All engineers will have to assess algorithms as part of their work, and many will actually develop them. But often these algorithms will be created inside special-purpose tools and expressed in special-purpose languages, ranging from the strange language of spreadsheets to the lisp extension language of computer-aided design tools; they might be written in the matrix-oriented languages of SciLab or Matlab, or in an object-oriented scripting language like Python. Often these algorithms will be designed to glue together other, already existing algorithmic tools, and so reforge those tools for a new purpose. Most of these algorithms will be intended to solve an immediate problem quickly and easily, and the tool will be selected with that impending priority in mind. But even here there is a need to create algorithms—to understand the fundamental notions of sequence, iteration, and selection, to understand the dynamic data transformations that algorithms carry out, to understand different ways of organizing data, and to have some sense of what algorithms can do, and what they can't. Because we rely on these programmable tools, we must have some understanding, more deep than superficial, of how they work and how they break.

Beyond this practical utility of getting a computer to solve a problem, learning to think about a problem algorithmically will give you more power over that problem. Even if you don't, in the end, solve a problem by writing a computer code, having an algorithmic perspective on it gives you another way to appreciate the issues involved.

Amazingly, the computer was designed to solve problems that its creators never envisioned and the computer will let you solve problems that no one else has ever even thought of. But causing a computer to carry out this feat requires creating algorithms and implementing them in a way that the computer can interpret. The implementing is comparatively trivial; the creating is very hard. But the ability to create algorithms is important, and the need to do so is inevitable: We have the power of a *programmable* execution machine at our fingertips. How can we choose not to use it?

THIS BOOK

I want you to develop a facility for algorithmic thought as one approach among many to engineering and scientific problems; I want you to think of problems in terms of the steps that can be scripted and then carried out to reach a solution. Once you can do that, the computer will take care of the boring part of actually performing those steps. This is therefore not a book *of* algorithms, but rather a book to make you think *about* algorithms.

This book is an introduction to the idea of the algorithm, and an introduction to creating them. It is aimed at beginning university students in engineering and the sciences. It is not particularly aimed at computer scientists. Although computer science students can certainly learn from this text, a computer science curriculum traditionally begins with a course on programming and builds on it through a whole series of courses that develop particular classical algorithms and data organization techniques. A computer science curriculum seldom focuses on calculus-based problems and basic physical mechanics.

This text, in contrast, is intended to support an engineering curriculum that contains only one first- or second-year course whose focus is primarily on algorithms and programming. Such a curriculum will build on this course by using simulation and computer-aided engineering design tools in later classes, classes whose primary focus is engineering and science rather than computing.

This text invites your exploration of ideas and provides a contemplative means to stimulate your thinking. Beyond this first introduction, you must commit to bringing algorithms to your other work, so that you can practice and build on the ideas introduced here. In our own curriculum at the University of Michigan, we have used this text to support a first-year course in algorithms and programming for engineers, and then built continuously on computing within later technical courses.

In order to think about algorithms, we must have problems to solve. First- and second-year students in engineering are concurrently taking calculus, physics, chemistry, and biology. These simultaneous studies provide us with a ready source of problems for which to build algorithmic treatments, so I will select from this fountain such problems as strike me both interesting and, perhaps with some effort, understandable to first-year university students. There are many wonderful algorithms that students of engineering and the sciences should learn, but this text is not the place to learn them all.

Throughout the text we will discuss alternatives. I will write many pieces of code more than once, and discuss the trade-offs and aesthetic issues involved in the various versions. You should similarly do so in your own creation of algorithms. I realize that you are reluctant to consider alternative ways of accomplishing a goal. After all, once something works, why look for another way, especially when you have a Russian exam tomorrow? But there is more to accomplishing a goal than simply obtaining something that works. We should consider aesthetics, flexibility, our certainty of correctness, ease of use, and robustness.

At the end of each section you will find questions; some of these are simple review questions, asking you to recall something of the recently read text. But some are intended to make you think about what you just read; indeed, some of these have no right answer, but ask you to consider or comment on choices. At the end of each chapter you will find projects, of varying length and complexity; most of these projects ask you to take up your keyboard and create codes. There is no better way to understand and appreciate algorithms than to write them, and execute them on a computer. And there is no better way to understand a problem than to develop an algorithm to solve it.

As you approach these end-of-chapter projects, you will note that often I don't lay out all the details; frequently the projects ask you to write functions or procedures, but do not specify an entire code. I want you to think about each assignment, formulate questions about it, and thereby take some intellectual ownership of it. I also want *you* to develop some means of testing your code. Further, I don't know how your instructor will prefer to work, so I try not to restrict her with details that may not be appropriate.[1]

THE EXPRESSION OF ALGORITHMS

When developing an algorithm, we must have some way to write it down. A few texts introduce only pseudocode, which is some means of algorithm expression intended only to be written and read by humans. The weakness of this approach is that it does not allow the algorithm to be tested on a real computer. Some other texts introduce pseudocode alongside a real programming language that can be used to control a real computer. I do this, but I use pseudocode sparingly, and use it less and less as the text progresses. My expectation is that you will become more proficient at simply reading code written in a real programming language.

Many practicing engineers create algorithms by first sketching out their ideas in a computer language, but they leave out details so as to concentrate on the big issues first. This is rather like making a rough draft of a story without worrying about the spelling or correctness of grammar, but focusing instead on the flow of plot and character. Despite this common practice, some textbook authors insist on scoping out all algorithms in pseudocode before writing them in a real language. I used to follow this practice, but after teaching algorithms and programming for a few years, I have come to see this "translation of pseudocode to real language" as counterproductive, especially for beginners. It is rather like requiring the rough draft in Latin, and then translating it into English to get the grammar right. Few students new to programming find their logic errors in pseudocode. They find their errors when testing their code. So I think it is

---

[1]In my own class I often give students a handout specifying the function and procedure interfaces quite precisely, because I often check assignments by linking their compiled code to my own test harness code. But other instructors will have their own preferences.

important for students to get their thoughts promptly into real code and executing on a computer. So I deemphasize pseudocode. My own observation is that students will naturally use this technique of code and test, no matter how much I might insist they do otherwise. Upon reflection, they are right to do so.

When developing algorithms, it is important to have a way to get those algorithms executed on that unimaginative, tyrannical hunk of doped silicon affectionately known as a computer's central processing unit. To do so, we must express our algorithms in a real programming language, not pseudocode. In this text I use C++. There are many reasons for this choice, not all of them objective. C++ is a good intermediate-level language, and is widely used. It is easy to find the software tools needed to use C++ on most any computer you may have. And it is easy to find, just down the hall, a member of the C++ literati whose brain you can pick at 1 A.M. in exchange for a slice of pizza and a coke.

The downside of C++ is that it can take years to fully know and understand the whole language. Fortunately, the language can be used, and used well, without knowing all there is to know about it. All the C++ that I will use in this book is presented in this book. But C++ is a huge language; it is fully, if incomprehensibly, described in ISO/IEC 14882, the 776-page tome that defines the language. It is also fully and somewhat more delicately described in the 1,040 pages of *The C++ Programming Language* by Bjarne Stroustrup, who is primarily responsible for creating the language. But I have no reason to create another 800-page book to bind between these covers. Indeed, to do so in the name of fully describing the language would be a confusing distraction from my primary aim. So I introduce only as much of the language as I need to describe the fundamental algorithmic and data organization ideas that I want to present.

ORGANIZATION OF THE TEXT

If you try to view this as simply a programming language text, and mistakenly compare it to others of that breed, you will note some unusual ordering of material. In Chapter 1, I introduce the idea of an algorithm as a set of steps that transform data from input to output, and I also give a whirlwind introduction to the organization of algorithms, and how a static description of an algorithm must control its later dynamic execution. The next three chapters cover the three pillars of algorithms: sequence (Chapter 2), iteration (Chapter 3), and selection (Chapter 4).

The most unusual feature here is the coverage of iteration before selection. Selection is often claimed to be simpler in concept than iteration, so conventional wisdom would mistakenly assert that I should discuss selection first. But to do so is to postpone the time when we can begin to take on really interesting problems and algorithms. Without iteration we can engage only in glorified formula evaluation exercises. My aim is to get you into the good stuff early, so you have time to consider it, to practice it, and to appreciate it.

Too much of the early engineering curriculum already presents a false picture of engineering as the practice of plugging numbers into formulas. Engineering is about creative design within the constraints imposed by nature, need, and society. Significant algorithms allow us to find creative solutions to engineering problems, but significant algorithms *always* exploit iteration.

Just as Chapters 2 through 4 describe the key concepts in organizing algorithms, Chapters 5 through 7 describe the organization of data. Part of Chapter 5 more fully describes the fundamental scalar data types of C++, a topic that would be explored earlier in a language-oriented text. But we really did not need that information earlier; earlier it would have been stuff to plow through only because we need it later, and it would not help us understand harder, more central concepts. Better, I think, to discuss such matters after you have the more difficult ideas of algorithmic organization fermenting in your thoughts.

The level of sophistication required to fully comprehend the examples and exercises varies. Some are quite straightforward, and some might greatly stretch your intellect. Example problems often involve discretization, time stepping of differential equations, solution of nonlinear equations, estimation of integrals, or the solution of a system of linear equations. We have taught all of this material in our first-year course at the University of Michigan, although we have never taught all of it in a single term. I expect your instructor will select material appropriate for your particular course.

Chapter 8 provides some introduction to the limitations of computers and of algorithms. Because algorithms must be executed on a finite computer with limited memory, there are limits to the accuracy and range of information that might be represented on the computer. Chapter 8 contains an extensive discussion of the representation of floating point numbers and floating point arithmetic. Although this material is easily understood with only an understanding of numbers and algebra, it does take some time to appreciate, and might easily be omitted from a course using the text. Chapter 8 also briefly discusses discretization and truncation errors, and estimating the time complexity of algorithms.

Two appendices provide a brief overview of some of the key C++ language constructs and library facilities used in the book. They also contain a few language constructs that were not used in the main body of the text. I encourage you to skim these appendices early on, and to then refer to them often. There are useful details to be found in them, but these are details that would be outside the main stream of the text, or else are scattered throughout the text yet gathered more conveniently together in the appendices. Think of the appendices not as optional supplements to your reading, but as critical material that needs to be read asynchronously.

ACKNOWLEDGMENTS

The choices made in creating this text are mine, but they have been influenced by conversations and a long association with many others. I must especially acknowledge the contributions of my fellow Engineering 101 instructors, especially Robert Beck, Alex Bielajew, and Kenneth G. Powell. I must also thank the many graduate student teaching assistants who have worked on the course, most especially Dan Osborne. Dan was born to teach, and has probably had more influence on this text than any other colleague.

I very much appreciate the support that I received in creating this text. Annie Borland from John Wiley & Sons was the key to taking this project from idle hallway chatter to a manuscript. My editor at Wiley, Joe Hayton, guided this project through several refinements, and was never *too* impatient, even though I was always late. My copy editor, Patricia Brecht, provided many excellent suggestions that appear in the final text, and was very polite in correcting my embarrassingly consistent confusion over "its" and "it's". I must also thank my department chairs, Gary Was and John C. Lee, who never begrudged the time I spent away from the department working on this course and this text.

ALGORITHMS AND ENGINEERING

I think that algorithms are important. I think you should know how to make *your* computer solve *your* problems, rather than the problems that some distant programmer thinks you should solve. I also think algorithms are insanely fun to create. When we create an algorithm, we start with a problem to solve and travel through the whole process of engineering: We design a solution, we implement it, we test it, we refine it, and we seek to make it beautiful. I hope that you see this beauty while reading this text.

James Paul Holloway
Chelsea, Michigan
December 31, 2002

CONTENTS

LIST OF CODES

CHAPTER 7   AGGREGATE SEMANTICS

CHAPTER 8   FINITE SPACE AND TIME

CHAPTER 1

INTRODUCTION

THIS IS a book about algorithms, and about implementing algorithms in a programming language. More particularly, this is a book about algorithms intended for engineers. This identification of purpose should fill your mind with questions: What's an algorithm? What's an implementation of one? What's a programming language? What's distinct about a book on algorithms for engineers? Why should I care? I'd like to explore these questions in this chapter, starting with a discussion of what algorithms are. But I know what happens when students look at books: You have much to do, you suspect this book will be boring, and you will want to know why you should have even bothered reading this far. But I can't tell you why you should care until I explain what I'm talking about. So let's make a deal: If you will please give me your attention for awhile (at least until the end of the chapter), I will try to provide you with a bit of motivation right now:

Claim

> Learning to design and implement algorithms will sharpen your logical thinking skills; it will give you a better basis to appraise the computer-generated results and simulations on which you will rely as an engineer; it will give you an early chance to engage in the analysis and design process that is at the heart of engineering education and practice; and it will give you a tool to better understand and explore science and mathematics.

1.1 ALGORITHMS

So, what's an algorithm? An algorithm is a list of instructions for accomplishing a task. Some say that a recipe for chocolate chip cookies is an example of an algorithm. But is it really? Is any list of instructions an algorithm? If this were so, it would hardly seem a significant concept. Certainly not worthy of a book title. Algorithms are lists of instructions with quite special and specific properties, and with some common structures to control the order in which the instructions are carried out.

Most important, an algorithm must be *executable by a mechanism.* To execute an algorithm means to actually carry out the instructions, like actually making the cookies. Executable by a mechanism means that it must be possible to construct a machine that executes the algorithm all by itself, without human intuition, cleverness, insight, or heart. This does not mean that working with algorithms is a soulless, cold activity. Quite the reverse—developing algorithms requires cunning, creativity, insight, and patience. But the cunning goes into creating the machine and into creating the algorithm. Once these are set in motion, the machine proceeds in its relentless way, executing the algorithm to make our cleverness manifest.

Definition

> An *algorithm* is a list of instructions that, when executed, transform information from input into output. The instructions are a *finite* set of steps that can be *executed,* in a definite order, by a deterministic mechanism. When these steps are actually executed, the execution must terminate after a finite time.

There are three key aspects to this definition:

Finite Expression   An algorithm is a list of instructions, but only finitely many of them. This requirement is a very practical one: It ensures that we can actually write the algorithm down (or express it in some form). If an algorithm had an infinite number of instructions in its list, we would spend all of our time writing it down, and never even get around to actually executing it.

Mechanistic Execution   There must be a machine that can carry out—execute— the steps of the algorithm. There is again a practical reason for invoking an execution mechanism in the definition of an algorithm: We want the work embodied in the steps of the algorithm to be done for us, quickly, reproducibly, and without error. But even more important, by defining an algorithm with respect to an execution mechanism, we ensure that the algorithm is unambiguous. If we have a deterministic mechanism that can do task T, then "do task T" is a well-defined step that needs no further detail. In this sense, the mechanism is a crucial part of the process of creating an algorithm. The execution mechanism's capabilities define the building blocks with which we must ultimately express our algorithms.

Finite Execution   The most subtle part of the definition is that when the algorithm is executed, only a finite number of things can actually be done—the algorithm executes in finite time. Since it takes time to do each step, only a finite number of steps can be *executed.* It might seem that this finite execution follows from the requirement that there only be a finite number of instructions, but in fact it does not. Consider an algorithmic step such as: "keep adding 10 to the sum until the sum exceeds 100." This single step causes something to happen over and over, until some condition becomes true. So a single step in the static expression of an algorithm might cause repetitions of some instructions when the algorithm is executed. This capability, to have a step that repeats some instructions many times, is critical for the creation of significant algorithms. But it introduces the possibility of a finitely expressible list of steps that never terminates.

The creation of significant algorithms can be quite taxing on the intellect. Often it's difficult to see how the solution to a problem can be found using an algorithm. Sometimes it's just difficult to express the obvious steps in terms of operations that a silicon chip can implement. Often it's hard to get the details right. But most generally, it is hard to see the implications of a set of algorithmic steps. Algorithms, as we will design and express them, are written in static symbols on a page (or in a computer file), but these same symbols are then given dynamic life when the algorithm executes. The changeless algorithm governs dynamic transformations of information during execution. When you create an algorithm, you are therefore trying to see the eventual *implications* of your instructions.

As a trivial example, if our execution machine can multiply numbers, then we can write an algorithm to square a number as:

ALGORITHM *Square*

Computes the square of a number
1: Request a value for x
2: Compute $x \times x$ and call this value s
3: Provide the value of s to the caller

At first sight this algorithm looks, well, ... boring. In fact, this one is pretty boring. But it will do for a start. Every time algorithm **Square** is executed by a machine, it asks, in step 1, for a number that we give the symbolic name x in the text describing the algorithm. *After* a numerical value is provided for x, the algorithm execution machine will execute step 2. In step 2 the machine computes the value of x times itself, calling the result s. And *then*, in step 3, it provides that value to whoever activated the algorithm. Note the sequence of events and the (at this point trivial) changes that we expect to occur when the algorithm executes. Before step 1 neither x nor s has any meaning. After step 1, x has a meaning (it's a symbolic name for the value that we are going to square). And after step 2 the symbol s has a meaning too; it's the value we wanted all along. But we can't execute step 3 before step 2, and we can't execute step 2 before step 1. Each step depends on the data that were introduced in the previous step.

This particular algorithm describes the transformation of input information x to output information s, which is supposed to be the value of x^2. The algorithms that are changing the world, and the algorithms that engineers encounter, are algorithms that, like this one, transform information. We fire up the algorithm execution mechanism, put in information, and out comes new information that we find even more interesting than the input. We input the shape of the airplane's wings, fuselage, and its airspeed into our algorithm, and at the end of execution out issues information on the lift and drag of the aircraft. This information might be in the form of pictures or endless lists of mind-numbing numbers, but either way it's great information that was not explicitly known before the algorithm was executed. It is such information-transforming algorithms that will engage us in this book.

1.1.1   The Calling Environment

Algorithms face the theological problem of creation: Something must start an algorithm's execution.

Definition

> The thing that causes an algorithm to be executed is known as its *caller*. The caller is usually another algorithm.

An algorithm is therefore always executed in an environment that's established by its caller, as cartooned in Fig. 1.1. Further, to be of use, an algorithm must usually take data from the environment into itself, and must always somehow emit data back into that external environment.

Definition

> *Input* is data that must be provided to an algorithm in order for it to execute and perform its function. *Output* is data that an algorithm provides to its external environment.

Although algorithms are always executed within the context of their caller's environment, they should be written to have only a minimal impact on this environment. For every algorithm we define an *interface* describing

1. what input data the algorithm needs, and how it will be passed into the algorithm.
2. what output data the algorithm will emit into the caller's environment, and how that output will be passed back to the caller.

Algorithm **Square** interfaces with its environment by taking one numerical value in, and by emitting one numerical value as output.

There are two general mechanisms for providing input to an executing algorithm: We can pass data by value, or by reference.

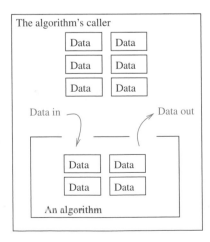

FIGURE 1.1 An algorithm executes in an external environment with which it exchanges data.

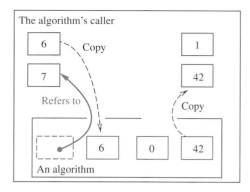

FIGURE 1.2 Here a caller passes one input datum (6) by value and the algorithm returns one datum (42). The caller has also passed one datum by reference; such data are not copied. Instead, the algorithm can refer to them directly.

Definition

> An algorithm's interface uses *pass by value* if it requires a copy of data from its caller's environment. It uses *pass by reference* if it requires direct access to data in its caller's environment.

You pass me data by value when you write a phone number on my palm. You pass me data by reference when you give me permission to enter your apartment and look in your address book; when you do this, you might give me permission just to read the book, but you might also give me permission to write it in.

These same two mechanisms, pass by value and pass by reference, can be used to provide output from an algorithm back to its caller, although pass by value is then called "returning" data:

Definition

> To *return* data from an algorithm is to provide the algorithm's caller with a copy of data values upon termination of the algorithm's execution.

Data returned to a caller are only *offered*; the caller might ignore them. In contrast, if an algorithm interfaces with its caller by providing output data by reference, then the algorithm is allowed to refer directly to data in the calling environment, and so can directly change data there. I return data to you by putting them in your mailbox. But we agree that I give you data by reference when you give me permission to enter your apartment and write in your address book. Figure 1.2 cartoons some of these possible means of interfacing an algorithm with its environment.

1.1.2 Two Multiplication Algorithms

The sorts of instructions that we can write when creating an algorithm are constrained by those that are built into the machine which will execute our algorithm. If it can multiply, we can use a multiply instruction. If it can't multiply, but can add and repeat tasks over and over, then we can build our own multiply algorithm. Here is a simple but inefficient multiply algorithm, suitable for multiplying nonnegative integers:

ALGORITHM   *Nonnegative Integer Multiply*

Takes nonnegative integers i and j and returns integer equal to $i \times j$

Require: : $i \geq 0$, $j \geq 0$

1: Set *product* to 0
2: Set *counter* to 0
3: **while** *counter* $<$ i **do**
4:      Set *product* equal to its current value plus j
5:      Add 1 to *counter*
6: **end while**
7: Return *product*

This algorithm works by starting with *product* $= 0$, and then adding j into *product* exactly i times. In expressing this, we need to arrange for the instruction on line 4 to be repeated i times. This requires us to describe the order in which instructions will be carried out in the eventual dynamic execution of the algorithm, but we must do so in our static written description of it. This is done here with a *while loop*, which is understood to specify the repeated execution of the code on lines 4 and 5, between the **while** and **end while** lines, until the condition *counter* $<$ i becomes false. We set up this repetition with the instruction on line 2, setting *counter* to zero. We then add 1 into *counter* each time line 5 is executed. After doing this exactly i times, we will have *counter* $= i$, and the condition *counter* $<$ i will therefore be false. The while loop will then be finished, and the algorithm is implied to continue with line 7. The overall effect is to ensure that line 4 will be executed exactly i times, so in the end *product* will equal $i \times j$.

Note that this algorithm, when it executes, keeps *changing* the value that is stored in *product*. This is a typical, and powerful, paradigm. We will build up, through a set of repeating steps, the required answer in the storage that I have named *product*. Consider multiplying $i = 3$ times $j = 20$. The loop executes three times, and each time the stored data are changed, as suggested in Fig 1.3. This approach to the desired result by repeated execution of some algorithmic steps is called iteration.

There is a danger in this algorithm. The value of *counter* is set to zero at the start. If it should happen that i is a negative integer, then *counter* $<$ i is false, and the while loop will do nothing. As a result, the algorithm will return zero, which is not $i \times j$. This is not really a defect: The algorithm promised to work for nonnegative integers only. It is to document this restriction that I have listed this limitation with a bold note of requirement at the top of the algorithm text. It is always the case that we create algorithms whose correctness is predicated on some assumptions about the input data. Often those assumptions are not obvious. It is therefore vitally important to explicitly identify such assumptions, because error often arises when we lose track of them.

Using iteration allows our multiply operation to work for *any* input nonnegative integers i and j. We can therefore consider the problem of multiplying nonnegative integers solved. **Nonnegative Integer Multiply** has a well-defined interface through which we pass two nonnegative integer values as input, and from which issues another nonnegative integer, which is the product of the two inputs. This interface is all we need to know in order to use algorithm **Nonnegative Integer Multiply**.

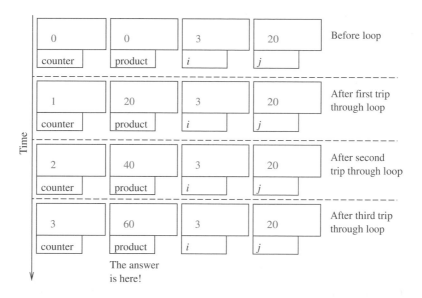

FIGURE 1.3   The changes of data as **Nonnegative Integer Multiply** executes.

Now that it works, how it works has become immaterial. We can just use it. We have *extended* the algorithm execution machine!

By building up a collection of such useful algorithms, we can take a machine that does relatively little and cause it to run algorithms that accomplish quite complex operations. Each algorithm, packaged behind its interface, becomes a component that we can use in a larger construction. This is a critical principle in organizing significant algorithms. We manage complexity by breaking down the solution of a large problem into a number of algorithmic components that interact only through well-defined interfaces. Each such component can be largely independent of the whole; there is no need for the individual parts to have any information about why they are being called or how their results will be used.

To see a small example of this, let's now create an algorithm to multiply together any two integers, rather than only nonnegative integers. To multiply negative integers, it is sufficient to multiply nonnegative integers, and to take care of negative integers by appropriately manipulating signs.

Suppose therefore that our algorithm execution mechanism has an instruction to reverse the sign of an integer i. This operation, when executed, actually changes the value that is associated with the name i. If i was -10, then i becomes 10, as illustrated in Fig. 1.4.

FIGURE 1.4   The instruction "reverse the sign of i" in action.

With such a sign-reversing instruction in hand, we can create an algorithm to multiply any two integers, whose signs might be negative or positive. Here is one possible algorithm based on this strategy:

ALGORITHM *Integer Multiply*

Takes integers i and j and returns integer $i \times j$

```
 1:  if i and j are both nonnegative then
 2:      use Nonnegative Integer Multiply to compute i × j and call this result product
 3:  else if i and j are both negative then
 4:      reverse the signs of i and j (so they are now positive)
 5:      use Nonnegative Integer Multiply to compute i × j and call this result product
 6:  else
 7:      if i < 0 then
 8:          reverse the sign of i (change i to −i)
 9:      else
10:          reverse the sign of j (change j to − j)
11:      end if
12:      use Nonnegative Integer Multiply to compute i × j and call this result product
13:      reverse the sign of product
14:  end if
15:  Return product
```

In expressing this, we don't need to repeat the steps of the **Nonnegative Integer Multiply** algorithm. We simply give witness when it's used, because **Nonnegative Integer Multiply** is now a well-defined step.

In organizing algorithm **Integer Multiply**, we need a mechanism to dynamically select which steps to execute based on conditions that are checked at the time of execution. In **Integer Multiply** this is expressed with a statement of the form:

```
if condition 1 is true then
   do task A
else if condition 2 is true then
   do task B
else
   do task C
end if
```

This text is meant to govern the set of steps that will be executed when the algorithm is run. Only one of tasks A, B, or C is meant to be carried out, but which it is will depend on the actual data on which the algorithm is acting. This is again a dynamic idea, describing how things must happen when the algorithm executes, but it must be expressed in the static description of the algorithm. The statement used to do so is called a *selection statement.*

The three algorithms introduced here are not particularly impressive in what they do. But they do illustrate many of the features that go into the manufacture of more interesting algorithms. They illustrate the notion of putting data into an algorithm, and getting data back. They show the symbolic naming of data, and its dynamic change as an algorithm executes. They illustrate the static description that must control a dynamic execution. Most important, they show the three main forms by which we control the order of execution of an algorithm's steps: sequence, iteration, and selection.

Questions

Question 1   In the algorithm **Nonnegative Integer Multiply**, how many times does the value called *product* change?

Question 2   Examine the algorithm **Nonnegative Integer Multiply**. If *i* is negative and *j* is nonnegative, it does not compute $i \times j$. What does it do if *i* is nonnegative but *j* is negative?

Question 3   Consider the following list of instructions for crossing the street:

while still in street **do**
    cross half the remaining distance
end while

Which of the three requirements of an algorithm does this fail to satisfy?

Question 4   Consider the algorithm

set *sum* to 0
while *sum* < 100 **do**
    add *increment* into *sum*
end while

For what values of *increment* will the algorithm terminate after a finite number of steps?

1.2   DYNAMIC CONTROL OF EXECUTION

The three algorithmic structuring concepts of sequence, iteration, and selection all describe the dynamic flow of control of the algorithm when it executes, and all three must somehow be expressed in the static written description of the algorithm. They are important enough to receive explicit definitions.

Definition

> *Sequence* specifies a linear order of execution in which one specific task is explicitly shown to follow another.

This is the simplest idea in algorithm execution. It is so simple it's easy to ignore, but beginning programmers often make sequencing errors. In a program text sequencing is often implied, in part, by the order in which statements appear on the screen. As suggested in Fig. 1.5, statements written higher up on the page are generally executed before statements written further down it.

Definition

> *Iteration* is the repetitive execution of a group of instructions until some condition is met.

Significant algorithms often require doing the same sort of work more than once. Consider the task of adding up a list of *N* numbers: We could write *N* instructions of the sort "add the next number to the sum," or we could write this instruction only once, but have it repeatedly executed *N* times. This allows us to write an algorithm to add up *N* numbers *when we don't even know what value N represents*. With iteration our description of the algorithm becomes a set of rules describing what steps to execute, rather an explicit list of steps to execute.

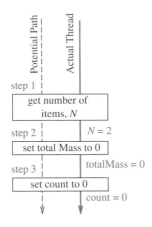

FIGURE 1.5 There is only one possible path through a list of sequenced steps in an algorithm. When a list of sequenced steps is executed, the actual order in which they are executed, shown in blue, is predestined.

Definition

> *Selection* is the selective execution of a group of instructions based on some condition.

The selective, or conditional, execution of instructions in an algorithm gives us the means to deal with cases in which the required data transformation steps differ depending on the data to be transformed. *If* it is a leap year, *then* the day after February 28th is the 29th; the instructions needed to address this extra day are only executed when it is indeed a leap year. Selection, like iteration, provides rules for determining what steps to execute.

The term "flow control" is often used to describe these organizing ideas in algorithm expression and execution. It's an evocative term, conjuring up an image of the execution of an algorithm as water flowing through a branching network of pipes, with some means to switch the flow into one, and only one, pipe at each junction. In more modern images we speak of the thread of execution of the algorithm. At each instant during execution the computer is doing one step of the algorithm, and this sequence of steps, strung out in order of execution, defines a path, a thread, through the algorithm. In the static expression of an algorithm there are many potential paths down which the thread might be strung, but at execution the flow control structures—sequence, iteration, and selection—direct the thread down one specific path, determined dynamically at execution time by the data being transformed.[1]

In describing a sequence, there is only one potential path through the steps of the algorithm, as shown in Fig. 1.5. With iteration a sequenced set of steps can be repeated, over and over, until some condition is met. The thread of execution can therefore loop back over a set of steps several times, as suggested in Fig. 1.6. In selection there

---

[1] A physical thread is not split as it is pushed through the fabric. Many modern computer codes can, in fact, split the thread of execution. But this interesting and most complicated possibility will not be considered in this text.

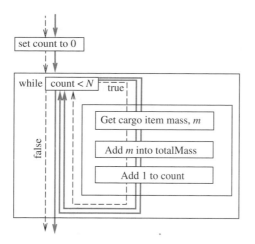

FIGURE 1.6 Iteration allows a set of steps to be repeated over and over, based on the data available when the algorithm is executed. The dotted line represents the potential paths through the steps, and the blue line an actual trip two times around the loop, for the case $N = 2$.

are multiple, branching potential paths through the steps of the algorithm, as shown in Fig. 1.7, but only one of these potential paths is followed at the time of execution.

Note also that these control constructs can appear nested within each other—an iteration could contain a selection statement, a selection statement will contain sequenced statements, an iteration statement could even contain another iteration statement. Such nested control structures will allow us to develop very useful algorithms for solving problems in engineering.

Questions

Question 5 Of the three forms of flow control—sequence, iteration, and selection—which are used in algorithm **Square** from Section 1.1? Which are used in **Nonnegative Integer Multiply?**

Question 6 The proper way for a salesclerk to make change involves returning the fewest possible number of bills and coins to the customer. What flow control constructs are needed to express an algorithm to do this? Does your answer depend on what operations you assume your computer can carry out?

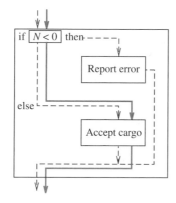

FIGURE 1.7 There are many potential paths through a selection construct, but only one is taken during any particular execution of the construct. The dotted line represents the potential paths through the steps, and the blue line an actual thread for the case $N = 2$.

1.3 COMPUTERS AND PROGRAMMING LANGUAGES

It is not difficult to build a machine to store and multiply numbers—a slide rule is such a machine, as is a calculator. The ability to execute a multiply algorithm is not all that special. A really useful algorithm execution machine should be able to carry out the steps of more than a *specific* algorithm; it should be able to carry out the steps of *any* algorithm.

Definition

A *computer* is a programmable algorithm execution machine. It is crafted so that we can feed both an algorithm and data into it, causing those data to be transformed by the executing steps of that algorithm.

Such a machine stores and operates on data, but it also stores the algorithm that is directing those operations. This is then a very powerful general-purpose machine: It can execute algorithms that were never envisioned by its creators. The task of the algorithm designer—our task—is to create sequences of instructions to usefully control the data manipulations of such a machine.

A computer must have several facilities, as suggested in Fig. 1.8, if it is to support our desire to execute information-transforming algorithms. It must be able to store information (both our data and our algorithms), it must be able to mechanistically transform information using some fundamental built-in operations, and it must be able to exchange information with its external environment. In order to create an algorithm and get a computer to execute it, we must somehow manage the interaction of all these systems—data storage, data operations, and data exchange with the real world.

A computer contains a data processor, often called a central processing unit or CPU, that can execute algorithms. This processor is designed to read information from the computer's memory and interpret these data as algorithmic instructions to transform

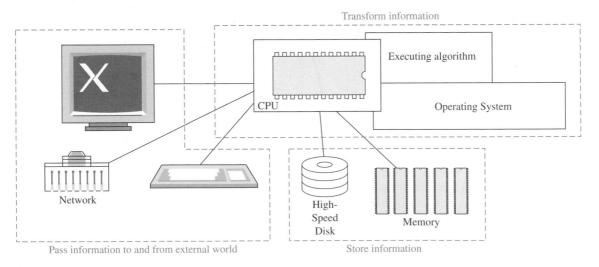

FIGURE 1.8 Computers provide a means to store information, to transform it under algorithmic control, and to exchange information with the rest of the world.

other data in its memory from input into output. But the processor can only understand a specific set of instructions, called its machine language. Machine language is neither human readable nor very expressive. The instructions of machine language are very primitive building blocks, including commands such as "load 8 binary digits from memory into the CPU," or "treat these two data as integers and add them together," or "if this datum is zero, skip the next instruction." To implement algorithms in machine language would be like building a car starting from bauxite and rubber trees.

We do not, in general, want to write our algorithms in machine language. Machine language is designed for machines, and we are humans. But our desire is to have our algorithms executed on a machine, and ultimately the machine can execute only machine code. So we must express the algorithm in a special, human writable, and human readable algorithm expression language that can then be translated into machine code.

Definition

A *programming language* is a well-defined language whose constructs have a precise form (syntax) and meaning (semantics) so that they can be mechanically translated into machine language. An algorithm expressed in a programming language or in machine language is often called a program.

Note that there is a distinction between syntax—how we express an idea in the language—and semantics—the meaning of what we express in the language. Many programming languages with distinct syntax nevertheless have similar semantics: We can say the same things with them, but must express our thoughts in a different syntax. You must work to understand the semantics of various programming language constructs. These semantics tell you what you can express in the language, what you can do. In the end, it is programming language semantics that define the basic instructions which we can use when creating algorithms. Syntax, while important, is secondary. Once you understand the semantic ideas and how to use them, you can learn languages with similar semantics rather easily, because you only have to learn the syntax.

It is not possible here to fully describe all the ways that programming languages get translated into actual steps executed on the physical mechanism of a computer. But I can describe one such way in cartoon form at least. We express an algorithm as a written text in a programming language and this written text is stored on a computer as a file. In order to actually have our algorithm executed, we must translate it into machine language. To this end there is actually an algorithm for translating anything written in the correct syntax of the programming language into machine language. You and I may not know that algorithm (and it's often a complex one), but we have been given a copy of this translation algorithm already written in machine language. This translation algorithm can therefore be run on our computer, and so we run it, providing our own source text as input. The translation algorithm executes, and transforms our source text into machine language, which is stored in a file, ready for execution. The translation algorithm is called a compiler.

Definition

A *compiler* is an algorithm for translating well-formed, syntactically correct programming language text into the machine language of a target computer.

A compiler, usually with the help of some other programs, can thus take our source text and transform it into a program ready to run on a computer.

Note that the job of the compiler is to take anything that's written in the syntax of the language and translate it into machine code. It will translate correct syntax into machine language while preserving the semantics of the code. But the compiler has no psychic powers, no intelligence, and it has no way of knowing if what we wrote will solve any problem whatsoever, let alone the specific problem we want it to solve. If the semantics are wrong, so be it. The compiler does not care one whit. After all, the psil was satherly fifleeing its ponthy is perfectly good English syntax.

In this text we will use a programming language called C++. C++ is a fairly modern language, and an important one, if only because of the revolution in programming practice that has accompanied it. C++ was designed based on lessons learned from 30 years of software development, and while it's not the most modern or most cleanly designed language available, it's a good language that is very widely used. There's a lot of information available about it, and any question you have on the language can be answered without too much effort expended on the search. There are many implementations of compilers for the language, some of which—even some of the best of which—are free.

It's important to realize, however, that computer languages such as C++ are a creation of the human mind. They are, in fact, the product of engineering design. As such, they are not perfect. Since design is a topic that I wish to discuss in this text, I shall not be shy about criticizing C++ where I think it deserves to be criticized. Such criticisms are certainly not meant to condemn the language, but these criticisms are meant to encourage you to critique your tools.

C++ is a large language. It has many constructs, many ways to express algorithmic steps. Many of these constructs are centered around the organization and management of data, some others exist to take care of important yet annoying details, while others are simply decorative embellishments. I will not introduce or use all this language. I will instead introduce a subset of the language and of its standard libraries, which simplify our work as we implement algorithms. A description of the language constructs we will use are provided in Appendices A and B.

Questions

Question 7   Here is an algorithm written in two different programming languages (C/C++ and Eiffel). What do you think it does?

```
int i = 4;
int j = 12;
int counter = 0;
int sum = 0;
while( counter < i )
  {
    sum = sum + j;
    counter = counter + 1;
  }
```

```
i: INTEGER
j: INTEGER
counter: INTEGER
sum: INTEGER
i := 4
j := 12
from
    counter := 0
    sum := 0
until counter = i loop
    sum := sum + j
    counter := counter + 1
end
```

Question 8   When we want an algorithm to be executed on a computer, why don't we just express it in English?

1.4 ALGORITHMS FOR ENGINEERS

So what algorithms are engineers interested in? Hopefully in all of them—in those written long ago, by people smarter than you and I, and those that have not yet been created, in whose birth you and I might have a hand. We engineers often create and exercise algorithms that model the physics of some system we are designing, giving us a way to partially test a design without actually building it. This gives us a means to explore alternative designs for a system based on the results of such simulations, without the expense or delay of physically building each design. For some problems you can even program the computer to itself select the optimal design. We also embed computers inside other machines, to control and monitor them.

But let me echo my earlier claim—the most important reason to study and create algorithms is not, in fact, their inherent utility, but instead is the thinking skills that their creation forces us to develop. The precise, logical thought required will stand you in good stead when you have problems to analyze, even if those problems cannot be solved by formally creating an algorithm. Beyond that, I will make connections to many problems from basic mathematics, including calculus and differential equations, and to problems in physics and other applied sciences. We will develop algorithms that solve some of the problems which arise in these fields, and these are of a sort that have immediate and direct benefit in engineering analysis and design. However, many of these algorithms rely on very similar algorithmic constructs, and they don't give a full picture of the sorts of algorithms that can be developed. I will therefore also bring in some other algorithms in data processing—algorithms that don't deal with modeling the physical world, but instead deal with manipulating some interesting information, for example, computer graphics. But I must also echo what was stated in the preface: This is not a book of algorithms, it is a book about creating algorithms. I do not intend to systematically show you all the algorithms with which, as engineers, you should be familiar; there are too many, and most require more advanced mathematics and science than is needed here. I know you will build on what you learn here in other courses, and in other reading.

Creating algorithms is exactly what we do. We *create* them. We start with a problem to solve, and a blank page, and must try to fill that emptiness with source text that, when translated and executed on a computer, will solve the problem. This creative process involves many design principles: We must understand the problem; we must analyze the problem to find a solution; we must analyze the solution to find how best to implement it; we must work within constraints (often most annoying); we must look for simplicity and elegance and reliability. An introduction to algorithms and their implementation can thus provide a rich introductory engineering design experience.

You can contrast this approach with traditional prefatory programming courses, and their related texts, which often focus on the preliminary mechanics of creating programs, with little attention paid to the creative design aspects of the process. Or you can contrast it with texts for introductory computer science courses, which often explore general classes of algorithms and data organization but which give scant attention to problems that arise in calculus, physics, and the broader fields of engineering. Here I want to give you problems that you will find challenging and that will start to suggest to you how computers can solve the same kinds of problems you are solving in your other introductory courses.

1.5   WHY SHOULD YOU KEEP READING?

This brief introductory chapter places many questions before you: What are some significant algorithms? What are some interesting problems we can solve with algorithms? How will we organize and express our algorithms? How will we organize and manage data while our algorithms transform it? How will we test our algorithms? How will we establish their correctness? When are algorithms or computers inadequate to a task? In the chapters that follow, we will take up these issues and more. You will discover some general and useful classes of algorithms, and if you make the considerable effort involved in writing and testing some algorithms of your own, you will experience the joy of creating something that actually works!

Projects

This chapter has but a few exercises, to get you started thinking about how algorithms might work and be organized.

PROJECT 1

Create an algorithm, and write it in a neat and unambiguous form that will tell you if an input integer is prime or not. The machine on which this algorithm will execute can add, determine remainders of integer division, and store numbers.

PROJECT 2

For the same machine as in Question 1, create an algorithm that will report all the prime numbers less than some input upper bound. Do you want to use the algorithm from Question 1 as part of this algorithm?

PROJECT 3

Create an algorithm that takes the time in hours, minutes, and seconds (each an integer) as shown on a standard 12-hour clock, and returns the number of seconds past 12:00 that this time represents.

PROJECT 4

Find a partner, take opposite sides, and argue the proposition: It is better to give your apartment key to the mail carrier than to have her use the mailbox. (If you can't find any positive arguments for this, you have not thought about all the possibilities.)

CHAPTER 2

SEQUENCE

IN THIS chapter we will continue our investigation of the idea of an algorithm, and create a few that manipulate data in a relatively straightforward way. These algorithms will be expressed in an algorithm-writing language called C++, and we will explore ways within C++ to express and control the most important aspect of an algorithm: sequence.

You should transcribe the algorithms you find here into appropriate files, compile them with a C++ compiler, and run the resulting program. This will provide you with firsthand experience with the compilation process and an appreciation of how the source code text becomes translated into action when executed on your algorithm execution machine—your computer. You should also *change* the algorithms written here. Making small changes and seeing the effect is the best way to get comfortable with both the language syntax and its semantics. Besides providing some introduction to C++, this chapter will encourage you to consider broader design principles that should be considered as you create and implement algorithms.

2.1 EXPRESSING ALGORITHMS

As I have briefly described, a computer program is expressed as a source text, which is a written document meant to be translated by another computer program (e.g., a compiler) into machine instructions that can then be interpreted by a computer's processor. But algorithms begin in the human mind with the analysis of a problem to be solved. The analysis of the problem and conceptual creation of an algorithmic solution are the most important steps in creating a program. Still, in order to create and analyze algorithms, we need some way to express them—to write them down.

There are two broad groups of languages for expressing algorithms. There are languages that are really intended only for human consumption, and there are languages that are sufficiently well specified and simple enough to be translated into machine code by a compiler. The former are often called pseudocode, while the latter are called programming languages. Much pseudocode is shockingly informal, allowing the loose expression of algorithms without any hope of really determining their correctness. Conversely, some are excruciatingly formal and support rigorous mathematical proofs of their properties. Most are in between, like the one I used to write the simple algorithms of Chapter 1. The primary utility of pseudocode is that it provides a means to express algorithmic ideas without worrying about the syntactical details needed to drive a compiler.[1] I will sometimes write pseudocode when I want to cut to the crux, but as you move deeper into the book, you will discover less and less of it.

The C++ language is a member of a language family rooted in a programming language called C. While C is essentially an abstract machine language, C++ is a multilayered language that at one extreme is simply the abstract machine language C, but at the other extreme is a strangely complex language that can directly support several modern programming paradigms. Unfortunately, it is a huge language expressed in a sometimes obscure syntax; if you want to use the whole language, there is much to know. In this text we will use C++ at an intermediate level: We will not generally use all of its most advanced mechanisms. We will instead use only a part of C++, along with part of a standard set of data management components known as the Standard Template Library (STL). These components will take care of most of our data bookkeeping needs, so that we can concentrate on higher levels of understanding. We will also use a few of the other standard C++ libraries, including the streams library, which is used to get data into and out of our programs, again sparing us many bookkeeping details.

2.2   HUMBLE BEGINNINGS

Let's begin with a simple algorithm, based on algorithm **Square** of Chapter 1, to square a number. To accomplish this, we need to get the number to square and store it, multiply it by itself, and provide this product back to the caller. Here is a simple C++ code to do this:

square1.cpp

```
1   #include <iostream>
2   using namespace std;
3
4   int main()
5   {
6
7       double x;
8       cin >> x;
9       cout << x * x;
10
11      return 0;
12  }
```

---

[1]Experienced programmers sometimes sketch out pseudocode in a computer language like C++, writing just enough to get the gist of the algorithm without worrying about the details, but this is a dangerous practice for many new students, because it can confuse you about the annoying yet important details of syntax.

The heart of the algorithm is written on lines 7–9. The rest of the program text is just scaffolding, stuff that must be there to hold the whole thing together, but which is not at the heart of the matter. Let's ignore the scaffold for the moment, and consider the key lines one by one.

We first need some container to hold the number that we are supposed to square. Line 7 reads

```
double x;
```

This creates, or *declares*, an *identifier*, which here is used to identify such a data container.

Definition

A name, given to an object, such as a data container, is known as an *identifier*.

On line 7 the datum associated with x is declared to be a number that can have a fractional part—this is the meaning of the special keyword `double` in C++. Line 7 is also an instance of an important C++ principle:

C++ Principle

Every identifier must be *declared* before it is used.

Such a declaration is an introduction: You are introducing the identifier (x in this case) to your reader. Without such an introduction, your reader would be uncertain as to what x means when it is used next on line 8. For a human reader, intuiting this meaning might not be a problem. But for a computer, such a guess is not so easy. And even a human reader might guess wrong. So we are explicit, and introduce the symbol x and say what kind of thing it is: It is a number (a `double`).

Line 8

```
cin >> x;
```

is essentially a command, "wait for the human who started this program to type in something that looks like a number," and once the human does that, "store the number in the data container identified by x." This step gets the input number that the algorithm is required to square; this is the expression of step 1 from algorithm **Square** of Section 1.1.

Finally, line 9 reads

```
cout << x * x;
```

This means take the number stored under the name x, multiply it, using the multiplication operator *, by the number stored under the name x, and show the result to whoever started this program. This essentially combines steps 2 and 3 of algorithm **Square** of Section 1.1. It squares the number identified by x, and it provides the value of x * x to the user of the program, which is the human who started the program and provided the input value of x.

Note that this implementation of the **Square** algorithm does all its input and output by side effect. The input data are requested directly from the caller's external environment, and the output data are written directly back to the caller. The C++ mechanisms being used for this data exchange, packaged behind the symbols << and >>, are not the ones typically used by an algorithm to interact with its caller. They are rather mechanisms used by algorithms in C++ to interact with the outside human world. We will discover other, more disciplined mechanisms for an algorithm to interchange data with its caller later in this chapter.

2.2.1   Statements and Sequence Points

Each of the lines 7, 8, and 9 of our code ends with a semicolon; this semicolon is really important. The semicolon denotes the end of a *statement*, the end of a complete thought, the end of a self-contained demand on the algorithm execution machine. In lines 7–9 there are two different types of statements: Line 7 is a simple declaration statement, and lines 8 and 9 are expression statements.

A simple declaration statement introduces and describes the meaning of an identifier.

C++ Principle

> A statement of the form
>
>   simple_type identifier;
>
> where `simple_type` is one of the keywords `double` or `int` is a *simple declaration statement*. It associates a symbolic `identifier` with data of the specified type. Such an identifier then describes mutable data, and is also called a *variable*.

The precise rules for forming an identifier are provided in Appendix A, but I bet you will have no problem creating valid identifier names as variations on those you see in this text.

Although there are many types of data that can be managed in C++, I shall make no attempt in this text to describe them all. For the moment at least we will content ourselves with two types that can describe numbers: `int` and `double`.

An `int` is a number that can take on only integer values. These are useful for counting, but are in practice somewhat limited in range (an `int` can hold a value from about −2 billion to 2 billion on many current 32-bit computers). In contrast, a `double` is a number that can have a fractional part, and that can take on a large range of magnitudes.[2] At first sight it might seem that `double` is more useful than `int`, but there are good reasons to have both. Most important, when developing an algorithm we should state exactly what we want of a variable—if we are counting, we don't want to suggest otherwise by using a number that *might* have a fractional part.

Claim

> We should select data types that most closely express our meaning.

In part, this helps other humans read our code; if we declare some variable to be an `int`, it is made clear to our readers that this thing will be used for counting, rather than to express a continuous quantity. We could declare it to be a `double` and just never store anything other than an integer in it, but then we are encouraging confusion when

---

[2]From about 2^{1023} to about 2^{-1074} on most 32-bit computers.

clarity should be our first goal. Less important, but important still, is that arithmetic on an `int` frequently is faster than on a `double` because it is not burdened with an unneeded fractional part. Further, an `int` usually takes up less storage in the computer.

Note that a declaration associates a type of data with an identifier, and commits us to that identification. We can't declare `int myage`, but then later think that `myage` is a `double`. Think of this in terms of a data container—if I have a hat box, I can't put a car in it.

Returning to our **square.cpp** source text, lines 8 and 9 are expression statements.

Definition

> An *expression statement* is a statement that will, when executed, cause data to be changed.

Most statements in a C++ code will, in fact, be expression statements, as these are the statements that actually get work done. The rest of the text in a C++ program is either flow control, declarations and definitions, or scaffold.[3]

C++ Principle

> An *expression statement* is of the form
>
>   expression;
>
> where `expression` is a combination of literal data, variables, and operators that transform data.

We will discuss expressions further in the next section; for the moment I note only that `cin >> x` and `cout << x * x` are both expressions in C++ syntax.

Note that both simple declaration and expression statements end with semicolons. Leaving out semicolons, or putting them in the wrong place, is a common error in expressing algorithms using languages from the C family. In fact, these semicolons are critical markers that describe the order of execution—the sequencing—of our source text statements. All work required by the statement in front of a semicolon will be completed *before* anything in a statement after the semicolon is begun. The semicolons in a C++ source text thus provide much of the sense of ordering that is required for a well-formed algorithm.

C++ Principle

> The semicolons that end simple declaration statements and expression statements are sequence points. The steps required by the statement in front of the semicolon are completed before any statement following the semicolon is executed.

Note finally that I have put one statement on each line of the source text; this is not required, but it is important. Although multiple statements can actually appear on a single line, it is a bad practice.

---

[3] According to the C++ language definition, expression statements in C++ don't actually need to change any data, but an expression statement that does no work serves no purpose, and is just a silly waste of keystrokes.

Claim

> Source text is written and read by humans, and should be made as readable as possible for humans.

It is important that source text be easily readable, not only by its author but also by others. A source text is not just input to drive a compiler; it is a means of communication between people. It should be presented in a pleasing way on the screen (or page), and it should be understandable by everyone who knows the language. By putting only one statement on each line, the ordering of the steps becomes manifest by simply scanning down the page.

2.2.2 Scaffold

So much for the heart of our code to square a number. Now let's look at the scaffold. Lines 1 and 2 of the source text **square1.cpp** are related. Line 1

```
#include <iostream>
```

is called a preprocessor include directive. It asks the compiler system to find the declarations of a whole host of important identifiers used to get data into and out of programs. This is actually done by pasting the contents of the named file, `iostream` in this case, right into the source text before it is run through the compiler.[4] Why is this done? It's a consequence of our C++ principle that every identifier must be declared before it is used. There are many objects that are provided to us in a library of ready-made algorithms, there are many objects to declare in most C++ codes. A convenient way to do so is to organize these into groups of related facilities, such as those used for dealing with input and output from a code, and place all the declarations needed to use such a group of facilities into a *header file*.

C++ Principle

> A preprocessor include directive of the form `#include <file>` causes the compiler to find the named file, usually called a *header file*, and paste its contents into that point in the source text.

A C++ compiler comes with a large number of such header files containing the declarations of facilities provided by the C++ standard library.

Two of the identifiers defined in `iostream` have the improbable names `std::cin` and `std::cout`. These provide a simple mechanism for getting data into your code (input) and getting data out of your code (output). These names have two parts, for example, `std` and `cin`. The first part, `std`, is a prefix placed on a great many standard facilities. We could use these long, formal names, but it is instead common to make the `std` part understood. This is the purpose of line 2

```
using namespace std;
```

which essentially tells the compiler to treat the first name `std` as understood.

---

[4]If you explore your computer system, you should be able to find and examine the file `iostream`.

Simple input (from a keyboard) and output (to a video display) for C++ codes are managed by the *standard input stream*, cin, and by the *standard output stream*, cout, respectively. We can extract data from cin using the >> operator; essentially, this operator causes our program to stop and wait for the human to type something on the keyboard of the computer. The characters typed are then *interpreted*, if possible, as information to be stored in the data container identified to the right of >>. So line 8 causes our program to halt its execution, waiting for some data to be typed on the keyboard. If those key presses can be understood as a number, for instance, -234.23, then that number will be stored in the container identified by x. If those key presses can't be understood as a number, for example, the human types in how are you?, then the input operation fails and unpleasant consequences ensue. We will deal with this problem later, but this is a case where the user has violated the required precondition of algorithm **Square** of Section 1.1, namely, that *x* must be a number.

Output can be displayed on the screen (or, if you want to sound impressive, on "the controlling terminal" of the program) with the << operator on cout. Whatever we put to the right of << is presented on the screen, formatted as characters for human consumption. Thus, line 9 is showing the results of the multiplication of x by itself, x * x, to the screen.

The next bit of scaffold occurs on lines 4, 5, and 12. On line 4 we introduce and define a special identifier called main. This is an example of a thing called a *function* in the C family of languages. A function is an encapsulated algorithm, named by an identifier; functions are extremely important and will be more thoroughly investigated later in this chapter. This particular function is special *because* it is named main: In C++ the function named main is called to start the execution of our algorithm. It is actually called for us by the computer's operating system when we run the compiled machine language code. The definition of main begins on line 4

```
int main()
```

This part says that function main takes no input from the operating system (the empty parentheses), and returns an integer to the operating system (int). This integer is, in most cases, of no fundamental importance whatsoever to modern operating systems, and its forced presence is a required and annoying anachronism.

Note that line 4 does not end with a semicolon. This is because it is neither a simple declaration nor an expression statement. Instead, it is a function definition, and the function name and argument list, main(), is followed instead by a compound statement, which is everything between a matched set of { and } braces.

Definition

> A *compound statement* is a means to collect together a group of statements. Any number of expression statements and simple declaration statements enclosed in braces { } is a compound statement.

The compound statement in **square1.cpp** starts on line 5 with {, and ends on line 12 with }.

Of the scaffold in the source text, that leaves line 11 which reads

```
return 0;
```

This is an expression statement that ends the execution of function main and returns the integer 0 to main's caller (the operating system).

There is now perhaps some confusion about this algorithm's caller and its input and output data. Although it is a human user who causes the algorithm to be executed, it is a computer operating system that actually calls main. The function main can therefore take input arguments from the operating system, and returns a value to the operating system. This leaves us looking for some way to get into the action—how do we get *our* data into the code, and *our* data out of it. This is the purpose of cin and cout in **square1.cpp**. The standard input cin and standard output cout provide one of the standard mechanisms to get data into and out of a code when it executes. Even these standard input and output streams are actually controlled by the operating system, so the interaction with a human user is really somewhat indirect, as suggested by Fig. 2.1. These standard streams are certainly not the only such mechanism for moving data around, and we shall discover more before long.

2.2.3 Compilation

What do we do with the source text **square1.cpp**? We must compile it into machine language. The details of this are very dependent on the compiler that you use; the C++ language standard defines the language, but not the details of how a compiler should be invoked. Typically, we put the source text in a file, named **square1.cpp**, although the name does not really matter. A compiler is then executed, and the name of this file provided as input, and if all is well the compiler creates a new file containing our algorithm translated into machine code, all ready to run on the computer.

In this text I will provide a few examples of running one particular compiler, the GNU C++ compiler.[5] To invoke the g++ compiler involves typing a command like (blue text shows what you type to compile the code):

```
1   [hagar@localhost]$ g++ square1.cpp -o square
2   [hagar@localhost]$
```

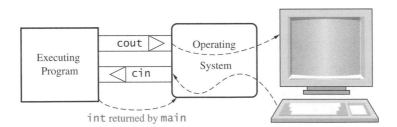

FIGURE 2.1   The operating system provides the overall execution environment for a running program, and mediates the exchange of data with the user.

[5]This excellent compiler is available free for most computer platforms, including Linux, Mac OS/X, Windows, and all versions of UNIX. See http://www.gnu.org for more information.

As cartooned in Fig. 2.2, this causes the compiler g++ to execute, read the source text from the file **square1.cpp**, translate it into machine code, combine it with necessary, preexisting, standard algorithms (for example to interact with a human), and write a complete program in machine language in the file square.[6]

The newly created collection of machine language code, square, can now be executed, as many times as you like, typically by simply typing its name (but this is again operating-system- and environment-dependent). Every time square is executed, nothing apparently will happen. This is correct behavior for the algorithm in **square1.cpp**, because the first thing the code does is to wait for you to type in a number (line 8). While it waits, it does nothing. But once you do type in a number (and typically hit the enter key), the code quickly squares the number you provided and writes this result back to the screen.

2.2.4 Analysis and Improvement

Now it's time for some analysis of our program. There are several things wrong with **square1.cpp**. Not wrong in the sense of giving the wrong results, but wrong in the sense of design. The code is simply not well designed. First off, when the code starts execution, it just sits still, waiting for a number to be entered. The human who invoked it probably just sits there too, wondering what's up. This code should *prompt* the user. It should present the user with a message, asking that the user type in a number.

Definition

> The *user* of a program is the human (or even other program) who causes it to be executed. The user invokes the program.

The user is effectively the caller of the algorithm implemented in the program, but as we have already seen, the way a program interacts with its user is mediated by the computer's operating system, and this special relationship needs to be distinguished

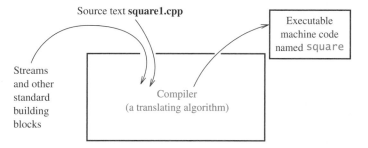

FIGURE 2.2 A compiler is itself an algorithm that translates a source text into executable machine code.

---

[6]Note that on a Windows-based operating system this file needs to have a .exe extension in order to be executed.

from the more common but restricted relationship between an algorithm and another algorithm that it calls.

Sometimes, you, the programmer, are the user. But often this is not the case. Usually, the user has no knowledge, and no wish for knowledge, of the algorithm behind the program. When you create an algorithm that will interact with a user, you must therefore consider how that interaction will appear. You must separate yourself from your special knowledge as the creator of the algorithm, and imagine yourself in the place of the user. And the user wants to be courted.

Claim

> If you design an algorithm to directly interact with a human, you should prompt for data.

Note that not all codes which are used by humans need to interact with humans. The compiler itself is an example. We start it up and let it do its work; it does not need to engage us in conversation, and it would be most annoying if it did.

But our code to square numbers does seem like one that should engage in a conversation:

"What's the number you want to square, my dear," said the computer.

"Twenty-nine point three," said Little Red Riding User.

Here is a version of the squaring algorithm that does this:

square2.cpp

```
1   #include <iostream>
2   using namespace std;
3
4   int main()
5   {
6
7       cout << "Enter_number_to_square:>_";
8       double x;
9       cin >> x;
10      cout << x * x;
11
12      return 0;
13  }
```

This new version adds one statement, which is shown in a box on line 7 of **square2.cpp:**

```
    cout << "Enter_number_to_square:>_";
```

The characters surrounded by double quotes comprise a *string literal*; it is a bit of text that is to be treated literally as it is, rather than interpreted as part of an instruction to translate into machine code. When showing string literals in this text, I show each and every space with the ⌣ symbol. This is simply so you can see where the spaces are. When actually typing such a string in your source text, you will hit the space bar and "see" a space. On line 7 of **square2.cpp** we are throwing the text Enter number to square:> into cout using the << operator, so that this informative prompt will appear on the screen *before* the code stops and waits for the user to type in a number.

A final improvement is worth considering here. The code's answer is a bit terse, and (as you know, since you've compiled and run the code by now, right?) awkwardly placed on the same line as whatever follows the execution of the code. We should never be surprised when the computer is very literal and displays no refinement: We did not put any instruction in our code to start a new line after displaying the answer, and so no new line was begun. Here is a final version of the squaring algorithm that does start a new line after displaying the answer, and indeed is downright chatty with the user.

square3.cpp

```
1   #include <iostream>
2   using namespace std;
3
4   int main()
5   {
6
7       double x;
8       cout << "Enter number to square:> ";
9       cin >> x;
10      cout << "The square of " << x << " is " << x * x << endl;
11
12      return 0;
13  }
```

The line to note now is line 10. This line shows several << operators in the same statement, some displaying literal text, one displaying the value of x, and one the result of the multiplication x * x. Finally, the mystery identifier endl is pitched into cout. endl tells cout to start a new line. Now when I run the code under the Linux operating system, it looks like this (blue text shows what you type to run the newly compiled program):

```
1   [hagar@localhost ]$ ./square
2   Enter number to square:> -29.3
3   The square of -29.3 is 858.49
4   [hagar@localhost ]$
```

We could probably refine square some more. There are certainly still design issues we can get into. But it's also a rather trivial application, whose purpose as an illustrative code does not warrant further improvement.

Questions

Question 1 Identify each of the following statements as an expression statement, a simple declaration statement, or a compound statement:

a. double x;

b. cin >> x;

c. cout << x * 0.5;

Question 2 In response to the prompt below, a user types 2.0 4.0. What does the code print on standard output?

```
cout << "Input_height_and_width_:>_"
double h;
cin >> h;
```

```
double w;
cin >> w;
cout << "Area_=_" << h * w;
```

Question 3 Change **Square3.cpp** so that it cubes a number. You must change two lines in the code.

2.3 EXPRESSIONS

Let's begin a more systematic study of expressions in the C++ language, with an eye toward seeing sequence within them. I will focus at first on a few ways that we can express numerical computations in C++. Numbers tend to be very important to engineers; this importance comes from our ability to model physical systems by manipulating numbers. For example, by saying $E = mc^2$, we note that if we square one number (called c in the formula) and multiply this result by another (known here as m), we get an interesting new number (called E). What we want to do with numbers, then, is store them, name them, use them in arithmetic expressions, and show them to the user. In this section we will explore how C++ allows us to express these ideas.

If I want to add two numbers, say, 9.1×10^{-31} and 1.7×10^{-27}, then I want to be able to write source text something like

```
9.1e-31 + 1.7e-27
```

and have the computer somehow make sense of it, and pop back with

```
1.70091e-27.
```

The text 9.1e-31 + 1.7e-27 is an example of an expression, yielding, in this case, an estimate of the mass of a hydrogen atom in kilograms. The expression consists, in this case, of two pieces of literal data—two numbers written in our beloved base 10 place value system using scientific notation—and an addition *operator* +. This expression can be *evaluated*, meaning that the operator can be made to act on the data and yield a value, the sum of the two operands. Although in this case we have applied the addition operator to two literal values, more generally we want to have a whole host of operators, including addition, subtraction, multiplication, and division. And we want to apply these operators not just to literal values but also to identifiers that have been associated with data (perhaps like m and c in $m \times c \times c$).

Definition

> An *expression* is a combination of operators, literal values, and identifiers that can be evaluated.

What are these things, operators, literal values, and identifiers? Identifiers we already defined in our first definition in this chapter.

TABLE 2.1   Binary and Unary Mathematical Operators in C++

Operator	Meaning	Arity	Placement	Precedence
–	Sign change	unary	prefix	15
*	Multiplication	binary	infix	13
/	Real division	binary	infix	13
/	Integer division	binary	infix	13
%	Remainder	binary	infix	13
+	Addition	binary	infix	12
–	Subtraction	binary	infix	12

Definition

A *literal data value* is a direct representation in our program text of a data value.

The number 256 is such a literal data value; Appendix A describes the rules for creating literal data values.

Definition

An *operator* is a machine that takes one (unary operator) or two (binary operator) data values and transforms them into a new data value.

The addition operator is such a machine, as are negation, subtraction, division, and multiplication. Some useful arithmetic operators are shown in Table 2.1.

Most of these operators are not surprising. The binary operators take two operands, which in the source text are placed on each side of the operator; such an operator is called an *infix* operator. So to add 1 and 2, we write 1 + 2. The unary operator – is placed before its operand in the source text (it is a *prefix* operator). It evaluates to the negative of its operand, so –2 evaluates to the negative of 2; surely no other semantics would do! But do consider this from the perspective of computation: Placing the sign change operator – in front of a piece of data is an instruction to do an active thing: "Negate the data please, oh computer, and use the result of that operation in this expression."

Two of the operators in Table 2.1 deserve special mention. Integer division / is an infix operator that when applied to two operands of type int yields the whole number part of the fraction, so, for example, 4/2 evaluates to 2, but 1/2 evaluates to 0, since 1/2 has no integer part. The remainder, or modulus, operator % provides the other piece of this puzzle; it yields the remainder of the fraction, so 1 % 2 evaluates to 1. In contrast, the real division operator /, which in most computer languages, including C++, unfortunately looks just like the integer division operator, yields its left operand divided by its right, so 1.0/2.0 is 0.5 as you would expect.

There is an apparent ambiguity then: How do we tell integer division from real division, when both are expressed with the same operator? Unfortunately in the C family, we (and the compiler) must tell by context. If both operands are of type int, then it is integer division. If either operator is of type double, then it is real division. When writing literal values, a number without a decimal point like 1 is considered to be an int, and a number with a decimal point like 1.0 is considered to be a double. When using identifiers as operands (as we shall presently), the declared type of each identifier provides the context to select between real and integer division.

This ambiguity, and its resolution by context, reflect a design principle of the C family of languages.

C++ Principle

> In C++ the types of operands determine the meaning of an operator and the type of the result.

Integer versus real division is the biggest headache in this situation, as everything else behaves pretty much as you would expect. But it is worth emphasizing that the type of the result is determined by the *types* of the operands, and not their values. When any of the binary operators is applied with two `int` operands, the result is an `int`. But if either operand is of type `double`, then the result will be a `double`. Thus, `2.0/1` is *not* an `int`; it is a `double` that happens to exactly equal the integer `2.0`.

C++ Principle

> Suppose that in an arithmetic expression `x op y`, where `op` is any of the binary operators from Table 2.1, `x` is of type `double` and `y` is of type `int`. Then the value of `y` is converted to `double` before the operator acts. The same is true if `y` is a `double` and `x` is an `int`.

In Chapter 5 we shall take up this issue yet again.

In expressions, sequence is important. For example, what does $2 + 3 / 5$ evaluate to? It could be $5/5$, which evaluates to 1. But, since $3/5$ evaluates to 0 (integer division), $2 + 3 / 5$ could also be $2 + 0$, which evaluates to 2. It all depends on the order in which the operators act. Does $+$ happen before $/$, or does $/$ happen before $+$? There is no inevitable answer to this—the order of evaluation is a choice that we humans must make. What we must have for the mechanistic execution of our algorithms is some fixed rules, so that in C++ the result should be *either* 1 or 2, but not sometimes 1 and sometimes 2. There are two routes out of such a quagmire. First, parentheses `()` can be used to force the order of operation to be whatever you want.

C++ Principle

> Parentheses group expressions: An expression inside parentheses is evaluated *before* the expression is used as an operand of any operator outside the parentheses.

Therefore in

        (2 + 3) / 5

the subexpression in parentheses $2 + 3$ is the left operand of the `/` operator. Thus, $(2 + 3) / 5$ evaluates to $5/5$, which is 1. Similarly,

        2 + (3 / 5)

evaluates to 2.

One of the great virtues of using parentheses is that there are no rules to memorize. When in doubt, simply put parentheses around things to specify the required order of evaluation. This advice is sometimes sneered at; after all, there are rules for the order of evaluation, and if we simply learn them, we can often dispense with parentheses. However, the C family of languages has over 36 binary operators, as well as a nice suite of unary operators for your programming enjoyment. This is all rather much; while remembering rules for what is evaluated first may be an entertaining mental exercise, it is of little intrinsic value. Using parentheses to make the order of evaluation clear is often of great help to your readers.

Claim

> You should use parentheses to make the order of evaluation clear in expressions. This enhances readability and makes it less likely that you will introduce defects in your code.

That said, it is worth knowing, and often worth using, the rules of precedence for the basic arithmetic unary and binary operators $+, -, *, /$, and $\%$; this is especially true in complicated arithmetical expressions (where there is a fine line between using parentheses liberally (to show the order of evaluation of operators) and creating parenthetical chaos). The rules that order the sequencing of mathematical operations, at least, are simple. A unary minus is always done first—it has the highest *precedence* of any operation in Table 2.1. Multiplication and division (which includes $\%$) have a medium precedence, so they are are done before any addition or subtraction, and otherwise everything evaluates left to right. Thus, in $5 + 3 / 3 - 9$ the division is done first, conceptually yielding $5 + 1 - 9$, and then the addition and subtraction are done from left to right (not that it matters here), yielding -3 as the value of the expression. Parentheses still come first, of course, so $(5 + 3) / 3 - 9$ evaluates to $8 / 3 - 9$, which is $2 - 9$ (don't forget that integer division business). Thus, the expression $(5 + 3) / 3 - 9$ evaluates to -7.

In general, the order of evaluation of operators is controlled by their *precedence* and their *associativity*.

C++ Principle

> The evaluation of operators is sequenced by their precedence, from high to low, so that higher-precedence operators operate on their operands before lower-precedence operators are able to act. Operators of equal precedence act according to their associativity. There are two associativities: left to right (as in reading English), or right to left (as in reading Arabic).

A left-to-right associativity means that an operator acts before other operators to its right, if they have equal precedence and the same parenthetical nesting. Operators with right-to-left associativity go the other way, with operators to the right acting sooner than those to the left. All the operators we have seen so far associate from left to right, except the unary minus $(-)$, which associates from right to left.

Not all operators have to do with arithmetic. Three examples are listed in Table 2.2. The insertion $<<$ and extraction $>>$ operators we have seen already. These throw data to, and extract data from, external data streams that might, for example, be connected to the screen or keyboard of a computer. The behavior of these input/output operators is actually dependent on the type of their operands, just like $/$ is. The operator

TABLE 2.2 **Some Other Interesting Binary Operators**

Meaning	Left Operand	Operator	Right Operand	Precedence
Insertion	output stream	<<	expression	11
Extraction	input stream	>>	identifier	11
Assignment	identifier	=	expression	2

<< is actually defined to take as its right operand a type of data with the unlikely name of ostream, which is short for "output stream." cout is actually an identifier whose value is just such an output stream. The left operand can be of type int or double, and the effect is to put a human text representation of this left operand into the standard output stream. What happens to that text is not really a part of the C++ standard. The operating system gets it, and might write it into a file, or might display it on the screen, or might even throw it away. In most cases you will encounter, standard output is by default sent to some computer display, but your operating system very likely provides a facility to redirect it to a file. If o is an ostream, the expression o << x causes a human readable representation of x to be sent into this ostream. But the expression o << x also evaluates to the value of o. This, together with the left-to-right order of evaluation of <<, allows an expression statement like

```
cout << 1.0 << 1;
```

to first put 1.0 into standard output *and* cause the expression to partially evaluate as

```
cout << 1;
```

then causing 1 to be placed into standard output.

Similarly, the >> operator can take as its left operand data of type istream, which is short for "input stream." Perhaps you will not be surprised to learn that cin is a variable whose type is istream. The right-hand operand can be an identifier[7] that names a variable of type int or double. If i is an istream, then an expression of the form i >> x causes the code to look at the standard input stream for characters that could represent a number of the type of x, and if they are there, to read them and place the corresponding value into x. In such an operation, white space characters (spaces, tabs, newlines) in the input are ignored. But i >> x also evaluates to the value of i, so i >> x >> y attempts to read two numbers from standard input. Because >> evaluates from left to right, a read is first attempted to place a number into x, and then a read is attempted to place a number into y.

Note that << and >> are evaluated from left to right, and their precedence is low enough that in cout << 1 + 3 the 1 + 3 happens first, and it is the result, 4, that is sent to the screen.

C++ unfortunately has 17 levels of precedence among its many operators. My advice: Learn the precedence of the operators in Tables 2.1 and 2.2, never use more than one assignment operator in an expression, and for all the rest, control the order of evaluation with parentheses.

The assignment operator = is an interesting beast also. This operator is used to *assign* data to its left operand. It associates right to left and has very low precedence so

[7]Strictly, its right-hand operand is a reference, but we will not discuss this detail just yet.

that expressions to the right get evaluated before any assignment takes place. Assignment is the primary mechanism by which we associate data with a symbolic name; this is important enough to merit a section of its own here.

2.3.1 Identifiers and Assignment

When working with numbers, or other data, it is useful, even crucial, to be able to store them somewhere and it is useful, even crucial, to refer to the stored quantity by a symbolic name. Such an identifier gives us a way to refer to a number without having to worry about what its value is. Conceptually, we want a way in our source text to demand that the computer set aside "space" to hold a data value for us, and that it associates a name—the identifier—with that data (see Fig. 2.3).

Although the computer itself may not associate a name with a memory location, you and I would rather refer to numbers by names like massElectron and massProton, and not by the values 9.1×10^{-31} and 1.7×10^{-27}. Then we could say

```
massElectron + massProton
```

and have the computer make sense of it, and compute

```
1.70091e-27.
```

The naming of variables simplifies the creation of algorithms, and is supported by high-level languages like C++. It is part of the compiler's job to convert between our human-oriented naming of data and the computer's reference to data by its location in memory. In order to do this, we need a way to set the values associated with massElectron and massProton. We can do this at the same time that the identifiers are declared, as shown in the following code:

hydrogenMass.cpp

```
1   #include <iostream>
2   using namespace std;
3
4   int main()
5   {
6
7       double massElectron = 9.1e-31;
8       double massProton = 1.7e-27;
9
10      cout << "The mass of Hydrogen is approximately: ";
11      cout << massElectron + massProton << endl;
```

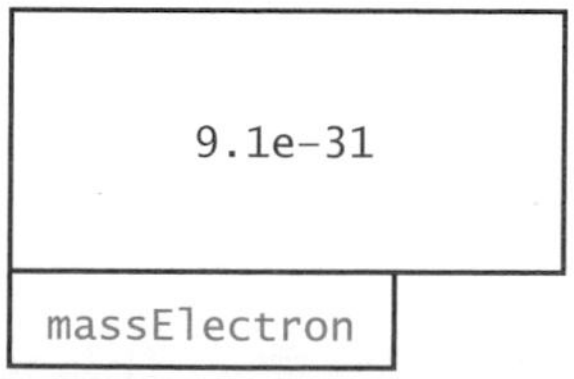

```
┌─────────────────┐
│                 │
│    9.1e-31      │
│                 │
├─────────────────┤
│  massElectron   │
└─────────────────┘
```

FIGURE 2.3 A data container—a variable—provides storage for a value and a means to symbolically identify it.

```
12
13      return 0;
14  }
```

C++ Principle

> A simple declaration can have the form
>
>   simple_type identifier = expression;
>
> A variable can thereby be initialized with the value of an expression when it is first declared.

For example, on the boxed line 7, the identifier massElectron is declared to be a double, and is given a value.[8]

On line 11 we have an expression statement. Part of this is the expression massElectron + massProton, in which we have a binary operator + acting on the two operands massElectron and massProton to compute their sum. Another binary operator on line 11 is <<, which operates on cout and the value of massElectron + massProton. The action of << is complex, but as we have already seen, it causes a human readable representation of massElectron + massProton to appear on the screen (cout).

In Table 2.2 I have introduced an important operation, assignment, expressed as = in many computer languages. This operation has little to do with the mathematical notion of equality, but the unfortunate use of the equality symbol for assignment was introduced long ago in FORTRAN and we have been unable to break free of it in the C family.[9] Remember: The symbol = denotes assignment, not an assertion of equality. I promise that you will, sometime or other, forget this, and use assignment where you don't mean to, or you will use it backwards. We all have.

Definition

> *Assignment* is the operation of placing data into a container.

It is important to think of assignment as an active operation. The symbol = in a C++ text is a *demand* to store data in the identifier to the *left* of the = operator; Fig. 2.4 suggests this action.

Assignment is an important (although not essential) notion in the expression of algorithms. It provides us with a way to denote the storage of a data value, and simultaneously provides us with a symbol by which we can refer, in our source text, to that stored value.

---

[8]It is worth noting that in C++ a variable *always* has a value; if a value is not explicitly assigned to a variable, its value is unknown to us and probably not useful.

[9]Languages such as Ada, Pascal, and Eiffel rooted in the Algol family did manage to jettison this misleading notation.

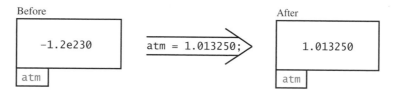

FIGURE 2.4 Assignment is an action. It causes data to be written into the data container named on the left-hand side of the = sign. The statement atm = 1.013250; puts the value 1.013250 into atm. Note that it does not matter if atm already holds a value or not; after the statement it holds only the value 1.013250.

C++ Principle

An expression statement of the form

```
identifier = expression;
```

causes the value of the expression to be stored in the container identified by the identifier on the left of the = operator.

Suppose that mass, height, and energy have previously been declared as identifiers of type double. The expression statement

```
mass = 80.0;
```

causes the value 80.0 to be stored in a container that is identified by the name mass, and similarly

```
height = 3.048;
```

causes the value 3.048 to be stored in a different container that is identified by the name height. And a subsequent statement

```
energy = mass * 9.81 * height;
```

causes first the expression mass * 9.81 * height to be evaluated,[10] and then this value to be stored in a container and identified by the name energy.

Note that the assignment operator = treats its right operand quite differently from its left operand. The right operand is anything that can evaluate to a datum value, but the left operand is an identifier. The expression statement

```
80.0 = mass;
```

will just cause the compiler to become annoyed with you, as would the statement

```
mass * 9.81 * height = energy;
```

---

[10]To 2218.944, if you care.

because in both cases the left operand of = does not identify or otherwise refer to a data storage location.[11] Unlike the symbol = that you know and love from mathematics, the assignment operator = is not symmetric. It cannot be, because its purpose is to demand an action from the computer; it demands that data be stored for us. In contrast, = in mathematics is a symmetric assertion of the equality of two things. The precise semantics of the C++ assignment operation are beyond the scope of this text, but the essence of it can be stated as follows:

C++ Principle

> The left operand of an assignment operation must identify an object that can hold data and whose value can be modified, and the right operand must be an expression.

The assignment operator has very low precedence, so that its right operand will be evaluated before the assignment is performed.

The semantics of assignment allow some very interesting, and at first sight surprising, statements to be written. Suppose that x has been declared as a numeric type like `double`, and assigned a value. The following statement is then valid and meaningful:

```
x = x * x;
```

Let's parse this. First the value stored under x is found, and that value times itself is computed; this happens first because the precedence of * is much higher than that of =. This product is the value of the expression on the right-hand side of the assignment operator, and this value is stored under the identifier x. Thus, this statement changes the value stored under x to the square of its former self. After the two statements

```
1   double x = 3.0;
2   x = x * x;
```

the value stored under x is 9.0.

Questions

Question 4　Given

```
double me = .511;
double mp = 9.38e2;
double mn = 9.40e2;
int Z = 4;
int A = 9;
```

what is the value of each of the following expressions?

a.　A/Z
b.　Z * mp + Z * me + (A-Z) * mn
c.　Z * mp + Z * me + (A-Z) * mn / A
d.　(Z * mp + Z * me + (A-Z) * mn) / A
e.　(1.0 * A)/Z

---

[11]Technically, the left-hand operand of the assignment operator needs to be a modifiable lvalue. We will not trouble ourselves with this level of technical C++ fussiness.

Question 5 Suppose the height $h(t)$ of a ball is given by $h(t) = v_0 t - gt^2/2$. Write an expression statement that will evaluate this formula and assign the appropriate value to a variable containing the height. Be sure to use good variable names for all the symbols in the formula.

Question 6 A machine requires n bolts, which are sold only in lots of m. Create good variable names and write a expression that writes to standard output the number of bolts which will remain unused after building the machine.

2.4 SOME EXAMPLE CODES

Let us now develop a few example C++ codes that carry out simple, but interesting computations. These codes are all simple formula evaluation exercises, and as such, do not yet hint at the true power of computing. But until we gain an understanding of iteration and its expression, as we shall in Chapter 3, such evaluation is all we can now manage. Still, these examples will help you develop a sense of how a basic C++ code should look, and I will comment on some issues in code layout.

2.4.1 Physics on the Computer

You all know this one: Suppose a ball of mass m is thrown upward at velocity v_0. What is its velocity $v(t)$ and height above release $h(t)$ at time t? The answer, if we neglect air resistance and a host of other tiny influences, is

$$v(t) = v_0 - gt \tag{2.1}$$
$$h(t) = v_0 t - gt^2/2 \tag{2.2}$$

where $g = 9.81$ m/s^2 is the acceleration due to gravity at the earth's surface. Let's write a C++ code that prompts for v_0 and t and then reports the ball's particulars. Here's a first go:

ball1.cpp

```
1   #include <iostream>
2   using namespace std;
3
4   int main()
5   {
6       double g = 9.81; // acceleration due to gravity
7
8       cout << "Input the initial velocity (m/s):> ";
9       double v0;
10      cin >> v0;
11
12      cout << "Input the time (s):> ";
13      double t;
14      cin >> t;
15
16      cout << "=============================================="//
17           << endl;
18      cout << "The velocity at time " << t << " is "
19           << v0 - g * t << endl;
```

```
20    cout << "and_the_height_is_"
21         << v0 * t - ( g * t * t ) / 2.0  << endl;
22
23    return 0;
24  }
```

Note that, as suggested in the last section, I prompt for input, and provide output that is fairly descriptive. Several of the C++ principles that you have now (hopefully!) learned are in evidence here, and I've snuck in a few new ones too.

First note on line 6 that a `double` is declared and initialized to hold the acceleration due to gravity. But also on this line is the strange annotation

```
// acceleration due to gravity
```

This is a *comment*, a bit of source code text intended only for human consumption, and ignored by the compiler.[12]

Claim

> You should use comments to increase the clarity of your source text.

Remember that a source text is as much a means of communication between humans as it is instructions for a compiler, so clarity should be one of your first goals.

The six lines 16–21 contain three expression statements, each spread out over two lines of source text. This is just fine—recall that expression statements end with a semicolon; their arrangement into lines is immaterial.

Note also that I have declared the variables `v0` and `t` right before obtaining values for them using `cin`. I could have declared these variables earlier, but I choose to declare them right before giving them useful values. When a variable is declared, but not initialized, it does have a value, but what that value is we can't know. The statement `double x;` implies that we want space to store a floating point value, but does not *give* it a *meaningful* value. Having variables with undefined values is often a source of errors in code, so it's a good idea to initialize variables as soon as possible.

Claim

> Give variables meaningful values as soon as possible.

You probably believe me to be hopelessly fussy, but wait until you have written a few broken codes with complex logic, and the root cause is discovered to be a variable that was declared and used before it was given a meaningful value, and wait until it takes you three hours to find the problem.

I know that, at this point, you will now compile and thoroughly test **ball1.cpp**.

2.4.2 Resistance in Parallel

Let's consider a problem from electronics. Suppose we have three electric resistors rigged up in parallel, as shown in Fig. 2.5, and we would like to treat them as one

---

[12]It is rather like a footnote: useful, but not part of the main text.

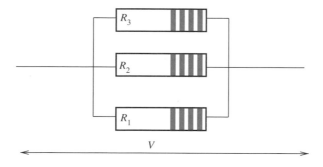

FIGURE 2.5 Three resistors hooked up in parallel can be treated as one resistor.

single resistor. Let's create an algorithm to compute the equivalent resistance of the three parallel resistors, but treated as one.

Ohm's law says that the current I_i through the ith resistor is proportional to the voltage drop V across the resistor, so these quantities are related by $V = I_i R_i$, where R_i is called the resistance of the resistor. The total current flowing through the three resistors is just the sum of the three currents and the voltage drop V is the same for all three, so

$$I_{\text{total}} = \frac{V}{R_1} + \frac{V}{R_2} + \frac{V}{R_3} = V\left[\frac{1}{R_1} + \frac{1}{R_2} + \frac{1}{R_3}\right]. \tag{2.3}$$

Thus, Ohm's law applies to the whole group of three resistors, with the resistance R_{parallel} given by

$$\frac{1}{R_{\text{parallel}}} = \frac{1}{R_1} + \frac{1}{R_2} + \frac{1}{R_3}. \tag{2.4}$$

Note that we had to analyze the problem before we could write any code; this is often the case, and the analysis of the problem and design of the solution are usually more difficult than the implementation.

Let's write a C++ code that prompts the user for three resistance values, and returns the resistance of those three in parallel:

parallelResistors.cpp

```
1   // ================================================================
2   // parallelResistors.cpp
3   // Prompts for three resistance values and computes the
4   // resistance of those three when in parallel
5   // ================================================================
6   #include <iostream>
7   using namespace std;
8
9   int main()
10  {
11
12      // Get resistance values from standard input
13      cout << "Please provide three resistance values:> ";
```

```
14    double R1;    // storage for the first resistance value
15    cin >> R1;
16
17    double R2;    // storage for the second resistance value
18    cin >> R2;
19
20    double R3;    // storage for the third resistance value
21    cin >> R3;
22
23    // Compute parallel resistance of these three
24    double Rparallel = 1.0 / (1.0/R1 + 1.0/R2 + 1.0/R3);
25
26    // Report back through standard output
27    cout << "The parallel resistance is " << Rparallel << endl;
28
29    // Give the operating system its bone
30    return 0;
31 }
```

Note the initialization using an expression in the boxed line of code. Also note the use of parentheses in the expression

```
1.0 / (1.0/R1 + 1.0/R2 + 1.0/R3)
```

These are required to ensure that the denominator is evaluated first.

Let's examine and think about this algorithm. Suppose the user provides a negative value for one of the resistances? This is meaningless, but the code will unfortunately press on without complaint. We really must provide a restriction on the values of R1, R2, and R3. We do not yet have the tools to express this in C++ source text, but our path is clear: If the user inputs a negative resistance, the code should complain, and then either give up, or give the user another chance to enter a meaningful value.

Suppose instead that the user inputs a zero value for one of the resistances? This actually has a physical meaning. A zero resistance allows current to flow unimpeded, and the parallel resistance in this case should be 0, but it is not certain that this code will produce the correct answer. The semantics of division in C++ are not exacting enough to ensure this, so we really should deal with this special case separately. But once again, we do not yet have the means to express this special case in our code; we need a selection construct, which I shall present in Chapter 4.

2.4.3 Manipulating Time

Suppose a time value has been stored as an integer number of seconds since midnight. As shown in Figure 2.6, we would like to convert this to the time on a synchronized, 24-hour, digital clock. The keys to solving this problem are integer division and the remainder operator. Let seconds represent the integer number of seconds since midnight. Since there are $60 \times 60 = 3,600$ seconds in 1 hour, the number of hours since midnight is seconds/3600. With / understood as integer division, this yields only the whole number part, with no remainder, and thus is the number of hours since midnight.

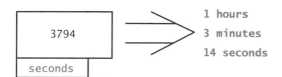

FIGURE 2.6 Mapping seconds since midnight into a human friendly form.

We can then extract the remaining number of seconds, the fractional part of the hour, as seconds % 3600. Repeating the same logic, we can extract from this remainder the whole number of minutes that it represents by again using integer division but now with a denominator of 60. Finally, we can extract the remaining number of seconds using the remainder operator.

The heart of this algorithm is integer division and the remainder operator. Here is a first attempt that's basically correct, but which could be better:

aclock.cpp

```
1   // ============================================================
2   // aclock.cpp
3   // A code to convert the number of seconds since midnight into
4   // a more human friendly form.
5   // ============================================================
6   #include <iostream>
7   using namespace std;
8
9   int main()
10  {
11    // Some basic constants from the distant past
12    int secondsPerMinute = 60;
13    int minutesPerHour = 60;
14
15    // Prompt for the number of seconds since midnight
16    cout << "Input the number of seconds since midnight:> ";
17    int seconds;
18    cin >> seconds;
19
20    // We can now compute the number of hours, minutes and seconds
21
22    cout << "The time since midnight is:> ";
23    cout << seconds / (secondsPerMinute * minutesPerHour)
24         << " hours ";
25
26    // Remove the hours and show the number of minutes remaining
27    seconds = seconds % (secondsPerMinute * minutesPerHour);
28    cout << seconds / (secondsPerMinute) << " minutes ";
29
30    // Remove the minutes and show the remaining seconds
31    seconds = seconds % (secondsPerMinute);
32    cout << seconds << " seconds" << endl;
```

```
33
34    return 0;
35  }
```

Note the use of the variables secondsPerMinute and minutesPerHour. These are intended to improve the readability of the code. I could just sprinkle the literal integer 60 and even 3600 through the code, but this is less clear to the casual reader, and it's hard to get it right since I have to type in those values in multiple places. When I make a mistake and accidentally type 6 someplace, I must search the code, looking at all the numbers and analyzing each to decide on its correctness. Worse, such an isolated error might only sometimes affect the results, which would decrease my chance of finding it through testing. By contrast, if I name my constants, with meaningful names, there is only one place to fix a mistyped value.

This code has a rough spot, albeit a minor one. Consider the following test run:

```
1  [hagar@localhost Code]$ ./aclock
2  Input the number of seconds since midnight:> 3661
3  The time since midnight is: 1 hours 1 minutes 1 seconds
4  [hagar@localhost Code]$
```

This is not good English, since singulars are being treated as plurals. We don't have a good means to address this yet. Once again, we need selection!

2.4.4 Correctness and Defects

Let's now expand the thrown ball code from Section 2.4.1 to provide the height and velocity of the ball in two different cases: first assuming it was launched on Earth, and then assuming it was launched on Mars, where $g = 3.63$ m/s^2. Here's an attempt:

ball2.cpp

```
1  // ================================================================
2  // ball2.cpp
3  // Code to compute the eventual height and velocity of a ball
4  // launched with given initial velocity on Earth and on Mars
5  // ================================================================
6  #include <iostream>
7  using namespace std;
8
9  int main()
10 {
11   double g = 9.81; // acceleration due to gravity on Earth
12
13   cout << "Input the initial velocity (m/s):> ";
14   double v0;
15   cin >> v0;
```

```
16
17      cout << "Input the time (s):> ";
18      double t;
19      cin >> t;
20
21
22      // Results on Earth
23      cout << "========================================"
24          << endl;
25      cout << "Earth:" << endl;
26      cout << "The velocity at time " << t << " is "
27          << v0 + g * t << endl;
28      cout << "and the height is "
29          << v0 * t + g * t * t / 2.0 << endl;
30
31      // now do Mars
32      g = 3.63;  // acceleration due to gravity on Mars
33      cout << "========================================"
34          << endl;
35      cout << "Mars:" << endl;
36      cout << "The velocity at time " << t << " is "
37          << v0 + g * t << endl;
38      cout << "and the height is "
39          << v0 * t + g * t * t / 2.0 << endl;
40
41      return 0;
42  }
```

Now I'm feeling very proud of myself—I have modeled a ball thrown on two planets! However, all is not well in gravityville. Have you yet noticed that this code is wrong? It compiles. It runs. It just happens to give the wrong answers. How do I know it gives the wrong answers? This is, in general, a very difficult thing to know. For interesting or important problems we never know the correct answer. If we did, why would we bother trying to solve the problem with a computer program? We can never be sure of an answer, but we can increase our confidence in a code's correctness by:

1. careful reasoning about our algorithms and examination of the implementation
2. checking special cases
3. intuition about a solution

We can seldom tell with certainty if something is right, but we can often tell for sure that it's wrong.

Claim

> You should continuously ask yourself, "how do I *know* I'm right?" And never easily accept any answer, not even your own.

With **ball2** we can tell that something is wrong with our code by compiling and running it:

```
1   [hagar@localhost Code]$ ./ball2
2   Input the initial velocity (m/s):> 1.0
3   Input the time (s):> 2.0
4   ==========================================
5   Earth:
6   The velocity at time 2 is 20.62
7   and the height is 21.62
8   ==========================================
9   Mars:
10  The velocity at time 2 is 8.26
11  and the height is 9.26
12  [hagar@localhost Code]$
```

There is something very funny here—in 2.0 seconds the ball supposedly reached 21.62 meters on Earth, while only reaching 9.26 meters on Mars. But Earth pulls on the ball more strongly than Mars. So this code's results are the opposite of what we should expect. Looking further, you might notice that the ball is moving faster at 2.0 seconds than it was moving at 0.0 seconds. Not only can we see that something is wrong, but the nature of the error may suggest the source of the problem. Don't look yet—think about it.

There must be some sort of sign error—I'm subtracting where I should add, or vice versa. The problem indeed is that I used a plus sign where I needed a minus sign; there was simple confusion about the sign of the acceleration due to gravity g. Here is a correct version of the Earth–Mars ball code, with the corrected lines of the source text boxed:

ball3.cpp

```
1   // ==============================================================
2   // ball3.cpp
3   // Code to compute the height and velocity of a ball
4   // launched with given initial velocity on Earth and on Mars
5   // ==============================================================
6   #include <iostream>
7   using namespace std;
8
9   int main()
10  {
11     double g = 9.81; // acceleration due to gravity on Earth
12
13     // Prompt user and get input data for initial velocity v0 and
14     // time t of interest
```

```
15
16     cout << "Input_the_initial_velocity_(m/s):>_";
17     double v0;
18     cin >> v0;
19
20     cout << "Input_the_time_(s):>_";
21     double t;
22     cin >> t;
23
24
25     // Results on Earth
26
27     cout << "============================================"
28          << endl;
29     cout << "Earth:" << endl;
30     cout << "The_velocity_at_time_" << t << "_is_"
31          << v0 - g * t << endl;
32     cout << "and_the_height_is_"
33          << v0 * t - g * t * t / 2.0 << endl;
34
35     // Now compute results for Mars
36
37     g = 3.63;  // acceleration due to gravity on Mars
38     cout << "============================================"
39          << endl;
40     cout << "Mars:" << endl;
41     cout << "The_velocity_at_time_" << t << "_is_"
42          << v0 - g * t << endl;
43     cout << "and_the_height_is_"
44          << v0 * t - g * t * t / 2.0 << endl;
45
46     return 0;
47   }
```

Whew, in order to fix this code, I had to remember to change four plus signs to minus signs. Did I get them all? Did I get the right ones? A common problem when correcting a source text is to only half-correct it. One way to partially avoid this problem is to factor code into reusable parts, so that any one expression needs be written only once: We shall take up this task in the next section. In the meantime, here is a repeat of the previous test:

```
1   [hagar@localhost Code]$ ./ball3
2   Input the initial velocity (m/s):> 1.0
3   Input the time (s):> 2.0
```

```
4   =========================================
5   Earth:
6   The velocity at time 2 is -18.62
7   and the height is -17.62
8   =========================================
9   Mars:
10  The velocity at time 2 is -6.26
11  and the height is -5.26
12  [hagar@localhost Code]$
```

Now these results show that the ball on both Earth and Mars, at 2.0 seconds after an upward launch of 1.0 m/s, has passed its zenith and is falling downward, and in fact has fallen below the launch point. The relative sizes make sense—Earth is pulling the ball back more rapidly than Mars.

Let's examine a special case: Some algebra will show that the time at which a ball reaches its maximum height is $t_{top} = v_0/g$. I can use this to provide another check:

```
1   [hagar@localhost Code]$ ./ball3
2   Input the initial velocity (m/s):> 9.81
3   Input the time (s):> 1.0
4   =========================================
5   Earth:
6   The velocity at time 1 is 0
7   and the height is 4.905
8   =========================================
9   Mars:
10  The velocity at time 1 is 6.18
11  and the height is 7.995
12  [hagar@localhost Code]$
```

I've picked the initial velocity and final time so that the ball should have just reached its zenith on Earth, and the code shows this. As I would expect, under the same conditions on Mars the ball is higher, and still going up.

I continue to have one minor concern with this code: I use the variable g to represent the acceleration due to gravity on both Mars and Earth. I initialize g to the value appropriate for Earth, and then later assign to it the value appropriate for Mars. This is not unreasonable; throughout the source text the symbol g represents *an* acceleration due to gravity. But it does not always represent *the* acceleration due to gravity. This now is a matter of stylistic judgment—is the source text more understandable the way it is, with g reused, or would it be better to introduce two different identifiers, say, gEarth and gMars? I have no definitive answer to this question. What do you think?

Questions

Question 7 Change **parallelResistors.cpp** to deal with four resistors in parallel.

Question 8 Write a C++ code that reads the number of seconds since midnight on January 1 from standard input and reports the number of days, hours, minutes, and seconds since the start of the year.

Question 9 Develop a set of tests for the code suggested in Question 8 above.

2.5 DECOMPOSITION

In implementing algorithms, decomposition is about order. It is the purely intellectual process of breaking an algorithm into manageable subparts, each of which is well defined by itself. Such decomposition is not logically necessary, but it is extremely useful in helping us imperfect humans manage the complexity of significant algorithms.

In Section 2.4 we computed the velocity and position of a particle subject to a constant gravitational acceleration on two different planets. This resulted in essentially identical expressions being repeated in multiple places in the source text. In consequence, when it was found to be wrong in one place, it was wrong in several. Further, when you read the source text, you are confronted with both the details of input and output, and the details of the physics calculation, even though these really have nothing to do with each other. Thus while designing and implementing input and output, you have the details of the physics calculation thrust in your face. And when considering the correctness of the physics calculation, you are forced to look in and among a forest of input/output statements. Surely we can organize this algorithm better.

Consider the physics calculation: It can really be understood as two functions in the mathematical sense. One is height as a function of initial velocity, time, and acceleration, and the other is velocity as a function of the same things. Wouldn't it be clearer if we could write something like

```
cout << "Height␣is␣" << height(g, v_0, t);
```

This statement demands less mental processing than the alternative

```
cout << "Height␣is␣" << v_0 * t - g * t * t/2.0;
```

whose purpose requires extensive interpretation of the mysterious expression on the right. The key idea here is that we would like to package the algorithm that computes the height of a ball inside a black box. Into this box we will pass values for g, v_0, and t, and the required height value will then pop back out. When using such a black box, we *don't care how it works*. We don't trouble our minds with it. We have separated our concerns: When dealing with data input and output, we worry about getting the right values and shoving them into our black box height machine. When creating the height machine, we don't worry about where data values came from; we only worry about getting the calculation right.

Most modern computer languages provide a facility to extend themselves by packing an algorithm into an independent entity accessible through a well-defined interface. When writing the `height` machine, we do not want to know that it will be used in that cout statement, or that it will be used once for Earth and once for Mars. We only want to specify that it needs three numbers, its input arguments g, t, and v_0. And that given those data, it calculates and provides as output the height that a ball will reach at time t.

Definition

> Algorithms packaged behind an interface are called variously *procedures, functions, commands, routines, subprograms,* or *subroutines.*

In C++ and the whole C family, such prepackaged algorithms are usually called functions. I will however make a common distinction: Routines that receive input data values, operate without side effects in their caller's environment, and return a value to their caller will be called functions.

Definition

> A *function* is an algorithm that returns data to its caller, and operates without reference to data in its caller's environment and without side effects.

Note that this does not mean a function has no input, but any input it has are just data values provided by the caller. You leave a note in my mailbox. In contrast, routines that take data values in, return no data, but which operate by side effects will be called procedures (they are also often called commands).

Definition

> A *procedure* or *command* is an algorithm that returns no data to its caller, but which directly references data in its caller, or otherwise operates by side effect.

You leave no data in my mailbox, I leave no data in yours, but I do enter your abode, read your bank statements, and leave a completed tax return on your desk. This is not really so bad, provided you had asked me to examine your finances and told me where to leave the form.

Routines that do both—return a value and act through side effects—will be called function-procedures, an intentionally ugly name for an ugly beast.

2.5.1 Library Functions

Let's now consider the realization of these ideas in C++. In this section we shall briefly introduce some functions that are always provided as part of the C++ standard library, a library of generally useful functions that are not part of the C++ language, but without which life would be most wearisome.

A library is a collection of ready-made routines that we can use when creating algorithms; these are procedures and functions that we can use without having to create them ourselves. I shall make no attempt to systematically list many of the standard library functions here[13]; a number of features of the C++ standard library are described

---

[13]To do so would require another 800 pages, Nicolai M. Josuttis's *The C++ Standard Library,* Addison-Wesley (1999) (ISBN 0-201-37926-0), provides a fairly complete reference on the subject.

in Appendices A and B, and you would be wise to skim those appendices. Here I will instead use some functions from the standard math library to illustrate function use, and to prompt a discussion of function call semantics.

One wonderfully useful grouping of predefined functions provide access to special-purpose mathematical functions such as sine, cosine, and exponentiation. In the listing of math functions in Appendix B you might discover the mysterious statement

double sin(double t) returns the sine of the angle t.

What does this mean? The basic idea should be clear: sin is a prepackaged algorithm that can be given an angle, measured in radians, and which will, somehow, estimate the sine of that angle and hand it back to whoever called sin. The syntax double sin(double angle) is meant to indicate that sine takes a double value as input (in the parentheses), and returns, or more exactly evaluates to, a double value. You put an input value in my mailbox, I return a value in your mailbox.

This description of sin suggests that it should be used as part of an expression, like

---

```
1  double theta = 1.5;            // angle theta is in radians
2  double hypotenuse = 2.0;
3  y = sin(theta) * hypotenuse;   // use the sine function
```

How is the expression on line 3 evaluated? When it is executed, the computer evaluates the expression on the left side of the assignment operator in the following order:

1. Function evaluation has very high precedence,[14] so first the function argument theta is evaluated—its value is just a number, 1.5. So the expression is first partially evaluated to

   sin(1.5) * hypotenuse.

2. The function evaluation—the function call—must now take place. The execution of the expression is set aside for the moment, and the algorithm execution machine fires up the sin algorithm, passing it the value 1.5 as data. Note that all sin gets is 1.5. It knows nothing about the identifier angle because that's in sin's caller, and sin knows nothing about its caller; sin just checks its mailbox and finds 1.5 waiting there. The sin algorithm does whatever it does for awhile, and eventually pops back with a data value of type double, say, 0.997494986604. The evaluation of the expression sin(1.5) * hypotenuse can now continue.

3. The original subexpression sin(theta) has now evaluated, so the value stored under hypotenuse is fetched and the expression is now

   0.997494986604 * 2.0.

---

[14]The ( ) of function evaluation has a precedence value of 16, higher than any of the mathematical operators of Table 2.1.

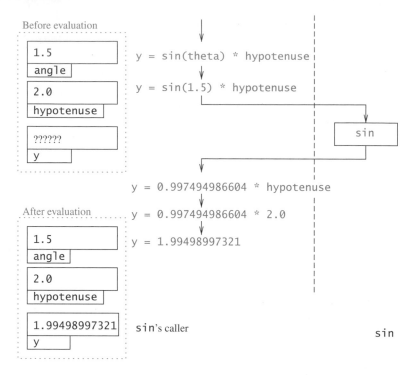

FIGURE 2.7 The thread of execution for evaluating an expression containing a function call.

The multiplication operator now has values to multiply, so this happens, and the expression has been fully evaluated to a double value of 1.99498997321.

4. Finally, this value is assigned under the identifier y.

Whew! For the visual learners among you, perhaps Fig. 2.7 will help. This shows the thread of execution being diverted into the sin algorithm, and then returning when that algorithm has finished its work.

Now frankly, you probably noted nothing surprising there, and would have had a clear and correct expectation of the result without my agonizing walk down parse tree lane. But something very important did, in fact, happen: sin(angle) was conceptually turned into sin(1.5). The sin machine was given the *value* 1.5 to work on, and that's all it ever knew about. It did not know anything about the identifier angle, or y, or hypotenuse; it just knew 1.5. The sin algorithm was given no knowledge of the environment in which it was used. It is a true function, and works without side effects. Further, we never needed to know how sin worked; we don't know what language it was written in, what identifiers were used, or what the algorithm is. The sin function just handed a number back to us. You left 1.5 in my mailbox, and in return I left 0.997494986604 in yours. Neither of us knows or cares how the other came up with his number. You know only that I promise to give you a good estimate of the sine of 1.5 radians.

Library Function Declaration   A fundamental C++ principle is that everything must be declared before it is used. So where is `sin` declared? In the header file `cmath`. To use any of the standard math functions, you must write the scaffold

```
#include <cmath>
```

in your C++ source text, near the top (perhaps just after `#include <iostream>`). Now let's create a complete code using functions, and see how this goes.

Snell's law   For your entertainment, here is a code that uses Snell's law to estimate the index of refraction of a piece of glass. The index of refraction n_g is the ratio of the speed of light in vacuum to the speed of light in glass. At an interface between glass and a vacuum, a ray of light traveling at angle θ_v in the vacuum will be bent, as it enters the glass, to an angle θ_g (see Fig. 2.8). According to Snell's law, these angles are related by $\sin(\theta_v) = n_g \sin(\theta_g)$. So, if we do a bit of algebra, $n_g = \sin(\theta_v)/\sin(\theta_g)$, and we can determine the index of refraction from the two angles θ_v and θ_g.

Here is a code that uses this to estimate[15] the index of refraction of the glass. Note the line `#include <cmath>` that is required to use functions from the standard math library.

indexRefraction.cpp

```
1  // ===============================================================
2  // indexRefraction.cpp
3  // Estimates the index of refraction of glass based on input
4  // angles of an incident ray of light and a refracted ray of
5  // light.
6  // ===============================================================
```

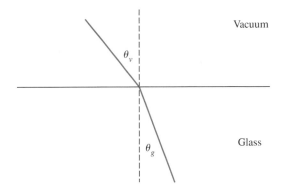

Vacuum

θ_v

Glass

θ_g

FIGURE 2.8   The geometry of Snell's law.

---

[15]Note that I said "estimate": I have no conceit that the angles will be perfectly measured, I have no expectation that the sines will be exactly computed, so I recognize that I will produce only an approximation to truth.

```
7   #include <iostream>
8   #include <cmath>
9   using namespace std;
10
11  int main()
12  {
13    cout << "Input angle of incidence in the vacuum: ";
14    double theta_v;
15    cin >> theta_v;
16
17    cout << "Input angle of refraction in the glass: ";
18    double theta_g;
19    cin >> theta_g;
20
21    double n_g = sin(theta_v)/sin(theta_g);
22
23    cout << "The index of refraction is " << n_g << endl;
24
25    return 0;
26  }
```

In this algorithm for determining the index of refraction we have decomposed the problem into three parts: getting data, finding sines of angles, and using the ratio of such sine values to find the index of refraction. Now the power of decomposition should be clear: Whatever the algorithm for computing sine looks like (and there are, in fact, several), it is of no concern to us when we deal with the index of refraction computation. No mistake that we make in the index of refraction computation affects the correctness of the sine algorithm. And, more surprisingly, an error in the sine algorithm does not make the **indexRefraction.cpp** algorithm incorrect. If the sine algorithm is wrong, no amount of fiddling elsewhere will make the algorithm right as a whole. The problems of making the algorithm work are separated into subproblems, which can be treated independently of each other. This separation of concerns is the primary benefit of decomposing a problem into separate routines.

Compiling with Library Functions Let's compile and run this **index-Refraction** code. Some compilers will require you to explicitly specify that you are using functions from the math library, and some will not. I did not write the sin function, but I use it in my code, so the compiler needs to find an implementation of it somewhere. Most compilers automatically look for implementations of some collection of library algorithms like the math function algorithms, and the common input/output algorithms, but there is no standard set of algorithms that every compiler will seek. Some compilers include the implementation of sin without special request, others need to be asked to look for it. None of these issues is part of the C++ *language* and they are not addressed by the C++ language definition. Different compiler writers take different approaches, and you will have to check with the documentation for your compiler to find out how to compile code that uses the standard math library. Here is an example using the common GNU g++ compiler:

```
1  [hagar@localhost]$ g++ indexRefraction.cpp -lm -o indexRefraction
2  [hagar@localhost]$ ./indexRefraction
3  Input angle of incidence in the vacuum:> 0.8
4  Input angle of refraction in the glass:> 0.7
5  The index of refraction is 1.11353
```

The text -lm tells the compiler to include the implementations of the math functions (m) from a standard library (l) of precompiled algorithms.[16]

Radioactive Decay   Unstable atomic nuclei—radioactive nuclei—are those nuclei that eventually cease to be. They convert themselves, often in several steps, to stable nuclei by spontaneously emitting stable particles. The fundamental rules of quantum mechanics imply that there is a decay constant λ, which is the probability per unit time that a particular nucleus will decay. It can be shown as a consequence of this definition that if we have N_0 nuclei at time 0, then we will have $N(t) = N_0 e^{-\lambda t}$ of these nuclei at time t. We can turn this around and measure the decay constant by measuring N_0 and $N(t)$, then implying $\lambda = \ln(N_0/N(t))$. Here ln is the natural log (with base e); the standard C++ math library provides the function log to compute the natural log.[17] Here is a code that uses the log function:

decayConstant.cpp

```
1  // ===============================================================
2  // decayConstant.cpp
3  // Estimates the decay constant of a radioactive nucleus
4  // from two observations, separated by a given time, of the
5  // number of nuclei in a sample.
6  // ===============================================================
7  #include <iostream>
8  #include <cmath>
9  using namespace std;
10
11 int main()
12 {
13     cout << "Input the initial number of nuclei:> ";
14     double Ninitial;
15     cin >> Ninitial;
```

[16]In recent versions of the GNU g++ compiler the -lm option is not needed; functions from the math library are included automatically.

[17]Don't confuse this with log10 that computes the log in base 10. See Appendix B.

```
16
17    cout << "Input␣the␣final␣number␣of␣nuclei:>␣";
18    double Nfinal;
19    cin >> Nfinal;
20
21    cout << "Input␣the␣time␣between␣those␣observations:>␣";
22    double time;
23    cin >> time;
24
25    double lambda = log(Ninitial/Nfinal);
26
27    cout << "The␣decay␣constant␣is␣" << lambda << endl;
28
29    return 0;
30  }
```

Tests, anyone?

Getting e and π In modeling the physical universe, we often need fundamental constants like e and π. We could look these up from some reference source, and type in, for instance, the first 20 digits of their values. But how tedious! And how many decimal places should be used? Is 20 enough? The math library functions give us a means to determine the values of these constants at run time, and in a way that is consistent with the library and the computer on which the code is running. Just use code like this:

```
1    double e = exp(1.0);  // get the value of the Euler number e
2    double pi = atan2(1.0, 0.0) * 2.0;  // get the value of pi
```

You can, and should, look up the functions exp and atan2 in the appendices.

Questions

Question 10   Write a C++ expression that computes the relativistic gamma factor $\gamma = 1/\sqrt{1 - (v/c)^2}$ for a velocity v, where $c = 2.99792458 \times 10^8$ cm/s^2. Feel free to check the appendices for any functions you may need. (*Note:* γ is the third letter of the Greek alphabet.)

Question 11   Write a code that asks the user for an angle θ and then presents to them the computer's value of $\cos^2(\theta) + \sin^2(\theta)$. Note that it might not be exactly 1.0 because the computer does not do arithmetic exactly.

Question 12   Given a positive integer n, write an expression that will determine its most significant base 10 digit. For example, for the integer 137 the expression should evaluate to 1. (Consider the functions log10 and pow to be your friends in this task.)

Question 13   Read about the standard library functions floor and ceil in Appendix B. Now write a code that asks the user for a number, rounds that number to the nearest integer, and presents the result to the user via standard output. Do you have any problems in making this work for both positive and negative numbers?

2.6   DEFINING FUNCTIONS

In the previous section we used a few functions from the standard math library. But our discussion of functions began with the problem of determining the height of a ball thrown in a constant gravitational field. I argued that there was need for a function called height that would take care of the formula evaluation $v_0 t - gt^2/2$. How can we create such a function? First, consider its interface. It must take three real numbers:

1. the acceleration due to gravity
2. the initial upward velocity of the ball
3. and the time at which we want to know the height

Then the function must evaluate to a number, which should be the height reached by the ball. With this understanding, we can now *declare* our function as

```
double height(double g, double v, double time);
```

In C++ such a declaration defines the function's *interface* without defining the algorithm that operates behind that interface. The declaration tells the compiler that the function takes three double values as input, and returns a double value. This declaration will have to be placed in our source text someplace *before* the first use of function height. As a matter of principle, it should be placed *outside* of all other functions, near the top of the source text. You will see an example of this placement shortly. A function declaration introduces an identifier (the name of the function), describes the type of data the function returns, and describes the types of data that it takes as input.

C++ Principle

A statement of the form

```
T identifier( formal_parameter_list );
```

is a declaration of a function identifier returning data of type T, and taking arguments of the types described by the formal parameter list provided in the parentheses. If the formal parameter list is absent, the function takes no input from its caller.

The return type can certainly be int or double, and it may, in fact, be most any of the types we will discuss later. A formal parameter list is basically a list of types and identifiers (in a function declaration these identifiers have no semantic content; it's the types that matter in a declaration).

C++ Principle

A formal_parameter_list is a list of type-identifier pairs, separated by commas. Such a list describes a set of types that can be input into a function, and defines their order.

In our height function declaration above, the formal parameter list is

```
double g, double v, double time
```

and this list indicates that `height` will require three values (`double`'s) as input parameters.

The declaration of the function describes something about how it is used: what sort of data it takes as input, and what sort of data it evaluates to when used in an expression. But such a declaration does not describe how the function works; we still need to *define* the function. This is the job of the function definition.

C++ Principle

A *function definition* is of the form

> `T identifier( formal_parameter_list )`
>   `compound_statement`

When the function is to be evaluated, the `compound_statement` provides the algorithm to do so. This `compound_statement` is called the *function body*.

The function definition contains the same information as the declaration, but it also provides an algorithm expressed in a compound statement that is to be executed when the function is called. Here then is such an implementation of `height`:

```
1   // ======>> height <<=========================================
2   // Returns height ball reaches when subject to constant
3   // gravitational acceleration.
4   // Arguments:
5   //   g - gravitational acceleration
6   //   v - initial velocity
7   //   time - time at which height is desired
8   // ==========================================================
9   double height(double g, double v, double time)
10  {
11    double h;  // height ball will reach
12    h = v * time - g * time * time * 0.5;
13    return h;
14  }
```

This is very much the sort of code we have already written; the only new items are lines 9 and 13. Even line 9 is not really new; it should remind you of `int main()`. Line 9, followed by the subsequent compound statement in { }, says that this is the implementation of a function called `height`. `height` takes three `double` values as input data, and names them g, v, and time, respectively. When `height` is called in a statement like `height(a, b, c)`, it is always provided with three values (not identifiers, values). It then implicitly executes the three declarations with initialization:

- `double g` = the first value provided (from a).
- `double v` = the second value provided (from b).
- `double time` = the third value provided (from c).

C++ Principle

> An expression of the form `f( expression_list )`, where `expression_list` is a comma-separated list of expressions, is a function call. The value of each expression in the `expression_list` is used in order to implicitly initialize the corresponding variable in the `formal_parameter_list` in the function definition, and the body of the function is executed. The function evaluates to the value provided by any `return` statement executed in the function body.

A function thus begins execution with the implicit initialization of the variables declared in the function's `formal_parameter_list`, using values provided by the function's caller, and ends execution with a `return` statement.

C++ Principle

> A return statement has the form
>
>   return expression;
>
> It causes the enclosing function to finish its execution, and it causes the function to evaluate in its caller to the value of the expression.

There are two key points to appreciate when creating and using functions:

1. The names of variables in the function have *nothing* to do with the names of variables in the function's caller.

2. A function *evaluates* to whatever value it returns. When a function executes a return statement, whatever value is provided there is used to replace the function call in the caller.

Consider this snippet of code:

```
1  double g = 9.81; // acceleration due to gravity m/s^2
2  double mass = 2.0;  // 2 kg object
3  double v0 = 10.0;   // initial velocity m/s
4  double energy = mass * g * height(g, v0, 1.0);
```

To evaluate the expression

    mass * g * height(g, v0, 1.0)

the identifiers g and v0 are first replaced by their values, so the expression conceptually becomes

    mass * g * height(9.81, 10.0, 1.0)

Execution then shifts to calling the `height` function, passing it the three data values `9.81`, `10.0`, and `1.0`, in order. No sense of variable names exists here—the three numbers are simply shoved into the `height` machine in order: one, two, three. The height machine now fires up, and implicitly executes the assignments

```
double g = 9.81;
double v = 10.0;
double time = 1.0;
```

We did not write these assignments; they are implied by the function declaration

```
double height(double g, double v, double time)
```

and the order in which the values are passed into the function: one, two, three. There is no connection between the identifiers in `height` and those in its caller. Some variables have the same names (e.g., g) and some do not, but *it does not matter* because these identifiers are known only within their respective algorithms, as suggested by Fig. 2.9.

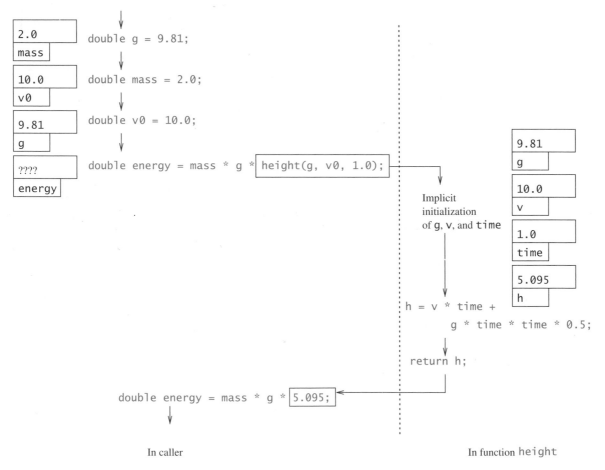

FIGURE 2.9 Data containers and thread of execution in `height` and in its caller. There are no common data containers between `height` and its caller.

Once the `height` function executes the return statement `return h;`, the value of h is made available to `height`'s caller, and replaces it in the original expression, which now is partially evaluated as

```
mass * g * 5.095
```

The function call is thus, in the end, replaced by the value that it returns, and this expression can now be fully evaluated in the caller.

The Ball Toss with Functions   Here is a new version of the ever-popular ball-throwing program, this time implemented with functions:

ball4.cpp

```
1  // ==============================================================
2  // ball4.cpp
3  // Code to compute the height and velocity of a ball
4  // launched with given initial velocity on Earth and on Mars
5  // ==============================================================
6  #include <iostream>
7  using namespace std;
8
9  double height(double g, double v, double time);
10 double velocity(double g, double v, double time);
11
12 // ========================>> main <<=========================
13 int main()
14 {
15   // define accelerations due to gravity
16   double gEarth = 9.81; // acceleration on Earth
17   double gMars = 3.63;  // acceleration on Mars
18
19   cout << "Input the initial velocity (m/s):> ";
20   double v0;
21   cin >> v0;
22
23   cout << "Input the time (s):> ";
24   double t;
25   cin >> t;
26
27
28   // Results on Earth
29   cout << "=========================================" << endl;
30   cout << "Earth:" << endl;
31   cout << "The velocity at time " << t << " is "
32        << velocity(gEarth, v0, t) << endl;
33   cout << "and the height is "
```

```
34            << height(gEarth, v0, t) << endl;
35
36     // Now do Mars
37     cout << "=========================================" << endl;
38     cout << "Mars:" << endl;
39     cout << "The velocity at time " << t << " is "
40            << velocity(gMars, v0, t) << endl;
41     cout << "and the height is "
42            << height(gMars, v0, t) << endl;
43
44     return 0;
45   }
46
47   // ===================>> height <<===========================
48   // Return height a ball reaches when subject to constant
49   // gravitational acceleration.
50   // Arguments:
51   //   g - gravitational acceleration
52   //   v - initial velocity
53   //   time - time at which height is desired
54   // ==========================================================
55   double height(double g, double v, double time)
56   {
57     double h;   // height ball will reach
58     h = v * time - g * time * time * 0.5;
59     return h;
60   }
61
62   // ===================>> velocity <<=========================
63   // Return velocity ball reaches when subject to constant
64   // gravitational acceleration.
65   //   g - gravitational acceleration
66   //   v - initial velocity
67   //   time - time at which height is desired
68   // ==========================================================
69   double velocity(double g, double v, double time)
70   {
71     double vf;  // final velocity of ball
72     vf = v - g * time;
73     return vf;
74   }
```

This version of the ball-throwing code is built out of three functions—components—called main, height, and velocity. The functions height and velocity perform the basic physics calculations. They can be written and read separately from and independently of each other, and separately from `main` as well. Similarly, `main` can be written and read and understood without peering into the details of `height` and `velocity`. This is the goal of decomposition—to allow us to separate the parts of a computation into independent parts. When reading such code, you should take advantage of this decomposition; read `main` first to get the overall thrust of the computation, and only then delve into those other routines that are pertinent to your study.

Note that the identifiers used inside a function, even in the parameter lists, have *nothing* to do with the names outside of that function. Inside the black box we don't need to know what folks outside call things—we are passed values, give those values names of our own, and return values, which those outside are welcome to name anything they like.

Questions

Question 14   Write a function that accepts three values of resistance and returns the equivalent resistance of those three in parallel. Be sure to use good names for everything.

Question 15   Write a function `double Cosine(double x)` that uses the relation $\cos(x) = \sin(x + \pi/2)$ to compute the cosine of an angle by calling the standard library `sin` function.

Question 16   Write a function that converts temperature from degrees Fahrenheit to degrees Centigrade.

Question 17   Write a function that takes as input the slope m and y-intercept b of a line, $y = mx + b$, and which also takes an x value. Have the function return the corresponding y value.

2.7   PROCEDURES

At the start of Section 2.5 I distinguished two kinds of routines: functions and procedures. Although the C++ literature calls both of these kinds of subprogram "functions," the distinction between functions and procedures is worth making.[18] Functions work purely by receiving input data, churning, and returning a value. Pure procedures do not return any value: They work by reaching outside themselves and somehow changing their environment. Functions are like a man in a box: He can take data in (hear it), and send data out (yell), but has no idea where the data came from, and does not know if anybody hears his response. In contrast to this lonely experience, procedures are like a man in a house: He can open the door and go walking about, treading on his neighbor's petunias while writing the results of his calculations on her garage door. She gets the data whether she wants it or not!

Procedures can do more than functions, but they are more dangerous. After all, the neighbor might sue.

A procedure declaration looks much like a function definition, except it returns no data. C++ provides a special word, `void`, to indicate the absence of a returned value.

---

[18]The reason for the missing distinction in much of the C++ literature is purely historic; very early versions of the C language, from which C++ later grew, provide *only* functions that return a value. Although C has long ago moved beyond this restriction, the terminology has unfortunately stuck.

C++ Principle

> A declaration of the form
>
> ```
> void identifier( formal_parameter_list );
> ```
>
> declares a procedure.

A procedure definition looks like a function definition, but with the return type replaced by the word void.

C++ Principle

> A procedure definition has the form
>
> ```
> void identifier( formal_parameter_list )
>     compound_statement
> ```
>
> The compound_statement is the procedure's body, and can contain return statements of the form return; only.

There are two forms that a procedure might take: It might take data in, use it, and write data external to the whole program (such as to the screen, or to a network connection), or it might take data in, and write data directly into its immediate caller's environment.

Consider, for example, the following procedure:

```
1  void printGreeting()
2  {
3    cout << "Hello,⎵race⎵fans!" << endl;
4    return;
5  }
```

This procedure does not return any data (its return type is declared as void), and it does not take any data (the parameter list in parentheses is empty). All it does is pitch data to cout, which in turn makes it somehow appear on the screen. Or consider, for another example, this procedure:

```
1  void printVelocity(double t, double v)
2  {
3    cout << "The⎵velocity⎵of⎵the⎵ball⎵at⎵time⎵" << t << "⎵is⎵"
4        << v << endl;
5    return;
6  }
```

This procedure takes two input values and prints an informative message about them on standard output, and then it returns to its caller, but it does not return any data.

These two examples provide simple facilities that encapsulate a program's interaction with standard output.

A second general form of procedure allows the procedure to directly affect data outside itself by working not with data values, but with references to data. The functions that we defined in Section 2.6 were, when called, given data values to work with, and when they were done, they returned data to their caller. You put data into my mailbox, and I put data into yours. But you could instead say to me, "I wrote the input data on my bathroom mirror, and could you please write your output data on the living room wall?" Why might you do this? Well, I can only put one piece of data in your mailbox (a function in C++ can only return one data object), so if there is lots of output data, then the living room wall might provide more space. And if there's lots of input data, and it's already written on your bathroom mirror, then it may be more efficient or convenient to simply let me read it there, rather than copying it into my mailbox.

This idea can be expressed in C++ with *reference variables* for which the following routine provides an example:

```
1  void squareMe(double & x)
2  {
3    // square a value in caller's environment
4
5    x = x * x;
6    return;
7  }
```

This procedure takes a *reference* to a double, squares the value stored under that reference, and stores this product back in the reference. This routine *returns* nothing, but it does have an effect on its caller through a pass by reference mechanism. The reference variable x is declared in the procedure's `formal_parameter_list` by placing a magic ampersand & after the variable's type.

C++ Principle

> A reference variable to a routine is declared in the routine's formal parameter list by the syntax T & name, where T is any type and name is the identifier by which the parameter will be known in the routine. This makes name within the function an alias for the actual parameter provided by the caller at execution time.

Consider this use of `squareMe`:

```
1  double y = 10.0;
2  squareMe(y);
```

When line 2 is executed, the value of y is not passed into `squareMe` because `squareMe`'s first argument was declared to be a reference to a `double`, rather than a `double`. Instead,

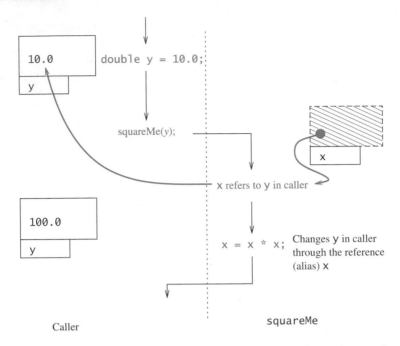

FIGURE 2.10 Data containers and thread of execution in squareMe and its caller. The reference parameter to squareMe provides a common data container between squareMe and its caller, although they refer to it by different names.

as shown in Fig. 2.10, the identifier x in squareMe refers to the data storage container that's identified as y in squareMe's caller.

Pass by reference is extremely useful; an example use in the never-ending ball-throwing code follows. This version is longer, but is yet more modular than the previous versions. Don't try to read the whole code from start to finish; it's not a novel. Read main to capture a high-level view of the algorithm. Then you should only need to read one of the other routines if its purpose is unclear, or you are particularly interested in how it does its deed.

ball5.cpp

```
1   // ================================================================
2   // ball5.cpp
3   // Code to compute the height and velocity of a ball
4   // launched with given initial velocity on Earth and on Mars
5   // ================================================================
6
7   #include <iostream>
8   using namespace std;
```

```
9
10   void trajectory(double g, double v0, double time,
11                   double & h, double & v);
12   void printVelocityHeight(double t, double v, double h);
13   void printSeparator();
14
15   // ===================>> main <<=============================
16   int main()
17   {
18
19     double gEarth = 9.81; // acceleration due to gravity on Earth
20     double gMars = 3.63;  // acceleration due to gravity on Mars
21
22     cout << "Input the initial velocity (m/s):> ";
23     double v0;
24     cin >> v0;
25
26     cout << "Input the time (s):> ";
27     double t;
28     cin >> t;
29
30
31     // Results on Earth
32
33     double v;  // final velocity
34     double h;  // final height
35     trajectory(gEarth, v0, t, h, v);
36
37     printSeparator();
38     cout << "Earth:" << endl;
39     printVelocityHeight(t, v, h);
40
41     // Now do Mars
42     trajectory(gMars, v0, t, h, v);
43
44     printSeparator();
45     cout << "Mars:" << endl;
46     printVelocityHeight(t, v, h);
47
48     return 0;
49   }
50
51
52   // =================>> trajectory <<===========================
53   // Compute height and velocity of ball thrown in constant
54   // gravitation acceleration
```

```
55    // Arguments:
56    //   g - acceleration due to gravity
57    //   v0 - initial velocity
58    //   time - time at which final velocity and height are desired
59    //   h - final height    (reference to container in caller)
60    //   v - final velocity  (reference to container in caller)
61    // ================================================================
62    void trajectory(double g, double v0, double time,
63                       double & h, double & v)
64    {
65      h = v0 * time - g * time * time / 2.0;
66      v = v0 - g * time;
67    }
68
69    // ==================>> printVelocityHeight <<==================
70    void printVelocityHeight(double t, double v, double h)
71    {
72      cout << "The velocity at time " << t << " is " << v << endl;
73      cout << "and the height is " << h << endl;
74      return;
75    }
76
77    // =================>> printSeparator <<==========================
78    void printSeparator()
79    {
80      cout << "=========================================" << endl;
81      return;
82    }
```

The code in `main` is now largely focused on interacting with the user, and organizing the rest of the computation, but without dwelling on the details, which are instead hidden in various procedures. It can be changed and modified with little concern for the physics hidden in `trajectory`, or in the `print` procedures. The entire code to compute the trajectory of the ball—all of the associated physics—has been packaged into a single procedure, `trajectory`. If it's wrong (is it?), it will only need to be fixed in one spot.

Questions

Question 18   Consider the following procedure:

```
void p(double x, double & y, double & z)
{
  y = x;
  x = 2.0;
  z = x;
}
```

What does the following snippet of code write to standard output?

```
double a = 3.0;
double b = 1.0;
double c = 1.0;
p(a, b, c);
cout << a << " " << b << " " << c
     << endl;
```

Question 19 Write a procedure that takes two numbers (by reference) and replaces both of them with their average.

Question 20 Write a procedure `void swap(int & a, int & b)` that swaps its arguments, so that the following code would print out 1 2 on standard output:

```
int a = 2;
int b = 1;
swap(a, b);
cout << a << "␣" << b << endl;
```

2.8 SEQUENCING AND SIDE EFFECTS

There is nothing in the C++ standard to prevent the definition of mixed function-procedures such as

```
1   int strange(int a)
2   {
3     cout << "Welcome,␣race␣fans!" << endl;
4     return 2 * a;
5   }
```

Such routines should be frowned upon. This one is plainly silly, but let's nevertheless analyze how its definition implies the intent of its use. It does something to the outside world—it prints a friendly message. But it also returns a number, so apparently it's intended to be used in an expression (and if it's not thus intended, it certainly can be so used despite the contrary intent). Things that are used in expressions should be designed carefully. Should the expression $x = \sin(x) \times \cos(z)$ change the value of z? I think not. Not only shouldn't it affect z, it shouldn't do *anything* other than compute an interesting number.

Claim

Functions have no business doing anything other than returning their value. Procedures have no business returning a value.

A procedure operates by side effect; it modifies data external to itself and should not participate in an expression. In contrast, a function simply returns some value and should not also aspire to the lofty status of a procedure. This notion is sometimes called command-query separation.

Come now, you say. What's wrong with a function with a side effect? A simple question in reply: Is $2 * f(x)$ the same as $f(x) + f(x)$? Of course, it is.

But there is nothing in the C++ standard that ensures $2 * f(x)$ will be equal to $f(x) + f(x)$. And yet, if they are not, it is contrary to our intuitions about how mathematics works. The notion that $2 * f(x)$ should equal $f(x) + f(x)$ is called referential transparency. We write functions that violate referential transparency at our peril, for they do not behave in a natural manner. Yet we can easily write such evil function-procedures in C++, as in

```
1   int fun(int & a)
2   {
3     a = a + 1;   // change a in caller
4     return a;
5   }
```

Consider starting with x = 1. The expression 2 * f(x) evaluates to 4, while, if we again start with x = 1, f(x) + f(x) evaluates to 5. This is the danger of functions that also produce side effects. This risk of confusion is reduced by separating routines into pure functions, and pure procedures, without mixing the two distinct concepts of function and procedure.

The function strange, defined above, is not referentially transparent either. I'm sorry to report that 2 * strange(x) does not do the same thing as strange(x) + strange(x). Other violations of referential transparency are equally subtle. Suppose you saw the pair of statements:

```
1   int n = 10;
2   int x = fun(n);
3   int y = fun(n);
```

Would you not assume that x and y then hold the same value? Referential transparency is what we naturally expect as humans; we do not *see* n change, so we naturally expect that it does not. And since n is passed into both functions, we expect that each will return the same value. Referential transparency requires that a function have no effect on its caller, and C++ does not guarantee this. Only our disciplined use of the language, by keeping procedures clearly separated from functions, can do so.

Questions

Question 21   Assuming the definition of fun given above, what value do the following statements assign to a?

```
int w = -1;
int a = fun(w) + fun(w) + fun(w);
```

Question 22   How is the statement x = 2 * strange(1); different from the statement x = strange(1) + strange(1);?

Question 23   Consider the following two routines to swap two numbers. Give an example of how each is to be used. Which is to be preferred? What are your reasons?

```
1   void swap(double & x,
2               double & y)
3   {
4     double tmp = x;
5     x = y;
6     y = tmp;
7   }
```

```
1   double swap(double & x,
2               double y)
3   {
4     double tmp = x;
5     x = y;
6     return tmp;
7   }
```

2.9 INPUT AND OUTPUT FUNCTIONS

We want our code to be able to get data from the outside world, and we also want it to be able to provide data to the outside world. Otherwise, the code is quite useless. So far, we have used the identifiers `cin` and `cout` in order to provide the external connection. These are actually variables of type `istream` and `ostream`, respectively. For variables of type `istream` the operator `>>` is defined. Its semantics are to extract data from the input stream, and to attempt to understand that data as a representation of a value to store under the identifier appearing on the right side of the `>>` operator. Similarly, for variables of type `ostream` the operator `<<` is defined, and it takes the value of the expression provided as its right operand, formats it as a series of characters for human interpretation, and sends those into the output stream.

2.9.1 Input and Output Streams

The C++ standard library implements a streams-based model of input and output. Data moving into or out of our code are treated as a stream of information flowing through a pipeline, with our code attached to one end, and the operating system pumping data into or out of the other end of the pipe. We will talk only about text-based streams in which all the data are considered to be organized into human readable representations as characters.

Consider input first. Data flow from a data source into our code. The operating system of the computer sits between the source and our code, as a kind of central pumping station. We gain access to our end of such a pipe by using a variable of type `istream` (or one of its relatives, to be described shortly). With this variable we can use the extraction operator `>>` to pull data out of the pipe. Once a datum has been pulled out, it's ours and is no longer in the pipe. Further, we can get only the datum that is sitting at the front of the pipe; if the datum we want isn't at the front, that's our problem. Figure 2.11 cartoons the idea of an `istream`.

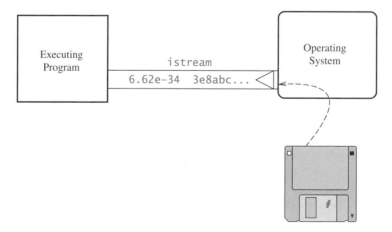

FIGURE 2.11 An `istream` provides a stream of characters to a running code.

So, consider the code:

```
1    double x;
2    cin >> x;
3    double y;
4    cin >> y;
5    double z;
6    cin >> z;
```

The expression cin >> x on line 2 looks in the standard input stream and tries to find enough information to build a number of type double. It throws away any leading whitespace characters first, then fetches characters as long as they make sense as part of a number of type double, such as 6.62e-34. It stops fetching characters as soon as they can no longer be part of a double. So if the input stream contains the characters 6.62e-34 3e8abc, then cin >> x will assign 6.62e-34 to x, and the input stream will be left containing 3e8abc. Then the expression cin >> y on line 4 will behave similarly, and assigns the value 3e8 to y, leaving the stream containing only abc. Finally, the statement on line 6 will do nothing to z, because when the standard input stream is examined, it is found to contain abc, which cannot be interpreted as a value of type double. The input stream is left alone, so it still contains abc, but cin is considered to be in the *failed* state.[19] It will no longer attempt to read any more data until it is reset. This sequence of data transformations is illustrated in Fig. 2.12.

Note the lack of referential transparency in the >> operator. Even though the expressions cin >> x and cin >> y appear identical, they will not, in general, result in x being equal to y. This is because the identifier cin is manipulating data that is invisible to us, and so apparently identical uses of it do not result in identical results. This lack of transparency might cause you some confusion; many students new to the notions of input in a computer code develop incorrect mental models of the process. It may help to focus consistently on the idea of a stream of data—no more, no less. We can suck data out one end while the operating system pumps it in the other, but we can't put it back, or get directly to something farther down the stream. We have only our end of the pipe to work with. Further, our removing data from the stream has no implications for what's going on in the operating system—just because we remove data from the stream does not mean that copies of those data are not retained elsewhere.

An output stream is similar to an input stream, but is somewhat easier to picture. We pitch data into the stream with <<, and it goes off to the operating system's data pumping station, to be sent from there wherever the operating system thinks it is supposed to go.

Data flow in and out of our code in streams. We get one end of the stream, and the operating system attaches the other end of the stream to wherever the data are supposed to come from, or go to. But how do we control those attachments? We are always given one istream and three ostream's, and these are available to us through the variables cin, cout, cerr, and clog, all declared in the header file iostream, as outlined in Table 2.3.

_____

[19]A means to check for this failure will be described in Chapter 3; see "fail" under "istream" in the index.

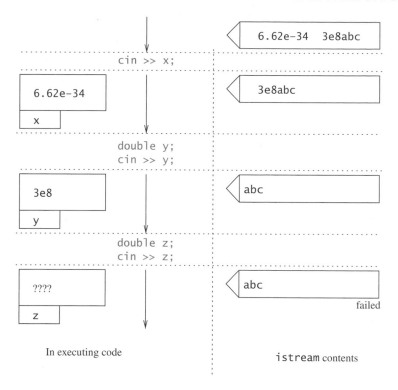

FIGURE 2.12   Reading data from an input stream into doubles. As data are read, they are removed from the stream. When data in the stream cannot be interpreted as the requested type, they are left in the stream.

There are, however, some interesting sequencing issues with the output streams. Data sent into an output stream do not have to appear at their destination before any particular sequence point in our code. Output data can be presented at its destination *asynchronously*, that is, without any specific sequencing with respect to our code. The output streams are either *buffered* or *unbuffered*.

Definition

> To *buffer* data means to collect it in a temporary storage location for later processing.

TABLE 2.3   The Standard Streams

Name	Type	Normally Connects to	Sequencing
cin	istream	keyboard	tied to cout
cout	ostream	screen	buffered
cerr	ostream	screen	unbuffered
clog	ostream	screen	buffered

This is often done in output operations because it is usually more efficient to send a large quantity of data to the operating system rather than a small quantity.

The unbuffered cerr is generally intended for data that is really important, and which should get to the user as quickly as it can; data written to cerr will be given over to the operating system before the next sequence point in our code (generally the next semicolon).

Although cout is buffered, it is also *tied* to cin. This means that any data sent to cout are guaranteed to be sent off to the user *before* the next use of cin. So in the following code:

```
1   cout << "Number␣please␣:>␣";
2   double x;
3   cin >> x;
```

the data Number please :> are guaranteed to be sent to the user before cin on line 3 tries to read data for x.

2.9.2   Redirection

In Table 2.3 I note the normal source and destination for each of the standard streams. However, most operating systems allow the standard streams to be redirected to or from files. This is not a C++ issue, and the details are operating-system-dependent, but the mechanism is becoming informally standardized under the command line shells of most operating systems.[20] For example, suppose we create a file named myinput that contains a single line:

myinput

```
1   1.23
```

Now when running the **square3.cpp** code, we can have it get input not from the keyboard but rather from the file **myinput**, and write output not to the screen but rather to the file **outfile**, by using a command line like

```
1   [hagar@localhost Code]$ ./square3 < myinput > outfile
2   [hagar@localhost Code]$
```

All the text that the code normally wrote on the screen can now be found in the file **outfile**. This redirection can be useful for catching a large amount of output and sending it to a file, instead of the screen, but the code is no longer directly interacting with a human. We might therefore want to design its interaction with the outside world

[20] At least the notation is identical in Unix, Linux, Windows, and Mac OS/X.

differently. Once we start down this path, we might simply want to read and write files directly from inside our code.

2.9.3 Files

A file is really an operating system concept. One job of an operating system is to manage *filesystems*, which are data repositories in which collections of data can be housed. Often such collections of data are physically stored on a spinning disk coated with magnetic material, but this is not an inherent requirement, and there are filesystems where the data are not so stored. A collection of data in a filesystem is called a *file*, and can be designated by its *pathname*, which is a string that is somehow mapped, in an operating-system-specific manner, to a particular set of data in the filesystem.

Thus, files are described to the operating system by their pathname, which is just a string that describes where the file is located within the available filesystems. A path name might be **/home/hagar/Book/TeX/data.tex**. In this **data.tex** is the file name, and **/home/hagar/Book/TeX/** describes the directory where the file is located.[21] Often the operating system has a notion of the *current working directory* and will look for a file within that directory if the directory information is left off the pathname. So we can usually designate files using just their name, like **data.tex**, and leave it at that.

The problem of reading data from, or writing data to, a file begins with attaching an `istream`, or an `ostream`, to an actual file managed by the computer's operating system. To do so, we need a C++ data type that we can connect to a file and subsequently use as an `istream` or `ostream`. These types are provided in the C++ standard library by `ifstream` and `ofstream`, which are declared in the standard header `fstream`. An `ifstream` is essentially an `istream` that can be connected to a file through the use of a special declaration syntax.[22] To connect an `ifstream` to a file named `myinput` in the current working directory, the declaration

```
ifstream in("myinput");
```

will do. Assuming that the operating system does successfully connect that file to a stream, then from this point on we can use `in` just like we would use `cin`. We can read data from it like `in >> x`, but instead of the stream being connected to the keyboard, it is connected to the file `myinput`.

C++ Principle

A declaration statement of the form

```
ifstream identifier(string_literal);
```

creates an `ifstream`. This is an `istream` that is connected to the file designated by the `string_literal` pathname.

---

[21] Under a Windows-based operating system, those slashes might be backslashes, although increasingly the libraries on the Windows operating systems are accepting either slash or backslash. Also, increasingly the word "folder" is being used as a synonym for directory.

[22] We will discuss this further in Chapters 5 and 7.

Note that this operation can fail. The file might not exist, or our code might not have permission to read the file. In either case, there would be no data to shove into the `ifstream`.

We have already considered the behavior of streams, and I noted that as we read data from a stream, they are removed and no longer there in the stream. Does this imply that creating and using an `ifstream` will suck the data out of a file, so there is nothing left when we are done? Not in the least. The operating system reads the data from the file and copies it into the stream. It is the stream that we empty, not the file.

Similarly, we can connect an object of type `ofstream` to a file in a declaration such as

```
ofstream out("myoutput");
```

after which

```
myoutput << "The␣square␣of␣" << x << "␣is␣" << x*x << endl;
```

acts just like

```
cout << "The␣square␣of␣" << x << "␣is␣" << x*x << endl;
```

except that data get directed to the file, rather than the screen.

C++ Principle

> A declaration statement of the form
>
> ```
> ofstream identifier(string_literal);
> ```
>
> creates an `ofstream`. This is an `ostream` that is connected to the file designated by the `string_literal` pathname.

This operation will either create a brand new file, or else destroy any preexisting file with that pathname. This operation, too, could fail.

Note that data of type `ifstream` are also data of type `istream`, and data of type `ofstream` are also data of type `ostream`, but the reverse is not true. Anything you can do with `cout` you can do with an object of type `ofstream`, but not the other way round. Objects of type `istream` and `ostream` cannot be assigned, so the following is not allowed:

```
istream in = cin;
```

But we can get a reference to a stream, so

```
istream & in = cin;
```

makes `in` a synonym for `cin`. Because streams cannot be assigned, they can only be passed into a routine by reference. To illustrate this, here is another version of my favorite ball-tossing program in which the output routines `printVelocityHeight` and `printSeparator` take a reference to an `ostream`, and write their data to this `ostream`:

ball6.cpp

```
1  // ==============================================================
2  // ball6.cpp
```

```
3    // Code to compute the height and velocity of a ball
4    // launched with given initial velocity on Earth and on Mars
5    // =============================================================
6    #include <iostream>
7    #include <fstream>
8    using namespace std;
9
10   void trajectory(double g, double v0, double time,
11                   double & h, double & v);
12   void printVelocityHeight(double t, double v, double h,
13                            ostream & out);
14   void printSeparator(ostream & out);
15
16   // ===================>> main <<============================
17   int main()
18   {
19     double gEarth = 9.81; // acceleration due to gravity on Earth
20     double gMars = 3.63;  // acceleration due to gravity on Mars
21
22     cout << "Input the initial velocity (m/s):> ";
23     double v0;
24     cin >> v0;
25
26     cout << "Input the time (s):> ";
27     double t;
28     cin >> t;
29
30     // Open a file
31     ofstream outfile("finalData");
32
33     // Results on Earth
34
35     double v;  // final velocity
36     double h;  // final height
37     trajectory(gEarth, v0, t, h, v);
38
39     printSeparator(outfile);
40     outfile << "Earth:" << endl;
41     printVelocityHeight(t, v, h, outfile);
42
43     // Now do Mars
44     trajectory(gMars, v0, t, h, v);
45
46     printSeparator(outfile);
47     outfile << "Mars:" << endl;
48     printVelocityHeight(t, v, h, outfile);
49
```

```
50    return 0;
51  }
52
53
54  // ================>> trajectory <<=============================
55  // Compute height and velocity of ball thrown in constant
56  // gravitation acceleration
57  // Arguments:
58  //   g - acceleration due to gravity
59  //   v0 - initial velocity
60  //   time - time at which final velocity and height are desired
61  //   h - final height    (reference to container in caller)
62  //   v - final velocity  (reference to container in caller)
63  // ============================================================
64  void trajectory(double g, double v0, double time,
65                  double & h, double & v)
66  {
67    h = v0 * time - g * time * time / 2.0;
68    v = v0 - g * time;
69  }
70
71  // ================>> printVelocityHeight <<==================
72  void printVelocityHeight(double t, double v, double h,
73                           ostream & out)
74  {
75    out << "The velocity at time " << t << " is " << v << endl;
76    out << "and the height is " << h << endl;
77    return;
78  }
79
80  // ================>> printSeparator <<=======================
81  void printSeparator(ostream & out)
82  {
83    out << "=====================================" << endl;
84    return;
85  }
```

Questions

Question 24   What does the following snippet of code write to the file **one** and to the file **two**?

```
ofstream a("one");
ofstream b("two");
a << 2 << endl;
b << 1 << endl;
a << 4 << endl;
b << 3 << endl;
```

Question 25   What is wrong with the following procedure declaration?

```
void print(ostream out, double data);
```

Question 26   Rewrite **ball6.cpp** to get its input from a file named **initData**. (Don't prompt—you are no longer interacting with a human.)

Projects

Here is a set of projects for which you must write code. Many of these say "write a function that...." Will you, wise as you now are in the ways of algorithm creation, just write these functions and leave it at that? No, of course not. You will naturally write a C++ code to test each such function. And you will worry about how to know if you are right. I provide few clues to help you in this. Welcome to engineering!

When you do write code to address these questions, you will often have to make decisions regarding the names of things and the types of data to be used. You should make good choices; it does matter.

PROJECT 1

Write a function that takes the y value, slope m, and y intercept b of a line described by $y = mx + b$, and which returns the corresponding x value. Are there any issues or concerns with this function?

PROJECT 2

Write a function that takes as input two points on a line [two (x, y) pairs], and an x value for which the function returns the corresponding y value.

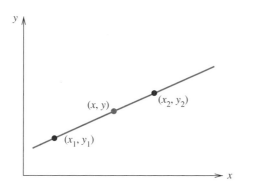

PROJECT 3

In many branches of science and engineering, quantities vary over a huge range of magnitude. It is often useful to consider such hugely varying quantities on logarithmic scales. One example is the measurement of power in decibels (dB). A power P measured in dBm is quantified as

$$dBm = 10 \ln(P/P_0)$$

where the reference power P_0 is 1 milliwatt or mW (1×10^{-3} Watts or W). Write a function that takes as in-

put a power level in Watts, and returns the corresponding dBm measurement. Is there any way you can ensure that the caller of this function has provided power in Watts?

PROJECT 4

The power used by an electrical load is given by $P_L = V_L I$, where I is the current through the circuit, and V_L is the voltage across the load. In the simple circuit shown, a voltage source provides a voltage drop of V_S as well as a resistance R_S. Write a function that will return the power used by the load, given V_S, R_S, and R_L. (*Note:* You will have to think this through first, in order to determine how to compute the power.)

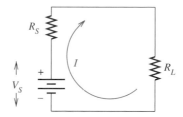

PROJECT 5

Write an electronic coin flipper! Write a function that will return a random integer between 0 and $N - 1$, with an equal probability of any integer being returned. To do so, you might explore the rand and srand functions described in Appendix A. (Look out for rand! It's a pure function, but not referentially transparent.)

PROJECT 6

A ball is initially at $(x(0), y(0))$ and has initial velocity $(v_x(0), v_y(0))$. It is subject to a constant acceleration g in the negative y direction. Write a function that can be used to provide the position and velocity of the ball at any time t.

PROJECT 7

Ancient remains of plants and animals can be dated by radiocarbon dating. This relies on the continuous creation of a radioactive form of carbon, known as C-14, from cosmic ray interactions in the earth's atmosphere. When a plant or animal dies, the ratio of C-14 to C-12 is initially this atmospheric ratio, but it starts to decrease because of the decay of C-14. At a later time, we can measure the amount of C-14 in ancient remains by measuring the rate A at which decay particles from C-14 are emitted; this is simply proportional to the number N of

C-14 nuclei in the sample ($A = \lambda N$, where λ is the decay constant of C-14).

To date ancient remains, we can take a carbon sample from it, and we also take a carbon sample—a comparitor—of known age T (ideally from a similar plant or animal tissue of about the same age as the sample), and measure A_{sample} and $A_{comparitor}$. We also weigh both the sample and the comparitor, giving us the mass of carbon in each as M_{sample} and $M_{comparitor}$. We can then find the age t of the sample from

$$\frac{A_{sample}}{A_{comparitor}} \frac{M_{comparitor}}{M_{sample}} = e^{-\lambda(t-T)}$$

(Can you see why?)

Write a code that prompts for appropriate input, and reports the age of the sample. The half-life of C-14 is 5,730 years, giving it a decay constant of $\lambda = \ln(2)/5730$ per year.

PROJECT 8

Consider a function $f(x) = a + bx + cx^2$. Write a C++ function that takes the coefficients a, b, and c as input and returns the value of x where the function f is at a minimum.

PROJECT 9

Consider two equations for the two unknowns x_1 and x_2:

$$a_{11}x_1 + a_{12}x_2 = b_1$$
$$a_{21}x_1 + a_{22}x_2 = b_2$$

where a_{11}, a_{12}, a_{21}, a_{22}, b_1, and b_2 are given. Solve these equations for x_1 and x_2 and write a routine called twoByTwoSolve that implements the solution of these equations. You should decide what data go into and come out of this routine.

Also write a main routine that reads the necessary data from a file called **linEqn** and writes the solution to a file called **solution**.

PROJECT 10

Consider a function $g(x, y)$ of two variables of the form

$$g(x, y) = a + bx + cy + dx^2 + exy + fy^2$$

with the restrictions $d > 0$, $f > 0$, and $4df > e^2$ (this restriction ensures that the function g is essentially bowl-shaped, and has a minimum).

Write a C++ function that takes the coefficients a, b, c, d, e, and f as input and provides as output the value of x and y where the function is at a minimum.

[*Note:* You don't need calculus to do this problem, just some thought and algebra. Think about the function $g(x) = a + bx + dx^2$ first. The previous two projects may be useful to you.]

PROJECT 11

Write a C++ procedure that fits a circle through three points, specified by coordinates (x_1, y_1), (x_2, y_2), and (x_3, y_3); the resulting circle should be specified by its center (x_c, y_c) and radius R. Also write a function that reports the distance d between a point (x, y) and the nearest point on a given circle specified by its center (x_c, y_c) and radius R. Write these functions as part of a code that also tests them by prompting a user for appropriate data, as shown below:

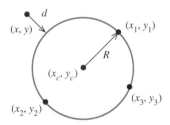

Here is a sample run of such a test code:

```
1  [hagar@localhost Assignment]$ ./circleGames
2  Three points on a circle please:
3  An (x,y) pair please: 3.41421356237 3.41421356237
4  An (x,y) pair please: 0.38196601125 0.8244294954157
5  An (x,y) pair please: 3.96013315568 1.60266133841
6  Center = (2, 2)
7  Radius = 2
8  An (x,y) pair please: -0.12132034356 4.12132034356
9  Distance from (-0.12132, 4.12132) to circle = 1
10 [hagar@localhost Assignment]$
```

PROJECT 12

A simple cylindrical lens is made by slicing the edge off a glass cylinder of radius R. Several parallel rays of light enter perpendicular to the flat side of the lens, at height y above the axis, and exit the curved side. Write a routine that can compute the angle with respect to horizontal α of the exiting rays, and the distance f from the front of the lens at which each ray will cross the axis. Your routine will need the index of refraction of the glass as input, among other things. Will this lens make objects placed on the flat side appear bigger or smaller, to an observer on the curved side?

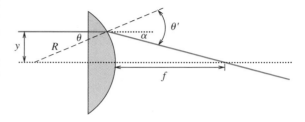

CHAPTER 3

ITERATION

THE ALGORITHMS that we can express based on the purely sequential constructs of the last chapter are somewhat limited. With sequence alone we can engage in formula evaluation exercises, but little creative thought is required in evaluating a formula. In this chapter you will learn to express iteration, and the power of algorithms will begin to reveal itself. With this will come more cunning algorithms, whose correctness is more difficult to establish.

Many introductory programming texts would present selection before iteration, but I will defer a discussion of selection until Chapter 4. We can develop far more interesting algorithms with sequence and iteration than we can with sequence and selection. Our number of applications will therefore explode in this chapter, compared to last. Once again, you should copy code from the book and try it. Change it and try it. Break it and fix it. Learning to develop algorithms requires that you actually develop some algorithms, so get out your pencil and paper and fire up your compiler.

3.1 REPETITION

Consider the question of producing the sum of the first N nonnegative integers. Let me decide that $N = 14$, so that I will write some C++ code to produce the sum of the first 14 nonnegative integers; perhaps something like `int sum = 93;`. But this solution is disappointing: It works fine for $N = 14$, but is useless for any other value of N. Even more important, there is no obvious way to determine if the solution is correct, other than by a comparison of the code's reported value against a known correct value. Such a test would itself be disappointing because it requires that I know the answer to check against the code's. But I wanted the code so that I could compute the answer. So either the code, or the test, is useless. This one-line code to determine the sum of nonnegative integers is a generally unacceptable approach; it is inflexible, and it is impossible to usefully verify.

Claim

An algorithm should be as generally useful as practical, and it should be possible to verify its correctness through reason alone.

One way to solve this problem of summing integers is in fact with reason alone. The sum of the first N nonnegative integers can be determined by some simple algebra, or some simple geometry. The result is $N(N - 1)/2$.[1] But for the purpose of illustration, let's consider a more algorithmic solution. I could write the code to sum up the first 14 nonnegative integers thus

```
int sum = 0;
sum = sum + 1;
sum = sum + 2;
sum = sum + 3;
sum = sum + 4;
sum = sum + 5;
sum = sum + 6;
sum = sum + 7;
sum = sum + 8;
sum = sum + 9;
sum = sum + 10;
sum = sum + 11;
sum = sum + 12;
sum = sum + 13;
```

Assuming that + and = are well defined, and correctly used, this code is at least verifiably correct. However, it is still useless for values of N other than 14, and it was quite tedious to write.

Claim

> Tedium is the enemy of quality work.

When work becomes tedious, consider please if there is not some better, more elegant, less dreary approach.

What to do, then, with our summing of integers problem? It needs to work for any N, and it needs to be clearly correct. Let's write the code using iteration!

sum.cpp

```
int sum(int N)
{
    int sum = 0;
    int counter = 1;
    while (counter < N)
    {
        sum = sum + counter;
```

---

[1] Easy for me to say, but how do you know I'm right?

```
 8          counter = counter + 1;
 9      }
10      return sum;
11  }
```

This provides a function, called `sum`, that will compute the required sum for any value of `N`. The key new syntactical construct is on line 5:

```
while (counter < N)
```

This starts a "while" loop. The compound statement that follows (between the { on line 6 and the } on line 9) is repeated as long as `counter < N`. The precise semantics of this loop are as follows: When the loop is executed, the condition `counter < N` is checked. If this condition is true, the body of the loop, a compound statement, is executed in its entirety. The condition `count < N` is then checked again. If it is true, the body of the loop is executed in its entirety, and the condition `count < N` is then checked again. This continues, on and on, until the condition is checked and found to be false. The loop is then done, and execution continues with the statement following the loop (line 10).

C++ Principle

A *while loop* is denoted by a statement of the form

```
while (condition) loop_body
```

where `condition` is an expression that evaluates to true or false, and `loop_body` is either an expression statement or a compound statement. During execution the following sequence of steps is followed: `condition` is evaluated, and if true, `loop_body` is executed, and then the loop begins again; if `condition` is false, then the loop is done and execution continues with the statement following the loop.

Note that there is a definite *sequence* to the execution of the loop. The `condition` is checked, and if true *then* the `loop_body` is executed. *Then* the loop cycles back to check the `condition` again. Thus it does not matter whether the `condition` is true or false *while* the `loop_body` is executed; it only matters when the `condition` is checked *at the start of each trip through the loop.*

At the heart of the **sum.cpp** code is a very common algorithmic construct known as a running sum. We begin by *initializing* the sum to zero, and then progressively add additional values to it with a statement of the form

```
sum = sum + new_value;
```

Does this statement surprise you? It should not. The expression to the right of the assignment operator is evaluated first, so the current value of `sum` is fetched and the value of `new_value` is procured; these values are then added together and this result is then assigned to the variable named on the left of the assignment operator. This variable happens to be `sum`. The effect is that we have added `new_value` into sum. Once again, = means evaluate the expression to the right and *assign* its value to the variable on the left. The symbol = most certainly does not mean equal.

The development of a running sum involves three parts:

- initialization, such as

```
sum = 0;
```

- iterative change, like

```
sum = sum + counter;
counter = counter + 1;
```

- and a termination condition, implied by

```
while (counter < N)
```

These same three parts will arise in all the repetitive constructs that we shall build in this chapter.

Note also that the loop can be understood as building up the desired answer (the sum of the first *N* nonnegative integers) through a set of intermediate approximations. Each trip through the loop the value stored in sum becomes a better approximation to the required value, until the last trip through the loop, when it becomes exactly right. All algorithmic loops effectively work toward the desired answer in an analogous way, and I will emphasize this throughout the remaining pages of this book.

Questions

Question 1 What is the value of i immediately after the execution of each of the following loops? How many times was the loop body executed in each case?

a.
```
int i = 0;
while ( i < 5 )
  {
    i = i + 1;
  }
```

b.
```
int i = 0;
while ( 0 < i%5 )
  {
    i = i + 1;
  }
```

c.
```
int i = 1;
while ( i < 10 )
  {
    i = i + 5;
  }
```

Question 2 What are the the values of x and y after the following loop terminates?

```
int x = 1;
int y = 10;
while ( x < y )
  {
    x = x + 1;
    y = y - 1;
  }
```

Question 3 Write a function int power(double x, int n) that will compute its first argument, x, raised to the power of its second, n, provided n is nonnegative.

3.2 RELATIONAL AND LOGICAL OPERATORS

In the previous section the notion of the while loop was introduced. Such a loop repeats a set of steps (the loop body) as long as a specified condition is true before each execution of the loop body. Let us now study the construction of such control conditions. A condition must be a logical expression, that is, an expression that evaluates to either true

TABLE 3.1 Relational Operators in C++.

Operator	Meaning	Precedence
<	less than	10
>	greater than	10
<=	less than or equal	10
>=	greater than or equal	10
==	is equal	9
!=	is not equal	9

All are binary operators using infix placement, and all associate left-to-right.

or false. To usefully build such loops we therefore need some means to write interesting logical expressions in C++.

One means to construct logical expressions is with relational operators.

Definition

> *Relational operators* are binary operators that test for a specific relation between their numerical operands.

The relational operators between numbers are well known to you; they include things like < (less than) and > (greater than). The expression 10 < 3 evaluates to false, while 10 > 3 evaluates to true. Table 3.1 lists the relational operators and their meanings for numerical data. The operands can be any numeric type, such as int, double, or others that we will discuss in Chapter 5. The semantics of each of these relational operators will check the truth of the indicated relation using the standard ordering of the real numbers. Note that the precedence of these operators is lower than that of the arithmetical operations, so 2 < 10 - 9 evaluates to false. But don't forget: A well-placed parenthesis is better than a memorized rule, so 2 < (10 - 9) is to be preferred.

The relational operators in C++ actually evaluate to either 0 or 1, with 0 being understood as false and 1 as true. Indeed, *any* nonzero integer is understood as meaning true.[2]

Here is a code that exercises the relational operators:

hiLo.cpp

```
1   //=================================================================
2   // hiLo.cpp
3   // Plays the ever popular high low game.
4   //=================================================================
5   #include <iostream>
6   #include <cstdlib>
7   using namespace std;
8
```

---

[2]Computer CPUs often have the instructions jump-if-zero and jump-if-not-zero that are intended to implement loops, so this association is a reflection of computer architecture in the C++ language.

```
9    int main(void)
10   {
11     int max = 100;   // max number for guessing
12
13     int seed;
14     cout << "Input a seed integer please :> ";
15     cin >> seed;
16
17     // get a somewhat random number between 0 and max;
18     srand(seed);
19     int target = rand() % (max+1);
20
21     cout << "Guess a number between 0 and "<< max << " :> ";
22     int guess;
23     cin >> guess;
24     while(guess != target)
25       {
26         cout << guess << " < target is " << (guess < target)
27               << endl;
28         cout << guess << " > target is " << (guess > target)
29               << endl;
30         cout << "Guess a number between 0 and " << max << " :> ";
31         cin >> guess;
32       }
33     cout << "Congratulations.  "
34           << "You've just wasted a few minutes of your life";
35     cout << endl;
36     return 0;
37   }
```

The loop in this code continues until the user inputs the correct guess for the target value. You have, of course, looked up the interesting standard library functions `srand` and `rand` in Appendix A.

The relational operators are quite nice—with them we can express four different sorts of logical expression,[3] and so can provide four different sorts of conditions to control a while loop. But does this really cover all the possibilities? Certainly not. One desire that you can probably imagine easily is to combine these conditions, and express a condition like $0 < x < 10$, which says that x is between 0 and 10. Such a condition is a combination of $0 < x$ *and* $x < 10$. What we need is some way to say "and" in C++. Well, how about `and`? The word `and` is a logical operator in C++, and there are two others, `or` and `not`. These are listed in Table 3.2 along with their precedence.[4]

---

[3]Greater than and greater than or equal are, of course, redundant.

[4]The logical operators have alternate forms: the twitchy `&&` for `and`, the strange parallel `||` for `or`, and the obscure `!` for `not`. I encourage you to use the more transparent, if wordy, `and`, `or`, and `not`. Unfortunately, until recently, most compilers only supported the older, bizarre versions of the logical operators, and it is possible that you will come across such older compilers. Appendix A has some advice on this matter.

TABLE 3.2   **Logical Operators in C++**

Operator	Meaning	Precedence	Alternate
not	not	15	!
and	and	5	&&
or	or	4	||

Both and and or are binary infix operators that associate left to right, although not is a unary prefix operator that associates right to left.

With these logical operators in hand, we can write logical expressions such as

```
(0.0 < x) and (x < 10.0)
```

to ask if x is between 0.0 and 10.0. Similarly, we could ask the converse, either as

```
not ((0.0 < x) and (x < 10.0))
```

or as

```
(x <= 0.0) or (10.0 <= x))
```

Sometimes it is useful to store logical values, and for this purpose there is a special data type called bool. Values of type bool can be either true or false, and the keywords true and false also provide a means to literally write Boolean values in C++.

Claim

> The proper way to express literal logical values in C++ is with the keywords false and true.

These are much clearer than 0 and not 0.

With variables of type bool we can store the results of a logical expression for later examination, as in

```
bool xInRange = (0.0 < x) and (x < 10.0);
```

This gives xInRange a value of either true or false. We can use such variables, for example, to control loops. You will sometimes see constructs such as this:

```
1  double x = 0.0;
2  double dx = 0.3;
3
4  // Do work with x values as long as they are between 0 and 10
5  bool xInRange = (0.0 < x) and (x < 10.0);
6  while(xInRange)
7    {
```

```
8      // do something with x
9      cout << sqrt(x * (10.0 - x));
10     // advance x to its next value
11     x = x + dx;
12     xInRange = (0.0 < x) and (x > 10.0);
13   }
```

Frankly, in this case, the use of `xInRange` offers us little over the explicit test

```
while((0.0 < x) and (x > 10.0))
```

other than giving the test a name. On the other hand, to do so we must write the test twice, once on line 5 and once on line 12. This duplication increases the chances of making a mistake. (Do you see the mistake?) But there is sometimes merit to giving a condition a name; if it is complicated, or reading it is a distraction from following the main thrust of the code, then hiding the details of the test behind a name could be useful. But if we really do want to give a condition a name, we should put it into a function that returns a `bool`, like

```
1   bool inRange(double x, double lowerBound, double upperBound)
2   {
3     return (lowerBound < x) and (x < upperBound)
4   }
```

Then the previous code could be written as

```
1   double x = 0.0;
2   double dx = 0.3;
3
4   // Do work with x values as long as they are between 0 and 10
5   while( inRange(x, 0.0, 10.0) )
6     {
7       // do something with x
8       cout << sqrt(x * (10.0 - x));
9       // advance x to its next value
10      x = x + dx;
11    }
```

This version is even right, unlike the previous one.[5]

[5] You might be concerned about introducing functions as small as `inRange`. Don't be. A function does not need to be big; indeed, smaller is generally better. Some authors worry about the inefficiency of such small functions, but that's really the compiler's problem. The human mind should not waste time worrying about small efficiency issues unless a definite performance problem is discovered.

Definition

A function that returns a `bool` value (`true` or `false`) is called a *predicate*.

Don't be reluctant to introduce predicates into your code. If a logical condition is complicated, it can greatly improve the readability and reliability of your code to isolate the condition into its own function.

Questions

Question 4   What is the value of each of the following logical expressions, given

```
int i = 10;
int j =  5;
double x = 12.0;
bool test = false;
```

a.   i < x

b.   (i < x) or (j == 3)

c.   false and (not test)

d.   true and (not test)

e.   i%j == 0

Question 5   What are the the values of x and y after the following loop terminates?

```
int x = 1;
int y = 10;
while ( (x < y) and (y > x) )
  {
    x = x + 1;
    y = y - 1;
  }
```

Question 6   What does the following loop do?

```
int x = 1;
int y = 10;
while ( x != y )
  {
    x = x + 1;
    y = y - 1;
  }
```

3.3   A COMMON EXAMPLE

Let's consider another algorithm, which will provide a rich set of algorithm design opportunities extending into the next chapter. Given two nonnegative integers, i, and j, find their greatest common divisor gcd(i, j). Here is an obvious, if inelegant, algorithm to do so:

ALGORITHM   *Simple gcd*

Computes the greatest common divisor of a pair of nonnegative integers
Require: $i \geq 0$ and $j \geq 0$
1:   Set $g = j$
2:   **while** g does not simultaneously divide j and i **do**
3:       Set $g = g - 1$
4:   **end while**
5:   Return g

This instruction list, like any instruction list, should not be accepted without question.

• Will it terminate?

• If it does terminate, does it give the right answer?

• If it does obtain a correct answer, does it waste significant time in getting there?

Every trip through the loop, g will be reduced by 1. This can happen only $j - 1$ times before g will equal 1, and since 1 certainly divides both i and j, the algorithm is guaranteed to terminate. Further, whenever this loop does terminate, g will be a divisor of both i and j because this is required by the termination condition. Finally, g will be the greatest such divisor because g began at the largest possible divisor of j and exhaustively checked every possible divisor below that. So we do have an algorithm, and it is even correct. How can this be expressed in C++? Here is a direct translation:

gcd1.cpp

```
1   int gcd(int i, int j)
2   {
3     int g = j;
4     while( not((i % g) == 0 and (j % g) == 0 ))
5       {
6         g = g - 1;
7       }
8     return g;
9   }
```

Note the logical expression (boxed in the code) that ensures the loop will stop only when g evenly divides (without remainder) both i and j. This algorithm has also been nicely packaged inside a function. One advantage of doing so is that we can now write a set of tests—sometimes called unit tests—for this gcd function *independent of how we might be otherwise using it*. Here is a test code that I wrote for the gcd function:

gcdDriver.cpp

```
1   // ============================================================
2   // gcdDriver.cpp
3   // Test code for a greatest common divisor function
4   // ============================================================
5   #include <iostream>
6   using namespace std;
7
8   // External routine declarations
9   int gcd(int, int);   // declare the gcd function
10
11  // ===========>> main <<================================
12  int main()
13  {
14    cout << "gcd(4, 2) = ";
15    cout << gcd(4, 2) << endl;
16
17    cout << "gcd(2, 4) = ";
18    cout << gcd(2, 4) << endl;
```

```
19
20    cout << "gcd(259,_111)_=_";
21    cout << gcd(259, 111) << endl;
22
23    cout << "gcd(1375,_218491)_=_";
24    cout << gcd(1375, 218491) << endl;
25
26    cout << "gcd(541,_3804853)_=_";
27    cout << gcd(541, 3804853) << endl;
28
29    cout << "gcd(0,_56)_=_";
30    cout << gcd(0, 56) << endl;
31
32    cout << "gcd(56,_0)_=_";
33    cout << gcd(56, 0) << endl;
34
35    return 0;
36  }
```

Note that we have two files containing source text, **gcd1.cpp** and **gcdDriver.cpp**. The source text in both of these files must be compiled together into a single sequence of machine language instructions. With many command line compilers this can be accomplished with a command like:

```
1   g++ gcdDriver.cpp gcd1.cpp -o gcdtest
```

In writing the **gcdDriver.cpp** file I have declared the gcd function, but not defined it. It must be declared, because everything in C++ has to be declared before it is used. But it does not need to be defined in **gcdDriver.cpp**. The compiler will find its definition in the file **gcd1.cpp**.

The test cases are designed to cover a range of possibilities, with an eye toward finding problems in the code. Here is the output of the test cases on a Sun machine running Solaris, and using the code produced by Sun's C++ compiler:

```
1   jplug$ ./gcd1
2   gcd(259, 111) = 37
3   gcd(4, 2) = 2
4   gcd(2, 4) = 2
5   gcd(0, 56) = 56
6   gcd(56, 0) = Arithmetic Exception
7   jplug$
```

and here is the result of running the same code on an Intel architecture machine running Linux and using the GNU g++ compiler:

```
[hagar@localhost Code]$ ./gcd1
gcd(259, 111) = 37
gcd(4, 2) = 2
gcd(2, 4) = 2
gcd(0, 56) = 56
Floating point exception (core dumped)
[hagar@localhost Code]$
```

Note that they agree, and the results are correct (how can I tell this?), but something funny happened with the last test, which looked for the GCD of 56 and 0. Time for some analysis and improvement!

What went wrong with gcd(56,0)? The greatest common divisor of 56 and 0 is 56. That is, 56 evenly divides both 56 and 0, and 56 is the largest such divisor. But my algorithm to find the GCD of two numbers does not get the right answer! What happened?

In fact the correct algorithm **Simple GCD** was not translated exactly to C++; the C++ implementation is very slightly different from the informal pseudocode of **Simple GCD**. The heart of the problem is English versus C++. Consider the first step of the algorithm, on line 3 of **gcd1.cpp**: for the case of i = 56 and j = 0 this will store the value 0 under the identifier g. The next step of the algorithm is the start of the while loop, on line 4 of the code. This includes the operations i % g and j % g, both of which now involve division by zero! This makes no sense; it is not possible to usefully define the remainder for a division by zero. At this point, the exact behavior of the executing code becomes unknown, and different computers/compilers/operating systems will respond in different ways. The messages printed out when the program runs provide hints as to what may have gone wrong, although here they are certainly not explicit. But it does not really matter. The problem is not the computer, it's the C++ algorithm.

This is a case where implementing the algorithm and testing it carefully can really be of benefit. We could have discovered this defect in the gcd implementation by human brainpower alone, but all too often we miss details such as this, or mentally fill in a missing step, without even realizing that we did so. The problem here is a boundary case: what the algorithm will do when one of its input values is on the boundary of allowed values. A carelessly designed algorithm will often break on such boundary cases. We knew from the start that the algorithm was only for nonnegative integers; in such a case, we should check the boundary value—zero—with great care.

To really fix this algorithm will require a selection construct, which we have not yet learned to express in C++. But let's not leave a broken code lying around. Let's fix it with a precondition forbidding zero as a value for j in function gcd. And let's go further—if a caller of this algorithm dares to pass zeros or negative values into it, they are breaking the rules we have established. So let's express these rules in the source text itself, using an *assertion*:

gcd2.cpp

```
1   #include <cassert>
2   using namespace std;
3
4   int gcd(int i, int j)
5   {
6     // Requirements
7     assert(j > 0);
8     assert(i >= 0);
9
10    int g = j;
11    while( not((i % g) == 0 and (j % g) == 0 ))
12      {
13        g = g - 1;
14      }
15    return g;
16  }
```

When run with our test code, the output is now:

Sample Run

```
1   [hagar@localhost Code]$ ./gcd2
2   gcd(259, 111) = 37
3   gcd(4, 2) = 2
4   gcd(2, 4) = 2
5   gcd(0, 56) = 56
6   gcd2: gcd2.cpp:5: int gcd (int, int): Assertion 'j > 0' failed.
7   gcd(56, 0) = Aborted (core dumped)
8   [hagar@localhost Code]$
```

Look carefully—the code still fails when given a value that the algorithm cannot deal with, but this time it tells us where and why. It failed on line 5 of the source text **gcd2.cpp**[6] and it failed because the assertion j > 0 was false. The careful use of assertions can help us find errors.

Claim

Assertions should be used to verify your assumptions about data.

Usually, we are making assumptions (hopefully knowingly) about our data, and assertions can be used to check these assumptions at key points in our source text.

---

[6]My compiler system showed this as qcd2.cpp:5. Others will show the same information, but the detailed appearance may differ.

We are definitely not done with our algorithm: it can certainly be improved. Note, for example, that gcd(2,1000) will return 2, as it should, but only after checking that 2 is not divisible by any number from 1,000 down to 3. That's a great many checks, when only one—is 1,000 divisible by 2—was really necessary. This inefficiency arose because I treat the second argument to gcd differently from the first: The second argument is used to initialize our guess g to the gcd. If the second argument is larger than the first, I waste much time walking the value stored under g down to the smaller value of the first argument before we have any chance of seeing a correct answer. We could avoid this by demanding that the first argument be the larger of the two, and ensuring this with an assertion. But this is a questionable approach—the algorithm works either way. It is just faster if the second argument is the smaller. A better approach would be to use selection to determine which argument is the larger, and act accordingly when picking an initial value of g. This is something we could do in the next chapter, when we learn how to express selection in C++. But in fact, with a way to express selection, we can actually write a much faster and more elegant algorithm.

Questions

Question 7 In testing **gcd2.cpp**, how can we be sure that our tests are correct? For example, how can I be sure that it is giving the correct answer for gcd(259, 111)?

Question 8 Write a single assertion that can replace the two assertions on lines 7 and 8 of **gcd2.cpp**.

3.4 LOOP INVARIANTS

Algorithms are written statically, but execute dynamically, so keeping all the potential threads of execution in mind can be difficult. Fortunately, finding something that is constant for all paths through a loop can give us the mental purchase we need to establish the correctness of the loop.

A loop is a way to approach the solution of a problem by successive approximations. Each trip through the loop we must make progress on the solution of the problem, so that we can guarantee the eventual correct and certain termination of the computation. I take it as clear that a loop exists within some part of an algorithm, and that it therefore has some environment of data that it can examine and manipulate. A loop can then be understood to have five ingredients: a goal, a body, an invariant, an initialization, and a termination condition.

A goal is a relationship among the data in the loop environment that we want to be true when the loop is done, for instance, when the loop terminates, g should be the greatest common divisor of i and j.

Definition

A loop's *goal* is a condition—a predicate relationship—among the data that must be true when the loop terminates.

A loop usually begins without the goal established, and must somehow perform repeated, iterative improvements until the goal is reached.

Moving toward the goal is the job of the loop body.

Definition

> A *loop body* is a set of algorithmic steps that transform data toward the goal.

It is the repeated execution of the loop body that must accomplish the work needed to establish the goal. It could be as trivial as g = g - 1, or it could be a hugely complex computation, but every time the loop body is executed the data that the loop is acting on must change, and change in a way that makes progress toward the goal.

Because the loop body changes data, potentially in a very complex way, it is difficult to keep track of its action. It is usually worth our effort to also develop some unchanging relationship between the data.

Definition

> A *loop invariant* is a relationship among the data that is always true at the start of the loop body, and for which the goal is a special true case.

An invariant defines some true relationship between the data used in the loop, and the loop body must maintain the truth of this relationship. When the goal is true, the invariant must also be true, but not vice versa. The job of the loop body is to move through the set of data for which the invariant is true, until the goal is reached.

In order to make an invariant true, we often need to set up some special relationship among the data before the loop body first executes.

Definition

> An *initialization* is a statement (or statements) that establishes the truth of the invariant before the first execution of the loop body.

The initialization of an iteration sets up our calculation; when we enter the loop, it's essential that our data be in a known state, satisfying some fixed relationships, or we have little hope of having a correct loop.

Definition

> A *termination condition* is a relationship among the data that, when true, causes the loop to stop with the goal established.

When a loop stops, the invariant is true, because it was true at the start (arranged by initialization) and it was kept true (by the loop body). And when a loop stops, the termination condition is true by definition. In a correct loop the intersection of the termination condition and the invariant must be the goal.

These five ingredients work together to move an algorithm from some starting point to completion. The initialization sets up a starting state and establishes the loop invariant. The iteration itself consists of repeatedly executing the loop body to transform the problem data progressively toward the termination condition, but to also maintain the truth of the loop invariant as it does so. Those data that simultaneously satisfy the

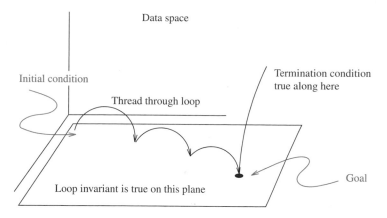

FIGURE 3.1   The general geometry of loop invariants in data space.

termination condition and the invariant had better satisfy the goal, because that's when the loop will stop.[7] This gives us a picture of a loop as acting on the set of data, as suggested in Fig. 3.1.

A loop invariant is a logical expression, a predicate, that is always true at some fixed point within the loop, typically just before the loop body is executed. Within the loop body the invariant can be temporarily broken—made false—but it must be restored by the time the loop body is finished.

Perhaps this all sounds a bit highfalutin in the abstract, but loop invariants are sometimes trivial. Consider a running sum:

ALGORITHM   *Running sum*

Computes the sum of a set of N numbers
1:   Set $s = 0.0$
2:   Set $count = 0$ (Invariant is established here.)
3:   **while** $count < N$ **do**
4:       Note: the invariant is always true here
5:       Get next number x
6:       Set $s = s + x$ (The invariant is not true anymore!)
7:       Set $count = count + 1$ (Whew! The invariant is true again.)
8:   **end while**
9:   Return s (It's the right thing, because the invariant is true.)

The predicate elements outlined above are:

- **The goal.** s is the sum of the N numbers.
- **The loop invariant.** s is the sum of the first $count$ numbers and $count \leq N$.
- **The termination condition.** $count \geq N$.

---

[7]Sometimes, the termination condition can simply be the goal.

The correctness of this loop is easy to see by looking at the invariant. The invariant is true at the top of the loop body. It is not true everywhere in the loop body, but it is always restored to truth at statement 7, so it's still true at the bottom of the loop body, and hence is true at the top when we cycle back around. When the loop terminates, *count* is equal to or greater than *N*. This and the loop invariant then tell us that *count* equals *N*, and that *s* is the sum of the first *N* numbers, which is what we want.

It is not uncommon for first-time programmers to get even this simple running sum loop wrong. A common mistake is to use the termination condition *count* ≤ *N*, which allows *count* to become equal to *N and still take another trip through the loop*. This is often called an "off-by-one" error, since it leads to the loop body being executed one time too many. Getting more difficult loops correct is often even trickier, and the concept of a loop invariant can help you get it right.

Here is another C++ function. This one implements a simple-minded algorithm to compute nonnegative integer powers of a real number, represented as a `double`.

power.cpp

```
1   //========================>> power.cpp <<====================
2   #include <cassert>
3   using namespace std;
4
5   double power(double x, int p)
6   {
7     // Computes x to a nonnegative integer power p.
8     assert(p >= 0);
9
10    double result = 1.0;
11    int counter = 0;
12    // invariant established: result = x^counter and counter <= p
13
14    while (counter < p)
15      {
16        // invariant: result = x^counter and counter <= p
17        result = result * x;
18        counter = counter + 1;
19        // invariant: result = x^counter and counter <= p
20      }
21    return result;
22  }
```

Is this loop right? Think about it first before you read on.

The loop invariant can be used to argue that it is. If p is zero, then the loop is never entered (because counter < p is never true), and the value 1.0 is returned. Otherwise, the loop is entered, with counter set to zero and result set to x to the power of counter (and so result is 1.0 as it should be). So the loop invariant is true the first time through the loop. On each subsequent pass through the loop, result is multiplied

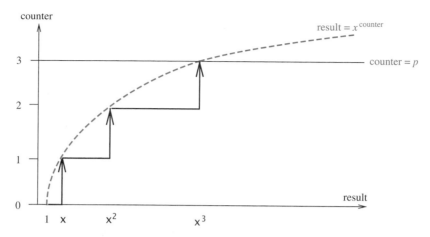

FIGURE 3.2   The geometry of data transformations through the power.cpp loop. The loop body moves the data along the arrows until the termination condition is reached. The loop invariant is true along the dashed line.

by x and the counter is incremented, so the loop invariant is maintained as true. Thus when the loop is exited, result does equal x to the power of counter, counter is less than or equal to p, and also counter must be greater than or equal to p (because this is the loop termination condition). So p, in fact, equals counter and the function power does what it is supposed to. Figure 3.2 shows the data transformations through the loop.

This is again not an especially tricky loop, although many a student has gotten it wrong by being off by one on the final value of counter. But it does illustrate the point: You can reason about loops using mathematical logic, and develop a high degree of certainty about their correctness.

Questions

Question 9   Consider the following algorithm for computing the product $n \times x$, where n is a nonnegative integer:

```
double product(int n, double x)
{
  assert(n >= 0);
  double p = 0.0;
  int i = 0;
  while( i <= n )
  {
    p = p + x;
    i = i + 1;
  }
  return p;
}
```

Develop a meaningful loop invariant and use it to argue for either the correctness, or the incorrectness, of the code.

3.5   ORDERING WORK IN A LOOP

Both the running sum loop of **Running sum** and the loop of **power.cpp** were while loops controlled by a counter. And in both loops I used basically the same structure:

```
1   counter = 0;   // establish initial value of counter
2   while( counter < max )
3     {
4       // do work
5       counter = counter + 1;
6     }
```

In both cases I am using `counter` in a disciplined way to count work done: First I do the work, and only then do I increment the counter. Incrementing the counter becomes a proclamation that I have successfully *finished* the current piece of work. I could write the loops as follows:

```
1   counter = 0;   // establish initial value of counter
2   while( counter < max )
3     {
4       counter = counter + 1;
5       // do work
6     }
```

but this is poor design. Now when `counter` is set to 1 during my first trip through the loop, its value will denote the step I am still hoping to complete, rather than a step that is done. This placement might make no difference to the correct functioning of the code, but does violate a principle I consider important.

Claim

> Do not count your chickens until after they are hatched.

Although the ordering of the statements in the loop body would make no difference in the **Running sum** and **power.cpp** algorithms, it can have a profound effect in some other loops. Suppose we have a list of a numbers, and want to sum them up. This is a typical task for a spreadsheet, a billing system, or any number of systems. This differs from **Running sum** because we don't know ahead of time how many numbers there are to sum up. We would like a loop something like this:

ALGORITHM *Exhaustive Sum*

Keeps a running sum of input data until there is no more data to process
1: Set sum = 0.0
2: **while** there are still numbers to deal with **do**
3:      Get the next number
4:      Add it to sum
5: **end while**
6: Return sum to caller

The question is, how do we deal with the condition "while there are still numbers to deal with"? Up till now we have assumed that we know how many numbers there are, and controlled the while loop with a condition like counter < N. But this requires that the number of items be known ahead of time. This is awkward, and if we rely on a human user to provide the value of N, it can be error prone.

In C++, input streams do not provide a means to tell if the next input operation is going to succeed. Instead they provide a mechanism to check if the previous input operation succeeded or failed. This means that we must attempt to get data, and then proceed to use it only if we succeed. Here is an algorithm in pseudocode that does this:

ALGORITHM   *Interactive Sum*

Maintains a running sum of data extracted from some data source
1:   Set *total* = 0.0
2:   Fetch *value* from data source
3:   **while** fetch was successful **do**
4:       Invariant: *total* is the sum of all previous numbers except *value*
5:       Add *value* into *total*
6:       Fetch *value* from user
7:   **end while**
8:   Return sum to caller

We are now fetching our numbers from some data source. This means that when we are in the loop body and want to add to the running sum, we want to be sure that we do have a valid new number to work with. The loop therefore runs as long as we do have valid data to work with; the loop *termination* condition is that the most recent attempt to fetch a number from the data source was *unsuccessful*. When the loop ends, *total* is the sum of all previously fetched numbers except for what's currently in *value*, and because of the termination condition whatever is stored in *value* is not valid data. So the loop is correct.

To implement this code in C++ we need a way to check if at attempt to get input using an istream was valid. Along with all istream data, such as cin, there come a host of interesting functions,[8] including one that will report if an attempt at input failed.

C++ Principle

> If identifier is of type istream, then the function bool identifier.fail() can be called to check the status of the stream. identifier.fail() will return true if the stream has failed to perform some operation.

So, for example, the call cin.fail() will return the value true if cin failed to get some input data, but otherwise it will return false. And since an ifstream is also an istream, we can use the same facility with streams attached to files. This allows us to write a function like this:

sumNumbers.cpp

```
1  // ================================================================
2  // sumNumbers.cpp
```

[8]About which I am sure you have read in Appendix A.

```
3    // A function to sum up numbers fetched via dataSource, until
4    // there are no more numbers forthcoming.
5    // ============================================================
6    #include <iostream>
7    using namespace std;
8
9    double sumNumbers(istream & dataSource)
10   {
11     double sum = 0.0;
12     double number;
13     dataSource >> number;
14     while( not dataSource.fail() )
15       {
16         sum = sum + number;
17         dataSource >> number;   // try for another
18       }
19
20     return sum;
21   }
```

This can be used in a code as follows:

addEm.cpp

```
1    // ============================================================
2    // addEm.cpp
3    // A code to add up numbers provided via cin and report the
4    // sum back via cout.
5    // ============================================================
6    #include <iostream>
7    using namespace std;
8
9    // Declaration of functions defined elsewhere
10   double sumNumbers(istream & dataSource);
11
12   // ==============>> main <<==============================
13   int main()
14   {
15     double sum = sumNumbers(cin);   // get the sum
16     cout << "The␣sum␣is␣" << sum << endl;
17
18     return 0;
19   }
```

You will note that I did not prompt for input in this code, in violation of my earlier dictum. But I don't really want to have a dialog with this code; I want to give it my data out of a file, rather than enter it interactively. A code like this is useful when we need to add up lots of numbers, not when we need to add up a few. But when we do need to add up lots of numbers, we can't hope to perfectly type them in by hand; a mistake would be likely, and the work tedious. Fortunately, most operating systems (e.g., Unix, Linux, Windows, and Mac OS/X) provide a way to connect standard input to a file, rather than the keyboard. This will allow us to get the required data directly out of a file, where it was likely placed by another program. The following illustrates this:

```
1  [hagar@localhost Code]$ ./addEm < numbers
2  The sum is 5
3  [hagar@localhost Code]$
```

The character < tells the operating system to attach (or redirect) standard input from the file whose name follows it, so I can put my data into that file, and the code will extract it from there. For the test case shown, the file named **numbers** contained

```
1.0
1.0
2.0
-1.0
-2.0
-1.0
5.0
```

It could just as easily have contained a list of one million numbers.

As shown in Fig. 3.3, redirection is an operating system service, having nothing to do with C++. But it is a convenient one. A code can be written to read its data from standard input using cin, and it can even be tested on small data sets interactively. But then, when a large data set must be processed, we don't type in those data by hand (a

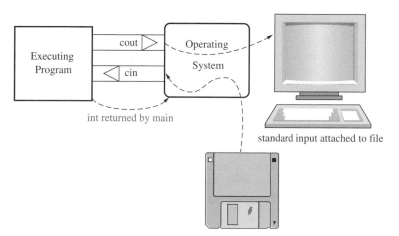

FIGURE 3.3 Standard input can be attached to a file instead of a keyboard. The characters from the file are fed into the code, rather than the characters from the keyboard.

tedious, and hence error-prone process), but rather ask the operating system to fetch the characters of input out of a file, rather than from a keyboard (see Fig. 3.3).

Questions

Question 10   Consider the following loop for adding up numbers read from an `istream` named `in`:

```
double sum = 0.0;
while( not in.fail() )
  {
    double x;
    in >> x;     // get number from stream
    sum = sum + x;  // add it into sum
  }
```

What's wrong with it?

Question 11   Change **addEm.cpp** to use a file for input, rather than `cin`.

Question 12   Consider the following loop for computing the average of numbers read from an `istream` named `in`:

```
double sum = 0;
int count = 1;
double x;
in >> x;
while( not in.fail() )
  {
    count = count + 1;
    sum = sum + x;
    in >> x;
  }
double average = sum/count;
```

What's wrong with it?

3.6   ITERATIVE SOLUTION OF EQUATIONS

Let's create an algorithm to compute the square root of a real number. The algorithm I shall present to you is based on a general technique called Newton's method, but we shall not consider that general idea here. We just want to compute the square root of x. The basic idea is to guess an answer, and use this guess to construct an improved estimate of the answer. Then we can do it over again, using the improved answer as the guess, and get a still better answer. Lather, rinse, repeat.

This is a very common idea: Our algorithm will construct an approximation of the thing we want, and then improve it, and keep doing so until some termination criterion is reached. Sometimes the exact answer can be found in a finite number of steps, but often (as in this square root problem) it cannot, and we must simply stop when we consider the result "good enough." When you examine, or create, a loop in a program, you should seek to understand it in this sense—how does each trip through the loop move us closer to the desired answer?

How shall we iterate toward $\sqrt{x}$? An iterative algorithm to solve this problem will advance from an old estimate r_{old} to a new one r_{new} via some formula of the form

$$r_{new} = f(r_{old}, x), \tag{3.1}$$

where the function f is as yet unspecified, but clearly must be built carefully if there is to be any chance of having r_{new} closer to $\sqrt{x}$ than r_{old}. However, without yet knowing what f is, let's sketch out the essentials of an algorithm. It will look like this:

ALGORITHM   *Square Root*

Compute the square root $\sqrt{x}$ of the input value x
Require: $x \geq 0$

```
1:   r_old = 1.0 (Hey, it's just a first guess!)
2:   while r_old * r_old ≠ x do
3:       r_new = f(r_old, x) (Compute new estimate.)
4:       r_old = r_new (Replace old estimate with new.)
5:   end while
6:   Return r_old
```

Cool! Looks perfect. But there's trouble. The termination condition demands that $r_{old} * r_{old}$ be *equal* to x. The loop only stops when r_{old} is *exactly* equal to the desired $\sqrt{x}$. What guarantee do I have that this precise termination condition will bless my algorithm with the property of finite execution? Will it ever stop? I have no such guarantee. In fact, you may know that a number like $\sqrt{2}$ cannot be written down with a finite number of digits—it takes an infinite amount of work to find $\sqrt{2}$ exactly. So I should not expect that an algorithm can exactly compute $\sqrt{2}$, and thus no algorithm can compute every square root exactly. I therefore need a stopping criterion for my loop that says, more or less, "keep going until the answer is good enough." I can only ask my iteration to yield an approximation to $\sqrt{x}$.

This is a common issue in engineering computing. Many of our problems have precise answers, but we cannot compute them. We can compute only approximations. Even such fundamental functions as $\sqrt{x}$, $\sin(x)$, and $\exp(x)$ cannot be computed in a finite number of steps, and so must be approximated.

So for our $\sqrt{x}$ computation, we must consider carefully the issue of stopping the iterative algorithm. In this problem we are trying to solve a mathematical equation, $r^2 = x$, involving continuous variables. But we are trying to do so with an algorithm that must run on a machine capable of only finite computation.

Definition

> A *numerical computation* is the approximate computational solution of a mathematical equation involving continuous variables.

In solving such problems iteratively, we need a way to decide if the iteration has *converged*, meaning that the iteration has improved the answer sufficiently to justify stopping.

Definition

> A *convergence condition* for a numerical computation is a condition, usually an inequality, that provides the termination condition for an iteration.

Typically, a convergence condition has some implication for the accuracy or precision of a computation. We will consider three different ways to terminate the root-finding algorithm in the next three sections.

Before doing so, let's provide a function to drive the iteration, so that we can implement the algorithms in C++ code and try them out. The function

$$f(r, x) = r - \frac{r^2 - x}{2r} \tag{3.2}$$

will do the trick. This can also be algebraically simplified to

$$f(r, x) = \frac{r^2 + x}{2r}. \tag{3.3}$$

Although the former form is more transparent for some purposes, the latter is more convenient to write in code. I shall therefore use the former form when I analyze the algorithm, but use the latter form when I implement the code.[9]

A key point to note about this function f is that $f(\sqrt{x}, x) = \sqrt{x}$. In other words, if we put in the correct answer, f hands the correct answer back to us. This is a necessary condition for a successful iteration, although it is not sufficient.

Iterate a Predetermined Number of Times I could stop the iteration when it has computed a fixed number of improved estimates (say, N). Such an algorithm would look like this:

ALGORITHM *Square Root with Fixed Iterates*

Estimate the square root of the input value x, using N iterates
Require: $x \geq 0$
1: $r_{old} = 1.0$ (Hey, it's just a guess!)
2: *counter* $= 0$
3: **while** *counter* $< N$ **do**
4:      Note: We have computed *counter* iterates
5:      $r_{new} = f(r_{old}, x)$ (Compute new estimate.)
6:      $r_{old} = r_{new}$ (Replace old estimate with new.)
7:      *counter* $=$ *counter* $+ 1$
8: **end while**
9: Return r_{old}

Here's the same algorithm rendered in C++:

squareRootN.cpp

```
1   // ================================================================
2   // squareRootN.cpp
3   // Function to approximate the square root using a fixed number
4   // of Newton's method iterations.
5   // ================================================================
6   #include <cassert>
7   using namespace std;
8
9   // ============>> squareRootN <<===================================
10  // Returns approximation to square root of x
11  // Arguments
```

[9]The advantage of Eq. (3.3) will also be explored again in Chapter 8.

```cpp
12  //    x -- number whose root we desire
13  //    N -- number iterates to take
14  // ================================================================
15  double squareRootN(double x, int N)
16  {
17    assert(x >= 0);
18
19    double rold = 1.0;  // estimate of root
20    int counter = 0;    // number of iterates completed
21
22    while( counter < N )
23      {
24        rold = (rold * rold + x) / (2.0 * rold);
25        counter = counter + 1;
26      }
27
28    return rold;
29  }
```

Note that I have dispensed with the variable r_{new} in the actual implementation of the code because it was not really needed.

Here is a test driver code, and a sample run. The test driver uses the sqrt function from the standard math library to provide an accurate comparison for my own square root values.

rootTesterN.cpp

```cpp
1   // ================================================================
2   // rootTesterN.cpp
3   // Code to test my first square root function.
4   // ================================================================
5   #include <iostream>
6   #include <cmath>
7   using namespace std;
8
9   double squareRootN(double x, int N);
10
11  // ===========>> main <<===================================
12  int main()
13  {
14    cout.precision(15);  // show lots of digits
15
16    double x;
17    int N;
18
19    cout << "Input x and number of iterates [q to quit] :> ";
```

```
20    cin >> x;
21    cin >> N;
22    while( not cin.fail() )
23      {
24        // we have valid input, so give it a try
25
26        cout << "squareRootN(" << x << ",␣" << N << ")␣=␣";
27        cout << squareRootN(x, N) << endl;
28        cout << "sqrt(" << x << ")␣=␣" << sqrt(x) << endl;
29        cout << "Difference␣=␣" << squareRootN(x, N) - sqrt(x)
30              << endl;
31        cout << "====================================" << endl;
32
33        cout << "Input␣x␣and␣number␣of␣iterates␣[q␣to␣quit]␣:>␣";
34        cin >> x >> N;
35      }
36
37    cout << "Thanks␣for␣playing!" << endl;
38    return 0;
39  }
```

Note the use of cout.precision(15) to cause cout to present lots of digits of precision; see Appendix A.

Here is a set of tests:

```
1   [hagar@localhost Code]$ ./rootTesterN
2   Input x and number of iterates [q to quit] :> 4.0 2
3   squareRootN(4, 2) = 2.05
4   sqrt(4) = 2
5   Difference = 0.0499999999999998
6   ====================================
7   Input x and number of iterates [q to quit] :> 4.0 5
8   squareRootN(4, 5) = 2
9   sqrt(4) = 2
10  Difference = 2.22044604925031e-15
11  ====================================
12  Input x and number of iterates [q to quit] :> 4.0 10
13  squareRootN(4, 10) = 2
14  sqrt(4) = 2
15  Difference = 0
16  ====================================
17  Input x and number of iterates [q to quit] :> 100.0 10
18  squareRootN(100, 10) = 10
19  sqrt(100) = 10
```

```
20  Difference = 0
21  ====================================
22  Input x and number of iterates [q to quit] :> 1000.0 10
23  squareRootN(1000, 10) = 31.6227766016838
24  sqrt(1000) = 31.6227766016838
25  Difference = 0
26  ====================================
27  Input x and number of iterates [q to quit] :> 1.0e6 10
28  squareRootN(1000000, 10) = 1296.19159270688
29  sqrt(1000000) = 1000
30  Difference = 296.191592706879
31  ====================================
32  Input x and number of iterates [q to quit] :> q
33  Thanks for playing!
34  [hagar@localhost Code]$
```

Each test shows the result of my squareRoot function, the result of the standard library sqrt function, and their difference. For numbers below 1,000 my function seems to be doing quite well with only 10 iterations. But as the number x gets larger, you will note that the error in my square root function, with a fixed number of iterates, is growing. Still, not too bad.[10] However, the number of iterates is in no way optimal; consider the case of $\sqrt{4}$. With 10 iterates the answer is very good. But it's just as good with 6 iterates. And with 5 iterates it's within 10^{-15} of the correct result.

The problem with this algorithm is that I have no rational basis to pick a value of N. Should I use $N = 10$? Or perhaps $N = 11$? I'm sort of clueless here. The only systematic approach would be to first use this squareRoot function with some value of N, and then use it again with a larger N, and see if the resulting root estimate changes by much. But even then I would not expect that a good value for N will be independent of the value of x; $N = 10$ might be adequate for $x = 2$, but insufficient for $x = 1,000$. So I'd have to carry out such a duplicate execution for every value of x.

Residual Control   Let's consider another approach. Suppose that my latest estimate of the root is r_{new}. If r_{new} did happen to be the exactly correct answer, then the quantity $|r_{new}^2 - x|$ would be zero. This quantity is called the residual; it's what's left of the error in satisfying the equation. Ideally, we should like this to be small (there are caveats about continuity and smoothness here, but hey, what's a missing caveat among friends?). So we could use the following algorithm, in which we keep iterating until the residual is small enough:

ALGORITHM   *Square Root with Residual Control*

Estimates the square root of the input value x, such that the residual is not greater than ϵ
Require: $x \geq 0$

---

[10] A library square root function is likely to do the square root with support from a built-in instruction in the CPU, and it certainly manipulates the hardware representation of the number x to avoid actually taking the square root of any number larger than 2. We will touch on this issue later in Chapter 8.

```
1:   r_old = 1.0 (Hey, it's just a guess!)
2:   residual = |r²_old − x|
3:   while residual > ε do
4:       r_new = f(r_old, x) (Compute new estimate.)
5:       r_old = r_new (Replace old estimate with new.)
6:       residual = |r²_old − x| (To see if we are done.)
7:   end while
8:   Return r_old
```

This is much nicer. We still need to specify an extra piece of data—the allowed residual difference ϵ—but at least this datum has some useful meaning. Further, a useful value of ϵ can be derived from the properties of the computer on which the code is executed (but we shall defer our discussion of this until Chapter 8).

The idea of the residual lets us do more than just control the algorithm. You have been asking yourself, "how do I know this whole crazy scheme works?" Let's start from the basic iteration

$$r_{\text{new}} = f(r_{\text{old}}, x) = r_{\text{old}} - \frac{r_{\text{old}}^2 - x}{2r_{\text{old}}} \tag{3.4}$$

and compute the residual $|r_{\text{new}}^2 - x|$. Squaring Eq. 3.4 yields

$$r_{\text{new}}^2 = r_{\text{old}}^2 - 2r_{\text{old}}\frac{r_{\text{old}}^2 - x}{2r_{\text{old}}} + \left[\frac{r_{\text{old}}^2 - x}{2r_{\text{old}}}\right]^2 \tag{3.5}$$

$$= x + \left[\frac{r_{\text{old}}^2 - x}{2r_{\text{old}}}\right]^2. \tag{3.6}$$

But this gives us

$$r_{\text{new}}^2 - x = \left[\frac{r_{\text{old}}^2 - x}{2r_{\text{old}}}\right]^2, \tag{3.7}$$

and this is remarkable is several ways. First, the left-hand side is the residual, without the absolute value sign, and the right-hand side is something squared, and so is always positive. So, in fact, $r_{\text{new}}^2 > x$, and this must be true for all iterates (excepting only the first, initial guess). Thus, $r_{\text{new}} > \sqrt{x}$ and we always approach the root from above! This is a special feature of this problem, but it's a powerful feature indeed. Our iterates always overestimate the value of the square root. At the same time, because $r_{\text{old}}^2 - x > 0$, Eq. (3.4) shows then that we are always decreasing our estimate from one step to the next.

The loop invariant is that $residual = |r_{\text{old}}^2 - x|$, and the termination condition is that $residual < \epsilon$. Since the residual decreases at every step, we have a guarantee that the algorithm will terminate in finite time, and when it does, we are sure that $|r_{\text{old}}^2 - x| < \epsilon$. The algorithm is correct.

Notice that this analysis shows there was no need for the absolute value when computing the residual, other than on the initial guess; I will exploit this in the C++ implementation below. But I must emphasize that many equation-solving algorithms do not have the properties of this one, and so computing a residual usually requires an absolute value to be used.

squareRoot.cpp

```cpp
// ==============================================================
// squareRoot.cpp
// Function to approximate the square root using a convergence
// criterion based on the residual in Newton's method.
// ==============================================================
#include <cassert>
#include <cmath>
using namespace std;


// ========>> squareRoot <<=======================================
// returns approximation to square root of x
// Arguments
//    x   -- number whose root we desire
//    eps -- desired residual
// ==============================================================
double squareRoot(double x, double eps)
{
  assert(x >= 0);

  double rold = 1.0;            // initial estimate of root
  double residual = abs(rold * rold - x);   // abs needed
  while( residual > eps )
    {
      rold = (rold * rold + x) / (2.0 * rold);
      residual = rold * rold - x;  // always positive
    }

  return rold;
}
```

Here is a test harness for this new square root code:

rootTesterResidual.cpp

```cpp
// ==============================================================
// rootTesterResidual.cpp
// Code to test my second square root function.
// ==============================================================
#include <iostream>
#include <cmath>
using namespace std;

double squareRoot(double x, double eps);
```

```
10
11   // =============>> main <<===================================
12   int main(void)
13   {
14     cout.precision(15);   // show lots of digits
15
16     double x;
17     double eps;
18
19     cout << "Input_x_and_the_desired_residual_[q_to_quit]:>_";
20     cin >> x;
21     cin >> eps;
22     while( not cin.fail() )
23       {
24         // we have valid input, so give it a try
25         double root = squareRoot(x, eps);
26
27         cout << "squareRoot(" << x << ",  "_<< eps << ")_=_";
28         cout << root << endl;
29         cout << "sqrt(" << x << ") _=_ " << sqrt(x) << endl;
30         cout << "Difference_=_" << root - sqrt(x) << endl;
31         cout << "Residual_=_" << root * root - x << endl;
32         cout << "===================================" << endl;
33
34         cout << "Input_x_and_the_desired_residual_[q_to_quit]:>_";
35         cin >> x;
36         cin >> eps;
37       }
38
39     cout << "Thanks_for_playing!" << endl;
40     return 0;
41   }
```

Here is a run of this test code:

```
1   [hagar@localhost Code]$ ./rootTesterResidual
2   Input x and the desired residual [q to quit]:> 4.0 1.0e-5
3   squareRoot(4, 1e-05) = 2.00000009292229
4   sqrt(4) = 2
5   Difference = 9.2922294747666e-08
6   Residual = 3.7168918762525e-07
7   ===================================
8   Input x and the desired residual [q to quit]:> 4.0 1.0e-15
9   squareRoot(4, 1e-15) = 2
```

```
10   sqrt(4) = 2
11   Difference = 0
12   Residual = 0
13   =================================
14   Input x and the desired residual [q to quit]:> 4.0 1.0e-100
15   squareRoot(4, 1e-100) = 2
16   sqrt(4) = 2
17   Difference = 0
18   Residual = 0
19   =================================
20   Input x and the desired residual [q to quit]:> 1.0e6 1.0e-5
21   squareRoot(1000000, 1e-05) = 1000.00000000001
22   sqrt(1000000) = 1000
23   Difference = 1.17097442853265e-11
24   Residual = 2.34194885706529e-08
25   =================================
26   Input x and the desired residual [q to quit]:> 1.0e6 1.0e-15
27   squareRoot(1000000, 1e-15) = 1000
28   sqrt(1000000) = 1000
29   Difference = 0
30   Residual = 0
31   =================================
32   Input x and the desired residual [q to quit]:> q
33   Thanks for playing!
34   [hagar@localhost Code]$
```

The results of this are quite nice. We only specify how good a result we want, and the algorithm takes the number of iterates needed to accomplish our aims.

Progress Control   The convergence criterion introduced in the last section, based on reducing the residual to a small enough value, is much better than simply guessing how many iterations will be needed. A residual-based method is frequently used in the solution of large systems of equations, and its use has much merit. But it is not the only possibility. In this section I will describe another means to determine convergence. This new method is not necessarily better than the residual-based method, and the selection of either often depends on context.

Using the residual focuses on how well the equation is satisfied. Another approach is to simply iterate until r_{old} is close to r_{new}. The algorithm is thus stopped when it ceases to make much progress. The idea behind this is that, as the root is approached, the quantities r_{old} and r_{new} get close to each other, because they are both close to the value of the root. Here is an algorithm that works this way:

ALGORITHM   *Square Root with Progress Control*

Estimates the square root of the input value x, proceeding until successive iterates differ by no more than ϵ

Require: $x \geq 0$

1: $r_{\text{old}} = 1.0$
2: $r_{\text{new}} = f(r_{\text{old}}, x)$ (Compute new estimate.)
3: $delta = |r_{\text{new}} - r_{\text{old}}|$ (To see if we are getting anywhere.)
4: **while** $delta > \epsilon$ **do**
5:      $r_{\text{new}} = f(r_{\text{old}}, x)$
6:      $delta = |r_{\text{new}} - r_{\text{old}}|$
7:      $r_{\text{old}} = r_{\text{new}}$ (Replace old estimate with new.)
8: **end while**
9: Return r_{old}

I shall leave the creation of a C++ implementation of this version to you.

Relative Criteria   The residual- and progress-based convergence criteria introduced in the previous two sections were both based on proceeding until a certain quantity was small, but no account was taken of the magnitude of the values being compared. We might compute the square root of 2 and demand a convergence tolerance of $\epsilon = 10^{-6}$. With either square root algorithm this will produce an answer that is correct past the sixth decimal place, providing an answer with about seven significant digits. On the other hand, if we are computing the square root of a very large number, say, 10^6, we probably don't care to have a value that is correct in the sixth place behind the decimal. This would imply something like nine significant digits in the result. Such high precision is seldom justified. There are very few numbers in the real world that are known to nine significant digits.[11] (They do *have* nine, in fact they have an infinite number of significant figures. We just don't know them.)

More often, we want to specify accuracy *relative* to the size of the numbers we are using.

Claim

Relative error criteria are more useful than absolute error criteria.

So if we are dealing with large numbers, we want the error to be small *relative* to the large number, but we don't want it to be absolutely small. Consider, because I love a good extreme, that I measure the width of my house as $91,400,000,000 = 9.14 \times 10^{10}$ Angstroms. I want to cut a new soffit board: Would I cut it to an accuracy of less than 1 Angstrom? No way. I'd be happy with an accuracy of 0.1% (which is about a centimeter, indicating perhaps that I'm a poor carpenter). The relative error criterion of 0.1% provides a more generally useful means to describe our desired level of precision.

To place the residual on a relative footing, we should use a quantity like $|r_{\text{new}}^2 - x|/|x| = |1 - r_{\text{new}}^2/x|$ or $|r_{\text{new}}^2 - x|/|r_{\text{new}}^2| = |1 - x/r_{\text{new}}^2|$. There is little to differentiate these two, unless the denominator might become zero.

squareRootRelative.cpp

```
1  // =================================================================
2  // squareRootRelative.cpp
```

---

[11] The speed of light is a rare exception, $c = 299,792,458$ m/s.

```
3    // Function to approximate the square root using a relative
4    // convergence criterion based on the residual in Newton's
5    // method.
6    // =============================================================
7    #include <cassert>
8    #include <cmath>
9    using namespace std;
10
11   // ======>> squareRoot <<===================================
12   // returns approximation to square root of x
13   // Arguments
14   //    x   -- number whose root we desire (nonnegative only)
15   //    eps -- desired residual
16   // =============================================================
17   double squareRoot(double x, double eps)
18   {
19     assert(x >= 0);
20
21     double rold = 1.0;            // estimate of root
22     double residual = abs(1.0 - x / (rold * rold));
23     while( residual > eps )
24       {
25         rold = (rold * rold + x) / (2.0 * rold);
26         residual = 1.0 - x / (rold * rold);  // always positive
27       }
28
29     return rold;
30   }
```

This can be tested with exactly the same test code that I used above. I shall leave this exercise to you.

You should be nervous when you write a code that divides one number by another, as I do in this function. How do I know that rold is never zero, so that the division operations on lines 25 and 26 are well defined?

Questions

Question 13 In **squareRootRelative.cpp**, how do I know that rold is never zero, so that the division operations on lines 25 and 26 are well defined?

Question 14 Consider the following variant of **Square Root with Progress Control:**

ALGORITHM   Square Root with Progress Control

Estimates the square root of the input value x, proceeding until successive iterates differ by no more than ϵ

Require: $x \geq 0$
1: $r_{old} = 1.0$
2: $delta = 2 * \epsilon$
3: **while** $delta > \epsilon$ **do**
4:      $r_{new} = f(r_{old}, x)$
5:      $r_{old} = r_{new}$
6:      $delta = |r_{new} - r_{old}|$

7: **end while**
8: Return r_{old}
There are two differences in this variant: one ok, and one wrong. Identify them.

Question 15 In **rootTesterN.cpp** the user could type the letter 'q' to quit, signifying that he or she was weary of taking square roots, and wished to cease. How did that work?

Question 16 Write a function to compute the square root of a number based on Newton's method, but using a convergence criterion based on the difference between two successive iterates for the roots.

3.7 TIME-STEPPING

We have previously created algorithms to compute the height and position of a ball falling in a constant gravitational field. That previous analysis left out air resistance, and so was not as refined as it could have been. Let's develop an algorithm that follows the progress of a ball falling in an atmosphere. This problem is hard, because modeling the effect of friction really requires studying the motion of the atmospheric gas as the ball pushes through it, and this is extremely difficult. However, a simple approximate model of the frictional effect says that friction produces a force that is directed *against* the ball's direction of motion, and is proportional to the speed of the ball squared. Thus, in the case where the ball moves only up or down in the y direction, the force on the ball is $F_y = -mg - Cv^2 v/|v|$. The first term is the acceleration due to gravity and the second is the frictional force. Note the job of $v/|v|$; this quantity is 1 if the ball is moving up ($v > 0$) and is -1 if the ball is moving down; this ensures that the friction force always acts *against* the direction of motion. Figure 3.4 shows the velocity and acceleration of the ball. The quantity C is known as a drag coefficient, which I will treat as constant.

It is convenient to eliminate C in favor of the terminal velocity of the falling object. Once the ball has fallen for a while, it will be moving downward with velocity v_∞, with $v_\infty/|v_\infty| = -1$. The friction force acting upward will balance the force of gravity, and so $F_y = 0$. This requires

$$Cv_\infty^2 = mg \tag{3.8}$$

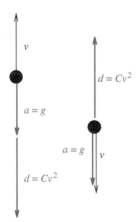

FIGURE 3.4 The acceleration of the ball is due to gravity, $a = g$, and due to drag, $d = Cv^2$. The drag is always directed against the motion of the ball.

and hence

$$v_\infty = \sqrt{mg/C} \qquad (3.9)$$

is the terminal velocity of the ball.[12] We can thus write the drag coefficient in terms of the terminal velocity as

$$C = mg/v_\infty^2. \qquad (3.10)$$

The acceleration on the ball, $a_z = F_z/m$, is thus

$$a_z = g\left[-1 - \left(\frac{v}{v_\infty}\right)^2 \frac{v}{|v|}\right] \qquad (3.11)$$

and contains only two parameters: the acceleration due to gravity g, and the terminal velocity characteristic of the falling object v_∞.

But how shall we find the velocity and height of the ball at various times after it is thrown? Let's consider only the discrete times $t_i = i\Delta t$, where Δt is a small time interval and $i = 0, 1, 2 \ldots$. We will then focus on finding $v(t_i)$ and $y(t_i)$, the velocity and height of the ball, at these times only. A good, if approximate, means to do so is to develop a method to step the ball from its initial condition at time $t_0 = 0$, forward to the time t_1. Once we have a means to do this, we can start over, treating the ball's velocity and height at time t_1 as its initial state, and stepping forward to time t_2. Repeating this process over and over (sounds like a loop!) will move the fall forward through its trajectory.

The process just outlined for determining the location and velocity of a ball at a set of discrete times is an example of time-stepping.

Definition

> *Time-stepping* is the process of iteratively (and usually approximately) determining the state of a system at a set of discrete times by stepping from one discrete time to the next.

There are systematic methods to develop time-stepping algorithms, but these are based on the study of differential equations and are beyond the scope of this text. I will simply introduce a few examples here and in the exercises; you should seek out a book on the numerical solution of differential equations for more insight. The fundamental idea, however, is to develop a formula or algorithm that will advance the state of the system, abstractly denoted here as x, from time t to time $t + \Delta t$, like $x(t + \Delta t) = f(x(t), \Delta t)$. Then, starting from some initial state x_0, we can advance to $x(\Delta t) \approx x_1 = f(x_0, \Delta t)$, then to $x(2\Delta t) \approx x_2 = f(x_1, \Delta t)$, and then to $x(3\Delta t) \approx x_3 = f(x_2, \Delta t)$ and so on into the future.

The particular method of time-stepping that I will present here is based on moving the ball for half of a time step as though the velocity and acceleration are constant, and then changing the velocity and acceleration of the ball for the entire time step based on what the ball is estimated to be doing at the half time step. So, starting from current

---

[12] The terminal velocity of an adult human falling out of an airplane is around 90–110 miles/hour.

information at time t_i, we will estimate some future information at time $t_i + \Delta t/2$, or $t_{i+1/2}$, and then use this information to move the ball from time t_i to time t_{i+1}.

Suppose that at time t_i the ball is at height y_i and it has velocity v_i. Then at a time $\Delta t/2$ in the future, the ball will have moved a distance of approximately $v_i \Delta t/2$, and will have changed its velocity by $g[-1 - (v_i/v_\infty)^2 v_i/|v_i|]\Delta t/2$, so we can write

$$y_{i+1/2} = y_i + v_i \frac{\Delta t}{2} \tag{3.12}$$

$$v_{i+1/2} = v_i + g\left[-1 - \left(\frac{v_i}{v_\infty}\right)^2 \frac{v_i}{|v_i|}\right]\frac{\Delta t}{2}. \tag{3.13}$$

These provide us with estimates of the position and velocity at a time half-way between t_i and t_{i+1}. We will now use these estimates to advance the ball from t_i and t_{i+1} as

$$y_{i+1} = y_i + v_{i+1/2}\Delta t \tag{3.14}$$

$$v_{i+1} = v_i + g\left[-1 - \left(\frac{v_{i+1/2}}{v_\infty}\right)^2 \frac{v_{i+1/2}}{|v_{i+1/2}|}\right]\Delta t. \tag{3.15}$$

This kind of two-step process, in which we first estimate some future information (like $v_{i+1/2}$) and then use this estimate to advance into the future, turns out to provide a better approximation than simply using current information directly.[13] The reasons for this lead into the fascinating study of the numerical integration of differential equations, and this is not the place for such a study. You might want to examine these formulae in the case of $v_\infty \to \infty$, however. This is the limit of no air friction, and the result in this friction-free case should impress you.

Let's develop a C++ code that time-steps a falling body in a gravitational field, and prints out the body's particulars at each time step. The object will start falling at $y = 0$ at time $t = 0$, but with a specified initial velocity (so it can be thrown up). The code will then allow the body to fall until a specified negative height is reached. (Why did I say negative?)

fallingBall.cpp

```
1    // ================================================================
2    // fallingBall.cpp
3    // Simulates a ball falling through an atmosphere, subject
4    // to constant gravitational acceleration (down) and
5    // a quadratic in velocity friction force.
6    // ================================================================
7    #include <iostream>
8    #include <fstream>
9    #include <cassert>
10   #include <cmath>
```

[13]The particular method used here is known variously as the modified Euler method, or the second-order Runge–Kutta (RK2) method.

```
11  using namespace std;
12
13  void getInput(double & g, double & vTerm, double & v,
14              double & dt, double & yFinal);
15  void oneStep(double g, double vTerm, double y, double v,
16              double dt, double & yNext, double & vNext);
17  double accel(double g, double vTerm, double v);
18
19  // =========>> main <<=====================================
20  int main()
21  {
22    double g;        // acceleration due to gravity
23    double vTerm;    // terminal velocity
24    double v;        // velocity
25    double dt;       // time step
26    double yFinal;   // final height of ball
27    getInput(g, vTerm, v, dt, yFinal);
28
29    // is data valid?
30    assert(yFinal < 0.0);
31
32    // connect to a file
33    ofstream out("trajectory.dat");
34
35    double y = 0.0;
36    double t = 0.0;
37    while( y > yFinal )
38      {
39        out << t << "␣" << y << "␣" << v << endl;
40        oneStep(g, vTerm, y, v, dt, y, v);
41        t = t + dt;
42      }
43
44    cout << "Done.␣␣Output␣file␣written" << endl;
45    return 0;
46  }
47
48  // =========>> oneStep <<=================================
49  // Takes one time step
50  // Arguments
51  //   g     - acceleration due to gravity
52  //   vTerm - terminal velocity of object
53  //   y     - current height
54  //   v     - current velocity
55  //   dt    - time step
56  //   yNext - place to write next height
57  //   vNext - place to write next velocity
```

```
58    // ================================================================
59    void oneStep(double g, double vTerm, double y, double v,
60                 double dt, double & yNext, double & vNext)
61    {
62      // compute velocity at half time step
63      double vHalf = v + 0.5 * dt * accel(g, vTerm, v);
64
65      // take a time step using data from half time step
66      yNext = y + dt * vHalf;
67      vNext = v + dt * accel(g, vTerm, vHalf);
68    }
69
70    // ===========>> accel <<==================================
71    // Returns acceleration
72    // Arguments
73    //   g     - acceleration due to gravity
74    //   vTerm - terminal velocity of object
75    //   v     - velocity
76    // ================================================================
77    double accel(double g, double vTerm, double v)
78    {
79      return g * (-1.0 - v*v*v/(vTerm * vTerm * fabs(v)));
80    }
81
82    // ====================>> getInput <<========================
83    // Get input data
84    // Arguments
85    //   g     - acceleration due to gravity
86    //   vTerm  - terminal velocity of object
87    //   v      - initial velocity
88    //   dt     - time step size
89    //   yFinal - height at which to stop simulation
90    // ================================================================
91    void getInput(double & g, double & vTerm, double & v,
92                  double & dt, double & yFinal)
93    {
94      cout << "Input_acceleration_due_to_gravity_:>_";
95      cin >> g;
96
97      cout << "Input_terminal_velocity:>_";
98      cin >> vTerm;
99
100     cout << "Input_initial_velocity:>_";
101     cin >> v;
102
103     cout << "Input_time_step:>_";
104     cin >> dt;
```

```
105
106     cout << "Input final height (negative):> ";
107     cin >> yFinal;
108   }
```

Here is a small sample run:

```
1   [hagar@localhost Code]$ ./fallingBall
2   Input acceleration due to gravity :> 9.81
3   Input terminal velocity:> 50.0
4   Input initial velocity:> 2.0
5   Input time step:> 0.2
6   Input final height (negative):> -1000.0
7   Done.  Output file written
8   [hagar@localhost Code]$
```

This code can produce a great deal of output. So rather than looking at these data directly, I am determined to write them to a file named **trajectory.dat**, and use this file to make plots with a nice plotting program. The sample run placed 119 lines of trajectory data into the file **trajectory.dat**. I've then used this file from three different runs of the code with different time steps to make the plot shown in Fig. 3.5. The figure shows

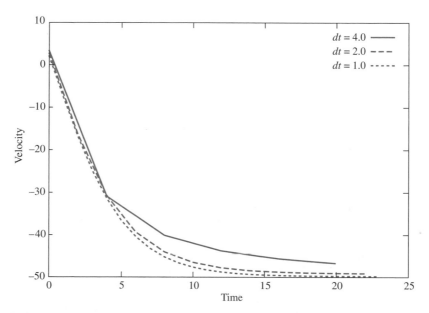

FIGURE 3.5 The velocity of a ball falling, subject to a drag force. Three different values of Δt have been used to compute these results. As Δt becomes small the velocity values converge to the correct answer.

the velocity, as a function of time, estimated using the `fallingBall` code. Note that as Δt is decreased, the results change. Is this reality? No, a real ball does what it does without regard for our approximate ways of describing it. But to arrive at Eq. (3.14), I assumed that the velocity did not change during the time step, and then to advance the velocity (inconsistently it might seem), I assumed in Eq. (3.15) that the acceleration did not change during the time step. These were approximations, which nature does not make, but which we must. For small values of Δt the approximations are excellent, and as Δt is made smaller and smaller, the results of our time-stepping algorithms will approach values independent of Δt. This is what we see happening in the figure.

This code does still have one dangerous problem. If a zero velocity is passed into `accel`, then the code will divide by zero on line 79, and subsequent results will be meaningless. We don't have a good way to fix this yet. Fortunately, it is unlikely that a zero velocity will be passed into `accel` unless you pick a zero initial velocity. But I do consider the code defective, and will ask you to fix it in Chapter 4 with a selection statement.

In describing the motion of the falling ball, we have *discretized* time. We went from the continuous variable t, which could take on any real value, to the discrete times t_i. So we went from a complete line of allowed t values to just a grid, as shown in Fig. 3.6. Along the way, we went from a continuously varying function like $y(t)$ to an approximation of its values on this grid of time values, $y_i \approx y(t_i)$. The independent variable, the time values, has been made discrete, but the dependent variables are still formally continuous—there is no explicit restriction on the *values* of y_i.[14] This is a common approach to mapping the continuous problems that mathematically model the real world into the finite and discrete world of computation. The allowed values of time t_i are called a time mesh or time grid.

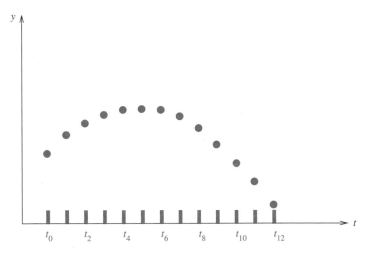

FIGURE 3.6   Time really is continuous, and so is graphically represented as a whole line of values. But for the purposes of computation, we restrict ourselves to a grid of times values, $t_0, t_1, t_2, \ldots$. The dependent variable y is not restricted to particular values—there is no y grid.

[14]Of course, when we compute, there is a restriction even on the values of the dependent variable y, because the machine can only represent a subset of the real numbers.

Definition

> A *mesh* or *grid* is a discrete set of independent variable values onto which a continuous problem is approximated.

This process of mapping functions or problems with continuous independent variables to a finite mesh is called discretization.

3.7.1   A Bit of Calculus

Let's rewrite Eqs. (3.14) and (3.15) as

$$\frac{y_{i+1} - y_i}{\Delta t} = v_{i+1/2} \tag{3.16}$$

$$\frac{v_{i+1} - v_i}{\Delta t} = g\left[-1 - \left(\frac{v_{i+1/2}}{v_\infty}\right)^2 \frac{v_{i+1/2}}{|v_{i+1/2}|}\right]. \tag{3.17}$$

Now let $t = i\Delta t$, and $y(t)$ and $v(t)$ be the height and velocity of the ball at time t. Consider then that $y_i = y(t)$ and $v_i = v(t)$, and also that $y_{i+1} = y(t + \Delta t)$ and $v_{i+1} = v(t + \Delta t)$. Since $y_{i+1/2} = y(t + \Delta t/2) \rightarrow y(t)$, we can take the limit $\Delta t \rightarrow 0$, yielding

$$\frac{dy}{dt}(t) = v(t) \tag{3.18}$$

$$\frac{dv}{dt}(t) = g\left[-1 - \left(\frac{v(t)}{v_\infty}\right)^2 \frac{v(t)}{|v(t)|}\right]. \tag{3.19}$$

The first of these equations is the definition of the instantaneous velocity of the ball, and the second is Newton's law of motion relating acceleration dv/dt to force, $m\,dv/dt = F = -mg + F_{\text{friction}}$. Our time-stepping algorithm has provided us with the means to approximately solve these differential equations for $x(t)$ and $v(t)$. Since our time-stepping equations, Eqs. (3.14) and (3.15), become these exact differential equations only when $\Delta t \rightarrow 0$, we can expect that our time-stepping algorithm will become increasingly accurate as we take smaller and smaller values of Δt.

Let f be a smooth function. A differential equation of the general form

$$\frac{dx}{dt}(t) = f(x(t)) \tag{3.20}$$

with the initial condition $x(0) = x_0$ uniquely defines a function $x(t)$.[15] Knowing that there is a solution $x(t)$ is one thing, actually finding it is another. The essential idea behind time-stepping is to replace the derivative on the left-hand-side by the slope of $x(t)$ between times $i\Delta t$ and $(i + 1)\Delta t$, so $dx/dt \approx (x_{i+1} - x_i)/\Delta t$, where $x_i = x(i\Delta t)$ and $x_{i+1} = x((i + 1)\Delta t)$. The issue is then to decide at what value of x to evaluate the right-hand-side, $f(x)$. The time-stepping algorithm that I have given you for the falling

---

[15] You will prove this in your sophomore-level differential equations course; if you do not, you should demand your money back.

ball problem is of the form

$$x_{i+1/2} = x_i + (\Delta t/2)f(x_i) \tag{3.21}$$

$$x_{i+1} = x_i + \Delta t f(x_{i+1/2}) \tag{3.22}$$

The purpose of the first equation is to get a rough estimate of the value of x half-way through the time step, and to use this to evaluate $f(x)$ at the middle of the time step. This is known as the modified Euler method, and in other contexts is known as the second-order Runge–Kutta method. This is by no means the only time-stepping method; a few others will be suggested in later exercises and examples.

Questions

Question 17   Modify `getInput` to read its data from a file called **fallingBallParameters** rather than `cin`.

Question 18   Consider Eqs. (3.14) and (3.15) in the limit $v_\infty \to \infty$ (which corresponds to no air resistance) and show that they are exact in this limit.

Question 19   Imagine a weight of mass m suspended from the ceiling by a spring with spring constant k. Here is a way to time step the motion of the spring, with y denoting the displacement of the spring away from its equilibrium position and v its velocity:

$$y_{1/2} = y_0 + \Delta t v_0/2$$
$$v_1 = v_0 - \Delta t y_{1/2}(k/m)$$
$$y_1 = y_{1/2} + \Delta t v_1/2.$$

Write a loop that will advance from y_i, v_i to y_{i+1}, v_{i+1} for a prespecified number of time steps.

Question 20   You have n_0 radioactive nuclei in your body. During a short time Δt the probability that such a nucleus will decay is $\lambda \Delta t$, where λ is a constant. Assuming that you take in no new radioactive nuclei, the number of nuclei left after time Δt can be estimated as

$$n_1 = n_0 - n_{1/2}\lambda\Delta t$$

where $n_{1/2}$ is itself estimated as

$$n_{1/2} = n_0 - n_0\lambda\Delta t/2.$$

Use this to write a code that will tell you how many nuclei are left at any later time of the form $i\Delta t$. You can use $\lambda = 5.42\times10^{-10}$/year, which is the value for all the radioactive potassium in your body (much of it from all those bananas, and that sodium-free salt).

3.8   ON THE STRUCTURE OF ITERATION

The loops that we have written so far have really come in two flavors. In solving for the square root of a number, we often used a loop of the form

```
1  double residual = tooBig;
2  while( residual > tooBig )
3  {
4    // do work to reduce residual
5  }
```

When we write this loop, we do not know how many times it will execute. But contrast this with the loop in **power.cpp**, which had the structure

```
1  int i = 0;
2  while( i < upperLimit )
```

```
3    {
4      // do work to complete i + 1
5      i = i + 1;  // count the step
6    }
```

Here there are an identifiable number of times that the loop will be executed. We might not know the value of the upperLimit when we create the algorithm, but there is a variable that will hold the number of times the loop body is to be executed. In the former iteration a general condition controls the execution of the loop body, while in the latter we really just execute the loop body a fixed number of times. This latter structure is commonly called a counting loop.

Definition

> A *counting loop* is an iterative construct in which a loop body is executed a certain number of times, and which, when executed, provides its loop body with a counter to specify which iteration is being executed.

Counting loops are very common, and many, but by no means all, computer languages have an idiom specifically designed to express them. In C++ counting loops are usually expressed using the *for loop*.

C++ Principle

> A statement of the form
>
> ```
>      for( initialization ; condition ; iteration_statement )
>          loop_body
> ```
>
> where initialization is an expression statement, condition is an expression with a Boolean value of true or false, iteration_statement is an expression statement, and loop_body is either an expression statement or a compound statement, is called a *for loop*.

The semantics of a for loop are identical to

```
1    initialization;
2    while (condition)
3    {
4        loop_body;
5        iteration_statement;
6    }
```

Although the for loop is a very general iteration construct, it is most often used to express counting loops in a form like this:

```
1  for(int i = 0; i < upper; i = i + 1)
2  {
3      // do some work
4  }
```

Its most significant advantage over the equivalent while loop is subjective: The idiom is very well recognized by most code authors. But there is an objective advantage. The for loop brings all the machinery for counting into one local place in the source text. A common error with expressing counting loops using the C++ while loop is to forget the statement $i = i + 1$;. Using a for loop, it is easier to remember and correctly express this increment.

Here is **sum.cpp** from Section 3.1 rewritten using a for loop:

sum2.cpp

```
1  int sum(int N)
2  {
3    int sum = 0;
4    for(int counter = 1; counter < N; counter = counter + 1)
5    {
6        sum = sum + counter;
7    }
8    return sum;
9  }
```

It is no more correct than the previous version, but once you get used to the idiom, it is easier to get right and easier to read.

Nested Loops   Consider a while loop:

```
while (condition) loop_body
```

where loop_body can be a compound statement. What can you put in a compound statement? Almost anything, including, certainly, loops. In other words, you can nest loops inside loops, and this is nothing special.

How would you write a code to print the multiplication table on the screen? If your code involves 100 statements, you've missed the point. No, you would write one loop to run over the rows of the multiplication table, and inside it you would place another loop to run over the columns, rather like this:

multTable.cpp

```
1  // multTable.cpp
2  // Code to print the multiplication table on standard output
3  #include <iostream>
```

```
4   using namespace std;
5
6   int main(void)
7   {
8     for(int i = 0; i < 11; i = i + 1)
9       {
10        for(int j = 0; j < 11; j = j + 1)
11          {
12              cout << i * j << "␣";
13          }
14          cout << endl;
15      }
16
17    return 0;
18  }
```

This code does not print a particularly pretty table, but I want to keep the code clean and free of distractions. For each value of i, the entire loop over j is run. So for each value of i, eleven values of j are used. The loop over j is nested within the loop over i.

Definition

A *nested loop* is a loop that appears within the loop body of another loop.

You should think of nested loops when you have repeated steps to carry out, each of which itself requires repeated steps.

Here is another example. Consider the task of enumerating all the ways to pair up N electrons. We can put electron 1 with electron 2, or with electron 3, and so on, or we can put electron 2 with electron 3, or with electron 4, and so on. Let's write a code to enumerate all the possible unordered pairs of electrons, where unordered means that pairing electron 1 with electron 2 is the same thing as pairing electron 2 with electron 1. Here is a scrap of C++ code that does the deed:

```
1   for(int i = 1; i <= N; i = i + 1)
2     {
3         for(int j = i + 1; j <= N; j = j + 1)
4           {
5               cout << i << "␣pairs␣with␣" << j << endl;
6           }
7     }
```

This code easily enumerates the 45 possible pairs of 10 electrons. Note, because you may not have thought of it, the boxed line of code that starts the inner loop. The loop index j is initialized using the value of i. Although you might not have thought of it, this coupling should not surprise you; inside the outer loop i has a value, and that value can be used in any expression.

We will nest many loops in the chapters that follow, so there is no hope of leaving the nest.

Questions

Question 21   What's wrong with the following loop?

```
double c = 0.0;
while( c < 100.0 )
  {
    c = c + c*c*sin(c);
  }
```

Question 22   How do I know that something is wrong with the following loop?

```
double pi = 2.0 * atan2(1.0,0.0);
double p = 0.0;
int c = 0;
while( c < 100 )
  {
    p = sin(c * pi);
    c = c + 1;
  }
```

Question 23   Write **power.cpp** from Section 3.4 using a for loop.

Question 24   Rewrite the following for loop using a while loop:

```
double g = -9.81;
double t = 0.0;
for( y = 0.0 ; y > yFinal ; t = t + dy)
  {
    y = y + v * dt;
    v = v + g * dt;
  }
```

Comment on the clarity, or lack thereof, for each version.

Question 25   Write a loop to compute the values of the polynomial $p(x) = 1 + x + x^2 + x^3 + x^4 + x^5 + x^6 + x^7 + x^8$, and then write an outer loop to evaluate this at the discrete x values $x_i = i\Delta x$, for $i = 0, 1, \ldots, 10$, with $\Delta x = 0.25$.

3.9 SLICING π

What is the area of a circle? The ancient Greeks were often interested in geometry problems of this sort. As the beneficiary of at least 3,000 years of mathematical progress, you know the most satisfying answer: πr^2, where r is the radius of the circle. But what is the value of π? Let's write a program that determines this, by computing the area of a circle.

The actual area of a circle cannot be computed exactly, in essence because the value of π is not exactly knowable. But we can, in principle, come as close as we wish. Figure 3.7 shows the basic tactic we will take (and it's a tactic that the ancient Greeks knew well): We approximate the circle by a polygon, and compute the area of the polygon as an approximation of the area of the circle. The area of the polygon is exactly knowable, because it is made up of rectangles and triangles, whose areas can be computed by multiplication and addition.

There is no one, unique way to approximate a circle by a polygon, but the approach that I will force upon you is shown in the figure. Let's characterize this polygonal approximation of a circle with care, in the hope that student interest soon will be there. Let's put a Cartesian coordinate origin at the center of the circle. We then divide the x axis into a grid of N intervals, each of width $h = 2r/N$. These mesh intervals can be numbered, starting at zero, by the integers $i = 0, 1, \ldots, N - 1$, and the ith interval is

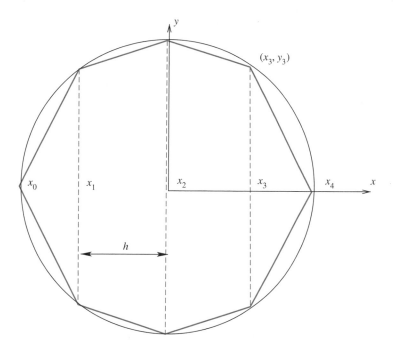

FIGURE 3.7 A circle, approximated by a polygon.

flanked by the points $x_i = ih - r$ and $x_{i+1} = (i + 1)h - r$. For each of the N values of x_i (we often call these ordinate values, in order to sound out the ordinary), there is a corresponding y value on the circle,

$$y_i = \sqrt{r^2 - x_i^2}, \qquad i = 0, 1, \ldots, N. \tag{3.23}$$

The four points $(x_i, -y_i)$, (x_i, y_i), (x_{i+1}, y_{i+1}), $(x_{i+1}, -y_{i+1})$ then define a quadrilateral whose area is its width times its average height, or

$$a_i = (x_i - x_{i+1}) * (y_i + y_{i+1}). \tag{3.24}$$

The area of the circle can then be approximated as the sum of these areas,

$$a = a_0 + a_1 + a_2 + \cdots + a_{N-1}. \tag{3.25}$$

Writing out such sums with all those plus signs and diddly dots is tedious, so instead we can write it with a summation sign (a capital Greek sigma) as

$$a = \sum_{i=0}^{N-1} a_i. \tag{3.26}$$

The polygon that I have used to approximate the circle is not a regular polygon, but it is a convenient polygon.

We now have a conceptual perch from which to approximate the area of a circle. We use a grid of $N + 1$ values of x to break up the circle into N polygons, each of

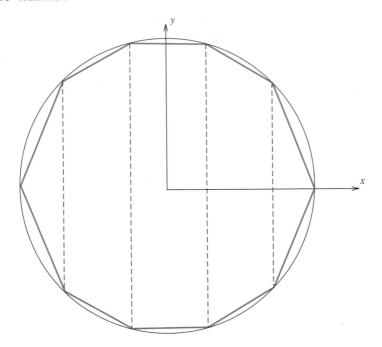

FIGURE 3.8   A circle, approximated by a finer polygon based on a finer *x* grid.

whose four vertices is on the circle, and which, taken together, nearly cover the circle. As the *x* grid is made finer, the number of such quadrilaterals is increased (see Fig. 3.8). They will more and more nearly cover the circle, and intuitively we should expect to get a better answer. You should be somewhat suspicious of this claim, but I will offer no proof here; the knowledge that you gain in real analysis or calculus will allow you to provide your own.[16] This construction, approximating a circle by a polygon, is useful in mathematics to explore the whole idea of area. But it's also useful as the basis for an algorithm to obtain a number. What do we need? We need basic mathematical operations (multiplication, addition) and we need to compute a sum, which is a job for a loop.

In pseudocode an algorithm to do the job might look like this:

ALGORITHM   *Circle Area*

Estimates the area of a circle
Require: $r \geq 0, N > 0$ is an integer
  1: $width = 2 * r/N$
  2: $area = 0.0$
  3: $i = 0$

---

[16]*Hint:* Show that the approximate areas are an increasing sequence in N, bounded above.

4: **while** $i < N$ **do**
5:      Set $x_{\text{left}} = -r + i * width$
6:      Set $x_{\text{right}} = -r + (i + 1) * width$
7:      Set $y_{\text{right}} = \sqrt{r * r - x_{\text{right}} * x_{\text{right}}}$
8:      Set $y_{\text{left}} = \sqrt{r * r - x_{\text{left}} * x_{\text{left}}}$
9:      Set $a = width * \left(y_{\text{left}} + y_{\text{right}} \right)$
10:     Set $area = area + a$
11:     Set $i = i + 1$ (Invariant: $area$ is area of i quadrilaterals.)
12: **end while**
13:   Return $area$

At the heart of this algorithm is our good friend, the running sum. The quantity *area* is first set to zero, and then with every pass through the loop more is added to it.

There is one subtle issue in this algorithm: It may be perfect if the arithmetic is done exactly, but may fail if the arithmetic is not perfect. Unfortunately, computers don't do arithmetic exactly, and they never will.[17] We shall explore this issue in some detail in Chapter 8, but for the moment note that we take square roots in order to find the height of each quadrilateral. If the argument of the square root should become negative, we would have results that the ancient Greeks could not even imagine. Where might this be an issue? During the last pass through the loop, we shall have $i = N - 1$, and therefore $x_{\text{right}} = -r + N*(2r/N)$. Although in exact arithmetic this yields $x_{\text{right}} = -r + 2r = r$, as desired, in inexact arithmetic it's conceivable that x_{right} will be just a hair larger than r.

This issue is easy to avoid here. Note that there is no worry about x_{left} becoming smaller than $-r$, because it starts at $-r$ on the first trip through the loop with $i = 0$,[18] and x_{left} just increases from there. So an obvious solution to my concern with x_{right} is to compute it by counting from the other direction, in order to ensure that it is exactly r on the final trip through the loop with $i = N - 1$. So let's write

$$x_{\text{right}} = r - (N - 1 - i) * width. \tag{3.27}$$

When $i = 0$, this yields

$$x_{\text{right}} = r - (N - 1) * width \tag{3.28}$$
$$= r - 2r + width \tag{3.29}$$
$$= -r + width, \tag{3.30}$$

as it should, but when $i = (N - 1)$, it yields

$$x_{\text{right}} = r - 0 * width = r, \tag{3.31}$$

even if *width* is not computed exactly. In between x_{right} just increases linearly by *width* from one trip through the loop to the next.

---

[17]*Proof:* Since the universe is finite, there are not enough atoms in the universe to build a computer large enough to do exact arithmetic.

[18]Assuming that computers do correctly multiply by zero, and if they don't, let's all go back to the slide rule.

Here is a C++ version:

circleArea.cpp
_____

```cpp
1   // ================================================================
2   // circleArea.cpp
3   // Code to approximate the area of a circle
4   // ================================================================
5   #include <iostream>
6   #include <cassert>
7   #include <cmath>
8   using namespace std;
9
10  double circleArea(double radius, int intervals);
11
12  // ===============>> main <<=================================
13  int main()
14  {
15     cout << "Input the radius of the circle:> ";
16     double radius;
17     cin >> radius;
18
19     cout << "Input the number of intervals to use:> ";
20     int intervals;
21     cin >> intervals;
22
23     double area = circleArea(radius, intervals);
24     cout << "The approximate area of the circle is "
25          << area << endl;
26     cout << "This corresponds to an approximation of "
27          << area/(radius * radius) << " for pi"  << endl;
28
29     return 0;
30  }
31
32  // ===============>> circleArea <<==============================
33  // Estimates area of a circle
34  // Arguments
35  //   radius    - radius of the circle
36  //   intervals - number of quadrilaterals to use
37  // ================================================================
38  double circleArea(double radius, int intervals)
39  {
40     assert(radius >= 0.0);
41     assert(intervals > 0);
42
```

```
43      double width = 2 * radius / intervals;
44      double area = 0.0;
45      int i = 0;
46      while (i < intervals)
47        {
48           double xLeft = -radius + i * width;
49           double xRight = radius - (intervals - 1 - i) * width;
50           double yLeft = sqrt(radius * radius - xLeft * xLeft);
51           double yRight = sqrt(radius * radius - xRight * xRight);
52
53           area = area + (yLeft + yRight); // multiply by width later
54           i = i + 1;
55        }
56      return area * width;
57   }
```

Running this code using different numbers of mesh intervals will suggest that the areas computed do indeed approach the area of a circle as more and more intervals are used. The rate of decrease in error is somewhat disappointing: With 1,000 intervals the results will correspond to an error of 10^{-5} in the value of π. It turns out that although the method I have given you is pretty good for many area computations, it becomes less accurate for circles. The difficulty arises at the edges at $x = \pm r$ where the circle is vertical and the quadrilaterals that we use to cover the circle degenerate into triangles.

An examination of the loop in circleArea shows that it's a counting loop. As such, it might be more typically implemented as

```
1   double circleArea(double radius, int intervals)
2   {
3     assert(radius >= 0.0);
4     assert(intervals > 0);
5
6     double width = 2 * radius / intervals;
7     double area = 0.0;
8     for(int i = 0; i < intervals; i = i + 1)
9       {
10          double xLeft = -radius + i * width;
11          double xRight = radius - (intervals - 1 - i) * width;
12          double yLeft = sqrt(radius * radius - xLeft * xLeft);
13          double yRight = sqrt(radius * radius - xRight * xRight);
14
15          area = area + (yLeft + yRight); // multiply by width later
16       }
17     return area * width;
18   }
```

You will also notice that I moved the multiplication by `width` outside the loop. The same quantity, `width`, multiplies every term in the running sum, so rather than multiplying each term in the sum by this quantity and then adding this product to the sum, we can compute the sum without this factor, and then multiply only once when the sum has been completed. This is mainly an optimization intended to make the code faster (avoid all those unnecessary multiplies); many compilers could actually make such an optimization automatically. I should weigh this possible increase in speed against the potential decrease in code readability that results.

Questions

Question 26   I will admit that the first time I wrote the code for the loop body of `circleArea`, I wrote it as

```
double xLeft = -radius + i * width;
double xRight = radius - (intervals - 1 -
                         i) * width;
double a = sqrt(radius * radius - xLeft *
            xLeft);
a = a + sqrt(radius * radius - xRight *
          xRight);
area = area + a;
```

Comment on this version, compared to the version appearing above.

Question 27   The perimeter of a circle of radius r is $2\pi r$. This could be approximated by computing the length of the perimeter of an inscribed polygon, of the sort shown in Fig. 3.8. Write a function that will estimate the perimeter of a circle in this manner, and use it to estimate π.

3.10   THE AREA UNDER A CURVE

Here is a question that abstracts the problem of finding the area of a circle: If we describe a curve by a function $y = f(x)$, and close off the area between this curve and the x axis by the vertical lines $x = a$ and $x = b$, as shown in Fig. 3.9, what is the area enclosed? In calculus this area is called the definite integral, and symbolically denoted as $\int_a^b f(x)\,dx$.

While pondering an approach to the problem, it's worth asking what use such an answer might be. Fantasize about the following: You drive down a long, straight road, but your odometer is broken. How far have you gone? Fortunately, your speedometer

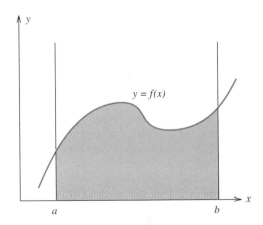

FIGURE 3.9   What is the area "under" the curve?

works, and so does your watch. Now you can tell how far you have gone by using the same inertial guidance method as a submarine or a satellite! Suppose you note the speed of the car every second, yielding a set of data points such as those shown in Fig. 3.10. If you assume the speed varies linearly between each such observation (equivalent to assuming constant acceleration between every point), then the distance traveled between the ith and $i + 1$st observation times is

$$x_{i+1} - x_i = v_i \Delta t + a_{i+1/2} \Delta t^2 / 2 \tag{3.32}$$

where Δt is the time between observations (e.g., 1 s), and $a_{i+1/2} = (v_{i+1} - v_i)/\Delta t$ is the acceleration of the car between observation i and observation $i + 1$. Using this definition of acceleration in Eq. (3.32) yields

$$x_{i+1} - x_i = v_i \Delta t + \frac{v_{i+1} - v_i}{2} \Delta t \tag{3.33}$$

$$= \frac{v_{i+1} + v_i}{2} \Delta t \tag{3.34}$$

$$= \text{area of the } i\text{th trapezoid.} \tag{3.35}$$

So the distance traveled between two observation points is the area of the trapezoid defined by those same two points, as shown in Fig. 3.10.

Since we can find the distance traveled between any two speed observation points, the total distance traveled may be found as the sum of these distances between points. Thus, using $N + 1$ observations, which corresponds to N distance intervals, yields

$$\text{Distance traveled} = \Delta t \left[\frac{v_0 + v_1}{2} + \frac{v_1 + v_2}{2} + \cdots + \frac{v_{N-1} + v_N}{2} \right] \tag{3.36}$$

$$= \Delta t \left[\frac{v_0}{2} + v_1 + v_2 + \cdots + v_{N-1} + \frac{v_N}{2} \right] \tag{3.37}$$

$$= \Delta t \left[\frac{v_0}{2} + \sum_{i=1}^{N-1} v_i + \frac{v_N}{2} \right]. \tag{3.38}$$

Since this is the sum of the areas of the trapezoids defined by each neighboring pair of observations, the distance traveled is the area under the curve in Fig. 3.10.

Now, the only thing we assumed here was that the acceleration was constant between speed measurements. If the observations were close enough together, that is, if

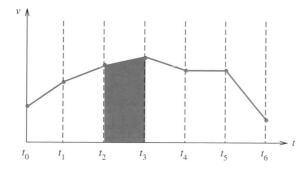

FIGURE 3.10 The distance traveled can be found from the area under the velocity curve. The distance traveled between t_2 and t_3 is the area of the shaded trapezoid.

Δt was small enough, then the error in this assumption must be small. After all, the car can't vary its acceleration by much in a very short time.

This example suggests a way to estimate the area under any curve. We divide the interval $a \leq x \leq b$ into N equal mesh intervals, and approximate the curve $y = f(x)$ by a series of straight-line segments across each of these mesh intervals. This breaks the region under the curve into N trapezoids, whose areas are easy to know. The area of the ith trapezoid is

$$A_i = \frac{1}{2}\left[f(x_i) + f(x_{i+1})\right]h \tag{3.39}$$

where $h = (b - a)/N$ is the width of each mesh interval, and $x_i = a + ih$ is the left edge of the ith mesh interval. Summing up the areas of all these trapezoids yields the area A under the curve as approximately

$$A = h\left[\frac{f(x_0)}{2} + \sum_{i=1}^{N-1} f(x_i) + \frac{f(x_N)}{2}\right]. \tag{3.40}$$

This is not, in general, an exact result for A, but as h is made smaller, we expect that this approximation should get better. The proof of this is again a task for calculus class.

This approach to computing the area under a curve is known as the trapezoidal rule. It is a fairly easy algorithm to write. We generally write it as shown in Eq. (3.40), in which we just have to sum up the function values at a set of points, but with the first and last points treated specially.

ALGORITHM   *Trapezoid*

Estimates the area under a curve defined by $y = f(x)$ for $a \leq x \leq b$, using N intervals
Require: $a \geq b, N > 0$ is an integer
1:   set $A = f(a)/2$
2:   set $i = 1$ (the number of points used so far)
3:   set $h = (b - a)/N$
4:   **while** $i < N$ **do**
5:     set $x_i = a + i*h$
6:     set $A = A + f(x_i)$
7:     set $i = i + 1$ (i is the number of points used so far.)
8:   **end while**
9:   set $A = A + f(b)/2$
10: return $h{\times}A$ as the desired area

Note that the loop runs over the points x_i that are *inside* the interval $[a, b]$. The edge points a and b must be treated specially because they only count half as much as an interior point.

Here is a C++ code to compute the area under the cosine, for angles from $-\pi/2$ up to $\pi/2$:

cosArea.cpp

```
1  // ================================================================
2  // cosArea.cpp
```

```cpp
3   // Code to compute the area under the cosine from
4   // -pi/2 up to pi/2
5   // ==============================================================
6   #include <iostream>
7   #include <cmath>
8   #include <cassert>
9   using namespace std;
10
11  double cosArea(double a, double b, int N);
12
13  // =====================>> main <<=============================
14  int main()
15  {
16    double a = -atan2(1.0,0);   // -pi/2
17    double b = -a;              // pi/2
18
19    cout << "Please_specify_the_number_of_intervals_:>_";
20    int N;
21    cin >> N;
22
23    cout << endl;
24    cout << "Using_" << N << "_intervals,_the_area_is_"
25         << cosArea(a, b, N) << endl << endl;
26
27    return 0;
28  }
29
30  // =====================>> cosArea <<=========================
31  // Estimates the area under cos(x) for x between a and b
32  // Arguments
33  //    a - left endpoint
34  //    b - right endpoint
35  //    N - number of intervals to use
36  // ==============================================================
37  double cosArea(double a, double b, int N)
38  {
39    assert(a <= b);
40    assert(N > 0);
41
42    double h = (b - a)/N;
43    double A = 0.5 * cos(a);
44    for(int i = 1; i < N; i = i + 1)
45      {
46        // invariant i = number of points used
47        double x = a + i * h;
48        A = A + cos(x);
```

```
49      }
50    A = A + 0.5 * cos(b);
51
52    return h * A;
53 }
```

Here is a set of sample runs:

```
1  [hagar@localhost Code]$ ./cosArea
2  Please specify the number of intervals :> 10
3
4  Using 10 intervals, the area is 1.98352
5
6  [hagar@localhost Code]$ ./cosArea
7  Please specify the number of intervals :> 20
8
9  Using 20 intervals, the area is 1.99589
10
11 [hagar@localhost Code]$ ./cosArea
12 Please specify the number of intervals :> 40
13
14 Using 40 intervals, the area is 1.99897
15
16 [hagar@localhost Code]$ ./cosArea
17 Please specify the number of intervals :> 80
18
19 Using 80 intervals, the area is 1.99974
```

If you look carefully, and know that the exact answer is 2, you will note that the error decreases by a factor of 4 every time I double the number of intervals used.

The trapezoidal algorithm is really quite general. It works with any well-behaved function $f(x)$. It would therefore be nice if our C++ code was just as general, but so far it only works with $f(x) = \cos(x)$. Must a function like cosArea be written for every case we may wish to try? To address this, we would like to be able to pass not just a, b, and N into our trapezoidal-rule-based area finder; we would like to pass the entire function f into it too. There are several ways to do this,[19] but here one approach is illustrated:

trapArea.cpp

```
1  #include <cassert>
2  using namespace std;
```

[19] And the more elegant approaches require the use of object-oriented programming techniques, which we are not seriously pursuing, but will touch on in Chapters 5 and 7.

```
3
4    // =====================>> trapArea <<=========================
5    // Estimates the area under f(x) for x between a and b
6    // Arguments
7    //    f - function to use
8    //    a - left endpoint
9    //    b - right endpoint
10   //    N - number of intervals to use
11   // =============================================================
12   double trapArea(double f(double), double a, double b, int N)
13   {
14     assert(a <= b);
15     assert(N > 0);
16
17     double h = (b - a)/N;
18     double A = 0.5 * f(a);
19     for(int i = 1; i < N; i = i + 1) // i: number of points used
20       {
21         double x = a + i * h;
22         A = A + f(x);
23       }
24     A = A + 0.5 * f(b);
25
26     return h * A;
27   }
```

Whoa! Do you see what the first argument to trap area is? It's a function that takes a `double` and returns a `double`! The `trapArea` function can be passed any other function as its first argument, provided that this other function takes only one `double` argument and returns a `double` value. Here is a use of this function:

areaFun.cpp

```
1    // =============================================================
2    // areaFun.cpp
3    // Code to compute the area under a number of functions
4    // =============================================================
5    #include <iostream>
6    #include <cmath>
7    #include <cassert>
8    using namespace std;
9
10   double trapArea(double f(double), double a, double b, int N);
11
12   // =============>> cosSin <<===============================
13   double cosSin(double x)
```

```
14   {
15     return cos(x) * sin(x);
16   }
17
18   // ===============>> main <<======================================
19   int main()
20   {
21     cout << "Please specify the interval [a, b] :> ";
22     double a;
23     cin >> a;
24     double b;
25     cin >> b;
26
27     cout << "Please specify the number of intervals :> ";
28     int N;
29     cin >> N;
30
31     cout << "Area under cos: " << trapArea(cos, a, b, N) << endl;
32     cout << "Area under sin: " << trapArea(sin, a, b, N) << endl;
33     cout << "Area under cos * sin: " << trapArea(cosSin, a, b, N)
34          << endl;
35
36     return 0;
37   }
```

And the following is a sample run:

```
1   [hagar@localhost Code]$ ./areaFun
2   Please specify the interval [a, b] :> 0 3.14159265358
3   Please specify the number of intervals :> 200
4   Area under cos: 9.79313e-12
5   Area under sin: 1.99996
6   Area under cos * sin: 1.25582e-16
7   [hagar@localhost Code]$
```

For reference, the exact areas are 0, 2, and 0, respectively. So we have done pretty well.

Questions

Question 28   Both **cosArea** and **trapArea** are defended with the assertion a <= b. Is a == b really ok? What, if anything, is wrong with a > b?

Question 29   Consider a function that is the product of two other functions, like $p(x) = f(x) g(x)$. The area under such products of functions is called an "inner product," and is very important (e.g., in quantum mechanics, such areas arise in measuring the strength of interaction of particles). Write a C++ function called **innerProduct**, analogous to **trapArea**, that computes the inner product of two functions f and g as the area under their product for x values $a \le x \le b$.

3.11   AN ADAPTIVE AREA ALGORITHM

In previous sections we developed some ideas to compute the area under a curve specified by a height function $f(x)$, and by x limits, $a \leq x \leq b$. One problem with the technique developed there was that we had to more or less guess into how many mesh intervals to subdivide the interval $a \leq x \leq b$. But there is a way to avoid this arbitrary choice: Develop an algorithm that itself subdivides the interval, and which quits subdividing when some error criterion has been met. The most direct algorithm would be something like:

ALGORITHM   *Adaptive Trapezoids*

Approximates the area under a curve using a simple adaptive technique with a tolerance of ϵ

```
 1:  Set N = 1
 2:  Compute area using Trapezoid(a, b, N)
 3:  Set done = false
 4:  while not done do
 5:      Set N = 2N
 6:      Compute area' using Trapezoid(a, b, N)
 7:      Set done = ϵ×|area'| > |area' − area|
 8:      Set area = area' (area is the area computed with N mesh intervals)
 9:  end while
10:  Return area as the result
```

This algorithm keeps doubling the number of mesh intervals used until the area change caused by such a doubling is sufficiently small. This is a stopping criterion of the sort introduced in Section 3.9, except that the criterion is based on the relative change in area from N to $2N$ mesh intervals. You should be concerned about what might happen if the exact area is zero, so that *area'* keeps getting smaller with each iteration.

This algorithm has an ugly feature, however. When it decides to double the number of grid intervals, it throws away all previous work and starts over, as though all that previous work was irrelevant and is now useless. This seems rather extravagant, and a bit of algebra reveals that indeed it is. Consider the area using N intervals as

$$A(N) = \frac{h(N)}{2} f(a) + h(N) \sum_{i=1}^{N-1} f(x_i(N)) + \frac{h(N)}{2} f(b) \qquad (3.41)$$

where

$$h(N) = \frac{b - a}{N} \qquad (3.42)$$

and

$$x_i(N) = a + ih(N). \qquad (3.43)$$

Now consider the area computed using $2N$ grid intervals:

$$A(2N) = \frac{h(2N)}{2} f(a) + h(2N) \sum_{j=1}^{2N-1} f(x_j(2N)) + \frac{h(2N)}{2} f(b) \qquad (3.44)$$

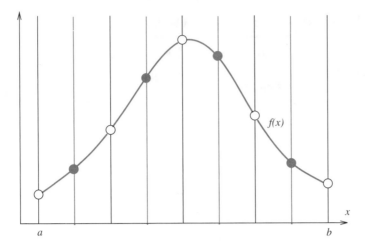

FIGURE 3.11   Going from N to $2N$ grid intervals requires evaluating the function f only at the midpoints of the N intervals. To go from four to eight intervals requires only four new function evaluations, at the solid (blue) points, while the old function values at the points marked with open circles are not needed again.

$$= \frac{h(2N)}{2} f(a) + h(2N) \sum_{\substack{j=1 \\ j\ \text{odd}}}^{2N-1} f(x_j(2N))$$

$$+ h(2N) \sum_{\substack{j=2 \\ j\ \text{even}}}^{2N-2} f(x_j(2N)) + \frac{h(2N)}{2} f(b) \qquad (3.45)$$

$$= \frac{1}{2}\left[h(2N)f(a) + 2h(2N) \sum_{\substack{j=2 \\ j\ \text{even}}}^{2N-2} f(x_j(2N)) + h(2N)f(b) \right]$$

$$+ h(2N) \sum_{\substack{j=1 \\ j\ \text{odd}}}^{2N-1} f(x_j(2N)) \qquad (3.46)$$

and so, using $h(2N) = h(N)/2$ and Eq. (3.41), we get

$$A(2N) = \frac{A(N)}{2} + h(2N) \sum_{\substack{j=1 \\ j\ \text{odd}}}^{2N-1} f(x_j(2N)). \qquad (3.47)$$

The point is that the area computed using $2N$ mesh intervals can be found from the area computed using N mesh intervals and the sum of the function values at the midpoints of those N original intervals. There is no need to redo the work of evaluating the function at the original N intervals; we need only to compute it at the midpoints of the original intervals. For some, a picture may be worth a thousand formulas, so consider Fig. 3.11.

Here is a C++ code that uses this idea with a nested loop:

adaptTrap.cpp

```
1   // ================================================================
2   // adaptTrap.cpp
```

```
 3   // Provides an adaptive trapezoidal rule function to estimate
 4   // the area under a curve.
 5   // ================================================================
 6   #include <cassert>
 7   #include <cmath>
 8   using namespace std;
 9
10   // ===========>> adaptTrap <<====================================
11   // Use an adaptive trapezoidal rule to compute the area under
12   // a function
13   // Arguments
14   //     f       -- the function under which the area lies
15   //     a       -- left end of the area
16   //     b       -- right end of the area
17   //     tolerance -- relative precision of area estimate
18   double adaptTrap(double f(double), double a, double b,
19                    double tolerance)
20   {
21     assert(a <= b);
22     assert(tolerance > 0.0);
23
24     int N = 1;
25     double h = (b - a);
26     double area = ( f(a) + f(b) ) * h * 0.5; // area from N intervals
27
28     bool done = false;
29     while( not done )
30       {
31         N = 2 * N;
32         h = 0.5 * h;
33
34         double functionSum = 0.0;
35         for(int j = 1; j < N; j = j + 2)  // use new grid points
36           {
37             functionSum = functionSum + f(a + j * h);
38           }
39
40         double newArea = 0.5 * area + h * functionSum;
41         done = tolerance * fabs(newArea) > fabs(area - newArea);
42
43         area = newArea;
44         // area is the area computed using N mesh intervals
45       }
46
47     return area;
48   }
```

I have tested this algorithm with a modification of the `areaFun` program from Section 3.10, and it generally works nicely. But it does have fundamental problems that can be revealed by thinking about a case like $f(x) = \cos(x)$ with $a = 0$ and $b = \pi$. What do you think the defect is?

It is a serious issue: Are we sure this function will terminate after a finite time? Perhaps N will keep increasing until it is too large to even be represented on the computer. This is likely to happen when the exact area under the curve is zero, since then `newArea` will be small, and the relative convergence test, in the boxed line of code,

```
tolerance * fabs(newArea) > fabs(area - newArea)
```

is likely to be false even when the estimate of area is very accurate. One approach to dealing with this is to put an upper limit on N, saying, for example, that if N becomes bigger than 10^5, then we should simply give up. Another would be to switch to an absolute convergence test if the estimated area seems to be small. The problem of automatically determining convergence of a numerical iteration is often full of such subtle issues, and often involves subjective choices on the part of the algorithm developer.

Questions

Question 30 Consider providing to **adaptTrap** a function f that satisfies the two conditions $f(a) = -f(b)$ and $f((a+b)/2) = 0$. What are the first two area estimates? What is the minimum number of times the function f will be evaluated? What would happen if the test on line 41 were

```
done = tolerance * fabs(newArea) >=
                   fabs(area - newArea);
```

What area would this compute for the case of $f(x) = \cos(x)$ with $a = 0$ and $b = \pi$ (for which the exact area is 0)? How about the case $f(x) = \cos^2(x)$ (for which the exact area is $\pi/2$)?

Question 31 What happens in **adaptTrap** if the function that defines the area being found satisfies the two conditions $f(a) \neq -f(b)$ and $f((a+b)/2) = 0$?

Projects

These questions are mostly on the loopy side, but some are not, and some can be but don't have to be. Which are which, I wonder?

PROJECT 1

The following function is very interesting, if you like white noise,

$$W_N(t) = \sin(t) + \sin(2t) + \sin(3t) + \cdots$$
$$+ \sin((N-1)t) + \sin(Nt) = \sum_{i=1}^{N} \sin(it)$$

Write a function called `whiteNoise` that takes t and N as arguments and returns $W_N(t)$.

PROJECT 2

Write a function `int factorial(int x)` that will compute the factorial of its argument x. In mathematics the factorial of a number is denoted using the exclamation point, !, and for x an integer $x! = 1\times2\times\ldots\times(x-1)\times x$, except that $0! = 1$. (Note: the function `factorial` is of limited usefulness because $x!$ grows very quickly with x. Even 13! is too large to be stored in an `int` on a 32 bit computer. For an extra challenge, rewrite your function as `double factorial(int x)`.)

PROJECT 3

Suppose the bacteria in a lake increase their number by a factor of p every second; so starting with n_0 bacteria at time zero, there are $n_1 = n_0 * (1 + p)$ after one second, and $n_2 = n_1 * (1 + p)$ after two seconds, and so on. Write a code that will print out the number of bacteria at specified time intervals, over a specified period. For example, if the code is given the values $n_0 = 10^6$ and $p = 0.001$, and asked to compute the bacteria population every 24 hours for one week, it should report:

```
1   n(0) = 1e+06
2   n(86400) = 3.1937e+43
3   n(172800) = 1.01997e+81
4   n(259200) = 3.25749e+118
5   n(345600) = 1.04034e+156
6   n(432000) = 3.32255e+193
7   n(518400) = 1.06112e+231
8   n(604800) = 3.38891e+268
```

PROJECT 4

Given a large set of numbers x_i, $i = 1, \ldots, N$, the mean m and standard deviation σ of these are defined to be

$$m = \frac{1}{N} \sum_{i=1}^{N} x_i$$

$$\sigma^2 = \frac{1}{N-1} \left[\sum_{i=1}^{N} x_i^2 - Nm^2 \right]$$

Write a code that computes the mean and standard deviation of a set of double values read from a file. You can only obtain the numbers once, so you may need to do some algebra.

PROJECT 5

The standard random number generator `rand` does not really produce random values. Just how apparently random its values are is therefore of some interest. The first simple test that we can apply is to compute the average and standard deviation of a large number of random values returned by `rand`. Write a code to do so. What should the answer be? Should you use `int`'s or `double`'s to compute the average and standard deviation? Why?

PROJECT 6

Write a code that prints out the triples t, $x(t)$, $y(t)$ which describe the position (x-horizontal, y-vertical) of a ball thrown at a specified angle θ with specified speed v,

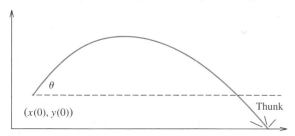

in a gravitational acceleration g, with starting position $x(0) = 0$, $y(0) = 0$. Neglect air resistance. The ball should be followed until it hits the ground at $y = 0$.

PROJECT 7

Write a code that estimates the distance that the ball modeled in the previous question traveled along its path (not along the ground, along its path, arcing through the air).

PROJECT 8

Write a code that prints out the triples t, $x(t)$, $y(t)$ which describe the position (x-horizontal, y-vertical) of a ball thrown at a specified angle θ with specified speed v, in a gravitational acceleration g, with starting position $x(0) = 0$, $y(0) = 0$. Include air resistance; remember that the friction force is directed *against the motion of the ball*. The ball should be followed until it hits the ground at $y = 0$.

PROJECT 9

Write a code that estimates the distance that the ball modeled in Question 8 traveled along its path (not along the ground, along its path, arching through the air). Compare this to the air-resistance-free case.

PROJECT 10

The function $\exp(x)$, which is the most important function in the universe, can be defined by the infinite series

$$\exp(x) = 1 + x + x^2/2! + x^3/3! + x^4/4! + \cdots + x^n/n! + \ldots$$

Write a function that will compute $\exp(x)$ using the first N terms of this series, where N and x are input by the user. Write a test code that will output its value for $\exp(x)$, as well as the value computed by the standard math library function `exp` declared in `cmath`. They should agree well for small x and N of moderate size (10–20).

PROJECT 11

The function $\cos(x)$, which is just the better half of $\exp(x)$ in heavy disguise, can be written using the infinite series

$$\cos(x) = 1 - x^2/2! + x^4/4! - x^6/6! + \cdots$$
$$+ (-1)^n x^{2n}/(2n)! + \ldots$$

Write a C++ function that uses N terms from this series to approximate $\cos(x)$. Check it out!

PROJECT 12

Redo the previous two projects but implement a convergence criterion that keeps adding terms to the sum until the last term added to the sum is larger than or equal to some tolerance, but so that the next term which would be (but won't be) added to the sum is smaller than the tolerance.

PROJECT 13

Write a code that will use Newton's method to find the pth root of a positive number x. The necessary iteration is given by

$$r_{new} = f(r_{old}, x) = \frac{(p-1)r_{old}^p + x}{pr_{old}^{p-1}}.$$

Select a reasonable means to determine if your result is converged.

PROJECT 14

We have looked at computing the area under a curve; now let's compute the length along a curve. Create an algorithm and implement it in C++ that will estimate the length along a curve $y = f(x)$ by approximating it with straight-line segments. Think of at least two clearly distinct tests for your code.

PROJECT 15

A simple model for the hull of a ship is given by

$$|y| = (B/2)[1 - (2x/L)^2][1 - (z/T)^2]$$

where y is the width of the hull, x is the distance along a line from bow to stern, and z is the depth of the hull. B is the beam, L is the length, and T is the draft. (*Note:*

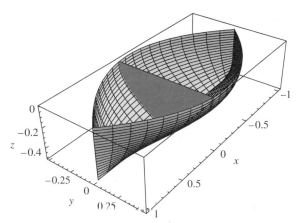

There are two values of y for each x and z, because the hull is symmetric from starboard to port.)

The cross-sectional area of the boat at a point x is called the "section" in nautical parlance. Write a function that will approximate the section $s(x)$ of this hull at any x using the trapezoidal rule. Then write a code that will use the trapezoidal rule to compute the integral under the curve of sections $s(x)$, and thus estimate the volume of the hull.

PROJECT 16

Start with a function like `trapArea` to compute the area under a function $f(x)$ using the trapezoidal rule. Use the function twice: once to compute an area $A(N)$ using N trapezoids and then again to compute an area $A(2N)$ using $2N$ trapezoids. Imagine that the area is a linear function of $1/N$, so $A(N) = m/N + b$, and use this to extrapolate the area to $N = \infty$. Write a C++ function to orchestrate this, and compare the results of using this extrapolated area to $A(2N)$. Which is better?

PROJECT 17

The function

$$f(x) = \frac{1}{1-x}$$

can be approximated by the series

$$f(x) \approx 1 + x + x^2 + x^3 + \cdots + x^n$$

as long as $|x| < 1$. We would like to explore how many terms are needed to make the difference between $f(x)$ and this series approximation smaller than some given tolerance.

For example, for an error of 1×10^{-1} and $x = 0$ only one term from the series is needed, while for $x = 1/2$

$$\frac{1}{1 - (1/2)} = 2$$

and

$$1 + \frac{1}{2} + \frac{1}{2^2} + \frac{1}{2^3} + \frac{1}{2^4} = 1.9375$$

so $n = 5$ terms is enough for an error of 1×10^{-1} and $x = 1/2$.

Write a procedure

```
void numTerms(double x, double error,
              int & n)
```

that will, for any value of x less than 1 in magnitude, compare the series to the exact function and determine the minimum number of terms needed to make their difference less than a specified `error`. Make sure you protect your procedure against bad inputs using assertions.

PROJECT 18

Suppose we have a population of creatures, call them prey, living together with another population of creatures, call them predators. The prey live a happy bucolic life, reproducing with abandon at a rate proportional to their numbers, but the predators are lonely and sad, and only reproduce if they can consume some prey. The predators only tend to starve ... unless, of course, they can find some prey to eat. Then prey disappear and predators reproduce. This is the heart of the Volterra–Lotka model of predator–prey interactions. This model is given by the differential equations

$$\frac{dx}{dt} = ax - bxy$$
$$\frac{dy}{dt} = -cy + dxy$$

where x is the number of prey and y is the number of predators. In the first equation the term ax represents the reproduction of prey, and $-bxy$ models the loss of prey due to predation. Similarly, in the second equation the term $-cy$ is the net loss of predators due to starvation and dxy gives the rate of predator reproduction that accompanies a good meal. Write a procedure

```
void predatorPrey(double a, double b,
                  double c, double d,
                  double dt, double tFinal,
                  double x0, double y0,
                  ostream & out);
```

that will time step these equations using the modified Euler method with time-step size `dt`. The procedure should advance the solution from time zero with the initial populations `x0` and `y0` up to the time `tFinal`. At each time step, the current time, population of predators, and population of prey should be written to `ostream`; each such set of three numbers should occupy one line in the file.

Write a test code to try out your `predatorPrey` routine. You might test your code with the values $a = 1.1$, $b = 0.4$, $c = 0.8$, $d = 0.1$, $x_0 = 2$, and $y_0 = 2$, and plot the prey x versus the predators y using your favorite plotting tool.

CHAPTER 4

SELECTION

SUPPOSE that I tell you today is 6-28-2001, the 6th day of June 2001. What day is tomorrow? Well, you may think me an idiot, because the answer is obviously 6-29-2001, but it actually takes a remarkable number of algorithmic steps to address this problem. The Gregorian calendar, which is now used in most places in the world, has a maddening mix of regularity and irregularity. Different months have different lengths, and one month even has a different length from year to year, changing in a complicated pattern designed to make the mean length of a Gregorian year exactly $365 + 1/4 - 1/100 + 1/400$ days. In order to determine algorithmically what day tomorrow is, we need to say things like "if today is the last day of the month, then tomorrow is the first day of the next month." That is, we need a way to express selection.

Like iteration, selection allows the conditional execution of a block of code based on the evaluation of data at execution time. But while iteration is intended to provide for the repeated execution of a set of instructions, selection is intended to allow for a simple choice among alternatives, causing one set of statements to be executed if a specified condition is true, and an alternative set to be executed if the specified condition is false. This control over alternatives provides the last major structure that we need to control the thread of execution through an algorithm.

4.1 SELECTING A SELECTION

As all programming languages must, C++ provides a selection statement:

C++ Principle

A *selection* or *if statement* can have the form

```
if (condition) statement_t else statement_f
```

where `statement_t` and `statement_f` are either compound statements, expression statements, or another if statement, and `condition` is an expression that evaluates to either true or false. `statement_t` is executed if `condition` evaluates to `true`; otherwise, `statement_t` is not executed and `statement_f` is executed instead. The entire `else statement_f` part is optional; if absent, it is equivalent to having a do-nothing `statement_f`.

So the following scrap of code starts an interplanetary war:

```
1  int numOfGreenCreatures = 10;
2  if( numOfGreenCreatures < 5 )
3  {
4    cout << "Hi,_y'all" << endl; // For a few GreenCreatures
5  }
6  else
7  {
8    destroyAlienInvaders();     // Too many.  Get Nasty.
9  }
```

A possibility that may not be immediately obvious to you, but which is simply a consequence of the semantics just outlined, is to write code of the following form:

```
1  if ( numOfGreenCreatures == 0 )
2  {
3    runSETI();
4  }
5  else if ( numOfGreenCreatures < 5 )
6  {
7    cout << "Hi,_y'all" << endl; // For a few GreenCreatures
8  }
9  else if ( numOfGreenCreatures < 1000 )
10 {
11   destroyAlienInvaders();     // Too many.  Get nasty.
12 }
13 else
14 {
15   runAndHide();               // Way too many.  Panic!
16 }
```

This tests a whole set of mutually exclusive alternatives. Note that if there are 500 of the little green guys, we will only destroyAlienInvaders, and will not runAndHide, because we only runAndHide if the condition numOfGreenCreatures < 1000 is false. There is some potential for ambiguity with the trailing else; an else always goes with the nearest, preceding else-less, if.

Of course, the right thing to do is this:

```
1  if (numberOfGreenCreatures > 0 )
2  {
3    lookForMovieCrew();  // Consider most likely case first
4  }
```

Questions

Question 1 What does each of the following scraps of code write to standard output?

a.
```
int i = 23;
if( i % 2 == 0 )
  {
    cout << "Even_so...";
  }
else
  {
    cout << "How_odd...";
  }
```

b.
```
double x = 20.0/2;
if( 0.0 < x and x < 10.0 )
  {
    cout << "In_range_";
  }
cout << "Out_of_range"
```

Question 2 Use selection to create an absolute value function that returns the absolute value of its argument, and express it in C++ for data of type `double`.

Question 3 Use selection to create a max function that returns the larger of its two arguments, and express it in C++ for data of type `double`.

4.2 SO WHAT DAY IS TOMORROW?

Selection requires discipline in its use. It is easy to write frightful fantasies of interacting selection statements whose correctness is worthlessly difficult to verify.

Let's write a procedure that will accept as input a date in the form of three integers, day, month, year, and will return tomorrow's date through the reference variables dayNext, monthNext, yearNext, for all dates in the Gregorian calendar. I'd like to deal with some big design issues first, so let's ignore leap years for the moment. Here is a first, and unfortunately typical, attempt at solving this problem (warning: Code that follows might be correct, but it is not necessarily good):

```
1   void tomorrow(int day, int month, int year,
2                 int & dayNext, int & monthNext, int & yearNext)
3   {
4     // deal with 31 day months
5     if( month == 1 or month == 3 or month == 5 or month == 7 or
6         month == 8 or month == 12)
7       {
8         if( day == 31 )
9           {
10            dayNext = 1;
11            if( month == 12 )   // deal with December 31st
12              {
13                monthNext = 1;
14                yearNext = year + 1;
15              }
16            else
17              {
18                monthNext = month + 1;
19                yearNext = year;
20              }
```

```
21              }
22          else
23              {
24                  dayNext = day + 1;
25                  monthNext = month;
26                  yearNext = year;
27              }
28          }
29
30      // deal with 30 day months
31      if( month == 4 or month == 6 or month == 9 or month == 11 )
32          {
33          if( day == 30 )
34              {
35                  dayNext = 1;
36                  monthNext = month + 1;
37                  yearNext = year;
38              }
39          else
40              {
41                  dayNext = day + 1;
42                  monthNext = month;
43                  yearNext = year;
44              }
45          }
46
47      // deal with 28 day month
48      if( month == 2 )
49          {
50          if( day == 28 )
51              {
52                  dayNext = 1;
53                  monthNext = month + 1;
54                  yearNext = year;
55              }
56          else
57              {
58                  dayNext = dayNext + 1;
59                  monthNext = month;
60                  yearNext = year;
61              }
62          }
63  }
```

Egads! What a mess. When we add leap years to this, it is going to get even worse.
I don't even want to test this piece of junk. This code considers everything as a special

case. It's not uncommon for such tortured special-case-chasing code to contain subtle defects, and it can be very hard to create tests that will expose all possible errors in such a rat's nest. There is far more regularity in the Gregorian calendar than this! Surely we can do better if we just look a bit deeper.

Consider the typical month, and call the number of days in that month daysInMonth. The following operation is expressed three times in the code above:

```
1  if( day == daysInMonth )
2    {
3      dayNext = 1;
4    }
5  else
6    {
7      dayNext = day + 1;
8    }
```

It would be far better to express this only once, and this is easy to do if we simply introduce daysInMonth and initialize it properly, depending on the value of month. In fact, what's the *typical* case going to be? We will add 1 to the day, and neither the month nor year will change. We should write the code so that this typical case is patently clear, and any special cases are clearly separated. Here is a second go:

tomorrow.cpp

```
1  #include <cassert>
2  using namespace std;
3
4  // Declare daysThisMonth function for use in tomorrow
5  int daysThisMonth(int month, int year);
6
7
8  // =================>> tomorrow <<=============================
9  // Returns the date of the day following the input date
10 // Arguments
11 //    day   - input day of month (1-31, depending on month)
12 //    month - input month of year (1-12)
13 //    year  - year
14 //    dayNext   - day of month for following date
15 //    monthNext - month for following date
16 //    yearNext  - year for following date
17 // ==========================================================
18 void tomorrow(int day, int month, int year,
19               int & dayNext, int & monthNext, int & yearNext)
20 {
21   int monthsInYear = 12;
22   int daysInMonth = daysThisMonth(month, year);
```

```
23
24      assert(0 < day and day <= daysInMonth);
25      assert(0 < month and month <= monthsInYear);
26      assert(0 < year);
27
28      // typical case
29      dayNext = day + 1;
30      monthNext = month;
31      yearNext = year;
32
33      // Month roll over
34      if( dayNext > daysInMonth )
35        {
36          dayNext = 1;
37          monthNext = month + 1;
38        }
39
40      // Year roll over
41      if( monthNext > monthsInYear )
42        {
43          monthNext = 1;
44          yearNext = year + 1;
45        }
46    }
```

This is much cleaner and easier to follow. In procedure tomorrow I use a function, daysThisMonth, that will return the number of days in the month of interest. This separates the rather messy work of determining the length of the month from the more straightforward task of using the length of the month. We will develop the daysThisMonth function in just a moment. With daysThisMonth in hand, we can also do some error checking to make sure the day, month, and year values are reasonable; this is done on lines 24–26.

The heart of the code is on lines 29–31, after which the special cases of a new month and new year are dealt with. The entire code is much smaller, and much easier to verify. Note also the relative absence of any special numbers, other than 1 and 12. The latter is used only to initialize a simple variable, so if (or should I say "when") I make a mistake, and type 21 for 12, there will be only one place to look for the error, and only one place to fix it. This version of the tomorrow function shows great regularity and structure because all the irregularities of the calendar are hidden in daysThisMonth.

Here is a version of daysThisMonth that does not deal with leap years:

daysThisMonth1.cpp

```
1   #include <cassert>
2   using namespace std;
3
```

```
4    // ================>> daysThisMonth <<============================
5    // Returns number of days in given month in given year
6    // ============================================================
7    int daysThisMonth(int month, int year)
8    {
9      assert(0 < month and month <= 12);   // valid month?
10     assert(0 < year);                     // valid year?
11
12     if( month == 1 or month == 3 or month == 5 or month == 7 or
13         month == 8 or month == 10 or month == 12)
14     {
15         return 31;
16     }
17
18     if( month == 4 or month == 6 or month == 9 or month == 11 )
19     {
20         return 30;
21     }
22
23     if( month == 2 )
24     {
25         return 28;
26     }
27
28     // should not get here, so fail if we do
29     assert(false);
30   }
```

This code *is* rather littered with special numbers, but here they are impossible to avoid, because we are now dealing directly with the irregularities of the Gregorian calendar. However, this function has one, small, well-defined task, so it's still fairly easy to check its correctness. Note also that I positively test every case. I could have left out the if(month == 2) case on line 23 because if we reach this place in the algorithm, the only possibility *is* that month is 2. However, this assumes I made no earlier mistake. Did I cover every month other than February in the two previous if statements? Just in case, I make the check if(month == 2) and arrange for the code to fail an assertion check if I advance past that point.

Here is a code that I wrote to test this version of the tomorrow function:

dayTomorrow.cpp

```
1    // ============================================================
2    // dayTomorrow.cpp
3    // Code reports the date following the input date, in
4    // day month year format.  Loops until invalid input
5    // is provided
```

```
6    // ================================================================
7    #include <iostream>
8    using namespace std;
9
10   void tomorrow(int day, int month, int year,
11                  int & dayNext, int & monthNext, int & yearNext);
12
13   // =====================>> main <<============================
14   int main()
15   {
16     // get initial input
17     cout << "Input day month year (separated by spaces) :> ";
18     int day;
19     cin >> day;
20     int month;
21     cin >> month;
22     int year;
23     cin >> year;
24
25     while( not cin.fail() )
26       {
27         // Figure out next day
28         int dayNext;
29         int monthNext;
30         int yearNext;
31         tomorrow(day, month, year, dayNext, monthNext, yearNext);
32
33         // Show it to user
34         cout << "After " << day << "-" << month <<  "-" << year;
35         cout << " there follows the glorious day ";
36         cout << dayNext << "-" << monthNext <<  "-" << yearNext;
37         cout << endl << endl;
38
39
40         // get input for next go around
41         cout << "Input day month year (separated by spaces) :> ";
42         cin >> day;
43         cin >> month;
44         cin >> year;
45       }
46
47     cout << "Thanks for your interest in the calendar." << endl;
48
49     return 0;
50   }
```

and here is a test run:

```
1  [hagar@localhost Code]$ ./dayTomorrow
2  Input day month year (separated by spaces) :> 1 1 2001
3  After 1-1-2001 there follows the glorious day 2-1-2001
4
5  Input day month year (separated by spaces) :> 31 1 2001
6  After 31-1-2001 there follows the glorious day 1-2-2001
7
8  Input day month year (separated by spaces) :> 28 2 2001
9  After 28-2-2001 there follows the glorious day 1-3-2001
10
11 Input day month year (separated by spaces) :> 31 12 2001
12 After 31-12-2001 there follows the glorious day 1-1-2002
13
14 Input day month year (separated by spaces) :> 28 2 1976
15 After 28-2-1976 there follows the glorious day 1-3-1976
16
17 Input day month year (separated by spaces) :> q
18 Thanks for your interest in the calendar.
19 [hagar@localhost Code]$
```

The code works well, except for leap years (there's a mistake in the framed line of output). Let's fix that. Notice that the tomorrow procedure, because it is written in a nice regular way, has no interest in leap years. It uses daysThisMonth to figure out how many days there are in a month, and that's all tomorrow needs. February is *not* a special case in tomorrow. To account for leap years, we need to modify daysThisMonth, and you will note that I prepared for this by passing year into daysThisMonth. Here is a version that takes proper care of all leap years (including the ever-interesting century leap-year case and its exception every 400 years):

daysThisMonth2.cpp

```
1  #include <cassert>
2  using namespace std;
3
4  // =================>> daysThisMonth <<========================
5  int daysThisMonth(int month, int year)
6  {
7    assert(0 < month and month <= 12);  // valid month?
8    assert(0 < year);                    // valid year?
9
10   if( month == 1 or month == 3 or month == 5 or month == 7 or
11       month == 8 or month == 10 or month == 12)
```

```
12      {
13          return 31;
14      }
15
16    if( month == 4 or month == 6 or month == 9 or month == 11 )
17      {
18          return 30;
19      }
20
21    if( month == 2 )
22      {
23          if( year % 4 == 0 and ( year % 100 != 0 or year % 400 == 0 ))
24           {
25             return 29; // a leap year
26           }
27          else
28           {
29             return 28; // not a leap year
30           }
31      }
32
33   // should not get here, so fail if we do
34     assert(false);
35   }
```

Running my test code again, we obtain good output all around!

```
1   [hagar@localhost Code]$ ./dayTomorrow
2   Input day month year (separated by spaces) :> 1 1 2001
3   After 1-1-2001 there follows the glorious day 2-1-2001
4
5   Input day month year (separated by spaces) :> 31 1 2001
6   After 31-1-2001 there follows the glorious day 1-2-2001
7
8   Input day month year (separated by spaces) :> 28 2 2001
9   After 28-2-2001 there follows the glorious day 1-3-2001
10
11  Input day month year (separated by spaces) :> 31 12 2001
12  After 31-12-2001 there follows the glorious day 1-1-2002
13
14  Input day month year (separated by spaces) :> 28 2 1976
15  After 28-2-1976 there follows the glorious day 29-2-1976
16
17  Input day month year (separated by spaces) :> 29 2 1976
18  After 29-2-1976 there follows the glorious day 1-3-1976
```

```
19
20 . Input day month year (separated by spaces) :> 28 2 2000
21   After 28-2-2000 there follows the glorious day 29-2-2000
22
23   Input day month year (separated by spaces) :> 29 2 2000
24   After 29-2-2000 there follows the glorious day 1-3-2000
25
26   Input day month year (separated by spaces) :> 28 2 1900
27   After 28-2-1900 there follows the glorious day 1-3-1900
28
29   Input day month year (separated by spaces) :> q
30   Thanks for your interest in the calendar.
31   [hagar@localhost Code]$
```

Very nice indeed. No problems with a regular leap year like 1976, no problems with the century leap year 2000, and no problem with a century nonleap year like 1900.

Questions

Question 4   Suppose that in **daysThisMonth2.cpp** I had neglected to include the check `month == 10` on line 11. Would the function return the wrong value?

4.3   SELECTION COMBINED WITH ITERATION

Iteration can be combined with selection to create unexpected and fascinating algorithms. Long before electronic computers existed, many algorithms were developed to reduce the work required to do arithmetic so that humans could effectively carry out the steps by hand. The heart of these algorithms was invariably the use of selection within iteration to cut down the number of steps required.

In Chapter 3 we developed a straightforward algorithm to determine the greatest common divisor (GCD) of two nonnegative integers. We can create a much better algorithm using selection; in fact, let's establish for ourselves the challenge of finding the greatest common divisor of integers i and j, gcd(i, j), without ever dividing any numbers!

Impossible, you say? Let's consider the goal: Given $i \geq 0$ and $j \geq 0$, with i and j not both zero, we want to find gcd(i, j). One interesting property of the function gcd is the trivial case

$$\gcd(k, k) = k \quad \text{for any } k \neq 0. \tag{4.1}$$

Another interesting pair of cases is

$$\gcd(0, k) = \gcd(k, 0) = k \quad \text{for any } k \neq 0. \tag{4.2}$$

If we can relate the general case to these special ones, without dividing any numbers, then we might have something.

Suppose $i \geq j$, and consider the value

$$g = \gcd(i - j, j). \tag{4.3}$$

We know that $\gcd(i, j)$ is a divisor of i and j, and therefore it is also a divisor of $i - j$. Can $i - j$ have any divisor larger than $\gcd(i, j)$? No, because

$$\frac{i - j}{g} = \frac{i}{g} - \frac{j}{g}, \tag{4.4}$$

and thus

$$\frac{i}{g} = \frac{i - j}{g} + \frac{j}{g}. \tag{4.5}$$

This implies that i/g is the sum of two integers, and hence i/g is also an integer, so $g = \gcd(i - j, j)$ is a divisor of i. Pulling all of this together, we see that $\gcd(i - j, j)$ is a divisor of both i and j, so

$$\gcd(i - j, j) \leq \gcd(i, j). \tag{4.6}$$

But $\gcd(i, j)$ is a divisor of both $i - j$ and j, so

$$\gcd(i, j) \leq \gcd(i - j, j). \tag{4.7}$$

Taken together, these two inequalities mean that

$$\gcd(i, j) = \gcd(i - j, j). \tag{4.8}$$

We can use this, starting from any i and j, to move toward one of the special cases $\gcd(k, k) = k$ or $\gcd(k, 0) = \gcd(0, k) = k$. We simply want to select the larger of i or j, reduce it by the smaller of i or j, and keep doing so until we reach one of the special cases. No division required! Here is an implementation:

gcd3.cpp

```
// ===========================================================
// gcd3.cpp
// Computes the greatest common divisor of two nonnegative
// integers a and b.
// ===========================================================
#include <cassert>
using namespace std;

int gcd(int a, int b)
{
   assert(not(a == 0 and b == 0)); // they can't both be zero
   assert(a >= 0);
   assert(b >= 0);

   int i = a;  // make local copies
   int j = b;

```

```
18    while( (i != j) and (j != 0) and (i != 0))
19      {
20        // loop invariant gcd(i,j) = gcd(a,b)
21        if(i > j)
22          {
23            i = i - j;  // reduce i but leave GCD unchanged
24          }
25        else
26          {
27            j = j - i;  // reduce j but leave GCD unchanged
28          }
29      }
30
31      // Now only special cases are possible
32      if( i == 0 )    // GCD(0, j) = j
33        {
34          return j;
35        }
36      return i;       // GCD(i, i) = i or GCD(i, 0) = i
37    }
```

Running this new version of **gcd** under the **gcdDriver.cpp** program from Chapter 3 results in

```
1    [hagar@localhost Code]$ ./gcd3
2    gcd(4, 2) = 2
3    gcd(2, 4) = 2
4    gcd(259, 111) = 37
5    gcd(1375, 218491) = 1
6    gcd(541, 3804853) = 541
7    gcd(0, 56) = 56
8    gcd(56, 0) = 56
9    [hagar@localhost Code]$
```

This code has no problems with the more difficult test cases, and is in fact much faster than any of the preceding versions of the algorithm, which were based on an exhaustive check of every possible divisor.

Note that the correctness of this code can again be established through the loop invariant $gcd(a, b) = gcd(i, j)$. Within the loop i and j are changed, but only in a way that maintains the invariant. Further, if they are not equal and neither is zero, then either i or j is decreased on each trip through the loop. Each can only be reduced a finite number of times until one of the easy cases ($i == j$, $i == 0$, or $j == 0$) is reached. So the algorithm will terminate, and the result will be correct.

In Chapter 3 we also wrote a very simple function to compute nonnegative integer powers of a number, **powers.cpp**. Here is another algorithm to accomplish the same task, but far more efficiently:

akpower.cpp

```
// ===============================================================
// akpower.cpp
// Computes x to the nonnegative integer power p using
// Al-Kashi's algorithm
// ===============================================================
#include <cassert>
using namespace std;

double akpower(double x, int p)
{
  assert(p >= 0);
  int n = p;
  double xn = x;

  double result = 1.0;
  // Invariant established: pow(x, p) = result * pow(xn, n)

  while(1 <= n)
    {
      if( n%2 == 0)
        {
          n = n/2;
          xn = xn * xn;
          // pow(xn, n) has not changed
        }
      else
        {
          n = n - 1;
          result = result * xn;
          // result * pow(xn, n) has not changed
        }
      // Invariant: pow(x, p) = result * pow(xn, n)
    }
  return result;   // pow(x, p) = result * pow(xn, 0)
}
```

The loop invariant is result * pow(xn, n) == pow(x, p). So the value of result * pow(xn, n) is always what we want to compute. Each trip through the loop leaves us with this invariant, but reduces the value of n, either modestly by 1, or greatly by dividing by 2. When the loop terminates, n == 0, so pow(xn, n) is trivially known to be unity, and `result` holds the value we seek. It's a lovely algorithm, whose correctness is nicely established by understanding a loop invariant.

Questions

Question 5 Modify `akpower` to work for negative values of p.

Question 6 By appropriate changes, `akpower` can be transformed into a routine for computing x * p, without multiplying. The desired invariant would be x * p == result + xn * n. Write a function `rpProduct` based on this.

4.4 BISECTION

In Chapter 3 we created an algorithm that computed square roots. That algorithm solved the equation $r^2 = x$, since the root $r = \sqrt{x}$ was the desired value. In this section we shall create a more general root-finding algorithm that is somewhat slower than the Newton's method used there, but which is very robust. Suppose we want to find the root r that satisfies $f(r) = 0$ for some continuous function f. The bisection algorithm that we will develop assumes we have an interval $x \leq r \leq y$ such that $f(x)f(y) \leq 0$. This peculiar condition ensures that generally $f(x)$ and $f(y)$ have opposite signs, and implies that someplace between x and y there will be a root r where $f(r) = 0$. So the condition $f(x)f(y) \leq 0$ ensures that there actually is a root r to find, and that $x \leq r \leq y$. If we can systematically move x toward y while maintaining the condition $f(x)f(y) \leq 0$, then we can move as close to the root as desired. Sounds like a loop invariant!

A systematic method to bring x toward y is to consider their average $(x + y)/2$ as a new candidate value for either x or y, and pair this candidate with either y or x in such a way that the condition $f(x)f(y) \leq 0$ is maintained, as suggested in Fig 4.1. Here is an implementation in C++:

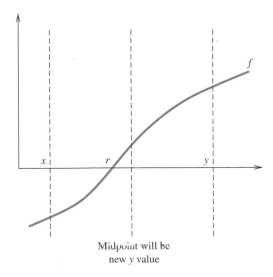

Midpoint will be
new y value

FIGURE 4.1 The bisection method works by trapping the solution within an interval whose size is halved at every iteration.

bisect1.cpp

```cpp
#include <cassert>
using namespace std;

//============================>> bisect <<=======================
// Seeks root of function double f(double r) using bisection
// in the interval [xStart, yStart].  A root must be verified
// in this interval or the code will abort.  Bisection proceeds
// until the root is bracketed by an interval of length less
// than tolerance.
// Arguments
//    xStart    -- left end of initial interval
//    yStart    -- right end of initial interval
//    tolerance -- maximum length of final interval
//    f         -- function whose root will be found
// ==============================================================
double bisect(double xStart, double yStart, double tolerance,
              double f(double))
{
  assert(tolerance > 0.0);
  assert(xStart <= yStart);
  assert(f(xStart) * f(yStart) <= 0.0);

  double x = xStart;  // point to left of root
  double y = yStart;  // point to right of root

  while( y - x > tolerance )
    {
      // invariant: f(x) * f(y) <= 0.0

      double midPoint = 0.5 * (x + y);
      if ( f(x) * f(midPoint) <= 0.0 )
        {
          y = midPoint;  // shorten interval, maintain invariant
        }
      else
        {
          x = midPoint;  // shorten interval, maintain invariant
        }
    }

  return 0.5 * (x + y);
}
```

This code was easy to write once the loop invariant was recognized. Here is a code that uses bisect to find a zero of the cosine:

cosRoot.cpp

```
1   // ==============================================================
2   // cosRoot.cpp
3   // Finds the root of cosine between 1.5 and 1.6 radians.
4   // ==============================================================
5   #include <iostream>
6   #include <cmath>
7   using namespace std;
8
9   // Declare functions
10  double bisect(double xStart, double yStart, double tolerance,
11                double f(double));
12
13  // ==================>> main <<==================================
14  int main()
15  {
16    cout.precision(14); // show lots of digits on output
17    cout << "The root of cosine between 1.5 and 1.6 is ";
18    cout << bisect(1.5, 1.6, 1e-6, cos) << endl;
19  }
20
```

and here is a test run:

```
1   [hagar@localhost Code]$ ./cosRoot
2   The root of cosine between 1.5 and 1.6 is 1.570796585083
3   [hagar@localhost Code]$
```

One complaint I have about the **bisect1.cpp** code is that it evaluates the function f more often than it needs to. Even if, from one trip through the loop to the next, the left boundary x remains unchanged, f(x) will still be evaluated again on the next trip through the loop. In fact, the bisect1.cpp code evaluates the function f twice on each trip through the loop, and this is twice as often as really needed. If the evaluation of f takes a long time, then the bisection code will be needlessly slow. Can you think of a way to avoid this extra work?

It is often advantageous to store data computed on one trip through a loop for later use on the next trip through the loop. In the present case, we want to store the values for f(x) and f(y), and reuse whichever we can on the next pass through the loop. In fact, we don't explicitly need the value of f(y), because it is never used; I have written the code to always consider the sign of f(x) * f(midPoint), so the following version will save unnecessary function calls:

bisect2.cpp

```cpp
1   #include <cassert>
2   using namespace std;
3
4   //=====================>> bisect <<============================
5   // Seeks root of function double f(double r) using bisection
6   // in the interval [xStart, yStart].  A root must be verified
7   // in this interval or the code will abort.  Bisection
8   // proceeds until the root is bracketed by an interval of
9   // length less than tolerance.
10  // Arguments
11  //   xStart    -- left end of initial interval
12  //   yStart    -- right end of initial interval
13  //   tolerance -- maximum length of final interval
14  //   f         -- function whose root will be found
15  // ===========================================================
16  double bisect(double xStart, double yStart, double tolerance,
17                double f(double))
18  {
19    assert(f(xStart) * f(yStart) <= 0.0);
20
21    double x = xStart;  // point to left of root
22    double y = yStart;  // point to right of root
23    double fx = f(x);   // function value to left
24
25    while( y - x > tolerance )
26      {
27        // invariant: fx * f(y) <= 0.0
28
29        double midPoint = 0.5 * (x + y);
30        double fMidPoint = f(midPoint);
31        if ( fx * fMidPoint <= 0.0 )
32          {
33            y = midPoint;  // shorten interval, maintain invariant
34          }
35        else
36          {
37            x = midPoint;  // shorten interval, maintain invariant
38            fx = fMidPoint;  // keep function value
39          }
40      }
41
```

```
42      return 0.5 * (x + y);
43   }
```

In this version we keep the value of f(midPoint), as needed, from one trip through the loop to the next. There is only one function evaluation on each trip through the loop. So, except for the most trivial functions f, this version will be roughly twice as fast as the previous one. It is also slightly harder to follow, because the absence of an explicit call like f(y) may seem slightly mysterious. The key to this is that the function value at the right endpoint of the interval was checked, only when necessary, on some previous trip through the loop when the current right endpoint was, in fact, the midpoint.

Questions

Question 7   What happens in the bisection algorithm if, by some chance, $f(x) = 0$ exactly at the left endpoint of one of the intervals?

Question 8   A phone book is stored as a long list of names, in alphabetical order. Sketch out an algorithm to find a specific name in the phone book.

4.5   A DESIGN EXERCISE

Selection is a wonderfully useful construct, but it is too often used in an undisciplined and confusing manner. I illustrated this in my first, disastrous attempt to deal with the calendar. Many students evolve their code into existence, implementing their first thoughts and then patching that implementation as various, apparently special, cases appear. Such evolutionary design is OK when first getting a handle on a problem, but once you go through this exercise, you should reconsider the problem in light of experience and see if you can't clean it up and make the core algorithm clear. I shall attempt such an exercise here, and along the way introduce a few additional C++ facilities.

Let's address a small, but important, defect in some of our previous software. Consider a program to compute the Arcsine of a value interactively input by a user. Suppose that value has been declared as a double. Then some code like

```
cin >> value;
```

might be used to get the input number from the user. But what if the user types Bob's_your_uncle, rather than a nice number like 0.5? Or what if the user types a nice number like 3.14159, for which the Arcsine is undefined? Such erroneous input can be checked using selection statements.

I had previously introduced the function cin.fail(), which returns true if something goes wrong when last reading data from standard input. If a user types something other than a number when a number is required, cin.fail() will subsequently evaluate true, and cin will, from that point on, do nothing. We can therefore check to see if the statement

```
cin >> value;
```

succeeded in placing a number into `value` with code like this:

```
1   cout << "Please input the value of sine: ";
2   cin >> value;
3   if( cin.fail() )
4     {
5       // we did not get a number -- what to do?
6     }
7   else
8     {
9       // we got a number
10      cout << "Arcsin(" << value << ") = " << asin(value);
11    }
```

But what should we do in the case of failure? One alternative is to simply give up. The function `void exit(int status)` declared in the standard header file `cstdlib` can be used to terminate the execution of the program, and return the integer value `status` to the operating system. Thus, `exit(1)`, called from anywhere, is more or less equivalent to `return 1` in `main`. Better yet, the predefined value `EXIT_FAILURE` is traditionally returned to the operating system if the code has run into some trouble, while `EXIT_SUCCESS` is often returned if all is well. Thus,

```
1   cout << "Please input the value of sine: ";
2   cin >> value;
3   if( cin.fail() )
4     {
5       // we did not get a number
6       exit(EXIT_FAILURE);
7     }
8   else
9     {
10      // we got a number
11      cout << "Arcsin(" << value << ") = " << asin(value);
12    }
```

Now when the user does not provide a useful value, the code simply quits. This is not unreasonable, since it cannot usefully proceed without a valid number to work with. However, it quits rather silently. Consider the perspective of the user: he has perhaps no idea that he input bad data; he just sees the code strangely quit. He probably then swears, and is embarrassed as the other computer lab users turn their heads and stare at him. To avoid this unwanted attention, we should at least write a message for the user before the code quits, explaining what's going on. One useful tradition is to print such error messages not to standard output (`cout`), but rather to reserve `cout` for normal data output, and use its friend, standard error `cerr`, for error messages. Although both `cout` and `cerr` send output to the screen by default, under many operating systems standard error and standard output can be redirected separately, so error messages may be separated from real data.

Claim

Error messages should be written to standard error, through `cerr`. Standard output `cout` should be used for expected output.

For example,

```
1   cout << "Please_input_the_value_of_sine:>_";
2   cin >> value;
3   if( cin.fail() )
4     {
5       // we did not get a number
6       cerr << "Did_not_get_a_valid_number.__Giving_up" << endl;
7       exit(EXIT_FAILURE);
8     }
9   else
10    {
11      // we got a number
12      cout << "Arcsin(" << value << ")_=_" << asin(value);
13    }
```

We still have not dealt with the possibility that the user does provide a number (so `cin.fail()` is false), but the number makes no sense. This is easily addressed:

```
1   cout << "Please_input_the_value_of_sine:>_";
2   cin >> value;
3   if( cin.fail() )
4     {
5       // we did not get a number
6       cerr << "Did_not_get_a_valid_number.__Giving_up." << endl;
7       exit(EXIT_FAILURE);
8     }
9   else
10    {
11      // we got a number
12      if( (-1.0 <= value) and (value <= 1.0) )
13        {
14          cout << "Arcsin(" << value << ")_=_" << asin(value);
15        }
16      else
```

```
17      {
18          cerr << "Did␣not␣get␣a␣number␣between␣-1␣and␣1.␣␣Giving␣up."
19          cerr << endl;
20          exit(EXIT_FAILURE);
21      }
22  }
```

We have now dealt with both possible bad input problems. If the user types in the wrong data for the value of sine, our code will catch it! But now look at this code with a fresh eye. If you had not come along for the ride, with this code evolving into existence, could you tell quickly what it is supposed to do? There are 22 lines of code, buried in the middle of which is the single key step `asin(value)`. In the typical case, the user will a number valid type, and with that only three lines of code are needed to deal.[1] So although this code is correct, and nicely defensive, it is ugly and obscure.

What's the solution? Forget all that error checking and just stick to the three crucial lines? The code will work most of the time. But it would be foolish to ignore the rare error. Many errors are rare, but have severe consequences when they do occur. I drive every day, and don't often make errors when driving. But that one time when I drove too fast on a winding country road, and my car went flipping end-over-end. . . .

We simply need to redesign this code, and separate the concern of obtaining and validating input from the concern of operating on valid input. Here is one approach:

```
1   // Get and validate input
2   cout << "Please␣input␣the␣value␣of␣sine:>␣";
3   cin >> value;
4   if( cin.fail() )
5     {
6         // we did not get a number
7         cerr << "Did␣not␣get␣a␣valid␣number.␣␣Giving␣up." << endl;
8         exit(EXIT_FAILURE);
9     }
10
11  // we got a number
12  if( fabs(value) > 1.0 )
13    {
14        cerr << "Did␣not␣get␣a␣number␣between␣-1␣and␣1.␣␣Giving␣up.";
15        cerr << endl;
16        exit(EXIT_FAILURE);
17    }
18
19  // we have a valid datum
20  cout << "Arcsin(" << value << ")␣=␣" << asin(value);
```

[1]Yep, I wrote this on purpose.

In this version I have simply made sure that the typical case is clear and identifiable on the page.

This version is better, but if I am going to be doing a lot of this sort of validation, I might want to wrap it up in a procedure:

getValidDouble1.cpp

```
1   // ================================================================
2   // getValidDouble1.cpp
3   // ================================================================
4   #include <iostream>
5   #include <cstdlib>
6   using namespace std;
7
8   // ====================>> getValidDouble <<====================
9   // Gets a double value from standard input and makes sure it's
10  // greater or equal to min and less than or equal to max.
11  // Forces exit on error.
12  // Arguments
13  //   min    -- minimum allowed value
14  //   max    -- maximum allowed value
15  //   goodValue -- reference through which to return value
16  // ================================================================
17  void getValidDouble(double min, double max, double & goodValue)
18  {
19
20    // try to get a value
21    double value;
22    cin >> value;
23
24    if( cin.fail() )
25      {
26        // we did not get a number
27        cerr << "Did_not_get_a_valid_number.__Giving_up." << endl;
28        exit(EXIT_FAILURE);
29      }
30
31    // we got a number
32    if( (value < min) or (value > max) )
33      {
34        cerr << "Did_not_get_a_number_between_" << min;
35        cerr << "_and_" << max << "._Giving_up.";
36        cerr << endl;
37        exit(EXIT_FAILURE);
38      }
39
40    // number is valid
```

```
41    goodValue = value;   // works by side-effect in caller
42  }
```

The heart of the Arcsine code is now downright clean:

```
1  cout << "Please input the value of sine:> ";
2  getValidDouble(-1.0, 1.0, value);
3  cout << "Arcsin(" << value << ") = " << asin(value);
```

You might wonder why getValidDouble is a procedure, rather than a function. I don't want you to be able to use getValidDouble in an expression, because it is not referentially transparent. To prevent its use in an expression, I wrote it as a procedure.

The use of a routine like getValidDouble greatly enhances the flexibility and stability of a code. We can use this same function every place where we want a single, range-checked double value, and obtain uniform behavior in all such cases. The alternative is to code a set of checks on the fly every time we write something like cin >> x; this is error-prone and tedious. And do you recall who tedium's enemy is?

Further, you can easily change the behavior of your code by altering getValid Double. For example, you may feel that I am being a bit harsh, quitting just because a human makes one mistake. Here is a different implementation of getValidDouble that is more user friendly:

getValidDouble2.cpp

```
1  // =================================================================
2  // getValidDouble2.cpp
3  // =================================================================
4  #include <iostream>
5  using namespace std;
6
7  // ====================>> getValidDouble <<====================
8  // Gets a double value from standard input and makes sure it's
9  // greater or equal to min and less than or equal to max.
10 // Keeps nagging for a valid value.
11 // Arguments
12 //    min   -- minimum allowed value
13 //    max   -- maximum allowed value
14 //    goodValue -- reference through which to return value
15 // =================================================================
16 void getValidDouble(double min, double max, double & goodValue)
17 {
18
19    // try to get a value
20    double value;
21    cin >> value;
```

```
22
23    while( cin.fail() or ((value < min) or (value > max)) )
24    {
25       cout << "The_number_must_be_between_" << min;
26       cout << "_and_" << max << endl;
27       cout << "Please_input_a_number_(like_";
28       cout << 0.5 * (min + max) << "):>_";
29
30       cin.clear();   // Reset cin in case cin.fail() was true
31       cin >> value;
32    }
33
34    // number is valid
35    goodValue = value;   // works by side-effect in caller
36 }
```

There is a new, and hidden, sequencing issue on line 23. Suppose, when evaluating the logical expression

```
    cin.fail() or ((value < min) or (value > max))
```

that cin.fail() is true. Then the logical expression is true, no matter whether ((value < min) or (value > max)) is true or false. The C++ compiler therefore makes sure that ((value < min) or (value > max)) is *not* evaluated. In fact, ((value < min) or (value > max)) is never evaluated unless it needs to be. This is called short-circuit evaluation.

Definition

> In *short-circuit evaluation* of a logical expression, the expression is evaluated in the normal order implied by the precedence, parentheses, and placement of the logical operators in the expression, but only until the truth or falsity of the expression becomes clear, after which no further parts of the logical expression are evaluated.

Thus, in an expression like

```
    a or b
```

there is no need to evaluate b if a is true, because no matter what b is, the expression evaluates to true. And in

```
    a and b
```

there is no need to evaluate b if a is false, because the expression is false no matter what b is. This short-circuit evaluation is important on line 23 of **getValidDouble2.cpp,** because we do not want to consider the condition ((value < min) or (value > max))) *unless* cin.fail() is false. Otherwise, we would be checking the validity of data we did not get!

Note now that I use standard output, rather than standard error, to converse with the user. This is an aesthetic choice; I generally think of standard error as a place to which notifications go, while standard output in an interactive code like this is the place for conversation.

One defect of this version is that if the user refuses to input valid data, the procedure will just loop forever, asking again and again for a valid number. It might be wise to install a maximum number of retries, which when exceeded causes the whole program to exit. I leave this as an exercise. A worse defect in this implementation is that if the user types something which is not a number, then, because of the default behavior of the standard input stream, this code will become trapped in an infinite loop.

Questions

Question 9 Rewrite **getValidDouble1.cpp** so that getValidDouble gets data from an istream passed in as an arugment, and does not prompt for input, but simply tries to read a double from that istream.

Question 10 In the following logical expressions, which clauses in parentheses are evaluated and which are not? You can assume double x = 10.0; and double y = 5.0;, if it makes any difference.

a. (1 > 2) and (x < y)
b. (1 < 2) and (x < y)
c. 0 or (x == y)
d. (30.0 < x) or (f(x, y))

4.6 RECURSION

Selection can be used together with function calls to create an interesting form of iteration known as recursion. Consider the factorial function, $n! = n \times (n-1) \times (n-2) \times \cdots \times 2 \times 1$, with $0! = 1$ by definition. Let's write the factorial function in a more "functional" form as fact(n). Then we know that

$$\text{fact}(0) = 1 \tag{4.9}$$
$$\text{fact}(n) = n \times \text{fact}(n-1). \tag{4.10}$$

This is called a recursion relation[2]; it defines the function fact in terms of itself, but in such a way that we can work our way up to fact(n) by knowing the special case fact(0):

$$\text{fact}(4) = 4 \times \text{fact}(3) \tag{4.11}$$
$$= 4 \times 3 \times \text{fact}(2) \tag{4.12}$$
$$= 4 \times 3 \times 2 \times \text{fact}(1) \tag{4.13}$$
$$= 4 \times 3 \times 2 \times 1 \times \text{fact}(0) \tag{4.14}$$
$$= 4 \times 3 \times 2 \times 1 \times 1. \tag{4.15}$$

Here I have simply expanded the recursion relation over and over until the explicit special case of fact(0) = 1 was reached, at which point the expression for fact(4) had been reduced to a series of multiplication operations. We can easily create an algorithm

---
[2] Also sometimes called a recurrence relation.

that automatically carries out this expansion based directly on the recursion relation, Eq. (4.10). The key is to have a function call itself, as in the following:

```
1   // ====>> fact <<=================================================
2   // Computes factorial of n
3   // ================================================================
4   #include <cassert>
5   using namespace std;
6
7   int fact(int n)
8   {
9     assert(n >= 0);
10    if(n == 0)     // special case that terminates recursion
11     {
12       return 1;
13     }
14    return n * fact(n-1);   // The recursion relation
15  }
```

Each call with a positive argument to function fact will automatically generate another call to fact, which will in turn generate another, which will generate another, and so on. Generally, every call to fact will generate a whole a series of calls to fact, with each successive call in the chain having a smaller value of the function argument. This chain of function calls will be terminated by the special case of a zero argument, since in this case the fact function simply returns 1 without calling itself. It is this direct evaluation of a special case that allows such recursive functions to terminate the chain of calls, and selection is therefore critical in completing a recursive function.

Recursive definitions arise often in the description of the physical world. For example, the shape of atomic orbitals is defined in part by a set of functions called the Legendre polynomials, $P_n(\mu)$. Imagine the atom as a planet with orbiting electrons; the independent variable μ describes where the electron is to be found in latitude.[3] In fact, $\mu = \cos(\theta)$ where θ is the polar angle, running from $\theta = 0$ at the North Pole down to $\theta = \pi$ at the South. So $\mu = 1$ represents the North Pole, $\mu = 0$ is the equator, and $\mu = -1$ occurs at the South Pole. In an atom, the integer index n describes the amount of angular momentum that an electron has, and $|P_n(\mu)|^2$ gives the relative probability that an electron in certain orbitals will be found near a latitude corresponding to μ.

However, the physics is not too critical in the current context. What is interesting to us is that the Legendre polynomials are defined recursively. The functions $P_n(\mu)$ are defined by the recursion relation

$$nP_n(\mu) = (2n - 1)\, \mu P_{n-1}(\mu) - (n - 1)\, P_{n-2}(\mu) \qquad (4.16)$$

---

[3]By the way, μ is the Greek letter "mu."

with $P_0(\mu) = 1$. This equation describes one of the Legendre polynomials, P_n, in terms of two others, P_{n-1} and P_{n-2}. Applying this recursive definition, we can easily compute

$$P_1(\mu) = \mu P_0(\mu) - 0 = \mu,\tag{4.17}$$

and

$$P_2(\mu) = \left[3\mu P_1(\mu) - 1P_0\right]/2 = \frac{3}{2}\mu^2 - \frac{1}{2},\tag{4.18}$$

and

$$P_3(\mu) = \left[5\mu P_2(\mu) - 2P_1\right]/3 = \frac{5}{2}\mu^3 - \frac{3}{2}\mu,\tag{4.19}$$

and we can continue to ascend to higher n as we wish. A moment's reflection on the recursion relation will reveal that P_n is indeed a polynomial of order n, and the particular cases just derived bear this out. The recursion relation is thus a very compact description of an infinite family of polynomial functions.

Although there are explicit formulae for the evaluation of $P_n(\mu)$, they are in fact not as useful for numerical computation as the recursion relation of Eq. (4.16). To write a C++ function to compute values of Legendre polynomials, an obvious approach is to use the recursion relation directly, along with the special cases $P_1(\mu) = \mu$ and $P_0(\mu) = 1$, to terminate the recursion. We need both because each application of the recursion relation requires values of two lower-order Legendre polynomials. Here then is a function that does the job:

legendre1.cpp

```
1   // ======>> legendre <<===========================================
2   // Computes values of Legendre polynomials P_n(mu)
3   // ==============================================================
4   #include <cassert>
5   using namespace std;
6
7   double legendre(int n, double mu)
8   {
9     assert(n >= 0);
10
11    double value = 0.0;
12    if(n == 0)
13      {
14        value = 1.0;   // P_0(mu) = 1
15      }
16    else if(n == 1)
17      {
18        value = mu;    // P_1(mu) = mu
19      }
20    else
21      {
```

```
22        value = (2*n - 1) * mu * legendre(n-1, mu) -
23                                    (n-1) * legendre(n-2, mu);
24        value = value/n;
25      }
26    return value;
27  }
```

I have, of course, tested this function, and I am sure you will do the same. It is, however, a very direct translation of the recursion formula into C++ code, and its correctness is easy to verify by reasoning alone.

However, this is not a particularly efficient implementation of the recursion. Consider the computation of $P_5(\mu)$: this involves the computation of P_4 and P_3. The former itself requires the computation of P_3 and P_2, but because there is no sharing of information, we will in fact do all the work to compute P_3 *twice*. Worse, we will compute P_2 *three* times: once when computing P_3 and twice when computing P_4. There is thus a great deal of redundancy in this implementation, and the amount of redundancy grows quickly with the value of n. In fact, the computation of P_5 will involve a total of 15 calls to the function legendre, when only 6 seem strictly necessary (to compute $P_0, P_1, \ldots, P_4, P_5$). The benefit of this implementation is not its efficiency, but rather is in the easy way that we could go from definition to implementation. This gives us certainty in the correctness of the algorithm, but it is not necessarily a fast algorithm.

A more efficient implementation of the legendre function would climb *up* the recursion relation from the bottom at P_0, and reuse the previously computed values needed for each step. It is perhaps easiest to think about this if the recursion relation is rewritten as

$$(n + 1)P_{n+1}(\mu) = (2n + 1)\mu P_n(\mu) - nP_{n-1}(\mu). \qquad (4.20)$$

We can implement an algorithm that starts with P_0 and P_1 and uses these with $n = 1$ to compute P_2. The algorithm can then use that newly computed value of P_2 along with the previously computed value of P_1 to compute P_3. This can continue, ascending toward the goal of knowing P_n for some higher n. Because we only need two previous Legendre polynomial values to move on to the next one, we can shuffle these previous data values through two variables using a loop:

legendre2.cpp

```
1  // ======>> legendre <<============================================
2  // Computes values of Legendre polynomials
3  // ================================================================
4  #include <cassert>
5  using namespace std;
6
7  double legendre(int n, double mu)
8  {
9    assert(n >= 0);
10
```

```
11    double      P = 1.0;    // P_0
12    double Pold = 0.0;
13
14    int i = 0;
15    while(i < n)
16      {
17        // Invariant:        P = P_{i}(mu)
18        //                i * Pold = i * P_{i-1}(mu)
19
20        double Pnew = ((2*i + 1) * mu * P - i * Pold)/(i+1);
21
22        // Pnew = P_{i+1}(mu) -- the next Legendre polynomial
23
24        Pold = P;       // Breaks invariant
25        P = Pnew;       // Invariant still broken
26
27        i = i + 1;      // Invariant restored
28      }
29
30    return P;
31  }
```

For large values of *n*, this version is *much* faster than the recursive implementation. It still uses the recursion relation, but does so without having a recursive C++ function. Although its greatly increased speed comes from avoiding repeated calculations, it takes careful thought to verify the correctness of this version; the loop invariant is again the key to doing so.

Recursion often allows for a simple and clearly correct algorithmic implementation of a problem solution. While in some cases recursion does not provide the most efficient solution:

Claim

> It is better to be right eventually, than wrong quickly.

So first make it right. But correctness and efficiency are coupled together in subtle ways, and, alas, some correct algorithms are so slow as to be useless in practice. Try the recursive legendre implementation with $n = 100$ and $\mu = 1$; the answer is $P_{100}(1) = 1$, but the code will take a really long time to discover this. Then try the second implementation; it will be quite fast. Unfortunately, we can neither dismiss nor blindly embrace recursion. Sometimes a recursive solution is too slow, and sometimes a recursive solution is the most efficient approach. For example, the merge sort algorithm that we will develop in Chapter 6 is naturally and efficiently recursive.[4]

---

[4] The topic of speed is touched on somewhat in Chapter 8, where we will explore the estimation of the speed of algorithms.

Questions

Question 11 Consider the function call `fact(10)`. How many times is `fact` actually called in order to evaluate `fact(10)`?

Question 12 Write the factorial function without using a recursive function call.

Question 13 In computing $P_8(\mu)$ using the recursive function `legendre`, how many times is P_2 computed? How many times in total is the function `legendre` called to compute $P_9(\mu)$?

Question 14 What does the following recursive function do?

```
int what(int n)
{
  if(n == 0)
    {
      return 0;
    }
  return n + what(n-1);
}
```

Question 15 Write a recursive function that computes a `double` raised to a positive integer power.

4.7 A SELECTION IDIOM

The purpose of selection is to pick instructions to execute based on the values of data at execution time. In the special case of selection based on exactly matching integer values, C++ provides a special construct called the switch statement. Consider, for example, the if-else ladder between lines 12 and 25 of **legendre1.cpp**. This code has the structure

> **if** *n* **is 0 then**
> Deal with this special case
> **else if** *n* **is 1 then**
> Deal with this special case
> **else**
> Deal with a default case
> **end if**

The selection statements are designed to use certain code if *n* is exactly equal to 0, and certain other code if *n* is exactly 1, and to otherwise use some default instructions. C++ provides the switch statement to deal with this arrangement of multiple if-else branches controlled by integer values.[5] So let me write the `legendre` function one more time, recursively but using a switch statement:

legendre3.cpp

```
1   // =====>> legendre <<==================================
2   // Computes values of Legendre polynomials
3   // =====================================================
4   #include <cassert>
5   using namespace std;
6
7   double legendre(int n, double mu)
8   {
```

[5] Such a special language construct is certainly not necessary, and many excellent programming languages do without it. I never use switch statements.

```
9      assert(n >= 0);
10
11     double value = 0.0;
12     switch(n)
13       {
14         case 0:
15           value = 1.0;   // P_0(mu) = 1
16           break;         // go to end of switch
17
18         case 1:
19           value = mu;    // P_1(mu) = mu
20           break;         // go to end of switch
21
22         default:
23           value = (2*n - 1) * mu * legendre(n-1, mu) -
24                                    (n-1) * legendre(n-2, mu);
25           value = value/n;
26       }  // end of switch body
27
28     return value;
29   }
```

The idea of the `switch` statement on line 12 is that the thread of execution will jump to one of the `case` labels, based on the value of n. If it should happen that the value of n is zero, then control will jump to the `case` label on line 14. And if it should happen that n equals 1, then the thread will proceed to line 18. But if n is not equal to either of these explicit values, then execution will flow to the `default` label on line 22. Whichever label the thread goes to, from then on it simply flows down the list of instructions as usual. However, the `break` statement, seen here on lines 16 and 20, allows the thread of execution to be redirected one more time to the end of the compound statement, on line 26, that the switch controls.

C++ Principle

A *switch* statement has the form

```
switch( integer_expression ) compound_statement
```

where `integer_expression` must evaluate to an integer and the `compound_statement` can contain *case* labels of the form `case integer_constant:`, with `integer_constant` an integer that is known at compile time. The `compound_statement` can also contain one default label, `default:`. The semantics of the statement are to evaluate the `integer_expression` and to then jump the thread of execution to that case label whose `integer_constant` equals the value of the `integer_expression`. If the `integer_expression` does not equal any of the case labels, then the thread of execution jumps to the default label, if it exists; otherwise, the `compound_statement` is skipped and execution continues from just after it.

The compound statement controlled by a switch is often called the switch body. Note that all the `switch` does is jump to a particular case label in its body; execution continues from that point as normal.

C++ Principle

> A *break* statement is a statement of the form `break;`. When appearing in a switch body, it causes the thread of execution to jump to the end of the switch body.

A break statement allows us to skip over statements associated with other case labels within a switch body, so that a switch can provide alternative sets of instructions to execute based on the value of an integer.

A break statement might be used with every case label, but not necessarily so. As another example use of the switch statement, we can use it to reorganize our `daysThisMonth` function as follows:

daysThisMonth3.cpp

```
1   // ===============>> daysThisMonth <<=========================
2   // Returns the number of days in a month
3   // ==========================================================
4   #include <cassert>
5   using namespace std;
6
7   int daysThisMonth(int month, int year)
8   {
9     assert(0 < month and month <= 12);   // valid month?
10    assert(0 < year);                    // valid year?
11
12    int days = 0;                        // number of days this month
13
14    switch(month)
15      {
16      case 1:       // January
17      case 3:       // March
18      case 5:       // May
19      case 7:       // July
20      case 8:       // August
21      case 10:      // October
22      case 12:      // December
23        days = 31;
24        break;
25
26      case 4:       // April
27      case 6:       // June
28      case 9:       // September
29      case 11:      // November
```

```
30          days = 30;
31          break;
32
33        case 2:
34          if( year % 4 == 0 and ( year % 100 != 0 or year % 400 == 0 ))
35          {
36             days = 29; // a leap year
37          }
38          else
39          {
40             days = 28; // not a leap year
41          }
42          break;
43
44        default:
45          assert(false);  // Should not get here!
46      }
47
48    return days;
49 }
```

I shall let you decide if this version is more or less clear than that in **daysThis-Month2.cpp**. Notice that the case statements do not have to be in any special order. Also note the use of break statements to jump control out of the switch body and thus avoid reassigning an incorrect value to days. This sort of jumping about can make code difficult to follow, although its use with switch statements is relatively disciplined. But be warned: Leaving out a break statement is a common error when implementing algorithms in C++.

Questions

Question 16   You have a treasure map that contains instructions like "Walk six paces north. Turn and walk 12 paces east. Then walk 7 paces north, followed by 3 paces west." Use the integers 1, 2, 3, and 4 to encode the directions north, south, east, and west. Write a switch statement that keeps track of your (*x, y*) location, measured in the non-SI unit "paces," as it is changed by one such walking instruction. The *x* axis points toward the east, and the *y* axis toward the north.

Question 17   What does the following code print on standard output?

```
int i = 4;
switch(i)
 {
  case 1:
    cout << "Huh?";
```

```
case 2:
  cout << "What?";
case 3:
  cout << "Say";
case 4:
  cout << "Uh...";
case 5:
  cout << "Eh";
default:
  cout << "_What?";
}
```

Question 18   What's wrong with the following switch statement?

```
double x = 1;
switch(x)
 {
```

```
case 1:                              case 3:
   cout << "x_is_one" << endl;          cout << "x_is_three" << endl
case 2:                              case 4:
   cout << "x_is_two" << endl;          cout << "x_is_four" << endl;
                                     }
```

Projects

Here are some selected exercises.

PROJECT 1

Write a function that takes two numbers and returns true if they are within 10^{-8} of each other, and false otherwise. Be sure to give your function a good name. You may find the fabs function, described in Appendix B, useful.

PROJECT 2

Write a function that takes three doubles and returns true if they are provided in ascending order, and false otherwise. So if called as

```
inOrder(1.0, 5.0, 1.0)
```

the function should return false, but if called as

```
inOrder(1.0, 10.0, 25.3)
```

the function should return true.

PROJECT 3

At the end of Section 3.7, I pointed out that the code **fallingBall.cpp** which I wrote to solve for the trajectory of a ball subject to gravity and air friction was defective, because of its potential division by zero. Fix this using selection, so that the sign of the velocity is computed without division by zero.

PROJECT 4

Write a code that prompts for the coefficients in the general quadratic function (with real coefficients) $f(x) = a_0 + a_1 x + a_2 x^2$, and uses the quadratic formula to report the roots back to the user. In the case of complex roots, the results should be reported as real and imaginary parts, such as $1.0 + 2.0i$. How will you deal with complex numbers, I wonder?

PROJECT 5

Write a code that prompts the user for the coefficients in the general cubic function (with real coefficients) $f(x) = a_0 + a_1 x + a_2 x^2 + a_3 x^3$, and uses the general formula for the roots of a cubic to report the roots back to the user. In the case of complex roots, the results should be reported as real and imaginary parts, such as $1.0 + 2.0i$.

PROJECT 6

The method of false position is an algorithm to find a root of a function, that is, to find r such that $f(r) = 0$. Like the bisection method, it begins with the root bracketed between two points $x \le r \le y$, in the sense that $f(x)f(y) \le 0$. The algorithm proceeds to select a point m such that $x \le m \le y$, and like the bisection method, it then reduces the interval to either $x \le r \le m$ or $m \le r \le y$, depending on the sign of $f(x)f(m)$. Although the bisection method picks $m = (x + y)/2$, the method of false position uses the function values $f(x)$ and $f(y)$ to select the value of m. In particular, m is selected to be the root of the line that passes from the point $(x, f(x))$ to the point $(y, f(y))$, as shown in the figure here.

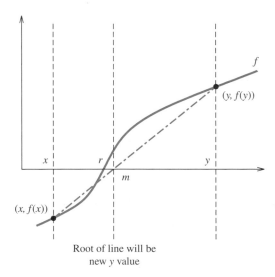

Root of line will be
new y value

Write and test a general-purpose method of false position routine for finding the roots of functions of the form double f(double).

PROJECT 7

Write functions `double MySin(double x)` and `double MyCos(double x)` that work as follows:

- For negative angles, use the fact that the cosine is even and the sine is odd to convert the argument to a positive angle.

- For angles larger than 2π, shift the angle to an equivalent one less than 2π.

- For angles x larger than $\pi/2$, relate $\cos(x)$ or $\sin(x)$ to their values in the first quadrant $0 \le x \le \pi/2$.

- For angles $\pi/4 < x \le \pi/2$, use trigonometric formulas to shift the problem to an angle no more than $\pi/4$.

- For angles less than $\pi/4$, use the series expansions

$$\cos(x) = \sum_{n=0}^{\infty} (-1)^n \frac{x^{2n}}{(2n)!}$$

$$\sin(x) = \sum_{n=0}^{\infty} (-1)^n \frac{x^{2n+1}}{(2n+1)!}$$

truncated at 8 terms.

You will find it convenient to introduce some additional functions to modularize your code.

PROJECT 8

Write a code that prompts a user for the number of pins knocked down with each ball in a standard 10 frames of bowling, and use these data to compute the player's score.

Here are the rules used to score bowling:

- Each "frame" of bowling allows the player two chances to knock down 10 pins.

- If a player knocks down less than 10 pins, then her score for that frame is the number of pins knocked down.

- But if the player knocks down all 10 pins in one frame, the scoring becomes more interesting.

There are two cases: a spare, in which the first ball knocks down fewer than 10 pins, and the second knocks down the remaining pins; and a strike, in which the first ball knocks down all 10 pins.

In either case, the score for the frame cannot be totaled until after the *next* frame is started. In the case of a spare in one frame, the score of the first ball of the *next* frame is added to the 10 points of the present frame, and the next frame is scored normally (so a spare lets the first ball of the next frame score twice). In the case of a strike, the score of the *next* two balls bowled, is added to the 10 points for the present frame, even if it takes two more frames to bowl those two balls.

Finally in the tenth frame, if you roll a spare you can bowl one extra ball in the tenth frame, and if you roll a strike, you can bowl two extra balls, in order to give the same scoring advantage to the balls of the tenth frame.

PROJECT 9

Here is an interesting way to compute π: Repeatedly generate pairs of random numbers (x, y) within the unit square, $|x| < 1$, $|y| < 1$. If the point (x, y) is inside the unit circle, score it as a hit. If S is the number of hits within the unit circle, and N is the number of tries overall (whether a hit or not), then $S/N \approx \pi/4$ (do you see why? it's a ratio of areas). The approximation tends to become more accurate as $N \to \infty$. Write a code that uses this method to compute an estimate to π; make sure you prompt for the number of trials N, and try several values of N.

PROJECT 10

Light is made up of particles known as photons. Photons move in straight lines through matter, except that every so often, at random, they scatter off of an atom and change their direction. We will perform a simplified simulation of this in which photons always stay in the (x, y) plane, and in which, when they scatter, they move off at any angle with equal probability (this is a gross simplification).

You will simulate a beam of light entering a slab of matter from the left, and compute:

1. The fraction of photons that are reflected (by exiting back through the left surface)

2. The fraction that are transmitted (by exiting through the right surface)

3. The average number of scatters per photon

4. The average of the y locations at which a photon exits the slab on the right, and the standard deviation of this

Your code will simulate the motion of a large number of individual photons. During a photon's travels, you will know its location (x, y) and direction θ of travel (measured anticlockwise with respect to the x axis). Every photon will be created at $(x, y) = (0, 0)$ and initially travel to the right at an angle of $\theta = 0$. The following figure shows the path of a single photon from birth to exit.

To compute the (random) distance d that a photon travels along the straight line from (x, y) at angle θ, you must simply generate a random number $0 < \xi \leq 1$, and then the distance d to the next scatter is

$$d = -\ln(\xi).$$

Knowing the distance d the photon will go, its direction of travel θ, and its starting point (x, y), you can easily compute the next point at which it will scatter (x', y'). Its new direction after that scatter will be an angle θ' randomly generated between zero and 2π.

Every photon will be created at $(x, y) = (0, 0)$ and travel to the right at an angle of $\theta = 0$. From this you can generate the photon's next location (x', y') and direction θ', as just described. Then from this you can generate its *next* location and direction, and so on. Every time you generate a new angle, the photon has scattered. If the photon leaves the slab to the right (x becomes greater than t), we will call it "transmitted." If it leaves to the left (x becomes smaller than zero), we will call it "reflected."

As soon as a photon is either reflected or transmitted, we are done with it, and can run a new photon. The number of photons to run and the thickness of the slab must be input to your code.

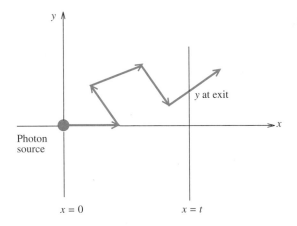

A photon that scatters four times in a slab of thickness t, and is then transmitted through the right-hand side of the slab.

CHAPTER 5

DEALING WITH DATA

WE HAVE dealt with the key issues of organizing algorithms, and now need to devote a few chapters to thinking about how to organize our data. There are really two issues here: how will we organize our data in a way that makes our algorithms clear and efficient, and how the information we want to transform may be mapped to some form that the computer can actually manipulate.

In the previous chapters we have paid scant attention to data types. We have used integers, real numbers, and Boolean values when needed, and on occasion we used literal strings to make output more user friendly. Now we will take a few pages to explore some additional data types, including unsigned integers, characters, floats (double's little cousin), and strings, and start to consider more complex data organization techniques.

5.1 ENCODING AND TYPES

When we write algorithms, we want to think about the information we will transform at a high and abstract level. But in the end, this data must actually be mapped to some physical realization when the algorithm executes on the computer. Generally, it's the job of the compiler and the CPU to manage this mapping of abstract information to some physical reality, and we need give it little thought when writing our own algorithms. But the details of such mappings are now partially exposed in the language of the information age in words like "bit" and "byte." I will briefly present the idea here to provide an illustration of the idea of encoding, and I will return to the topic in Chapter 8, where the encoding of information in a finite computer will be seen to lead to some limitations on what the computer can do.

Information is, in some way, always abstract. I note that it is August; this has meaning because of the associations that it conjures up in your mind. August implies the eighth month, the height of summer in the Northern Hemisphere, a span of time named after the Roman Emperor Augustus. My understanding of August is always based on connecting it with other information; these associations are actually rather slippery, but the human mind is apparently well suited to this mapping of ideas to ideas. But now, to manipulate information in a physical device, we must somehow connect our ideas to the state of a physical device.

The digital computer, internally, deals with bits. These are simple binary values; a bit can take on one, or another, of two possible states. Quite frankly, we do not care what those two "states" are. We often represent them as 0 and 1, but just as often we speak of false and true. This is already an encoding. Zero or one, false or true; neither reveals to us the physical means by which these binary values are stored deep in the guts of the machine. They are just logical representations of how some circuit is set; it can be set this way, or that, and we encode these in our minds as 0 or 1.

Bits are usually organized into groups of 4 bits, called a nybble, and into groups of 8 bits, called a byte. So, here are some bytes:

```
00000000
00000001
00000011
00000111
00001111
00011111
```

The computer can store these patterns for us because, for example, it is loaded with numerous capacitors that can store charge (1) or not store charge (0). A running computer's memory is full of these 8-bit patterns; they were written there by various programs to encode the information that those programs want to manipulate. So if you look at a section of computer memory, and decode the physical reality into bits, you will see something really useless, like this:

```
01001000 00001110 00111111 11101010 00011010 11100011 ...
```

But what do all these zeros and ones hidden in the innards of a computer mean? They mean whatever the programmer who wrote them wants. For example, here is a meaning that I could choose for some byte patterns:

This pattern	*Means*
00000000	A
00000001	stitch
00000011	in
00000111	time
00001111	saves
00011111	nine

This mapping between a pattern of bits and a meaning is an encoding.

Definition

An *encoding* is a one-to-one mapping between two sets of symbols.

It is seldom useful to make up a new encoding for simple data types. When you make up your own encoding, you must expend a great deal of effort just managing the mapping of data to and from your encoding. In general, for commonly used things like letters and numbers there are *standard* encodings, encodings that have been agreed on as reasonable, and for which supporting software and hardware exist. This support is so complete that we seldom even think about the encoding of basic data such as numbers and letters; it is well hidden from us.

Some encodings can be very systematic: Nonnegative integers can be encoded by writing their base 2 representation. Other encodings must be more arbitrary: The encoding of an alphabet requires mapping letters to bit patterns, and there is no inevitable mapping. One standard mapping of characters to bit patterns is ASCII encoding, part of which is

The 8 bits	Encode as the character
01000001	'A'
01100001	'a'
01000010	'B'
01100010	'b'
00110001	'1'

Note that in any such encoding, we can always interpret the bit pattern as an unsigned integer, written in base 2 place-value notation. With such an interpretation, we see that 'A' has been mapped to 65, 'B' to 66, and so on. While this orderly progression would seem logical, it is not inevitable, and not all encodings of characters enjoy it. Even this encoding maps 'A' somewhat mysteriously to 65. Why not 13, or 129? It was simply a choice. Note most importantly that the character '1' is not mapped to the integer 1; it is mapped to a bit pattern that can also be read as the integer 49. This too was simply a choice that has now become standardized.

So far in this text we have mostly worked with two data types: int and double. But we also have worked with some other types: cin is actually a variable of type istream, and cout and cerr are variables of type ostream. But what is a data type?

Definition

> A *type* consists of an encoding of information to the underlying computer and a set of allowed operations on that information.

Consider a double; there is some mapping of numbers to bit patterns (which we will explore more fully in Chapter 8), and there are allowed operations on those data like +, *, /, <=, and so on. Similarly, data of type istream must keep track of some information related to its function, and this information is mapped to some bit pattern in the machine. Further, the type supports a set of operations like << and istream.fail().

The benefits of data types are both practical and aesthetic. By selecting a data type that matches our needs, we can obtain a more efficient (in both time and storage space) means to our end. A double can be used to count, but an int is specialized for this purpose, and it probably is faster and uses less space. Also, selecting a data type that matches needs makes the purpose of that data more clear, so that the code is easier to understand. Further, a well-designed data type may provide operations that produce quite complex effects in a simple expression. This may allow an algorithm to explicitly show its high-level behavior while hiding complex details. To make these notions more clear, we will exploit several data types in this chapter, and explore the various ways that operations on those data can be expressed in C++.

Questions

Question 1   As you can easily confirm, there are 2^N unique arrangements of N bits. How many numbers can I encode using 8 bits? If I want to encode 12 different things into bit patterns, what's the fewest number of bits I need?

Question 2   Do some research and find out what integer is equivalent to `'Z'` in ASCII. Now find out what integer is equivalent to `'Z'` in EBCDIC (also known as *extended binary coded decimal interchange code*).

5.2   NUMERIC TYPES REVISITED

We have already used the numeric types `int` and `double` in all of our algorithmic implementations. It is worth taking a few pages to describe some related numerical types and their uses, as we might explore them presently. Each of these types encodes a particular subset of the real numbers, and provides a basic set of operations on them, including the fundamental four (+, -, *, /) and relational operators.

5.2.1   Integer Types

We have already met `int`. This is the C++ data type that is designed to hold signed integer values. A compiler, when it compiles our C++ source text into machine instructions, must choose how to implement this data type using the capabilities of the CPU that will execute our code. CPUs have a native integer data type on which they can operate very quickly, and it is often this native integer type that is used by a compiler to implement `int`. For this reason, many software designers will use `int` for a data type unless there is a very clear and compelling reason to do otherwise.

However, the C++ language defines several other *integral types*. We shall not explore all of these, but will take up the study of only four: `int`, `unsigned int`, `char`, and `bool`.

Unsigned Integers   An `unsigned int` is rather like an `int`, but it is, would you believe, unsigned. An `unsigned int` variable can be used to store nonnegative integer values only. Why should we have such a type? One advantage of an `unsigned int` over a regular `int` is that it can usually store larger values. Because the implementation of an `unsigned int` does not need to store information about the sign, it can typically be twice as large as the largest `int` value. However, another reason to use unsigned integers is simply to make some intention more clear. If the purpose of a data value is to contain a count of something, then it can't be negative, and an `unsigned int` expresses this intention more clearly. However, despite this sound philosophical argument, too few who implement code in C++ use an `unsigned int` when counting. Too many stick to `int`, mostly by tradition, and perhaps also in the belief that `int`'s are faster.[1]

---

[1]Which might not be so; it really depends on the computer architecture. In any event, as Knuth says, "Premature optimization is the root of all evil."

Characters   A char is a small integral type that requires 1 byte of storage.[2] Although a char is an integer, its standard use is to store a single character (hence its suggestive name). This use to store characters depends on an implied mapping between integers and characters, and such a mapping must be selected by the compiler implementer. The C++ language does *not* specify any particular mapping between characters and the integer values that can be stored in a char. The only restriction made is that the integer value zero cannot be mapped to any character (this allows zero to be used to represent a sort of noncharacter, called null, when it must be named). Many compilers and operating systems use a mapping known as ASCII, but there certainly are computers/compilers/operating systems that do not use the ASCII mapping of characters to char.

C++ therefore provides a special way to write literal char values. A character placed in single quotes is interpreted as an integer value of type char. So the following declares and stores a character:

```
char c = 'A';
```

It's possible that 'A' means 65, but who cares? Unless there is a clear and compelling reason not to, we just use the more readable 'A' and let the compiler do its job of mapping this character to an integer value. The >> and << operators read and write char values as characters, automatically converting the character to or from the associated integer value. So cin >> c causes execution to wait for the human to type in (at least) one character, which it gets, converts to the corresponding integer, and stores in the char c. But there is a small wrinkle with this: By default cin, indeed all istream's, ignore whitespace.

Definition

> *Whitespace* characters are characters that produce only space, and no other visual evidence of their presence. Often they include spaces, tabs, and newline characters.

Consider, for example, this code, which is supposed to echo characters to the screen, with each character surrounded by vertical bars ||.

getChars.cpp

```
1  // =============================================================
2  // getChars.cpp
3  // Echo characters from standard input to standard output,
4  // ignoring whitespace, until a 'q' is seen.
5  // =============================================================
6  #include <iostream>
7  using namespace std;
8
```

---

[2]Typically 8 bits, but in the C++ standard the word byte does not have this now conventional meaning. Rather, "byte" is defined to be however much space a char takes up.

```
9   // ===========================> main <=============================
10  int main(void)
11  {
12    char c;
13    cin >> c;
14    while( (not cin.fail()) and (c != 'q') ) // quit if q
15    {
16      cout << "|" << c << "|"; // write |c|
17      cin >> c;
18    }
19  }
```

```
1  [hagar@localhost CodeScraps]$ ./getChar
2  abcd    efg    hij    q
3  |a||b||c||d||e||f||g||h||i||j|[hagar@localhost CodeScraps]$
```

The spaces in my input (between d and e, between g and h, and between j and q) do not appear in the output. A newline character would be similarly ignored. This behavior can be changed by calling the function `cin.unsetf(ios::skipws)`. This will cause `cin` to deliver whitespace characters in the stream, rather than ignore them. In contrast, calling `cin.setf(ios::skipws)` will cause `cin` to once again skip them. These functions are described in Appendix B.

Another issue, that is not new to us, but which becomes more obvious with character input, is that the execution of this code clearly halts until the user presses the enter key at the end of each input line. This is not C++. It is the operating system that holds up input until the user presses the enter key. This delay is an operating system service intended to allow us to edit the input line before it is sent to the waiting program. This behavior too can be changed, but that is an operating system issue, not a C++ issue, and there is no standard (operating-system-independent) way to address it in C++.

Boolean Values   The data type `bool` is designed to store only the Boolean values `true` and `false`. These are not strictly integral types, but values of type `bool` are converted to and from values of type `int` at the drop of a hat. If used where an integer makes sense, a value of `true` is converted to 1 and a value of `false` is converted to 0. Similarly, if used where a value of type `bool` is expected, a nonzero integer value is converted to `true` and a zero integer value is converted to `false`. So I can write

```
bool a = 10; // a == true
```

and

```
bool b = 0; // a == false
```

The values `true` and `false` are preferred, because they make the meaning more clear.

Limits   Information about the representation of integer types can be found using the code declared in the header file `limits`. This file defines the data objects

```
numeric_limits<int>,
numeric_limits<char>
```

and

```
numeric_limits<unsigned int>,
```

which provide functions that return information about the corresponding data types. Complete documentation can be found in the C++ standard, but the following code illustrates some of the information available about the integer types:

integerLimits.cpp

```
1   // ================================================================
2   // integerLimits.cpp
3   // Report some basic information on an implementation's
4   // integer types
5   // ================================================================
6   #include <iostream>
7   #include <limits>
8   #include <cstdlib>
9   using namespace std;
10
11  int main()
12  {
13    numeric_limits<int> intLimits; // Declare numeric_limits
14                                   // object. It is initialized
15                                   // automatically
16    numeric_limits<unsigned int> uintLimits;
17
18
19    cout << "Integer information" << endl;
20    cout << "Maximum integer: " << intLimits.max() << endl;
21    cout << "Minimum integer: " << intLimits.min() << endl;
22    cout << "Maximum unsigned integer: " << uintLimits.max()
23         << endl;
24    cout << "Minimum unsigned integer: " << uintLimits.min()
25         << endl;
26
27    return EXIT_SUCCESS;
28  }
```

Note that declaring a numeric_limits object causes it to be automatically initialized. This is one of those annoying inconsistencies in C++; some things are automatically initialized, and some are not. The use of intLimits should remind you of cin; there are functions whose names contain periods. I shall speak more of these later in this chapter. Here is the output of the **integerLimits.cpp** code on a 32-bit workstation. Note that, for this machine and its compiler, the largest unsigned int is one larger than twice the largest int value.

```
1  jplug$ ./integerLimits
2  Integer information
3  Maximum integer: 2147483647
4  Minimum integer: -2147483648
5  Maximum unsigned integer: 4294967295
6  Minimum unsigned integer: 0
7  jplug$
```

5.2.2 Floating Point Types

Floating point numbers are a means to approximately represent some real numbers within the finite storage of the computer. As you know, there are an infinite number of real numbers. Indeed, there are an infinite number of real numbers just between zero and 1. It is therefore not possible to represent all real numbers, or even a finite range of all real numbers, on a machine designed for finite execution (i.e., a computer). Instead, we must represent only a finite subset of the real numbers, and live with the inherent approximations this implies. We shall study this issue more thoroughly in Chapter 8. For the moment I shall mention and explore only two types: `float` and `double`.

These two types are designed to represent real numbers with a large but finite range of magnitudes and a finite number of digits of precision. Since the numbers are generally represented using base 2, it is not possible to exactly specify a number of decimal digits being represented. Furthermore, the limits that do exist on the floating point types are not thoroughly specified by the C++ standard. The standard says that a float will use at least 4 bytes, and that a double will use at least 8 bytes. This expresses the intent that a `double` will be more precise and allow a larger range of magnitudes than a `float`, but this is not a requirement of the standard. The standard allows a `float` to be exactly the same as a `double`![3]

Information on the floating point and integer representations can be found from the data objects declared in the `limits` header file. The very interesting-looking function call `numeric_limits<double>::max()` will return the largest number that can be represented by the data type `double`, and `numeric_limits<double>::min()` will return the smallest number that can be represented. Similar calls, replacing `double` by `float`, will provide this information for the `float` type, and similarly for `int` and `unsigned int`.

5.2.3 Type Conversions

I have previously described the integer division operator /, and the floating point division operator /, and remarked that since the same symbol is used for both, the compiler must determine by context which operator is called for. This it does by looking at the types of the operands. If both are integers, then integer division is called for. If both are

---

[3]This is not an oversight. Different computers efficiently support different floating point capabilities, and forcing a particular floating point representation, as is done, for example, in Java, can be very inefficient.

floating point, then floating point division is called for. But what if one is an integer and the other is a floating point datum?

C++ Principle

> When a binary operator is used with numeric operands of different types, the data are converted to a common type before the operand acts, and its result will be of that common type.

The conversion rules are, in part,

1. If either operand is of type `double`, then the other operand is converted to a `double` representing the same numeric value (if possible).

2. Otherwise, if either operand is of type `float`, then the other operand is converted to a `float` representing the same numeric value (if possible).

3. Otherwise, if either operand is of type `unsigned int`, then the other operand is converted to an `unsigned int` representing the same numeric value (if possible).

The conversion of one numeric type to another also occurs if a value of one type is assigned to an identifier that was declared to store the other. This conversion is done without changing the numerical value *if possible*. But sometimes it is impossible to convert between types without a loss of information, for example:

```
1   double a = -1.8345;
2   float b = 1.0e16;
3   int c = -100;
4   unsigned int d = 10;
5
6   // all the following assignments result in a change or loss of
7   // information
8   c = a; // double assigned to int -- fraction lost, c stores -1
9   d = c; // negative int assigned to unsigned int -- problem
10  c = b; // large float assigned to int -- may fail
```

C++ Principle

> When a floating point type is assigned to an integer, the fractional part is always thrown away (no rounding occurs — the fraction is simply left off). If the floating point value is too large in magnitude, the conversion is undefined.

This often allows us to remove the fractional part of a number simply by assigning it to an `int` variable. The reverse conversion is also common:

C++ Principle

> When an integer type is assigned to a floating point type, the result is exact if possible. Otherwise, the integer is converted to either the next lower or next higher possible floating point value.

I will not discuss the semantics of other problematic conversions, but such conversions can also occur if one numeric type is passed into a function that expects a different numeric type, provided the compiler can unambiguously determine an appropriate conversion.

Conversions from one data type to another can also be controlled explicitly using a static_cast operator.

C++ Principle

The expression

    static_cast<T>(expression)

causes expression to be evaluated and that value to be converted to type T, if the conversion is defined.

So in

```
1   int i = 1;
2   int j = 2;
3   double x = i/j; // x = 0
4   double y = static_cast<double>(i)/static_cast<double>(j);
5                                          // y = 0.5
6   double z = static_cast<double>(i)/j;  // z = 0.5
```

x is zero because i/j on line 3 involves integer division, but y and z are 0.5 because / on both lines 4 and 6 involves floating point division. Using the static_cast operator may be verbose, but it is usually better to clearly proclaim "I am changing my mind" than it is to silently hope the compiler reads it as intended.

Questions

Question 3   What data types would you consider using to store each of the following quantities:

a.   The number of kilowatts used by a factory

b.   The number of machine screws in stock

c.   The mass of an 87, 000-kilogram airplane

Question 4   Time is designated in a simulation as $i\Delta t$, where i is an integer. What type would you use for i? Briefly explain.

Question 5   Given the following declarations, identify the type of each expression:

```
double x = 2.0;
double y = sqrt(x);
int i = 2;
int j = sqrt(i);
```

a.   x + i

b.   x * y + i

c.   j / i

d.   i / x

e.   j - i

5.3   CONSTANTS AND ALIASES

Besides the basic numeric data types described above, C++ provides a means for introducing an identifier that is an alias of an already existing one. It also provides a way to say that the data designated by an identifier cannot be changed using that identifier. These introduce new data types that are directly related to the basic types, but distinct from them.

5.3.1 Making Data Constant

I have often referred to identifiers as "variables," reflecting the notion that an identifier attached to a data container provides a means to model the mathematical notion of a variable, a symbol that takes on a changeable value. But some quantities just can't change. The ratio of a circle's diameter to its circumference, the base of the natural logarithm (also called the Euler number), and the number of frames in a game of tournament bowling—all are constants. Therefore, it is often useful to note that a piece of data in an algorithm cannot be changed by that algorithm. In C++ we can express this with the type qualifier `const`. Prepending this to any of the simple variable declarations affirms the following for the compiler: The declared identifier cannot be used to change the associated data value.

C++ Principle

A declaration of the form

```
const T name = expression;
```

declares and defines an identifier `name` for a data container holding constant data of type `T`, and places the value of `expression` into it. The data stored under `name` cannot later be changed.

After such a declaration the compiler will not allow any statement that appears to change the value stored under the identifier `name`. The data stored in such a data container must therefore be initialized in the declaration, since it won't be possible to do this later. Thus in

```
1  const int binaryBase = 2;
2  const double pi = 2.0 * atan2(1.0, 0.0);
3
4  binaryBase = 3;
5  pi = 2.0;
```

both boxed lines of code attempt to assign values to constants, and the compiler will not permit this.

While it is seldom strictly necessary to declare data to be `const`, it is a very good idea.

Claim

If a datum should not be changed, declare it `const`.

This makes it clear to your readers that this data is special, and it will allow the compiler to catch accidents later, like when you mistakenly try to change monthsInYear from 12 to 52.

5.3.2   References

A reference allows us to introduce into our source text a new identifier that is an alias for some already existing and identified data. We have discussed references already in Chapter 2, in our description of procedures that can change the values of variables in their calling environment. But we can also create a reference in a declaration statement.

C++ Principle

A declaration with initialization of the form

```
T & name = other_name;
```

makes name a synonym for the identifier other_name, which must have already been declared and be of type T.

A reference is not like the variables that we have thus far declared. A reference does not identify a data container of its own, but rather it refers to an existing data container. If a variable is a box with a name, a reference is just another name for that same box. And because it must refer to an existing container, a reference *must* be initialized when it is declared, rather like an identifier that is declared const. Also like a const identifier, once a reference is initialized, it can never be changed.

The code

```
1   int i = 10;
2   int j = 5;
3   int & eye = i; // eye is a synonym for i
4
5   cout << i << endl;
6   cout << eye << endl;   // does the same thing
7   eye = j;
8   cout << i << endl;     // i is now 5
```

illustrates the use of a reference. It also makes you wonder what good they are, since eye is just another way to say i.

The most common use for references is certainly as procedure parameters, where they give us a means to pass a reference to a variable in the caller's environment into a command. When we declare an identifier to be a reference in the formal argument list of a routine, we say that the identifier is *pass by reference*; this distinguishes it from the *pass by value* behavior in which it is a data value that is copied and passed into the routine. A pass by reference argument, by contrast, provides to the routine an alternate name for a data container in the routine's caller.

Suppose we have data values stored in a and b, and want to make sure that a does not contain the larger of the two values. Code to do so could be written like this:

```
1   double a = 6.0e2;
2   double b = 100.0 * atan2(1.0,0.0);
3
4   // make sure b does not hold the smaller of the two
5   if (b < a)
6     {
7       double tmp = b; // save b for a moment
8       b = a;          // put bigger into b
9       a = tmp;        // put smaller into a
10    }
11
12  // now a and b are ordered
13  cout << "The interval is from " << a << " to " << b << endl;
```

The selection statement that is used to reorder a and b, when necessary, is going to be somewhat out of place. It won't be the heart of whatever algorithm is being written, so it really should be wrapped up in a procedure. A procedure to do so must use references to a and b in order to effect the swap of these values in its caller. A procedure to do so would look like:

orderPairDouble.cpp

```
1   void orderPairDouble(double & first, double & second)
2   {
3     if (second < first)
4       {
5         double tmp = second; // save second for a moment
6         second = first;      // put bigger into second
7         first = tmp;         // put smaller into first
8       }
9   }
```

and the original code can now look like this:

```
1   double a = 6.0e2;
2   double b = 100.0 * atan2(1.0,0.0);
3
4   // now a and b are ordered
5   orderPairDouble(a,b);
6
7   cout << "The interval is from " << a << " to " << b << endl;
```

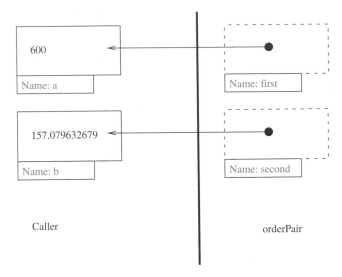

FIGURE 5.1 Pass by reference parameters to a procedure allow the procedure to directly access data containers in its caller. The reference variables do not contain their own data; rather, they are identifiers that refer to other data containers.

The procedure **orderPairDouble** works by manipulating data *in its caller*. It can do this because its caller provided it with references to a and b. Figure 5.1 suggests this interaction.

Since references can't be changed after they are created, the question naturally arises as to what `const` might mean for a reference. What meaning would you choose for `const int & i`?

Declaring a reference variable to be `const` means that the data being referenced cannot be changed through the alias, so

```
1   const int binaryBase = 2;      // can't change binaryBase
2   const int & i = binaryBase;    // can't change binaryBase using i
3   int & j = binaryBase;          // Not allowed, binaryBase is const
4
5   double pi = 2.0 * atan2(1.0, 0.0);    // pi not const
6   const double & piref = pi;            // ok
7
8   piref = 1.0;                   // not allowed, piref is const
9   pi = 1.0;                      // allowed (but not ok)
```

Such constant references are often used in function and procedure parameter lists to provide the routine with access to data in its caller's environment, while simultaneously forbidding any change to that data. It's as though you let me into your apartment to read your writings on the walls, but you frisk me and take away any pens before I enter, so that I won't add writings of my own. This `const` reference mechanism allows us to create functions that do look into their caller's environment, but only look. This gives us a way to avoid copying large amounts of data from the caller into a function or procedure. We shall see examples of this soon enough.

Questions

Question 6 What, if anything, does each of the following snatches of code write to standard output?

a.
```
double vth = 0.0;
double & v = vth;
vth = 2200.0;
cout << v;
```
b.
```
int i = 6;
int & j = i;
int & k = j;
```
```
k = 10;
cout << i;
```
c.
```
const int i = 6;
int & j = i;
j = 10;
cout << i;
```

Question 7 Suppose I have written a wonderful chunk of code to write data into an ostream called output. There are over 100 lines of the sort output << data;, but now I want to send all that data to standard output instead. What one line of code will accomplish the deed?

5.4 SCOPE AND LIFETIME

One more basic data management idea is worth a brief discussion. Every named object, be it data, a function, or a routine, has a scope and a lifetime.

Definition

> The *scope* of an identifier is the textual context in a source text within which it is semantically meaningful to refer to that identifier.

This is a purely static idea. When we write a program in C++, we create a static text that declares and then refers to various identifiers. There are only certain places within this text where we can refer to the identifiers we declare.

Let me introduce you to a scope:

C++ Principle

> An identifier declared within a compound statement has *local scope*. The identifier is in scope from its point of declaration to the end of the enclosing compound statement, unless it is hidden by an identical identifier in an enclosed compound statement. A function parameter is in local scope starting at the beginning of its function body.

You will recall that a compound statement starts with a { and ends with a }. So in the function

```
1   void f(double x)
2   {
3     int i = 1;
4     cout << i << "␣";
5     int j = 2;
6     cout << j << endl;
```

```
7      cout << x << endl;
8    }
```

i and j have local scope, because they are declared and defined in the compound statement that is the body of the function. The identifier x also has local scope, from the start
of the function body until its end.

The notion of hiding an object may not be immediately apparent. Consider the
following code:

```
1    int i = 1;
2    cout << i << "␣";
3    int i = 2; // No can do!
4    cout << i << endl;
```

This will not compile because the identifier is declared and defined twice within the
same block of code—an identifier can be defined only *once* within a given compound
statement. But the following code is valid:

```
1    int i = 1;
2    {
3      cout << i << "␣";    // i = 1
4      int i = 2;          // Ok.
5      cout << i << endl;  // i = 2
6    }
```

and this will write 1 2 to standard output. On line 3 the identifier i refers to the data
object i declared on line 1. But on line 4 the identifier i is again declared and defined,
but within the compound statement. The declaration on line 4 is valid, but the identifier
i so introduced is different from, and hides, the identifier i declared on line 1. From
its declaration on line 4 until the end of the enclosing compound statement, i hides i.
If you feel confused by this, you should be: It's confusing. And therefore, you should
never write code like this.[4]

Global Constants   Most of the variables we have worked with have had local
scope, but occasionally we need to define variables that have a much bigger scope.
So with some trepidation I introduce the dangerous notion of an identifier with global
scope. We have, in fact, already seen some of these: When we declare functions and procedures, we are actually introducing identifiers—the function and procedure names—
that are in scope anywhere from their point of declaration to the end of the file where
they are declared.

---

[4]Just because the language allows you to do something, doesn't mean it's a good idea to do it. This ability
to hide one identifier with another is a horrible and strange vestigial language design "feature" from the
1960s. Let it lie.

But I will introduce one more genus of this sort of creature, a constant with file scope. Suppose I want various routines in my code to have access to some useful constants like π, e, and the charge on the electron in Coulombs. Rather than repeat these values in every routine that might have need for them, I can introduce them as identifiers whose scope is the point of declaration to the end of the code file. Consider the following example:

globalConst.cpp

```
1   // ================================================================
2   // globalConst.cpp
3   // Demonstrates some global constants
4   // ================================================================
5   #include <cmath>
6   #include <iostream>
7   using namespace std;
8
9   const double qElectron = 1.9e-19; // charge on electron
10  const double pi = 2.0 * atan2(1.0, 0.0);
11  const double e = exp(1.0);
12
13  int main()
14  {
15    cout << "pi␣=␣" << pi << endl;
16    cout << "e␣=␣" << e << endl;
17    cout << "q␣=␣" << qElectron << endl;
18  }
```

In this code the identifiers pi, e and qElectron are in scope from their point of declaration to the end of the file **globalConst.cpp** in which they are declared. So even though these identifiers are not declared in main, they are within scope in main, and can be referred to there. Their lifetime is the entire life of the code, from birth to death.

Consider the following source file:

massEnergy.cpp

```
1   // ================================================================
2   // massEnergy.cpp
3   // Computes energy of particles
4   // ================================================================
5   #include <iostream>
6   #include <cmath>
7   #include <cstdlib>
8   using namespace std;
9
10  // Global namespace variable -- better be const!
11  const double c = 299792458.0; // speed of light [m/s]
```

```
12
13    // Function declarations ========================================
14    double restEnergy(double m);
15    double energy(double p, double m);
16    void getValidDouble(double min, double max, double & value);
17
18    // ======================>> main <<============================
19    int main()
20    {
21      const double maxMass = 1.0e53; // mass of universe [kg]
22      const double maxP = maxMass * c; // largest momentum [kg m/s]
23
24      cout << "Input_particle_mass_(kg)>_";
25      double mass;
26      getValidDouble(0.0, maxMass, mass);
27
28      cout << "Input_particle_momentum_(kg_m/s)>_";
29      double p;
30      getValidDouble(-maxP, maxP, p);
31
32      cout << "The_rest_mass_energy_of_that_particle_is:_";
33      cout << restEnergy(mass) << "_(J)" << endl;
34
35      cout << "The_total_energy_of_that_particle_is:_";
36      cout << energy(p, mass) << "_(J)" << endl;
37
38      return EXIT_SUCCESS;
39    }
40
41    // ======================>> restEnergy <<========================
42    // compute the rest mass energy of m in SI units
43    // ==============================================================
44    double restEnergy(double m)
45    {
46      return energy(0.0, m);
47    }
48
49    // ======================>> energy <<============================
50    // compute the total energy of particle with mass m and
51    // momentum p, all in SI units.
52    // ==============================================================
53    double energy(double p, double m)
54    {
55      return sqrt(m * m * pow(c, 4) + p * p * c * c);
56                                              // relativity rules!
57    }
```

This code introduces several identifiers, including `restEnergy`, `energy`, `getValidDouble`, and `main`, with *global scope*.[5] These identifiers can be referred to any place from their point of declaration to the end of this file. Even things like `cin` and `cout` have global namespace scope, since they are declared in `iostream`. However, the identifier `maxP` has *local scope* (sometimes called block scope). It can be referred to only within the compound statement—the body of `main`—within which it is defined; more precisely, it can be referred to from its point of declaration to the end of the enclosing compound statement. Variables like `m` and `p`, declared as parameters in the function definitions of `restEnergy` and `energy`, have *local scope*; they are implicitly declared (and initialized) at the top of the function body. They can be referred to any place within, and only within, the body of the function where they are defined.

For Loop Scope   There is one interesting special case of scope of a variable that is worth knowing about. In the statement

```
1   for(int i = 0; i < 10; i = i + 1)
2     {
3       cout << i << endl;
4     }
5   cout << i << endl; // no good -- i is not in scope
```

the identifier `i` has scope only within the for loop body and within its controlling condition and iteration statement. The framed line of code therefore is not referring to the index `i` of the for loop.[6]

Lifetime   Scope is a static shadow of the dynamic property of lifetime.

Definition

> A variable's *lifetime* is the span of time along an algorithm's thread of execution during which the variable's value can be read or written.

The lifetime of a data object begins when storage is allocated for it, and it ends when that storage is released for use by another data object. As a consequence, trying to refer to a datum after its lifetime has ended will lead to strange and unfortunate results, because the storage that was associated with it might have been reused for something else. For parameters (other than references) of a function or procedure, the lifetime starts when the function is called and the parameters are implicitly initialized, and it ends when the function or procedure returns to its caller. Similarly, for variables declared in a compound statement their lifetime begins when (and only if) the appropriate declaration is reached, and it ends when the execution of the enclosing compound statement is done. Thus in

---

[5] Actually called global namespace scope in the C++ standard.
[6] Although the C++ standard defines this for loop scope, some C++ compilers do not strictly enforce it.

```
1  int i;
2  cin >> i; // get a value for i
3
4  {
5    int j = 2;
6    if ( i == 3 )
7      {
8        int k = 4;
9      }
10  }
```

the lifetime of i will follow execution from line 1 until sometime after line 10. But j, with block scope, will come into existence at line 5 and its life will end at line 10. And k will have no lifetime at all, unless i == 3 is true. Thus, on one execution of this section of code, k might have a finite lifetime, but on another execution it might never even come into existence.

Questions

Question 8   Why does the compiler complain about the following code:

```
int i = 2 * j;
int j = 4;
```

Question 9   What are your thoughts on the following loop, intended to compute the sum of the squares of the first 10 integers:

```
int i = 0;
int sq = 0;
while(i < 10)
  {
    int sq = sq + i * i;
```

```
  }
cout << sq;
```

Question 10   What is wrong with this code?

```
int sum = 0;
for(int i = 1; i <= 10; i = i + 1)
  {
    sum = sum + i;
  }
cout << "The_sum_of_the_first_" << i
     << "_integers_is_" << sum << endl;
```

5.5   DATA OBJECTS

The data types that I have described so far are all relatively obvious in their purpose—there are numbers, there are characters (even if in C++ they are integers in disguise), there are Boolean values. But we have also been using other data types for some time, and with little comment: Both cin and cout are, in fact, global variables, whose types are istream and ostream, respectively. The istream and ostream types are not part of the C++ language; rather, they are defined *using* the language. C++ is called an *object oriented programming language* in part because it allows such complicated data types to be defined, constructed, and manipulated within the language itself, without the language designers' knowledge or assent. We will not extensively explore object-oriented programming in this book, but we will use its fruits. It is therefore appropriate to expose some of its terminology and semantics, and its syntax within

C++. We will do so here, and then later in Chapter 7 we will delve into this subject just a bit more deeply.

The numeric data types are called fundamental types, and these, along with a few other fundamental data types, can be assembled by the programmer into various compound types. There are several kinds of compound data in C++, but among these the *class* stands out. A class provides a means to declare an object whose semantics are defined by the programmer, rather than by the designers of the C++ language. This is no mean feat; the language offers a means for you to define an object that the language designers never even imagined. The language is thus, in a disciplined way, extensible. These programmer-defined objects are more than mere bags of basic data. When we define a class, we define not only data, but also the operations allowed on those data. Such a programmer-defined assembly of data and its allowed operations are called a class.

Definition

A *class* is a compound data structure made up of fundamental data, and even other compound data, combined with a set of allowed operations. The internal data objects in a class are called its data members, and the allowed operations are called its methods.

The word *object* is sometimes used as a synonym for "class," but it is more often used more broadly, and somewhat subtly, to mean any actual data of a specific type, so in `int i;` we call `i` an object because it is a specific realization of an `int`.

An object is declared just like any of the fundamental data types, but because an object can contain complex internal data, its declaration often includes a simultaneous procedure call to initialize this internal state. In C++ this special procedure is called a constructor.

C++ Principle

If `T` is a class, then an object `x` of type `T` is often declared as

```
T x(argument_list);
```

where `argument_list` is a comma-separated argument list as would appear in a function call.

We have used this sort of declaration already in constructing `ifstream` and `ofstream` objects, like `ofstream output("results.dat");`. In an attempt to be uniform in its declaration syntax C++ also allows such initialization for fundamental data objects, as in `int i(0);`, which does the same thing as `int i = 0;`. We shall see another concrete example of this in the next section when the `string` class is introduced.

A programmer-defined data type must define some ways to manipulate itself; otherwise, it is of little use. A class can therefore define methods that look like functions and procedures, and it can also define methods that are operators. To access method routines, a special syntax is used. This syntax is founded on the member selection operator, which looks like a period. If object `x` has a member named `m`, then we access it with the syntax `x.m`. We have seen this already in calls like `cin.fail()`, which calls a function that looks at the state of the variable `cin`.

C++ Principle

Class methods can be called using the member selection operator `.` (period). In the syntax `x.fun(argument_list)` the member function or procedure `fun` has direct access to the internal data of object `x`.

This access is one of the primary advantages to introducing a special syntax for member routines. This special syntax is not strictly necessary (the language could have been defined without it), but it serves to emphasize the connection between the member routine and the data upon which it acts, and it makes the syntax for calling a member routine uniform.

Those who create a class must organize its internal data according to some carefully crafted design—they must establish the encoding of information into a form the computer can manipulate. All use of the class must then employ a publicly provided interface designed for the purpose. All member routines are defined along with the class, and are fully privy to the implementation details of the class, so they can provide the interface for those of us who use the class. Operators, such as + and <, can also be defined to act on programmer-defined classes, and may again provide part of the publicly available interface for manipulating the information encoded into the class. We shall see some examples of this when we examine the `string` class in Section 5.5.1.

One bit of object-related C++ technicality is appropriate: We have so far blithely included lines of code like `#include <iostream>` in our C++ source texts. These `#include` lines cause the specified file (e.g., `iostream`) to be literally pasted into our source text before the compiler attempts to compile it. These header files contain the declaration and sometimes even the definitions of various standard identifiers, classes, and variables. It is quite common for the allowed operations on an object of type `T` to be declared in a file named `T`, which is then included in our source text with a directive like `#include <T>`. This then gives us access to the facilities and capabilities of objects of class `T`.[7]

This whirlwind introduction to objects is only intended to set the stage for our increasing use of them in the rest of this text. We have already used some of this machinery with `istream` and `ostream` objects, and we will use more of it presently.

5.5.1 The String Class

I will now introduce a genuinely new and useful data type: the string class. Strings are used in programming languages to manage collections of characters. They are not necessarily well suited to complicated text processing applications, but they do provide a basic facility to work with text. We have already used *string literals*, which are collections of `char`'s enclosed in double quotes, like `"When␣I␣get␣a␣little␣money␣I␣`

---

[7]This reliance on explicitly named header files is a wart on C++. It was made necessary by the early development of C++ as an extension of the C language, and its resulting reliance on old compiler technology. Other object-oriented languages, including Eiffel, Python, and Java, have managed to avoid the header file nightmare.

buy␣books".[8] But the C++ standard library provides a very good data object for the storage and manipulation of strings, and we will examine this data type here. Besides demonstrating its intrinsic utility, this discussion will provide us with an opportunity to explore the organization and use of a class.

As I suggested earlier, the more complex data objects in C++ provide a means to package related collections of data together with functions and procedures that can operate on them. This coupling is arranged so that the identifier used to name the data object will also be the base name for any routines acting on its internal state. We have actually seen the syntax for this already in our use of the standard streams identifier cin, where the function cin.fail(), for example, is visually connected to the data cin on which it must operate. Such an object, in which data is directly associated with the operations on it, is often called a *class*. Let's examine this structure further with the string class.

To use string objects in a C++ code, we must include the header file string in our C++ source text. String objects can then be declared much like other data types. The following code illustrates three different string declarations and initializations:

stringExample.cpp

```
1   // ================================================================
2   // stringExample.cpp
3   // Some games with strings
4   // ================================================================
5   #include <string>
6   #include <iostream>
7   using namespace std;
8
9   int main()
10  {
11    // declare some strings
12    string firstName;                     // an empty string
13    string lastName("Baggins");           // nonempty string
14    string occupation = "Hobbit␣of␣leisure";  // initialize string
15
16    cout << "Name:␣" << firstName << "␣" << lastName <<
17            ",␣" << occupation << endl;
18
19    occupation = "Ringbearer";  // change his occupation
20
21    cout << "Name:␣" << firstName << "␣" << lastName <<
22            ",␣" << occupation << endl;
23
24    string drogoSon("Frodo");   // Frodo son of Drogo
```

[8]The rest of Erasmus' quote is "and if any is left, I buy food and clothes."

```
25    firstName = drogoSon;        // give him a first name
26
27    cout << "Name:␣" << firstName << "␣" << lastName <<
28            ",␣" << occupation << endl;
29
30    return 0;
31  }
```

Running this code produces exciting output:

```
1  [hagar@localhost Code]$ ./stringExample
2  Name: Baggins, Hobbit of leisure
3  Name: Baggins, Ringbearer
4  Name: Frodo Baggins, Ringbearer
5  [hagar@localhost Code]$
```

Note first the three declarations on lines 12–14. Each of these declares an identifier of type string. The first creates an empty string, one that contains no characters. The second creates a string that contains the characters "Baggins", and the third creates an empty string but immediately initializes it with the characters "Hobbit␣of␣leisure". All of these are allowed ways to create a string.

Like a double or an int, once a string is created, we can assign another value to it, and this I do on line 19. On that line I assigned a literal string, but on line 25 I assign from one string directly to another. Both of these work, and do so by copying the value of the string on the right into the one on the left.

A string is not a single static entity, however. A string is really a collection of char's, and the string type gives us a rich set of operations. We can concatenate strings together, we can extract pieces of strings, we can search strings, and more. These operations are accessed via both operator methods and routine methods.[9] Routine methods are accessed using the member selection operator, which in C++ looks exactly like a period. So, for example, if s is a string, then s.size() returns the length of the string s. Note that s is not passed into the size() function as an argument, but rather is attached to it with the member selection operator. Table 5.1 lists some interesting member functions and procedures for string objects.

stringExamplePart2.cpp

```
1  // ================================================================
2  // stringExamplePart2.cpp
3  // More games with strings
4  // ================================================================
5  #include <string>
6  #include <iostream>
7  using namespace std;
```

[9]Not routine as in ordinary, but routine as in functions and procedures.

TABLE 5.1 Some Basic String Methods.

Method	Semantics
s.size()	Returns number of char's in string s
s.append(s2)	Appends string s2 to string s
s.push_back(c)	Appends char c to string s
s.find(s2)	Searches for string s2 within s
s.npos	Value returned by s.find if s2 is not found
s < s2	Evaluates true if s is less than s2
s > s2	Evaluates true if s is greater than s2
s == s2	Evaluates true if s is equal to s2
s <= s2	Evaluates true if s is less than or equal to s2
s >= s2	Evaluates true if s is greater than or equal to s2
s != s2	Evaluates true if s is not equal to s2
s + s2	Evaluates to a new string that contains s concatenated with s2

Ordering of strings is lexicographical (as in a dictionary), but case-sensitive and with all characters significant.

```
8
9    // Declare procedures
10   void lookFor(const string & s, const string & pattern);
11
12   // =======================>> main <<===========================
13   int main()
14   {
15     // declare some strings
16     string name("Eowyn");
17     string fatherName("Eomund");
18     string relation;
19
20     relation.append(name);
21     relation.append("_daughter_of_");
22     relation.append(fatherName);
23
24     cout << relation << endl;
25
26     cout << "There_are_" << name.size() << "_characters_in_"
27          << name << endl;
28
29     string pattern("i");
30     lookFor(name, pattern);
31
32     pattern = "e";
33     lookFor(name, pattern);
34
35     pattern = "E";
36     lookFor(name, pattern);
37
```

```
38    pattern = "bitter";
39    lookFor(relation, pattern);
40
41    pattern = "aug";
42    lookFor(relation, pattern);
43
44    return 0;
45  }
46
47  // =====================>> lookFor <<============================
48  // Looks for a match to the pattern in the string s
49  void lookFor(const string & s, const string & pattern)
50  {
51    if (s.npos == s.find(pattern))
52      {
53        cout << "There is no \"" << pattern << "\" in " << s << endl;
54      }
55    else
56      {
57        cout << "Found an \"" << pattern << "\" in " << s << endl;
58      }
59  }
```

And here is the output of this code:

```
1  [hagar@localhost Code]$ ./stringExamplePart2
2  Eowyn daughter of Eomund
3  There are 5 characters in Eowyn
4  There is no "i" in Eowyn
5  There is no "e" in Eowyn
6  Found an "E" in Eowyn
7  There is no "bitter" in Eowyn daughter of Eomund
8  Found an "aug" in Eowyn daughter of Eomund
9  [hagar@localhost Code]$
```

Note that searching for an "e" in "Eowyn" failed, because a lowercase letter is not matched by an uppercase letter. Note also the use of const references in the procedure lookFor; the use of a reference avoids passing a (potentially) large amount of string data, while the use of const ensures that lookFor can't change the contents of either of its string arguments.

Besides creating strings and acting on them with the member functions and procedures listed in Table 5.1, we can compare them using the standard relational operators <, <=, >=, >, ==, and !=. These behave much as expected, with the notion of less than being based on lexicographical ordering (alphabetical order, essentially) and case-sensitive. Play with it, and see what happens!

The string data type, usually called the string class, is a relatively new creation. Long before it came into existence, C programmers had created a different data type, now often called the C string, to manage string data. These are the strings that we have so far created as literal values like "This␣is␣a␣string!". Some functions and facilities, even in C++, still expect this older style of string data. To accommodate this, a string object named s also provides a member function called s.c_str() that will return a copy of the string s stored in this older format. This copy of the string cannot be altered, but it is useful for passing to functions that do not yet accept the newer string objects as arguments. Thus, to ask for a filename and open it for reading, we can use code like this:

```
1   cout << "Input␣file␣name␣please␣:>␣";
2   string filename;
3   cin >> filename;
4   istream input(filename.c_str());
5   if( input.fail() )
6     {
7       cerr << filename << "␣did␣not␣open" << endl;
8       exit(EXIT_FAILURE);
9     }
```

5.5.2 Files

We have already seen how to open files, and now we have strings to manage text, so let's put these together in a simple code that will take everything the user types and write it into a file. One new function from the standard string library will be useful: void getline(istream in, string & line) will read a whole line from the specified istream, and write it into line.

typeIn.cpp

```
1   // ================================================================
2   // typeIn.cpp
3   // A code to echo characters into a file
4   // ================================================================
5   #include <iostream>     // cin and cout
6   #include <fstream>      // to write to text files
7   #include <string>       // to use strings
8   using namespace std;
9
10  // Declare procedures
11  void typeIn(ofstream & out);
12
13  // =========================>> main <<=========================
14  int main()
```

```
15    {
16      cout << "What do you want your file called: ";
17      string filename;
18      cin >> filename; // read a string (no whitespace allowed)
19
20      ofstream output; // an output stream
21      output.open(filename.c_str()); // attach it to a file
22
23      cout << "Type your text lines, or \"quit\" to quit" << endl;
24
25      typeIn(output);
26      output.close(); // we are done with the file, let OS clean up
27      cout << endl;
28      return 0;
29    }
30
31    // ======================>> typeIn <<=========================
32    // Reads lines from standard input until line reads "quit" or
33    // input fails. Writes each line to the output file stream out.
34    // ===========================================================
35    void typeIn(ofstream & out)
36    {
37     string line; // the most recently read line
38     getline(cin, line); // read a whole line into a string
39     while( not cin.fail() )
40       {
41         if (line == "quit")
42           {
43             return;
44           }
45         out << line << endl;
46         getline(cin, line);
47       }
48    }
```

Note that the boxed lines of code, which declare the ofstream, attach a file to it with open, and then later detach the file with close. In line 21 I use the c_str method of the string object filename to extract a C string version of the filename. This is not strictly necessary if the library complies with the C++ standard, but it is one area where most of the libraries are not yet up to date. The purpose of line 21, in any event, is to attach the ofstream object to an actual file managed by the operating system of the computer. Output data written to the stream is passed to the operating system, destined for that file, as suggested in Fig. 5.2. Note that, using the facilities of standard C++, I only know that the operating system is given the data, and I know that I asked for that data to be sent to a file whose name I provided. But I don't know for sure what the operating system actually does with the data, or

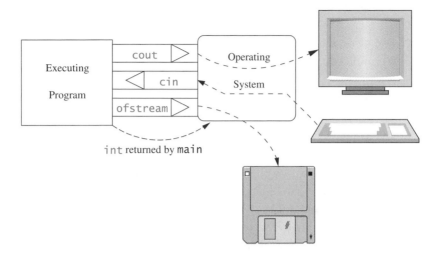

FIGURE 5.2   A file, destined for output, is attached to our code through the operating system.

when. Indeed, once the data is passed into the output file stream, all sense of sequencing for it is lost. The stream is buffered, so there is no guarantee that it will actually be written to the file before the next sequence point in my C++ code; indeed, there is no guarantee of when data added to the stream will be given to the operating system. For this reason it is wise to include the call to close as soon as you are done with a file; this asks the output stream to pass any data that it is still holding over to the operating system, which (if error-free) should get it written to the file in a timely fashion.

I had mentioned in Chapter 2 that istream's and ostream's cannot be copied or assigned. So statements like the following are not allowed:

```
1  ifstream file;
2  file.open("bobsfile");
3  ifstream fileCopy;
4
5  fileCopy = file; // can't be done
6
7  ifstream & fileRef = file; // this is ok
```

An ifstream object is associated with some external resource managed by some operating system, like a file on disk. If we copied file into fileCopy, then we would have two separate objects in our code, both of which are trying to put data into the same external resource. This would be quite contentious. But we can get a reference to an ifstream, since a reference is just an alias for another object, so fileRef just refers to the same istream as file does. This issue most often arises when we want to pass an input or output stream into a function or procedure; we must pass these objects as references, and cannot pass them as values.

It is worthwhile also to discuss the notion of a text file.

Definition

> A text file is a file containing data that are interpreted as characters, and which are logically partitioned into groups of lines.

How such a file is actually organized is operating-system-dependent, and of no interest to us. It will be presented to a C++ code as a stream of data in which special characters known as newline characters are embedded. These characters, which can be written '\n' (that's a single char), are understood by the C++ library and/or operating system to mark the end of lines in the file. So a text file is nothing more nor less than a collection of bytes grouped into lines by newline characters.

Searching for a Pattern in a File   Let's consider a code to solve a common problem in computing. I'd like to look at every line of text in a file and report if that line contains a specified string of characters. Here is a first attempt:

searchFor.cpp

```
1  // ================================================================
2  // searchFor.cpp
3  // Searches a file for a given pattern
4  // ================================================================
5  #include <iostream>
6  #include <fstream>
7  #include <string>
8  #include <cstdlib>
9  using namespace std;
10
11 // Function declarations ========================================
12 void getInStream(ifstream & file, string & fileName);
13 void getPattern(string & pattern);
14 void searchFor(const string & pattern, ifstream & file);
15
16 // ==============>> main <<======================================
17 int main()
18 {
19   string fileName;  // file to search
20   ifstream file;    // file to search
21   getInStream(file, fileName);
22
23   string pattern;   // string to search for
24   getPattern(pattern);
25
```

```
26      cout << "Searching_" << fileName << "_for_" << "\""
27          << pattern << "\"" << endl;
28
29      searchFor(pattern, file);
30      file.close();
31
32      return EXIT_SUCCESS;
33  }
34
35  // =============>> getInStream <<============================
36  // Gets the name of a file and opens it for input
37  // Arguments
38  //    file -- reference to istream to be opened
39  //    fileName -- reference to to filename to be opened
40  // =========================================================
41  void getInStream(ifstream & file, string & fileName)
42  {
43    cout << "File_to_search :> ";
44    cin >> fileName;
45
46    file.open(fileName.c_str());
47    if( file.fail() )
48      {
49          cerr << "File_" << fileName << "_did..not_open" << endl;
50          cerr << "Giving_up..." << endl;
51          exit(EXIT_FAILURE);
52      }
53  }
54
55  // =============>> getPattern <<=============================
56  void getPattern(string & pattern)
57  {
58    cout << "Pattern_to_search_for:>_";
59    cin >> pattern;
60  }
61
62  // =============>> searchFor <<=============================
63  // Searches each line of file for pattern
64  // =========================================================
65  void searchFor(const string & pattern, ifstream & file)
66  {
67    string line;
68    getline(file, line);
69    while( not file.fail() )
70      {
71          if( line.npos != line.find(pattern) )
```

```
72        {
73          cout << line << endl; // found it -- show the line
74        }
75      getline(file, line);
76    }
77  }
```

Note the order of the `getline` calls in `searchFor`. I acquire a line *before* entering the loop, so that within the loop `line` is always a valid line of text extracted from the file. This is a common pattern; we have a loop that looks like this:

```
1  get data
2  while( data is valid )
3  {
4    do work
5    get data
6  }
```

We could have written this as

```
1  fake up valid garbage data
2  while( data is valid )
3  {
4    get data
5    if( data is valid ) do work
6  }
```

This loop is semantically equivalent to the first, but it requires us to fake out the `while( data is valid )` condition to achieve the first entry into the loop. This loop also requires an essentially redundant test `if( data is valid )`. Not very pretty. Unfortunately, many a student has written this sort of loop as

```
1  fake up valid data
2  while( data is valid )
3  {
4    get data
5    do work  // we may be using invalid data here!
6  }
```

in which work is done even though the data may be invalid. The check in `while( data is valid )` will not be invoked until the loop body is completely executed.

There are at least two issues with the **searchFor.cpp** code. First, the `pattern` we are searching for cannot contain a space. Thus, we could not search for "To␣be,␣or␣

not_to_be." This can be addressed by using `getline(cin, pattern)` on line 59 to read a whole line of input, including whitespace. Second, this code needs two pieces of data from its user: a file to search, and a pattern to search for. Once those are in hand, it does its work and does not need to interact with a human again. It is therefore not clear that engaging in a conversation—prompting for data—is the best way to interact with this code. But to avoid the conversation, we need some new tools, and that will have to wait for a discussion of arrays and pointers in Chapter 6.

Questions

Question 11 Write a routine `readline(istream in, string & s)` that reads a line of text from the input stream and stores it in the string s. Be sure to get all the whitespace, and consider the value of `s.push_back(c)`. Do not use `getline`.

Question 12 Write a procedure `void copy(istream in, ostream out)` that copies the contents of `in` to `out`. Make sure to get all the whitespace.

Question 13 Consider an object like `string s`. What is the advantage to writing `s.size()` over `size(s)`?

5.6 GENERIC ROUTINES AND GENERIC TYPES

In Section 5.3.2 I defined the function

```
void orderPairDouble(double & a, double & b)
```

which would swap its arguments, in its caller, to ensure that the first argument was the smaller of the two. This function worked fine for `double`'s, but what if I want to use it with `int` data? I am out of luck. Even though C++ defines the conversion from an `int` to a `double`, it does not define the conversion from a reference to an `int` to a reference to a `double`. The following code will not compile, because a and b were declared as `int`, rather than `double`:

badCode.cpp

```
1   // ================================================================
2   // badCode.cpp
3   // Some code that will not compile
4   // ================================================================
5   #include <iostream>
6   using namespace std;
7
8   // ==================>> orderPairDouble <<====================
9   // Makes sure first argument is <= second argument
10  // ================================================================
11  void orderPairDouble(double & first, double & second)
12  {
13    if (second < first)
14      {
15        double tmp = second; // save second for a moment
```

```
16          second = first;      // put bigger into second
17          first = tmp;         // put smaller into first
18      }
19  }
20
21  // ================>> main <<================================
22  int main()
23  {
24      int a = 10;
25      int b = 1;
26
27      orderPairDouble(a, b);
28      cout << a << "_" << b << endl;
29
30      return 0;
31  }
```

The problem is that the rules of C++ do not specify what it would mean to place an int where a reference to a double is expected.

The solution seems obvious:

orderPairInt.cpp

```
1  void orderPairInt(int & first, int & second)
2  {
3      if (second < first)
4          {
5              int tmp = second;      // save second for a moment
6              second = first;        // put bigger into second
7              first = tmp;           // put smaller into first
8          }
9  }
```

And we could write one for unsigned int and float, and, oh, one for string, like

orderPairString.cpp

```
1  #include <string>
2  using namespace std;
3
4  void orderPairString(string & first, string & second)
5  {
6      if (second < first)
7          {
8              string tmp = second;   // save second for a moment
9              second = first;        // put bigger into second
```

```
10        first = tmp;              // put smaller into first
11     }
12  }
```

But wait a minute! This is getting ridiculous. All these functions are the same, with only the types of the data being changed from one source text to the next. Is there no better way?

C++ provides for *generic routines*; a generic routine is one whose source code text is parameterized by the types of data it is intended to manipulate. Here's how the orderPair procedure looks as a generic procedure:

orderPair.cpp

```
1  template <class T> void orderPair(T & first, T & second)
2  {
3     if (second < first)
4     {
5        T tmp = second;        // save second for a moment
6        second = first;        // put bigger into second
7        first = tmp;           // put smaller into first
8     }
9  }
```

For this definition of orderPair, the compiler has been told to treat the symbol T as a *generic type*, which will be effectively replaced with an actual data type when the compiler discovers a need to generate the corresponding procedure.

In the following code, the compiler implicitly generates a

```
orderPair(double &, double &)
```

procedure, and a

```
orderPair(string &, string &)
```

procedure, but I did not have to write either of these explicitly. I just wrote a generic version.

orderSamples.cpp

```
1  // ============================================================
2  // orderSamples.cpp
3  // Generic procedure to order a pair of numbers in its caller
4  // ============================================================
5  #include <iostream>
6  #include <string>
7  using namespace std;
8
9  // Generic declaration of procedure orderPair
10 template <class T> void orderPair(T & first, T & second);
```

```
11
12    // =================>> main <<=================================
13    int main()
14    {
15      int a = 10;
16      int b = 1;
17
18      cout << "Before:␣" << a << "␣" << b << endl;
19      orderPair(a, b);
20      cout << "After:␣" << a << "␣" << b << endl;
21
22      string one("All␣your␣base");
23      string two("are␣belong␣to␣us");
24      cout << "Before:␣" << one << "␣" << two << endl;
25      orderPair(one, two);
26      cout << "After:␣" << one << "␣" << two << endl;
27
28      return 0;
29    }
30
31    // =================>> orderPair <<=============================
32    template <class T> void orderPair(T & first, T & second)
33    {
34      if (second < first)
35        {
36          T tmp = second;        // save second for a moment
37          second = first;        // put bigger into second
38          first = tmp;           // put smaller into first
39        }
40    }
```

There are some limitations to this generic routine template construct. First, the operations in the generic function or procedure must make sense when applied to the actual types used in the code. Thus,

```
1    double x = 10.0;
2    double y = -10.0;
3
4    orderPair(x, y); // makes sense
5
6    ifstream inOne;
7    ifstream inTwo;
8
9    inOne.open("fileA");
10   inTwo.open("fileB");
```

```
11
12   orderPair(inOne, inTwo); // makes no sense
```

The call `orderPair(inOne, inTwo)` makes no sense, because most of the operations in `orderPair` have no meaning for data of type `ifstream`. We can't compare `ifstream`'s with the relational operator <; indeed, we can't even assign `ifstream`'s with = (the assignment operator).

It can be slightly tricky to use generic routines. If such a routine is used in one source file, but is defined in a different source file, the compiler must devine this, and generate the correct routine by referring to both source files. Many C++ compilers still have not implemented all of the mechanisms for supporting this. When I use generic routines in this text, I will therefore make sure they are defined in the same source text file where they are used, either explicitly, as in **orderSamples.cpp**, or else by using the preprocessor #include mechanism.

Complex Numbers   C++ also uses the `template` mechanism to support generic types. These are classes that manage the storage of data, but do not explitly specify the type of the data being stored. One very useful generic type in the C++ standard library is `complex`, declared in the header file `complex`. This class represents complex numbers as a real part and an imaginary part, and defines all the standard mathematical operations (like +, -, *, /) for them. The library also defines the standard algebraic and transcendental functions (like `sqrt`, `cos`, `cosh`, `sin`, and so forth) for `complex` data. However, if a `complex` type is declared as a real and imaginary part, what type is used for these parts? The type used is selected as a template parameter, as in the following code:

complex.cpp

```
1    // =============================================================
2    // complex.cpp
3    // Just some sample manipulations using the complex class
4    // =============================================================
5    #include <iostream>
6    #include <complex>
7    using namespace std;
8
9    int main()
10   {
11     complex<double> a(0,1); // a = 0 + i
12     complex<double> b(1,2); // b = 1 + 2 i
13     complex<double> c(1.0, 2.5); // c = 1.0 + 2.5 i
14     complex<double> d;
15
16     d = a + c - b; // an expression statement using complex<double>
17     cout << d << endl; // output works too
18
```

```
19    cout << "Real_part_of_d_=_" << d.real() << endl;
20    cout << "Imaginary_part_of_d_=_" << d.imag() << endl;
21
22    const complex<double> i(0,1); // a useful constant
23    complex<double> f = 2.5 + i * 6.0;
24    cout << f << endl;
25
26    cout << "sin(" << d << ")_=_" << sin(d) << endl;
27    cout << "sin(" << f << ")_=_" << sin(f) << endl;
28
29    complex<double> minusOne(-1.0,0.0);
30    cout << "Square_root_of_-1_=_" << sqrt(minusOne) << endl;
31
32    complex<float> g(1.0, 2.0);
33    // g + d fails. complex<float> + complex<double> not defined
34
35    return 0;
36  }
```

Pairs   Another generic type from the standard library is the pair, which is simply a container for a pair of values of some other types. The pair is defined in the header file utility, and supports a declaration of the form

```
    pair<T1, T2> identifier;
```

where T1 and T2 are any types. The pair then has the data members first and second, which represent the first and second member of the pair. After declaring pair< int , double > p, we can write p.first = 23 and p.second = 56.4. The pair can also be initialized with a value v1 of type T1 and a value v2 of type T2 by using a declaration of the form

```
    pair<T1, T2> identifier(v1, v2);
```

Here is a silly example use of pair:

sillyPair.cpp

```
1   // ===============================================================
2   // sillyPair.cpp
3   // Demonstration of the pair class.
4   // ===============================================================
5   #include <iostream>
6   #include <utility>
7   #include <string>
8   using namespace std;
0
10  int main()
11  {
```

```
12    pair<int, string> a; // a holds an int and a string
13    a.first = 1;
14    a.second = "Hello";
15    cout << a.first << endl;  // writes 1 to standard output
16    cout << a.second << endl; // writes "Hello" to standard output
17
18    return 0;
19  }
```

Questions

Question 14   Write a generic function called `min` that will take two generic arguments, both of the same type and assumed to support <, and which returns the smaller of the two.

Question 15   Rewrite `orderPair` so that it reorders a `pair`. It can have a declaration like `template<class`

`T> orderPair(pair<T, T> & p)` and should ensure that `p.first <= p.second`.

Question 16   Declare complex constants that represent $1 + i$, $1 - i$, and 0.

Question 17   Declare a pair of complex numbers and store the pair $(1 + i, 1 - i)$ in it.

Projects

These projects all ask you to write codes that manipulate the various data types that I have presented in this chapter. In Chapter 8 I shall dwell on the details of encoding some of these data, and you can expect more exercises there.

PROJECT 1

Write a function `int round(double x)` that rounds a `double` to the nearest `int`. Do so without using any functions from the standard math library (i.e., don't use `floor`, `ceil`, or any of those things). Your functions do not need to deal with the case where the result would be too large to represent as an `int`.

PROJECT 2

Write functions `int ceil(double x)` and `int floor(double x)` that behave like the functions `ceil` and `floor` from the standard math library, but which return `int` values. Do this without using any functions from the standard math library. Your functions do not need to deal with the case where the result would be too large to represent as an `int`.

PROJECT 3

Write a code that tests the proposition that $\sin^2(x) + \cos^2(x) = 1$, by computing the value of the left-hand

side for a range of real x values. Be sure to print out lots of digits of precision. Make a plot of the left-hand-side value, as computed by your code, versus the value of x. What do you see?

PROJECT 4

Write a code that tests the proposition that $\sin^2(x) + \cos^2(x) = 1$, by computing the value of the left-hand side for a range of *complex* x values.

PROJECT 5

Write a function that accepts the real coefficients of a quadratic equation $ax^2 + bx + c$ and returns its roots as a `pair` of `complex`.

PROJECT 6

Write a function that reads `char`'s from standard input, interprets these as the base 10 representation of a positive integer, and writes the binary representation of that number to standard output.

PROJECT 7

Write a code that prompts the user for an input base integer, between 2 and 16, and an output base integer, also between 2 and 16, both represented as usual in base 10, and which then reads `char`'s from standard input and interprets these as the representation of a positive integer number in the input base. The code should then write the number in standard place value notation using the output base. The digits to use for bases 2–16 are 0123456789ABCDEF. Your code should deal with errors in input. Your code should not store the digits for either input or output (to do so would require tools from a later chapter anyway). Here is a sample run:

```
1  [hagar@localhost Code]$ ./baseSwitch
2  Input base: 15
3  Output base: 10
4  Number: A3E
5  A3E (base 15) is 2309 (base 10)
6  [hagar@localhost Code]$ ./baseSwitch
7  Input base: 15
8  Output base: 10
9  Number: A3F
10 A3F is not a valid number in base 15.
```

PROJECT 8

Change the **searchFor.cpp** code to print a nicely formatted line number next to every matched line, and also to allow whitespace to appear in the pattern. Something like the following sample output should appear:

```
1  [hagar@localhost Code]$ ./searchFor
2  File to search :> searchFor.cpp
3  Pattern to search for:> getPattern <<
4  Searching searchFor.cpp for "getPattern <<"
5  55:// ==============>> getPattern <<=======
6  [hagar@localhost Code]$
```

Here 55 is the line number for the line that matched the pattern.

PROJECT 9

Change the **searchFor** code yet again, this time making the search case insensitive (so that "Aaron" will match "aaron"). *Hint:* Look in Appendix B at the character manipulation functions.

CHAPTER 6

ARRAY SEMANTICS

IMAGINE THAT you needed to store and manage one million data values. Would you be inclined to give them all individual identifiers, something like `data1`, `data2`, `data3` ... `data1000000`? I certainly would not, because tedium is the enemy of quality work. We need a different way to manage such a large collection of data. Arrays are that way!

Arrays provide one means to manage a collection, large or small, of like data. An array can manage a collection of one million `double`'s, or one million `int`'s, or even one million `string`'s. Such a data management system must provide us with the means to identify the collection as a whole, as well as provide us with access to its individual elements. Many compound data types provide such mechanisms, but arrays are distinguished by storing only items of like type, and by allowing access to any element of the array based on its location within the array. We will explore these ideas in this chapter.

6.1 ARRAY SEMANTICS WITH STRINGS

Let's develop the fundamental ideas for arrays by using the `string` class, first introduced in Chapter 5. A `string` is a data type that manages a collection of `char`'s. But this structure as a *collection* was treated somewhat subliminally in Chapter 5; we never really accessed the individual `char`'s of which the string was made. Consider the string operations listed back in Table 5.1; these operations all act on the string as a whole, and do not provide access to the individual `char`'s of which the string is constructed. Only one of those operations, `s.push_back(c)`, works with the individual `char`'s of which a string is composed, and this operation simply appends a single character to an existing string. Using the operations of Table 5.1, we cannot take apart a string.

If we do want to take apart a `string`, we need some way to refer to the individual characters from which it is built. This can be done using *offsets*, as suggested in Fig. 6.1.

Definition

The *offset* of an element of a string is an integer that specifies how many characters from the front of the string that element lies.

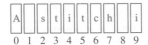

FIGURE 6.1   A string as a collection of characters, identified by offset from the start of the string. The first character 'A' is at offset 0; it is zero from the front. The *i*th character is at the offset *i* − 1. The character at offset 9 is 'i', and is the tenth character in the string.

So in the string "All␣Neptune's␣oceans", the character at offset 4 is 'N', and the character at 0 is 'A'. Note that the first character is at offset 0; it is zero characters away from the first one. The use of offsets, rather than ordinal indices, first, second, third, et cetera, sometimes causes confusion, but this preference for offsets over ordinals is common in many programming languages.

By using an offset to locate each character within a string, we can access the individual characters by using the *array indexing* operator [ ], as illustrated here:

```
1   string s = "Will␣all␣great␣Neptune's␣ocean␣wash␣"
2               "this␣blood␣clean␣from␣my␣hand?";
3   char c;
4
5   c = s[0]; // s[0] is 'W', so this assigns 'W' to c;
6   c = s[5]; // s[5] is 'a' (in all), so this assigns 'a' to c;
7   s[0] = 'n' // puts 'n' in to the first location in the string
```

Using offsets, we can get at the individual parts of the string by asking for the char at any particular offset. This is the heart of array semantics.

Definition

> An aggregate object supports *array semantics* if all of its elements are of the same type and if each element can be accessed individually by specifying an integer, such as an *offset* from the start of the array. This integer is called an index, and the range of integer indices must be contiguous. The number of elements in an array is called its length or its size.

Note that an index uniquely identifies each element in an array. Although indices are not required to be offsets, running from zero to 1 less than the length of the array, in the C++ tradition offsets are generally used for indices.

The string class in C++ supports array semantics using offsets from the start of the string to uniquely specify each char in the string; this offset is the index of the individual char. The string, and other objects with array semantics in C++, support the indexing operator [ ], which is used to fetch an individual element of an array based on its index. Figure 6.2 shows an array as a tower of data storage containers all having a common name, but each individually accessible using an index.

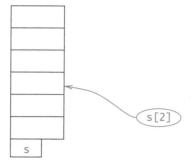

FIGURE 6.2 The object s supports array semantics, and s[2] is a reference to the third element of the array.

C++ Principle

> If identifier is an object that supports array semantics, an expression of the form
>
>   identifier[integer_expression]
>
> evaluates to a reference to an element of the array. Here integer_expression is an expression that evaluates to an unsigned integer.

It is essential that identifier[ ] evaluates to a *reference* to some data object. This allows identifier[ ] to be used in our source text to refer to the individual element of the array. It allows indexing to be used on either the left-hand or right-hand side of an assignment operator.

So, we can indeed use indexing to replace an existing character in a string, as in lines 14–19 of this code:

notWill.cpp

```
1   // ================================================================
2   // notWill.cpp
3   // From quality to corruption
4   // ================================================================
5   #include <iostream>
6   #include <string>
7   using namespace std;
8
9   int main()
10  {
11      string s = "Will_all_great_Neptune's_ocean_wash_"
12                 "this_blood_clean_from_my_hand?";
13
14      s[0] = 'B';   // 'B' is put into the string at offset 0
15      s[30] = '.'; // '.' is put into the string at offset 30
16      s[30 + 1] = 'W';
17      s[30 + 11] = 'f';
```

```
18   s[s.size()-1] = '.';     // last char in the string
19   s[s.size()-5] = 's';
20   s.push_back('\n');        // Append a char to end of string
21
22   cout << s;
23   return 0;
24 }
```

This causes rank poetry `Bill all great Neptune's ocean.Wash this flood clean from my sand.` to be written to standard output.

Indexing is wonderful, but with great power comes great prospect of error. What happens if I use an invalid array index? For example, suppose I write `s[-1]` in my C++ source text? The number `-1` makes no sense as an offset—there is no character one before the first—so something bad is sure to happen. Unfortunately, we cannot say exactly what; we only know that it will be bad.

```
1   string macbeth = "Will all great neptune's oceans...";
2
3   // try something bad -- can't say what will happen
4   cout << macbeth[ -1 ];              // offset is one too small;
5   cout << macbeth[ macbeth.size() ];  // offset is one too big;
```

Lines 4 and 5 both use invalid index values. Although you might hope that a compiler could catch these particular errors, it cannot, in fact, be counted on to do so. For consider, does `macbeth[i]` use an invalid index or not? It is impossible to say until `i` has a value, and all the values that `i` will actually take cannot be known until the code is executed. And even then, the values assumed by `i` might differ from one execution to the next, depending on the data that the algorithm gets from its environment.

It is hard to describe what devastation might occur when improper indices are used with the indexing operator `[ ]`. Most often, the behavior is *undefined*, meaning that the authors of the C++ standard did not want to be responsible for whatever unfortunate events ensue. So while we cannot say what will happen if we execute `macbeth[ -1 ]`, we can be sure that it will not be good. Worse, whatever evil does unfold may occur silently. Like a cold presence creeping through our code, an incubating sickness will take root. The rot will grow, causing our program to mysteriously succumb. Get the picture? It will be bad.

Most of us who have used a desktop computer have seen one of the eventual outcomes of using an invalid array index: the *general protection fault*. This error goes by somewhat different names under different operating systems, including the variants *segmentation violation* and *general protection violation*. In a modern operating system with protected memory, each code is run as a process with access to its own memory space; each code is given a certain range of memory into which it can write data, or from which it can read. If the process should dare to look outside of its own sandbox, the operating system will crush it before any damage can occur. After killing the process, it is the operating system that reports the error, as a general protection fault. The words are intended to suggest that the code tried to circumvent the memory *protection* provided by the operating system.[1] A protection fault is a *good* symptom of an invalid array index; unfortunately in C++ using an invalid index can easily result in a silent error because the invalid index might refer to other data within the same process. In this case no memory protection error has occurred and the operating system does not get involved. But an error has still occurred and our data is corrupted.

There is another way to index into the string object, using the `at` member function. Basically, `s.at(i)` is the same as `s[i]`, unless `i` is greater than or equal to `s.size()`, in which case the code will noisily generate an error. This is a better outcome than a segmentation violation, because the cause—an invalid array index—will be clearly identified. Unfortunately, the case of a negative index is still not addressed.[2]

```
1   string macbeth = "Will_all_great_neptune's_oceans...";
2
3   // try something bad -- will be caught at execution
4   cout << macbeth.at(macbeth.size());   // offset is one too big;
5
6   // try something bad -- still can't say what will happen
7   cout << macbeth.at(-1);               // offset is one too small;
```

In this case, the use of an index that is too large, on line 4, causes the code to abort execution when the inappropriate index is passed into the `at` method of `string` `macbeth`.

6.1.1 Substrings

Strings support another mechanism for extracting a part of a string that, while not strictly part of array semantics, also relies on indexing. Every `string s` includes a member function `s.substr(startOffset, length)`, which returns a new string that contains the characters from `s[startOffset]` up to `s[startOffset + length]`. So

```
1   string s = "All_Neptune's_oceans...";
2   string spart = s.substr(3, 5);
```

assigns `"_Nept"` to `spart`. This is but one of many facilities provided by the `string` class that allow access to parts of a `string` by using offsets into the `string`. Table 6.1 briefly introduces some `string` operations that rely on offsets from the start of the string.

---

[1]The message "segmentation violation," preferred by some operating system authors, is intended to suggest that the process looked outside of its own *segment* of memory.

[2]A mistake in the design of the `at()` function, in my view.

TABLE 6.1   **Some String Methods Based on Indexing.** s **is a** string, **While** offset **and** len **are Unsigned Integers.**

Method	Semantics
s.erase(offset, len)	Removes len characters from s, starting at offset
s.find(s2)	Returns offset of s2 in s, or s.npos if s2 is not found
s.insert(offset, s2)	Inserts string s2 into s starting at offset
s.resize(len)	Resizes the string to length len, truncating or padding it with null characters as needed
s.size()	Returns number of elements in string s
s.substr(offset, len)	Returns new string identical to s[offset]...s[offset + len]
s.replace(offset, num, s2)	Replaces num characters in string s with the whole string s2, starting at offset in string s

Questions

Question 1   Indicate, for each of the following expressions, if the indexing is valid or not. Assume that

```
double x = 1.0;
double y = 1.5;
int i = -5;
int j = 3;
unsigned int k = 4;
string s("Gauss Rules");
```

a. s[j]

b. s[i]

c. s[x]

d. s[y]

e. s[y]

f. s[k - j]

g. s[k/i]

h. s[s.size() + i]

Question 2   What does the following code write to the output stream output?

```
string s("alpha");
s[2] = 'm';
s[0] = 'g';
s[3] = 'm';
s[1] = 'a';
output << s;
```

Question 3   Given string s =_"The_lands_opened _wide_about_him.";, what strings or characters does each of the following expressions evaluate to?

a. s.substr(10, 6)

b. s.substr(s.size()-4,3)

c. s.substr(0,9)[2]

d. s.substr(4,1)[0]

6.2   INTERFACES TO ROUTINES USING ARRAYS

As we work increasingly with arrays of data, we will want to pass arrays into routines; we will want to have routines create new data and somehow get this data back to their caller in an array; and we will want to have routines modify arrays in their callers. Let's consider each of these possibilities in turn.

Let T be a type that supports array indexing, and suppose first that we want a routine to simply take an array from its caller and use the data in it for some computation. We could design the interface to that routine as

```
void useArray(T a)
```

This will result in the standard implicit initialization when this routine executes, so the data from the caller will be *copied* into a. Often this is quite wasteful, and while efficiency has not been a central theme in this text having multiple copies of potentially huge arrays lying around is often beyond the pale. The alternative is to declare the routine as

```
void useArray(const T & a)
```

Now when the routine is called, it is simply given a reference to data in its caller, and must work within the prohibition provided by `const`.

When we want to get array data back from a routine, we similarly have two choices. We can have a function like

```
T buildArray()
```

or a procedure like

```
void buildArray(T & a)
```

In the former case, the array will be built inside `buildArray`, and then copied into the caller in some expression like `T result = buildArray()`. In contrast, when the routine is designed as a procedure taking a reference parameter, the array, already declared in the caller, can be directly filled in by the routine, like

```
T result;
buildArray(result); // Changes result
```

This is somewhat less pretty than `T result = buildArray()` but it is often the right thing to do in order to avoid copying huge amounts of information.[3]

The third possibility is that we require a routine to change an existing array in place. For this case, there is no choice: We need the array to be passed into the routine through a reference variable, like

```
void changeArray(T & a)
```

The routine `changeArray` can then modify the array in its caller as required, through the alias `a`.

Let's consider some of these cases in the concrete. Let's create and implement an algorithm that takes a string and converts all of its characters to uppercase letters. So when fed the string `"Alas,_poor_Yorick."`, the algorithm will yell back, `"ALAS,_POOR_YORICK."` There are at least three ways we could design the interface of such an algorithm. We could pass a reference to the string into a procedure and act only through this reference; this would cause the string, actually stored in the procedure's caller, to be converted in place to uppercase, and the original string would be destroyed. Or, we could pass a copy of the string into the algorithm, convert that copy to uppercase characters, and pass a copy of this uppercase string back to the caller. This could be done either through a reference, or by returning the string. In this later case, we would define a function

```
string upperCase(string s);
```

---

[3]Some objects supporting array semantics provide very efficient means to copy and assign large objects, using a technique known as reference counting. But this topic is outside the scope of this text.

with the expectation that we are going to use the uppercase string in an expression. Since strings can be concatenated with +, compared with the relational operators (like < and ==), or thrown to standard output with <<, such a function would make sense. So let's write this version first:

upperCase.cpp

```
1   // ===============================================================
2   // upperCase.cpp
3   // Convert s to uppercase letters and return a copy
4   // ===============================================================
5   #include <string>
6   #include <cctype>
7   using namespace std;
8
9   string upperCase(string s)
10  {
11    for(int i = 0; i < s.size(); i = i + 1)
12      {
13        s[i] = toupper(s[i]);
14      }
15    return s;
16  }
```

Here is a code to test this function:

upperCaseTest.cpp

```
1   // ===============================================================
2   // upperCaseTest.cpp
3   // ===============================================================
4   #include <iostream>
5   #include <string>
6   using namespace std;
7
8   string upperCase(string s);
9
10  // ===============>> main <<===============================
11  int main()
12  {
13    cout << "Type a line please:";
14    string line;
15    getline(cin, line);   // read a line from the user
16    cout << upperCase(line) << endl;  // print it in uppercase
17    return 0;
18  }
```

Let's now consider a different machine to accomplish the same goal; let's write a procedure of the form

```
void upperCaseByRef(const string & source, string & target)
```

In this version, I will provide to the procedure a string called source. This shall be done through a constant reference, so that I cannot accidentally change the source string. I shall then copy this source string through a reference into a target string in the caller, with all the letters converted to uppercase characters.

upperCaseByRef.cpp

```
1   // ==============================================================
2   // upperCaseByRef.cpp
3   // Replace target by uppercase version of source string
4   // ==============================================================
5   #include <string>
6   #include <cctype>
7   using namespace std;
8
9   void upperCaseByRef(const string & source, string & target)
10  {
11     target.resize(source.size());
12     for(int i = 0; i < source.size(); i = i + 1)
13       {
14         target[i] = toupper(source[i]);
15       }
16  }
```

The code must now start by resizing the target string, as is done on line 11. We must do this because we have no idea what size target was given in the caller of upperCaseByRef. We could instead insist that target already be of exactly the correct size, and could even enforce this with an assertion. But there is no compelling reason for such a demand; we can resize target in the upperCaseByRef procedure, so let's simply do so. The call target.resize(source.size()) resizes target to be the same length as source. The loop is the same as in upperCase, but there is nothing to return. This version of the algorithm is not meant to be used in an expression. It can be called as follows:

```
1   string s("Johnny Appleseed");
2   string t;
3
4   upperCaseByRef(s, t);
5   cout << t; // shows "JOHNNY APPLESEED" on standard output
6
7   upperCaseByRef(s, s);  // same as s = upperCase(s);
```

Note that the target string must be declared, in the caller, *before* the procedure upperCaseByRef is called. Also note that whatever used to be in the target string is destroyed by the procedure. This version of the uppercase algorithm has little functional advantage over the upperCase function. But it is more efficient; the source string only needs to be copied once, as it is converted to uppercase, and the target string only needs to have characters placed in it, and is never copied. This provides some savings in time and memory during execution. Note also that upperCaseByRef can actually change the source string, as shown in line 7.

Here, finally, is a somewhat different procedure that *converts* an existing string to uppercase characters:

```
void upperCaseInPlace(string & s)
```

This version will take the string by reference, and actually change that string in the caller. It destroys the old content of the string and replaces it with new content:

upperCaseInPlace.cpp

```
1   // ================================================================
2   // upperCaseInPlace.cpp
3   // Convert s to uppercase in the caller
4   // ================================================================
5   #include <string>
6   #include <cctype>
7   using namespace std;
8
9   void upperCaseInPlace(string & s)
10  {
11    for(int i = 0; i < s.size(); i = i + 1)
12      {
13        s[i] = toupper(s[i]);
14      }
15  }
```

In this version, only one string is manipulated, and that string is actually changed in the caller. This version therefore provides rather different semantics than the previous two versions. Those previous versions constructed a new string from an old one, while this version only modifies an existing string. Figure 6.3 shows the different patterns of data management used in the three different uppercase implementations.

Here is a code that uses these various uppercase algorithms:

upperCaseEffects.cpp

```
1   // ================================================================
2   // upperCaseEffects.cpp
3   // ================================================================
4   #include <string>
5   #include <iostream>
```

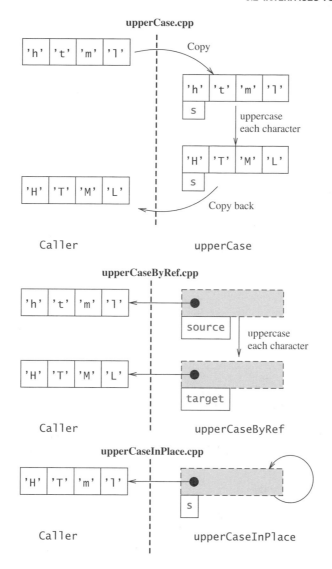

FIGURE 6.3 upperCase, upperCaseByRef and upperCaseInPlace each has a unique pattern of data use between the routine and its caller (upperCaseInPlace is shown in the middle of its loop, after having changed two of the characters in its caller).

```
6   #include <ctime>
7   using namespace std;
8
9   void upperCaseInPlace(string & s);
10  void upperCaseByRef(const string & source, string & target);
11  string upperCase(string s);
12
```

```
13   int main()
14   {
15       // build a long source string
16       string a = "abcdefgh...qrstuvwxyz1234567890,.;<>";
17       cout << "a_=_" << a << endl;
18
19       string b = upperCase(a);
20       cout << "b_=_upperCase(a)_=>_b_=_" << b << endl;
21
22       string c;
23       upperCaseByRef(a, c);
24       cout << "upperCaseByRef(a,_c)_=>_c_=_" << c << endl;
25
26       upperCaseInPlace(a);
27       cout << "upperCaseInPlace(a)_=>_a_=_" << a << endl;
28
29       return 0;
30   }
```

It produces the output

```
1   [hagar@localhost Code]$ ./upperCaseEffects
2   a = abcdefgh...qrstuvwxyz1234567890,.;<>
3   b = upperCase(a) => b = ABCDEFGH...QRSTUVWXYZ1234567890,.;<>
4   upperCaseByRef(a, c) => c = ABCDEFGH...QRSTUVWXYZ1234567890,.;<>
5   upperCaseInPlace(a) => a = ABCDEFGH...QRSTUVWXYZ1234567890,.;<>
6   [hagar@localhost Code]$
```

Questions

Question 4   I have written a procedure void encrypt(string s) that will replace a string s with an encrypted version of itself, using encryption so powerful that even the National Security Agency won't be able to decipher it. Give me one good reason why you won't use my procedure?

Question 5   I need a function that will read a word of input from an input stream, where a word is defined to be anything that does not include whitespace. How will you declare this procedure? Justify your choice.

Question 6   Write a function that will take a string and remove all whitespace from it. The standard library function isspace may be of use to you.

6.3   MORE COMPLEX INDEXING

The power of array indexing comes not from our ability to simply walk down the array, starting at offset 0 and progressing up to the last offset. This is useful, indeed, but such a simple linear traversal from start to finish can be easily accomplished with other data

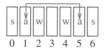

FIGURE 6.4 Comparing the second and last-but-one character in a string as part of deciding that it is a palindrome.

structures as well.[4] The true power of arrays comes from our ability to address any element at any index, in any order.[5]

Let's write an algorithm that performs somewhat more interesting index manipulations. The string "was␣saw" is a palindrome; it is the same if reversed as it is if read forward. Let's write a function that checks if a string is a palindrome. The basic idea is to look at each character of the string in turn, and compare it to an appropriate character at the other end of the string, as suggested in Fig. 6.4. So if the first and last characters are not the same, the string is not a palindrome. If the second and last-but-one characters are not the same, the string is not a palindrome, and so on. Here is a first try at implementing this idea:

palindrome1.cpp

```cpp
// ===============================================================
// palindrome1.cpp
// A function to test that a string is a palindrome
// ===============================================================
#include <string>
using namespace std;

bool palindrome(string s)
{
  bool isPalindrome;
  for(int i = 0; i < s.size(); i = i + 1)
    {
      if( s[i] != s[s.size() - i] )
        {
          isPalindrome = false;
        }
    }
  return isPalindrome;
}
```

But this code has at least two defects. Can you see them?

The first problem is that isPalindrome will not be given a value unless one of the tests fails. So if the string is a palindrome, the value of isPalindrome will be returned, but we don't know what value it will have. This is easily fixed with a declaration like bool isPalindrome = true;. Another defect is in the indexing

[4]For example, with the very cool structure known as a linked list.

[5]Additionally, most data structures that support array indexing allow us to get at the individual data elements within a fixed time, irregardless of their location within the array.

s[s.size() - i]. When i = 0, this says s[s.size()], but s.size() is not a valid index because string's are indexed using offsets from the first character. The largest possible index, the index of the last character, is s.size() - 1. Once again, checking a boundary case pays off. Since indices are offsets, the index of the element that is offset i *from the end* of the string is s.size()-1 - i. So the correct test is

```
        if (s[i] != s[s.size() - 1 - i])
```

Here is a better (and at least correct) version, with the appropriate changes shown:

palindrome2.cpp

```
1  // ================================================================
2  // palindrome2.cpp
3  // Returns true if the string s is a palindrome, and false
4  // otherwise
5  // ================================================================
6  #include <string>
7  using namespace std;
8
9  bool palindrome(string s)
10 {
11    bool isPalindrome = true;
12    for(int i = 0; i < s.size(); i = i + 1)
13    {
14       if( s[i] != s[s.size() - 1 - i] )
15       {
16          isPalindrome = false;
17       }
18    }
19    return isPalindrome;
20 }
```

The code is still a bit unsatisfying. We know that a string is not a palindrome if the test on line 14 fails for *any* valid index i. So as soon as we find one failure, we are really done, and the string is not a palindrome. This is easily dealt with by returning false as soon as the test fails. So here is another version that returns, from the inside of the loop, as soon as possible:

palindrome3.cpp

```
1  // ================================================================
2  // palindrome3.cpp
3  // Returns true if the string s is a palindrome, and false
4  // otherwise
5  // ================================================================
6  #include <string>
```

```
7   using namespace std;
8
9   bool palindrome(string s)
10  {
11    for(int i = 0; i < s.size(); i = i + 1)
12      {
13        if( s[i] != s[s.size() - 1 - i] )
14          {
15            return false;
16          }
17      }
18    return true;
19  }
```

Note how this works. If all the tests are passed, the code will fall from the bottom of the for loop and return `true` (the string is a palindrome). But if just one test fails, the code will execute `return false`, causing the `palindrome` function to quit right then and return the value `false` to its caller.

There is a particularly interesting "feature" of our two working palindrome testers. They both report that an empty string is a palindrome.[6] This is a tough call—certainly if a string is of size 1, then it is a palindrome because its first character is the same as its last. But is the empty string `""` a palindrome? It is hard to decide what to do with an empty string, especially without more context about how the palindrome tester is to be used in some larger algorithm. But my instincts tell me that if someone passes an empty string into my palindrome tester, they are either being careless, or trying to spoof me. I can easily guard against this with an assertion of the form `assert(s.size() > 0)`.

Our palindrome-checking algorithm is fairly nice—short, verifiable, robust, and correct. But it does still miss some of my favorite palindromes, like the classic `"Able_was_I,_ere_I_saw_Elba"`, and the less known but more intriguing `"Rats_live_on_no_evil_star."` Neither of these strings will be recognized as a palindrome by the `palindrome` function in **palindrome3.cpp**. Furthermore, it's about half as fast as it should be. But let's leave these questions for some exercise.

Questions

Question 7 All the palindrome codes in this section took a string as an argument. Modify any one of them to take a reference to a string instead. Should it be `const` or not?

Question 8 Write a function

```
void everyOther(const string & s,
                ostream & out)
```

that writes every other character of s, starting from the first, to the output stream.

Question 9 Devise a meaningful loop invariant for the code in **palindrome2.cpp**.

Question 10 You can make **palindrome3.cpp** about twice as fast by adding two characters to one line of the source text. Do it.

Question 11 Write a generic procedure that will take any object v that supports array indexing and the `v.size()` method (returning the number of elements in the array), and will reverse it *in place*. So if v has elements {1, 2, 3, 4}, then the procedure will replace it with {4, 3, 2, 1}.

---

[6] Yep, those boundary cases are always interesting!

6.4   VECTORS

A favorite pastime in engineering analysis is to model a physical system and assess its ability to perform some function. Another enjoyable activity is to gather data concerning some technological or physical system, either from measurement or from simulation, and analyze it. In either case, we are faced with lots of numbers, and need a way to store and manage them. Sounds like a job for an array of numbers! There are many suitable data structures in both the C++ language and in the C++ standard library; here I shall introduce one such data structure: the `vector` class.[7]

The `vector` class is a rather full-featured data management class that supports array semantics (indexing), as well as a number of useful enhancements, bells, and even some whistles. As an arraylike object, a `vector` consists of a number of distinct elements of some stored data type, and these elements can be accessed individually using their integer offset from the start of the array. The kinds of data that an individual element can hold are wide and varied, ranging from a `double` all the way to another complete `vector`. So we can use a vector of `double`'s to store a list of numbers, or even a `vector` of `vector`'s to store a whole table of data! A vector can be resized to hold any number of objects (if there is enought space in the computer to do so).

The `vector` class is declared in the `vector` header file. The `vector` class provides a means to manage a collection of objects, all of the same type, using array semantics. It provides facilities to set the size of these data collections at execution, to add and remove elements to the collection, and, of course, provides array indexing. The `vector` class uses the generic template mechanism described in Chapter 5 to allow `vector`'s to hold most any data type, even other `vector`'s.

There are a number of ways to declare a vector; let's explore three of them.

C++ Principle

The simplest vector declaration is of the form

```
vector< T > identifier;
```

where `T` is some data type and `identifier` is an identifier. This declares a vector of zero size that contains no data.

A vector can also be given a size when it is declared, although it can be resized, up or down, later.

C++ Principle

Consider a declaration of the form

```
vector< T > identifier(integer_expression);
```

where `integer_expression` evaluates to a nonnegative integer `len`. In this declaration, `identifier` is declared as a vector of `len` objects of type `T`. The elements of the vector are initialized in some default way dependent on `type`.

---

[7]The `valarray` is another, as is the language's native array, but these array objects are less flexible than the `vector` class.

Again, this vector can later be resized, up or down. This vector is initialized with the specified number of data objects, each of which is created in a default, data-type-dependent way. That's a bit scary—when we create a vector like

```
vector< dodads > dv(10);
```

we have created dv as a vector of 10 dodad's (whatever those are), but have no clear idea of what values those dodad's have been given. It is usually safer to specify a data value with which to initialize a vector:

C++ Principle

In a vector declaration of the form

```
vector< T > identifier(integer_expression, e);
```

where integer_expression evaluates to a nonnegative integer len and e is of type T, identifier is declared as a vector of len objects, all of which are initialized as copies of e.

These three declarations do not exhaust the possible ways to declare a vector, but these will suffice for us.

Once a vector has been created, we will want to do something with it. A vector v of course supports the indexing operation v[i], since that is its main excuse for existing. So we can write code like this:

```
1  unsigned int num = 100;              // number of points
2  double dx = atan2(1.0,0.0)/(num-1);  // distance between points
3  vector< double > sineValues(num);    // values of sine, of course
4
5  for(unsigned int i = 0; i < sineValues.size(); i = i + 1)
6  {
7    sineValues[i] = sin(i * dx);
8  }
```

and thereby create a table of sine values. But vector's support many other operations as well; Table 6.2 lists but some of the basic vector operations that C++ provides for our programming pleasure.

Here, for example, are declarations of vectors of double's, int's, string's and even vector's of vector's:

vectorCreation.cpp

```
1  // =================================================================
2  // vectorCreation.cpp
3  // A code illustrating the creation of vectors
4  // =================================================================
5  #include <iostream>
```

TABLE 6.2 **Some Basic Operations on Objects of Type** vector. **In These** v **is a** vector< type >, e **Is an Element of Type** type, **and** i **Evaluates to an Unsigned Integer.**

Method	Semantics
v.assign(num, e)	Replace the contents of v with num copies of e
v.at(i)	Refers to the element at offset i
v[i]	Refers to the element at offset i (with no check on i)
v.back()	Refers to the last element of the vector
v.clear()	Empties the vector
v.empty()	Returns true if the vector is empty
v.front()	Refers to the first element of the vector
v.pop_back()	Removes the last element of the vector
v.push_back(e)	Appends the element e to the vector
v.resize(newSize)	Changes the vector to be of size newSize
v.resize(newSize, e)	Changes the vector to be of size monotextnewSize and puts e into any newly created elements
v.size()	Returns number of elements in vector v

```
6   #include <vector>
7   #include <string>
8   using namespace std;
9
10  // Declare functions for printing some vectors on
11  // standard output
12  template<class T> void printVector(vector< T > v);
13  template<class T> void printVectorOfVector(
14                      vector< vector< T > > v);
15
16
17  // =======================>> main <<=============================
18  int main()
19  {
20    // Declare some empty vectors
21    vector< int > counters;          // vector of ints
22    vector< double > data;           // vector of double
23    vector< string > quotes;         // vector of strings
24    vector< vector< double > > table; // vector of vectors
25
26    counters.push_back(10);  // push some integers into counters
27    counters.push_back(5);
28
29    // put 10 values, all equal to 2.5, into vector data
30    data.assign(10, 2.5);
31
32    // push some strings into vector quotes
33    quotes.push_back("Alas,_poor_Yorick.");
```

```
34     quotes.push_back("Hey,⎵it's⎵just⎵a⎵skull");
35
36     table.push_back(data);   // put copy of vector data in vector table
37     table.push_back(data);   // put another copy of data into table
38
39     // print some of the vectors created so far
40     cout << "counters⎵:\n";
41     printVector(counters);
42     cout << "data⎵:\n";
43     printVector(data);
44     cout << "quotes⎵:\n";
45     printVector(quotes);
46
47     cout << "table⎵:\n";
48     // printVector(table);   Tempting, but it won't work
49     printVectorOfVector(table);
50
51     // Make vector of 15 int's
52     int i = 10;
53     vector< int > A(i + 5);   // make vector of 15 ints
54
55     // Make vector of 10 doubles, fill with 1.0's
56     vector< double > B(10, 1.0);
57
58     // Make vector of 10 strings, fill with string "Hi!")
59     vector< string > C(10, "Hi!");
60
61     // Make vector of 10 vector's of double, fill with
62     // copies of data, which is a vector of double
63     vector< vector< double > > D(10, data);
64
65     // print these new vectors
66     cout << "A⎵:\n";
67     printVector(A);
68     cout << "B⎵:\n";
69     printVector(B);
70     cout << "C⎵:\n";
71     printVector(C);
72     cout << "D⎵:\n";
73     printVectorOfVector(D);
74
75     return 0;
76  }
77
78  // ===============>> printVector <<=========================
79  template<class T> void printVector(vector< T > v)
```

```
80  {
81    for(int i = 0; i < v.size(); i = i + 1)
82    {
83       cout << "Element " << i << " = " << v[i] << endl;
84    }
85  }
86
87  // ==============>> printVectorOfVector <<====================
88  template<class T> void printVectorOfVector(vector< vector< T > > v)
89  {
90    for(int i = 0; i < v.size(); i = i + 1)
91    {
92       cout << "Element " << i << " = " ;
93       for(int j = 0; j < v[i].size(); j = j + 1)
94         {
95            cout << v[i][j] << " ";
96         }
97       cout << endl;
98    }
99  }
```

The vector< vector < double > > (read that as "vector of vector of double") deserves some discussion. Two of these objects are declared in **vectorCreation.cpp**, the first on line 24 and the second on line 63. A vector< vector < double > > is just a vector object that contains other vectors. Let's think of an object like vector< double > as a list of numbers, laid out horizontally as columns across a single row, as shown in Fig. 6.5. A vector of vectors can then be thought of as a whole collection of such rows, conceptually aligned vertically, as in Fig. 6.6; a vector of vector of double is,

1.0	2.0	4.0	8.0	16.0	32.0	64.0
0	1	2	3	4	5	6

FIGURE 6.5 A vector< double > seen as a row of, in this case, seven numbers.

	0	1	2	3	4	5	6
0	1.0	2.0	4.0	8.0	16.0	32.0	64.0
1	1.0	3.0	9.0	27.0	81.0	243.0	729.0
2	1.0	4.0	16.0	64.0	256.0	1024.0	4096.0

FIGURE 6.6 A vector< vector < double > > interpreted as a table of numbers, in this case with three rows, each containing seven columns.

conceptually, an entire two-dimensional table of data. But this image is in our human minds, not in the computer. We *interpret* the vector of vectors as a table of data.

The vector-of-vector construct is very powerful, and we shall use it in a number of example applications later in this chapter. Note now, however, that there is really nothing very special about manipulating it. Applying the C++ principles outlined above to such an array will yield the expected behavior. For example, if we declare

```
1  vector< double > row(10, 1.0);  // vector of 10 ones
2  vector< vector< double > > table(5, row); // 5 rows, 10 columns
```

then we have created a table of 5 rows and 10 columns, which happens to be filled with 1.0's. We can fetch a whole row (a `vector< double >`) using indexing, like

```
table[3]
```

This refers to the entire fourth row of the table. And we can fetch a single element using indexing like

```
table[3][9]
```

which goes to the fourth row (offset three) and fetches the tenth element (offset nine).

Note, however, that I did not use the generic procedure `printVector` to print the `vector< vector< double > > table`. In the body of `printVector`, I use the statement `cout << v[i]` to ask `cout` to display the element `i` of vector `v`. If applied to `table`, this would ask `cout` to print an entire row of `table`. But a row of `table` is itself an entire array, and `cout <<` is not defined for an entire array. Once again, a generic procedure like `printVector` will only work if the data types it is passed support the operations used in the procedure. Because output streams do not directly support writing out vectors, I had to write a different procedure to print vectors of vectors.

Questions

Question 12 You have a vector `v`, and need it to hold exactly ten items. How can you make sure it will do so?

Question 13 Declare a table of strings with ten rows and five columns.

Question 14 How would you describe the shape of the vector of vectors created in the code below?

```
vector< vector< double > > L(50);
vector< double > row(25, 1.0);
for(unsigned int i = 0; i < L.size()/2;
    i = i + 1)
  {
    L[i] = row;
  }
row.assign(2 * row.size(), 0.0);
for(unsigned int i = L.size()/2;
    i < L.size(); i = i + 1)
  {
    L[i] = row;
  }
```

Question 15 Will the generic procedure that you wrote for Question 11 work on a `vector`?

6.5 SORTING BY MERGING

Sorting is a common need in computing. Indeed, it is a common need in life, and developing excellent sorting algorithms is a continuing task in computer science. Let us therefore develop a reasonably efficient sorting algorithm here. The task is to take an array of elements that can be compared pair-wise by the less than operator <, and rearrange the elements of the array into ascending order. More precisely, let x be an array, and let i and j be valid indices; then if x[i] < x[j], it must be that i < j.

How shall we develop an algorithm to sort an array? There are many simple, but rather inefficient sorting algorithms. I'd like to lead you toward a reasonably efficient one, and along the way illustrate a general approach that can be applied to many problems. When faced with a problem, it is often useful to develop the solution to a simpler, but related problem, and then develop the solution to the original problem by using the solution to this simpler problem.[8] As a simpler problem, let me pose the following question: Suppose that I have *two* arrays, left and right, each of which is already sorted. How can I merge these into a single sorted array x? This problem is not so hard: We simply walk up the arrays left and right, pull out the smallest available element from either, and put it into x. Here is an algorithm to do it:

merge.cpp

```
1   // ================================================================
2   // merge.cpp
3   // Merge two sorted arrays into a single sorted array.
4   // ================================================================
5
6   template<class T>
7   void merge(const T & left, const T & right, T & x)
8   {
9     x.resize(left.size() + right.size());
10    unsigned int leftIndex = 0;  // next element to get from left
11    unsigned int rightIndex = 0; // next element to get from right
12    for(unsigned int i = 0; i < x.size(); i = i + 1)
13      {
14        if(leftIndex == left.size())
15          { // nothing left in left, get data from right
16            x[i] = right[rightIndex];
17            rightIndex = rightIndex + 1;
18          }
19        else if(rightIndex == right.size())
20          { // nothing left in right, get data from left
21            x[i] = left[leftIndex];
22            leftIndex = leftIndex + 1;
23          }
```

[8]Genius is often displayed by those who connect a simple problem to a hard problem when the rest of us see no connection.

```
24        else if(left[leftIndex] < right[rightIndex])
25          {
26            x[i] = left[leftIndex];
27            leftIndex = leftIndex + 1;
28          }
29        else
30          {
31            x[i] = right[rightIndex];
32            rightIndex = rightIndex + 1;
33          }
34      }
35  }
```

This code loops over the elements of the merged array x, and for each element selects the smallest element available from left or right. Some care is needed to make sure that only valid array indices are used. Note most carefully that merge will produce a sorted array x out of two smaller *sorted* arrays. If left and right are unsorted then x will not be sorted either.

To test this procedure, I wrote a small code. Because it needs access to the generic procedure merge from **merge.cpp**, I have included the latter file into the test code using the #include preprocessor directive on line 7 of the following code.

mergetest.cpp

```
1   // ================================================================
2   // mergetest.cpp
3   // Tests the merge procedure.
4   // ================================================================
5   #include <iostream>
6   #include <vector>
7   #include "merge.cpp"
8   using namespace std;
9
10  int main()
11  {
12    vector< int > a(10);
13    vector< int > b(a.size());
14    for(unsigned int i = 0; i < a.size(); i = i + 1)
15      {
16        a[i] = 2*i;      // even numbers
17        b[i] = 2*i+1;    // odd numbers
18      }
19
20    vector< int > c(10);
21    merge(a, b, c);
22
23    for(unsigned int i = 0; i < c.size(); i = i + 1)
```

```
24      {
25        cout << c[i] << endl;
26      }
27
28    return 0;
29  }
```

Running this test will write the numbers 0 through 19, in order, to standard output.

Let us now return to the original problem of sorting a single array. Suppose this list is of length N. Let's split it evenly into two other arrays, which I will call left and right, and let's sort each of those. Then we can use the merge procedure to combine them together into a final, sorted list. Hey, presto! We are done.

"Wait a minute," I hear you cry. "How will you sort left and right?" The same way, of course: Split and sort each half. I'll sort every array in this same way, unless the array is of length zero or 1, in which case it is already sorted. So what I am planning to do is to chop the array in half, and sort each half by chopping *it* in half, and so on, until the piece I am sorting is so short that there is nothing left to sort. Then I will merge these parts back together, maintaining any sort they already have; this merge is where the sorting actually occurs. Figure 6.7 shows the steps in sorting an array of four elements. It's actually very simple, and it's easy to implement the algorithm using its natural recursive structure.

mergeSort.cpp

```
1  // =================================================================
2  // mergeSort.cpp
3  // Sorts the array x, in place
4  // ================================================================#include
   "merge.cpp"
5
6  template<class T>
7  void mergeSort(T & x)
8  {
9    if( x.size() <= 1)
10     {
11       return;   // there is nothing to do
12     }
13
14    // get storage for left and right parts of x
15    T left;
16    T right;
17    left.resize(x.size()/2);
18    right.resize(x.size() - left.size());
19
20    for(unsigned int i = 0; i < left.size(); i = i + 1)
21      {
22        left[i] = x[i];
```

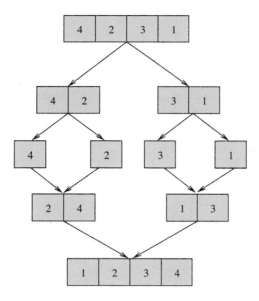

FIGURE 6.7 Merge sort, applied to an array of four integers. Sorting actually occurs when arrays are merged together.

```
23      }
24      for(unsigned int i = 0; i < right.size(); i = i + 1)
25      {
26         right[i] = x[left.size() + i];
27      }
28
29      // sort left and right halves
30      mergeSort(left);
31      mergeSort(right);
32
33      // merge sorted data back together
34      merge(left, right, x);
35  }
```

Observe the simplicity of this algorithm: the input array is split into two parts, each is sorted by a recursive call to mergeSort, and these two sorted parts are combined into a sorted whole by merge. Here is a test of this routine on two different types of array:

sortTest.cpp

```
1  // ============================================================
2  // sortTest.cpp
3  // Tests the merge sort procedure.
4  // ============================================================
5  #include <iostream>
6  #include <vector>
7  #include <string>
```

```
8    #include "mergeSort.cpp"
9    using namespace std;
10
11   int main()
12   {
13     vector< int > a(10);
14     for(unsigned int i = 0; i < a.size(); i = i + 1)
15       {
16         a[i] = a.size() - i;   // count down
17       }
18
19     mergeSort(a);
20
21     cout << "Sorted_vector:_";
22     for(unsigned int i = 0; i < a.size(); i = i + 1)
23       {
24         cout << a[i] << "_";
25       }
26     cout << endl;
27
28     string s("smhtirogla");
29     mergeSort(s);
30     cout << "Sorted_string:_" << s << endl;
31
32     return 0;
33   }
```

Here is the output of this test:

```
1    [hagar@localhost Code]$ ./sortTest
2    Sorted vector: 1 2 3 4 5 6 7 8 9 10
3    Sorted string: aghilmorst
4    [hagar@localhost Code]$
```

Questions

Question 16   Apply the merge sort algorithm, by hand, to sort the array {7, 8, 6, 5, 3, 4, 2, 1}.

Question 17   Note that mergeSort calls itself twice when passed any array of length 2 or longer. The longest possible array on a 32-bit computer is 2^{32} elements long. How many times will mergeSort be called when sorting an array of this maximum length?

Question 18   Why didn't I write lines 18 and 18 of mergeSort as follows?

```
left.resize(x.size()/2);
right.resize(x.size()/2);
```

Question 19   Why didn't I write lines 16 and 16 of mergeSort as

```
T left(x.size()/2);
T right(x.size() - left.size());
```
and dispense with lines 18 and 18 entirely?

6.6 SMOOTHING

Let's develop a procedure to smooth a set of data in one dimension. This is a common problem in data analysis—we have a set of data, from a measurement perhaps, and it is rather noisy, filled with jiggles and jaggles that obscure some long-term trend. A common and useful practice is to *smooth* such data to remove the rapid fluctuations (see Fig. 6.8). The secrets of smoothing data are the subject of the very sophisticated field of filtering; here I shall employ only rather straightforward smoothing techniques that are neither the most efficient nor the most effective, but they are workable and adequate for my presentation.

Imagine some discrete noisy data; it consists of a series of data values d_i, which might represent the ith measurement in a series of measurements. The noise problem rears its ugly head when there is some error or uncertainty in d_i, so that even though the values of d may generally be increasing, there is no definite trend from one point to the next. We want some means to smooth out such fluctuations while leaving the general upward trend apparent. We can do so by averaging the nearby values, in the hopes that the fluctuations are random and will tend to cancel out.

There is no one way to do this. Let's consider the simplest method first: Let d_i, $i = 0, 1, \ldots$ represent the raw data, and let D_i, $i = 0, 1, \ldots$ represent the smoothed data. We will compute D_j simply by averaging the values of d_{j-1}, d_j, and d_{j+1}, so

$$D_j = \frac{d_{j-1} + d_j + d_{j+1}}{3}. \tag{6.1}$$

What are the merits of such a filter? Suppose that the original data are of the form $d_i = im + b + \epsilon_i$, which represents an exact straight line (of slope m and intercept b) with some extra random junk ϵ_i added to it. Then a bit of simple algebra shows

$$D_j = jm + b + \frac{\epsilon_{j-1} + \epsilon_j + \epsilon_{j+1}}{3}. \tag{6.2}$$

So the filtered data also represent a line $D_j = jm + b + \delta_i$, with the right slope and intercept, but with the noise

$$\delta_j = \frac{\epsilon_{j-1} + \epsilon_j + \epsilon_{j+1}}{3}. \tag{6.3}$$

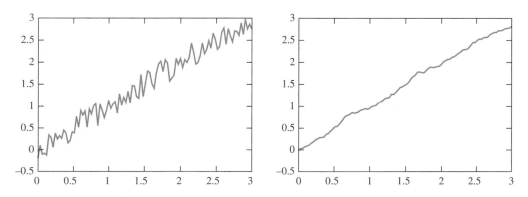

FIGURE 6.8 Noisy data, and the same data after being smoothed.

If the noise ϵ_i is indeed random, then $\epsilon_{j-1} + \epsilon_j + \epsilon_{j+1}$ will tend to be smaller than any one value of ϵ_i, because the ϵ_i values will sometimes be positive and sometimes be negative. I shall not do so here, but it can be shown that the fluctuations in the filtered data are only about one-third the size of the fluctuations in the raw data.[9]

Let's implement this simple averaging filter in a C++ procedure. To do so, we must first select a container to hold our data. A vector< double > looks good for this. We will, of course, work with only a finite set of data values. The formula, Eq. (6.1), will be implemented more or less like this:

```
1   D.resize(d.size());  // size D to hold the result
2   for (unsigned int i = 0; i < d.size(); i = i + 1)
3   {
4     D[i] = (d[i-1] + d[i] + d[i+1])/3.0;  // problem with boundary
5   }
```

But there is a wrinkle to this. How shall we treat the first point, d[0], and how shall we treat the last, d[d.size()-1]? We cannot automatically say

```
D[0] = (d[-1] + d[0] + d[1])/3.0;
```

because d[-1] does not exist. There are only three choices possible here:

1. Invent a value for d[-1].
2. Do not compute D[0] at all.
3. Use a different formula for computing D[0].

It is quite common to deal with this problem, conceptually, by making up a value for d[-1]. Often d[-1] = 0 is used, or sometimes d[-1] = d[0]. But both are effectively making up data, which is rather distasteful. The second approach, not computing D[0] at all, has some merit, but is frequently annoying because we start with d.size() pieces of data and would like to end up with the same number, if only because of potential confusion about what D[0] will mean if we don't compute it at all. That leaves using a different formula. But what should we use? I shall take this third approach, and simply write D[0] = (d[0] + d[1])/2.0. In this way D[0] is still a simple average of its neighbors. The last point, D[d.size()-1] can then be similarly treated.

threePointAverage.cpp

```
1   // ================================================================
2   // threePointAverage.cpp
3   // Computes a simple three-point moving average of a signal
4   // Arguments
5   //    d -- noisy signal
6   //    D -- smoothed signal
7   // ================================================================
```

[9]This requires that the fluctuations be uncorrelated, that is, the value of the fluctuation ϵ_i does not affect the value of the next fluctuation ϵ_{i+1}.

```
8    #include <vector>
9    #include <cassert>
10   using namespace std;
11
12   void threePointAverage(const vector< double > & d,
13                                 vector< double > & D)
14   {
15     assert(d.size() > 0);
16     D.resize(d.size());  // size D to hold the result
17
18     D[0] = 0.5*(d[0] + d[1]);
19
20     for (unsigned int i = 1; i < d.size()-1; i = i + 1)
21       {
22         D[i] = (d[i-1] + d[i] + d[i+1])/3.0;
23       }
24
25     D[d.size()-1] = 0.5*(d[d.size()-1] + d[d.size()-2]);
26
27   }
```

This three-point averaging technique is an example of a *moving average*. It generates a new array in which each point is the average of its neighbors from the original array. There is no reason why such an average should be restricted to three neighboring points. Why not five or seven, or more? Why not, indeed, make the width of the averaging neighborhood an input to the procedure? The only restriction I make, for the moment, is that the number of points used must be odd, since otherwise we would have to use a different number of neighbors to the right than we do to the left.

We can deploy such a variable-width average by using a nested loop, so that instead of averaging only three neighboring points, we can average a number of points determined at the time of execution. This will give us a more powerful filter than the simple three-point average used in **threePointAverage.cpp**. The following procedure implements such a variable-width filter:

movingAverage.cpp

```
1    // ================================================================
2    // movingAverage.cpp
3    // Computes a simple moving average of a signal
4    // ================================================================
5    #include <vector>
6    #include <cassert>
7    using namespace std;
8
9    // A couple of utility functions
```

```
10   unsigned int firstIndex(unsigned int i, unsigned int width);
11   unsigned int lastIndex(unsigned int i, unsigned int width,
12                          unsigned int size);
13
14   // =====>> movingAverage <<===================================
15   // Filters the signal in d into the vector D using a moving
16   // average of specified width.  The width must be odd.
17   // Arguments
18   //   d      -- noisy signal
19   //   D      -- smoothed signal
20   //   width -- width of filter
21   // ==========================================================
22   void movingAverage(const vector< double > & d,
23                            vector< double > & D,
24                      const unsigned int width)
25   {
26     // Requirements ------------------------------------------
27     assert(d.size() > 0);
28     assert(width % 2 == 1);   // only odd filter widths allowed
29     // ------------------------------------------------------
30     D.resize(d.size());  // size D to hold the result
31
32     for(unsigned int i = 0; i < d.size(); i = i + 1)
33       {
34         D[i] = 0.0;
35         unsigned int start = firstIndex(i, width);
36         unsigned int stop  = lastIndex(i, width, d.size());
37
38         for(unsigned int j = start; j <= stop; j = j + 1)
39           {
40             D[i] = D[i] + d[j];
41           }
42         D[i] = D[i]/(stop - start + 1);
43       }
44   }
45
46   // ======>> firstIndex <<====================================
47   // Returns the index <= i at which signal values can start to
48   // contribute to the filtered value of data element i
49   // ==========================================================
50   unsigned int firstIndex(unsigned int i, unsigned int width)
51   {
52     if(i >= width/2)
53       {
54         return i   width/2;
55       }
56     else
```

```
57    {
58       return 0; // start with first piece of data
59    }
60  }
61
62  // ======>> lastIndex <<============================
63  // Returns the index >= i beyond which signal values cease to
64  // contribute to the filtered value of data element i
65  // ============================================================
66  unsigned int lastIndex(unsigned int i, unsigned int width,
67                         unsigned int size)
68  {
69    if(i + width/2 < size)
70      {
71        return i + width/2;
72      }
73    else
74      {
75        return size - 1; // end with last piece of data
76      }
77  }
```

Note the use of the auxiliary variables start and stop to control the limits of the inner loop. It is these that actually implement the width of the filter, but setting their values is slightly tricky because we must act differently when the filter tries to go beyond the edges of the existing signal data. I therefore wrote two utility functions, firstIndex and lastIndex, to determine the necessary values of start and stop for any particular value of i.

Here is a code that I've written to test this. It computes the sine of angles from 0 to 30 radians, adds some random noise to these values, and then smooths the noisy data. This code also calls several other interesting procedures to manipulate vectors; these you can peruse at your leisure. The procedure writeRowsAsCols is particularly long, because it is rather general.

averageTester.cpp

```
1   // ============================================================
2   // averageTester.cpp
3   // Creates some noisy data, and then smooths it
4   // ============================================================
5   #include <iostream>
6   #include <fstream>
7   #include <vector>
8   #include <cmath>
9   #include <string>
10  using namespace std;
11
12  // Declare functions
```

```
13  void funFill(vector< double > & d, vector< double > & x,
14               double xLeft, double xRight, unsigned int N,
15               double fun(double));
16  void addNoise(vector< double > & d, double magnitude);
17  void movingAverage(const vector< double > & d,
18                     vector< double > & D,
19                 const unsigned int width);
20  void writeElementsAsCols(const vector< vector<double> > & d,
21                     ofstream & out);
22
23  // =========================>> main <<=========================
24  int main()
25  {
26    // basic data for the problem
27    unsigned int N = 1000;    // number of data points
28    double start = 0.0;       // first angle
29    double stop = 30.0;       // last angle
30    double amplitude = 0.3;   // size of noise
31    unsigned int width = 11;  // width of average
32    string filename("sinedata.dat");  // file to write data into
33
34    vector< double > data;
35    vector< double > angles;
36    funFill(data, angles, start, stop, N, sin);
37
38    vector< double > noisyData;
39    noisyData = data;    // copy the original data
40    addNoise(noisyData, amplitude);  // add noise to it
41
42    vector< double > smoothedData;
43    movingAverage(noisyData, smoothedData, width); // smooth it
44
45    // write all the data to a file
46
47    vector< vector<double> > d;
48    d.push_back(angles);
49    d.push_back(data);
50    d.push_back(noisyData);
51    d.push_back(smoothedData);
52
53    ofstream out;
54    out.open(filename.c_str());
55    writeElementsAsCols(d, out);
56    out.close();
57
58    return 0;
59  }
```

```
60
61    // ================>> funFill <<================================
62    // Computes a uniform grid of N points (N > 1) running from
63    // xLeft to xRight, inclusive, and stores this into vector x.
64    // Also evaluates fun(x) at each of those points, and stores
65    // the function values into d.
66    // ============================================================
67    void funFill(vector< double > & d, vector< double > & x,
68                 double xLeft, double xRight, unsigned int N,
69                 double fun(double))
70    {
71      assert(N > 1);
72
73      double dx = (xRight - xLeft)/(N-1);
74      x.resize(N);
75      d.resize(N);
76      for(int i = 0; i < N; i = i + 1)
77        {
78          x[i] = xLeft + i * dx;
79          d[i] = fun(x[i]);
80        }
81    }
82
83    // ================>> addNoise <<================================
84    // Adds random noise between -magnitude and magnitude to the
85    // data in vector d.
86    // ============================================================
87    void addNoise(vector< double > & d, double magnitude)
88    {
89      for(int i = 0; i < d.size(); i = i + 1)
90        {
91          // get a random number between -1 and 1
92          double r = 1.0 - 2.0 * static_cast<double>(rand())/RAND_MAX;
93          d[i] = d[i] + magnitude * r;
94        }
95    }
96
97    // ================>> writeRowsAsCols <<========================
98    // Writes a vector of vector of doubles as a table of numbers
99    // with each vector in d as a column in the output.
100   // ============================================================
101   void writeElementsAsCols(const vector< vector<double> > & d,
102                            ofstream & out)
103   {
104     if( d.size() == 0 )
105       {
106         return;  // no data -- nothing to do
```

```
107        }
108
109        // Set up output formatting and create padding strings
110
111        out.setf(ios::scientific);    // use scientific notation
112        out.setf(ios::right);         // right adjust the output
113
114        string separator("␣␣");       // two spaces separate columns
115        out.precision(8);             // digits after the decimal point
116        int extra = 7;                // 7 + 8 = total width
117
118        string pad;  // string of blanks to print in absence of data
119        for(int i = 0; i < extra + out.precision(); i = i + 1)
120          {
121            pad.push_back(' ');
122          }
123
124        // find the length of the longest row
125        unsigned int mostRows = 0;
126        for(int i = 0; i < d.size(); i = i + 1)
127          {
128            if( d[i].size() > mostRows )
129              {
130                mostRows = d[i].size();
131              }
132          }
133
134        // Write the data
135        for(int i = 0; i < mostRows; i = i + 1)
136          {
137            for(int j = 0; j < d.size(); j = j + 1)
138              {
139                if(i < d[j].size())
140                  {
141                    out.width(out.precision() + extra);  // reset width
142                    out << d[j][i];
143                  }
144                else
145                  {  // no data -- print enough spaces
146                    out << pad;
147                  }
148                out << separator;
149              }
150            out << endl;  // time for a new row
151          }
152    }
```

Figure 6.9 shows the noisy sine data generated by this code, and Fig. 6.10 illustrates this same data after smoothing with an 11-point moving average. The resulting curve is relatively smooth, although still somewhat noisy around the peaks.

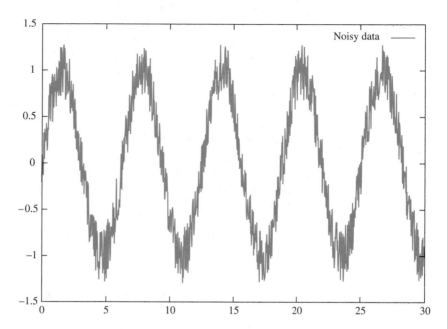

FIGURE 6.9   A noisy sine curve.

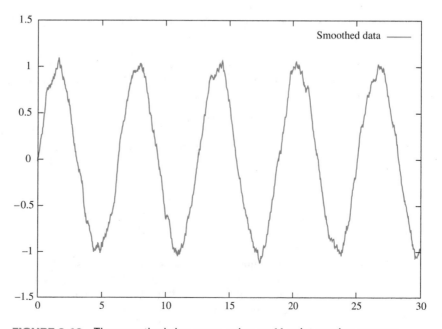

FIGURE 6.10   The smoothed sine curve, using an 11-point moving average.

Questions

Question 20   Is the assertion

```
  assert(d.size() > 0);
```

necessary in `threePointAverage`? How about in `movingAverage`?

Question 21   Rewrite the `threePointAverage` procedure to treat the boundary values by assuming that nonexistent data like d_{-1} and d_N are equal to the boundary values d_0 and d_{N-1}, respectively, where N is the number of data values.

Question 22   Write a simpler version of `writeRowsAsCols` by assuming that the input `vector< vector< double > > d` has rows all of equal length.

6.7   MATRIX-VECTOR MULTIPLICATION

Let's examine once again the moving-average smoothing operation: Suppose we have eight data values $x_0, x_1, \ldots, x_7$, and wish to filter them using a three-point moving average. Denoting the smoothed data by $b_0, b_1, \ldots, b_7$, we can say that the x's are related to the b's by the system of equations

$$
\begin{aligned}
b_0 &= \tfrac{1}{2}x_0 + \tfrac{1}{2}x_1 + 0x_2 + 0x_3 + 0x_4 + 0x_5 + 0x_6 + 0x_7 \\
b_1 &= \tfrac{1}{3}x_0 + \tfrac{1}{3}x_1 + \tfrac{1}{3}x_2 + 0x_3 + 0x_4 + 0x_5 + 0x_6 + 0x_7 \\
b_2 &= 0x_0 + \tfrac{1}{3}x_1 + \tfrac{1}{3}x_2 + \tfrac{1}{3}x_3 + 0x_4 + 0x_5 + 0x_6 + 0x_7 \\
b_3 &= 0x_0 + 0x_1 + \tfrac{1}{3}x_2 + \tfrac{1}{3}x_3 + \tfrac{1}{3}x_4 + 0x_5 + 0x_6 + 0x_7 \\
b_4 &= 0x_0 + 0x_1 + 0x_2 + \tfrac{1}{3}x_3 + \tfrac{1}{3}x_4 + \tfrac{1}{3}x_5 + 0x_6 + 0x_7 \\
b_5 &= 0x_0 + 0x_1 + 0x_2 + 0x_3 + \tfrac{1}{3}x_4 + \tfrac{1}{3}x_5 + \tfrac{1}{3}x_6 + 0x_7 \\
b_6 &= 0x_0 + 0x_1 + 0x_2 + 0x_3 + 0x_4 + \tfrac{1}{3}x_5 + \tfrac{1}{3}x_6 + \tfrac{1}{3}x_7 \\
b_7 &= 0x_0 + 0x_1 + 0x_2 + 0x_3 + 0x_4 + 0x_5 + \tfrac{1}{2}x_6 + \tfrac{1}{2}x_7.
\end{aligned}
\tag{6.4}
$$

There is a tremendous amount of regularity in these equations. Each equation, on the right, contains a sum of eight terms, each of which is one of the x's multiplied by a coefficient. These coefficients depend on which of the x's is being multiplied and which of the b's appears on the right-hand side. For example, the fourth equation could be written as

$$
\begin{aligned}
b_3 &= A_{30}x_0 + A_{31}x_1 + A_{32}x_2 + A_{33}x_3 + A_{34}x_4 \\
&\quad + A_{35}x_5 + A_{36}x_6 + A_{37}x_7,
\end{aligned}
\tag{6.5}
$$

where the A_{ij} are just symbolic names given to each of the coefficients, with i denoting the equation (in other words, which of the b_i is being computed), and j denoting the coefficient of x_j in that equation. The action of the filter can be completely specified by the rectangular table, or *matrix*, of these coefficients:

$$\begin{matrix}
\frac{1}{2} & \frac{1}{2} & 0 & 0 & 0 & 0 & 0 & 0 \\
\frac{1}{3} & \frac{1}{3} & \frac{1}{3} & 0 & 0 & 0 & 0 & 0 \\
0 & \frac{1}{3} & \frac{1}{3} & \frac{1}{3} & 0 & 0 & 0 & 0 \\
0 & 0 & \frac{1}{3} & \frac{1}{3} & \frac{1}{3} & 0 & 0 & 0 \\
0 & 0 & 0 & \frac{1}{3} & \frac{1}{3} & \frac{1}{3} & 0 & 0 \\
0 & 0 & 0 & 0 & \frac{1}{3} & \frac{1}{3} & \frac{1}{3} & 0 \\
0 & 0 & 0 & 0 & 0 & \frac{1}{3} & \frac{1}{3} & \frac{1}{3} \\
0 & 0 & 0 & 0 & 0 & 0 & \frac{1}{2} & \frac{1}{2}.
\end{matrix}$$

$$(6.6)$$

There are 64 of these coefficients, so if we want to give symbolic names to them, individualized names are out of the question; instead, we need a systematic naming scheme. Let's agree to call them all by a single name, say, **A,** and use row and column indices to denote specific ones. The number in row i and column j can then be denoted A_{ij}.

The equation in row i of Eq. (6.4) can be written as

$$b_i = \sum_{j=0}^{N-1} A_{ij}x_j, \qquad (6.7)$$

where $N = 8$ is the number of data values x_j, $j = 0, 1, \ldots, 7$, and $\sum$ denotes summation, as always. This operation, which takes a vector **x** of length N and transforms it into another vector **b,** is called matrix-vector multiplication. Symbolically, in mathematical notation we write

$$\mathbf{b} = \mathbf{Ax}. \qquad (6.8)$$

Matrix-vector multiplication is one of a number of basic matrix operations that commonly arise in dealing with systems of linear equations. Although the matrix in Eq. (6.6) is square—it has the same number of rows as it does columns—there is nothing in the definition of matrix-vector multiplication, Eq. (6.7), that requires this. In general, we can multiply a matrix of M rows and N columns—called an $M \times N$ matrix—by a vector of size N,[10] and thereby get a new vector of size M. Denoting the elements of **A** by A_{ij}, we obtain

$$b_i = \sum_{j=0}^{N-1} A_{ij}x_j, \qquad i = 0, 1, \ldots, M. \qquad (6.9)$$

For example, in the system of equations

$$\begin{aligned}
b_0 &= 1x_0 + 1x_1 + 1x_2 + 1x_3 \\
b_1 &= 0x_0 + 1x_1 + 1x_2 + 1x_3 \\
b_2 &= 0x_0 + 0x_1 + 1x_2 + 1x_3
\end{aligned} \qquad (6.10)$$

---

[10]Indeed, we can regard a vector of length N as a matrix with one column and N rows; such a $N \times 1$ matrix is often called a column vector.

we are multiplying a vector **x** of size 4 by a matrix with three rows and four columns. We often write this as

$$\begin{bmatrix} b_0 \\ b_1 \\ b_2 \end{bmatrix} = \begin{bmatrix} 1 & 1 & 1 & 1 \\ 0 & 1 & 1 & 1 \\ 0 & 0 & 1 & 1 \end{bmatrix} \begin{bmatrix} x_0 \\ x_1 \\ x_2 \\ x_3 \end{bmatrix} \tag{6.11}$$

and in this you might consider the structure of the equations: we scan across a single row of the matrix while zooming down all the rows of the vector **x**, multiplying each A_{ij} from the row i of the matrix **A** by a value x_j from row j of **x**. For example, to compute b_1 in Eq. (6.11), we use row 1 of the matrix and all rows of **x**, as shown here:

$$\begin{bmatrix} b_0 \\ b_1 \\ b_2 \end{bmatrix} = \begin{bmatrix} 1 & 1 & 1 & 1 \\ 0 & 1 & 1 & 1 \\ 0 & 0 & 1 & 1 \end{bmatrix} \begin{bmatrix} x_0 \\ x_1 \\ x_2 \\ x_3 \end{bmatrix} .$$

To express the mathematical operation of matrix multiplication in an algorithm, we need to select some means of encoding matrices and vectors using the structures provided by our programming language. There is no one unique way to do this. Indeed, one of the marvelous contributions of the object-oriented language C++ to scientific computing is the realization that such matrix data can be represented in many different ways, each tailored to some specific circumstance. We shall not try to explore all of these ways. There are many general and special-purpose matrix and vector libraries available for C++,[11] but to proceed in this text, we must develop at least one way of mapping matrices and matrix-vector computations to C++.

It seems quite reasonable to map the mathematical notion of a column vector to the C++ standard library type of `vector`, and often more specifically to `vector<double>`. But note that in doing so, a `vector` does not provide any sense of a "row" or "column." A `vector` is just a list of numbers. If we do consider such a list to be a column vector, this is an *understanding* that we have when expressing the algorithm, but it is not an understanding that has any place in the C++ language. Similarly, it seems reasonable to use a `vector< vector< double > >` to represent a matrix. Such a vector of vectors provides a pair of indices that we can interpret as row and column indices. So given the declaration

```
vector< vector< double > > A(M, vector<double>(N, 0));
```

we can consider `A` to be a matrix of numbers with `M` rows and `N` columns, and use `A[i][j]` to refer to row `i` and column `j`. But the C++ language is not enforcing any conventions about matrices; C++ does not "know" that we are thinking of `A` as a matrix, or that it has "rows" and "columns." The matrix nature of `A` lies primarily in *our interpretation* of it. In the computer's memory the data that we store in `A` is not laid out in a large rectangle of rows and columns.

---

[11]Lapack++, Blitz, and the MTL are but three of the interesting general-purpose libraries available for storing and manipulating matrices and vectors in C++.

Using this encoding of mathematical vectors to the vector class, and of matrices to vector< vector< > >, let's write a C++ procedure to compute the product of a matrix of double's and a vector of double:

matvecDouble.cpp

```
1   // ================================================================
2   // matvecDouble.cpp
3   // A procedure to perform a matrix vector product
4   // ================================================================
5   #include <vector>
6   #include <cassert>
7   using namespace std;
8
9   // ====>> matvecDouble <<===================================
10  // Does a matrix vector product
11  // Arguments
12  //   A  -- a matrix
13  //   x  -- vector by which to multiply it
14  //   y  -- vector in which to place result
15  // ================================================================
16  void matvecDouble(const vector< vector< double > > & A,
17                          const vector< double > & x,
18                          vector< double > & y)
19  {
20    // Requirements
21    assert(A.size() > 0);
22
23    y.resize( A.size() );   // resize y to hold the result
24
25    for(unsigned int i = 0; i < y.size(); i = i + 1)
26      {
27        // Requirements: num columns of A == size of x
28        assert(A[i].size() == x.size());
29
30        y[i] = 0.0;
31        for(unsigned int j = 0; j < x.size(); j = j + 1)
32          {
33            y[i] = y[i] + A[i][j] * x[j];
34          }
35      }
36  }
```

With this routine in hand, we can filter a signal by simply building the required matrix and multiplying the signal by it. Let's consider this plan; we might write code much like this:

movingAverage2.cpp

```
1    // ============================================================
2    // movingAverage2.cpp
3    // Computes a simple moving-average of a signal.
4    // This version uses an explicit matrix vector multiply.
5    // ============================================================
6    #include <vector>
7    #include <cassert>
8    using namespace std;
9
10   // Declare matvecDouble from matvecDouble.cpp
11   void matvecDouble(const vector< vector< double > > & A,
12                     const vector< double > & x,
13                           vector< double > & y);
14
15
16   // =======>> firstIndex <<=====================================
17   // Returns the index <= i at which signal values can start to
18   // contribute to the filtered value of data element i
19   // ============================================================
20   unsigned int firstIndex(unsigned int i, unsigned int width)
21   {
22     if(i >= width/2)
23       {
24         return i - width/2;
25       }
26     else
27       {
28         return 0; // start with first piece of data
29       }
30   }
31
32   // =======>> lastIndex <<======================================
33   // Returns the index >= i beyond which signal values cease to
34   // contribute to the filtered value of data element i
35   // ============================================================
36   unsigned int lastIndex(unsigned int i, unsigned int width,
37                          unsigned int size)
38   {
39     if(i + width/2 < size)
40       {
41         return i + width/2;
42       }
43     else
44       {
```

```
45      return size - 1; // end with last piece of data
46    }
47  }
48
49  // =====>> buildFilterMat <<=================================
50  // Builds a matrix A to perform a moving-average filtering.
51  // size is the number of data points to filter, and width is
52  // the width of the moving average.
53  // ==========================================================
54  void buildFilterMat(vector< vector< double > > & A,
55                      unsigned int size, unsigned int width)
56  {
57    // empty A
58    A.clear();
59
60    // Now resize it to fit
61    A.resize(size, vector<double>(size, 0.0));
62
63    // Now fill it in
64    for(unsigned int i = 0; i < size; i = i + 1)
65     {
66       unsigned int start = firstIndex(i, width);
67       unsigned int stop = lastIndex(i, width, size);
68
69       for(unsigned int j = start; j <= stop; j = j + 1)
70        {
71          A[i][j] = 1.0/(stop - start + 1);
72        }
73     }
74  }
75
76  // =====>> movingAverage <<=================================
77  // Filters the signal in d into the vector D using a moving
78  // average of specified width.
79  // ==========================================================
80  void movingAverage(const vector< double > & d,
81                     vector< double > & D,
82                     const unsigned int width)
83  {
84    // Requirements ------------------------------------------
85    assert(d.size() > 0);
86    assert(width % 2 == 1);   // only odd filter widths supported
87    // -------------------------------------------------------
88
89    // Build filter Matrix
90    vector< vector< double > > A;
```

```
91    buildFilterMat(A, d.size(), width);
92
93    // actually filter the signal
94    matvecDouble(A, d, D);
95  }
```

What does this version offer us over the previous one?

It is true that the new `movingAverage` routine is very short and easy to follow. But this simplicity exists only at the surface. All of the detailed work has been pushed into the routines `buildFilterMat` and `matvecDouble`. Once those routines are considered, this version is revealed as more complicated than the original **movingAverage.cpp**. Indeed, this version is also slower, and it uses more storage space in the computer. So is this new version without merit? No, it does have merit—it exposes the general structure of filtering as a matrix-vector multiplication. So when we want to move beyond the moving average, we can build other filters simply by changing the filter matrix.

Examining the filter matrix of Eq. (6.4), we see that each row of the matrix sums to 1. The responsibility of each row of the filter matrix is to average together various signal values from **x** into a single value of the smoothed signal. Let us therefore generalize the notion of a filter. Given a list of data values, the signal, $x_i, i = 0, 1, \ldots, N-1$, we can transform it by matrix multiplication, yielding the values

$$b_i = \sum_{j=0}^{N-1} A_{ij} x_j.$$

If the rows of the matrix A satisfy the condition

$$1 = \sum_{j=0}^{N-1} A_{ij} \qquad \text{for each } i,$$

then a constant signal is unchanged by such a transformation, and each b_i is called a weighted average of the x_i's. I will ask you to explore this further as part of a project at the end of this chapter.

The Forward Problem in Tomography   As another application of matrix-vector multiplication, let's examine a simplified form of the computed tomography problem. As you may know, in a computer-aided tomography (CAT) scan a penetrating beam of radiation is used to produce a picture of the interior of an object. Be it a human or an archaeological artifact, the picture is in fact a map of the spatially varying mass density within the object.

For a simplified version of the problem, imagine an object that is made up of concentric square rings of matter, with different rings possibly having different density, as suggested in Fig. 6.11. Tomography works by measuring the mass of slices through an object, such as those shown by the dashed cuts through Fig. 6.12. This mass measurement could be done by physically cutting the object and weighing each slice, but human patients might object. The mass of each segment can also be measured by passing x-rays or other radiation through the object, because the number of radiation particles that

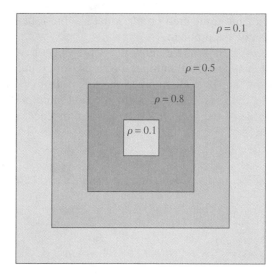

FIGURE 6.11 An object made up of concentric square rings of mass. Each concentric ring has its own density. The central square is still considered a ring.

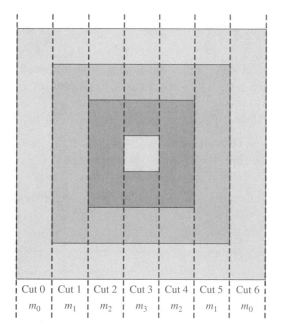

FIGURE 6.12 Seven cuts are made through the object, and the mass of each slice is determined. The masses of the slices on the right are the same as those on the left, so there are really only four masses to know: m_0, m_1 m_2, and m_3.

get through the material is related to the mass through which they pass. With such a set of mass measurements in hand, the tomography problem involves using these measured masses to determine the density of each of the rings.[12] This is called the *inverse problem*; its opposite number is the *forward problem* of computing the mass of each slice through the object, assuming that the density of the rings is known. This forward

[12]What distinguishes this simplified problem from the general tomography problem is my assumption here that the object is made up of rings of constant mass. This greatly simplifies the algebraic problem, but retains its fundamental features.

problem is a matrix-vector multiplication problem; let's solve it here, and in the next section we will solve the inverse problem.

So suppose for the moment that we know the density ρ_j of each ring, and want to find the mass m_i of each slice. I shall number the rings from 0 to $N - 1$, going from outside toward the center, and I shall number the slices from 0 to $N - 1$, going from the left side toward the center. The mass of the first slice is the density of the outer ring times the volume of the slice. If a ring is one unit thick and one unit wide, then the volume of the slice is $1 \times 1 \times (2N - 1)$, and so

$$m_0 = (2N - 1)\rho_0. \tag{6.12}$$

The mass of the second slice involves two chunks of ring 0, and $(2N - 1 - 2)$ chunks of ring 1, so

$$m_1 = 2\rho_0 + (2N - 1 - 2)\rho_1. \tag{6.13}$$

Similarly,

$$m_2 = 2\rho_0 + 2\rho_1 + (2N - 1 - 4)\rho_2, \tag{6.14}$$

and we can generalize this to

$$m_i = \sum_{j=0}^{i-1} 2\rho_j + (2N - 1 - 2i)\rho_i, \qquad i = 0, 1, \ldots N - 1. \tag{6.15}$$

Do you see the matrix-vector multiplication in this? The vector of slice masses $\mathbf{m}$ is given by multiplying a matrix $\mathbf{A}$ by the vector $\boldsymbol{\rho}$ of ring densities. For the case of four rings, the equation $\mathbf{m} = \mathbf{A}\boldsymbol{\rho}$ is

$$\begin{bmatrix} m_0 \\ m_1 \\ m_2 \\ m_3 \end{bmatrix} = \begin{bmatrix} 7 & 0 & 0 & 0 \\ 2 & 5 & 0 & 0 \\ 2 & 2 & 3 & 0 \\ 2 & 2 & 2 & 1 \end{bmatrix} \begin{bmatrix} \rho_0 \\ \rho_1 \\ \rho_2 \\ \rho_3 \end{bmatrix}. \tag{6.16}$$

Creating the required matrix in C++ is a straightforward process. Here is a routine to do so:

sliceMassMat.cpp

```
1   // ================================================================
2   // sliceMassMat.cpp
3   // Builds the matrix that can compute the mass of slices through
4   // a set of concentric square rings.
5   // ================================================================
6   #include <vector>
7   #include <cassert>
8   using namespace std;
9
10  void sliceMassMat(unsigned int numRings,
11                    vector< vector< double > > & A)
12  {
13    assert(numRings > 0);
14    A.resize(numRings);
```

```
15   for(unsigned int i = 0; i < numRings; i = i + 1)
16   {
17     A[i].assign(numRings, 0.0);
18     for(unsigned int j = 0; j < i; j = j + 1)
19     {
20       A[i][j] = 2.0;
21     }
22     A[i][i] = (2 * numRings - 1 - i * 2);
23   }
24 }
```

We could then solve the forward problem, determining the masses of the slices from known density data, with a simple pair of calls:

```
1  // vector< double > rho is known
2
3  vector< vector< double > > A;
4  sliceMassMat(rho.size(), A);
5
6  vector< double > m;   // masses
7  matvecDouble(A, rho, m);
```

Figure 6.13 shows a possible density distribution, and Fig. 6.14 the mass of the corresponding slices, computed by matrix-vector multiplication using 100 rings of constant density.

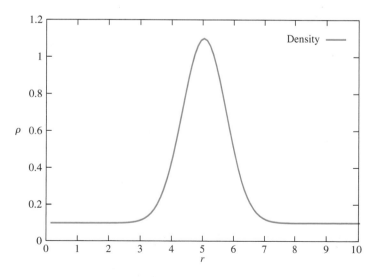

FIGURE 6.13   A density distribution as a function of distance r from the center of a square object.

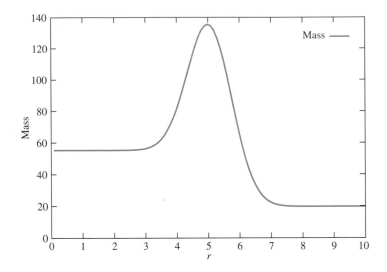

FIGURE 6.14   The mass of slices through the object with the density distribution from Fig. 6.13, as a function of the distance from the center of the object.

Questions

Question 23   Consider the declaration:

```
vector< vector< double >> A(M,
        vector<double>(N, 0));
```

In this section I interpreted this as a matrix with M rows and N columns. Why should we not instead consider A to be a matrix of N rows and M columns?

Question 24   Why is the code in **movingAverage2.cpp** slower than that in **movingAverage.cpp**? Why does **movingAverage2.cpp** use more storage than did **movingAverage.cpp**?

Question 25   Using templates, write a procedure matvec that computes a matrix-vector product of matrices whose elements are any numeric type. For the

sake of this question, a numeric type is any type that supports the arithmetic operators * and + (e.g., double, int, complex, and so forth).

Question 26   Write a procedure

```
sliceMass(
        const vector< double > & density,
        unsigned int numRings,
        vector< double > & sliceMasses)
```

that will compute the masses of numRings slices through the object made up of square rings whose densities are given in density, but do not compute or store a matrix, or explicitly use a matrix-vector multiplication routine.

6.8   SOLUTION OF LINEAR SYSTEMS

Now that we have the matrix for the tomography problem, we can take up the more interesting inverse problem: Given the mass of the N slices, what are the masses of the N rings? This is determined by solving the system of linear equations $A\rho = \mathbf{m}$ for the vector of N unknowns, ρ. The special form of the matrix A makes this relatively straightforward. The matrix A has only zeros above its diagonal, so we can instantly solve the first equation for

$$\rho_0 = \frac{m_0}{A_{00}}, \tag{6.17}$$

and once that is done, we can easily solve the second equation for

$$\rho_1 = \frac{m_1 - A_{10}\rho_0}{A_{11}} \tag{6.18}$$

and then

$$\rho_2 = \frac{m_2 - A_{20}\rho_0 - A_{21}\rho_1}{A_{22}} \tag{6.19}$$

and so on.

This repetitious pattern looks ripe for algorithmic implementation. Because it is traditional, I will call the unknown **x**, and the known vector **b**. A matrix **A** that has nonzero elements only on and below the diagonal is called lower triangular. Here is a C++ procedure that solves the system **Ax** = **b** for a lower triangular matrix **A**.

lowerTriangularSolve.cpp

```
1   // ==================================================================
2   // lowerTriangularSolve.cpp
3   // Solves A x = b with A square and having only zeros above
4   // the diagonal, and no zeros on the diagonal.
5   // ==================================================================
6   #include <vector>
7   #include <cassert>
8   using namespace std;
9
10  void lowerTriangularSolve(const vector< vector< double > > & A,
11                                    vector< double > & x,
12                            const vector< double > & b)
13  {
14    assert(A.size() == b.size());
15    x.resize( b.size() );
16
17    for(unsigned int i = 0; i < A.size(); i = i + 1)
18      {
19        assert(A[i].size() == b.size());
20        // Invariant: x[j] = solution for all 0 <= j < i
21
22        double numerator = 0.0;
23        for(unsigned int j = 0; j < i; j = j + 1)
24          {
25            numerator = numerator + x[j] * A[i][j];
26          }
27
28        // solve for x[i]
29        x[i] = (b[i] - numerator)/A[i][i];
30      }
31  }
```

On each trip through the outer loop, this code solves for the next unknown, x[i]. To do so, it first runs an inner loop that computes the known product $\sum_{j=0}^{i-1} A_{ij}x_j$ and subtracts this from the right-hand side b_i. Simply dividing this difference by the diagonal matrix element A[i][i] yields the desired result.

Just for a test, here is a simple test code:

lowerTriangularTest.cpp

```
1    // =================================================================
2    // lowerTriangularTest.cpp
3    // Tests the lowerTriangularSolve procedure
4    // =================================================================
5    #include <iostream>
6    #include <vector>
7    using namespace std;
8
9    void lowerTriangularSolve(const vector< vector< double > > & A,
10                                    vector< double > & x,
11                              const vector< double > & b);
12
13   int main()
14   {
15     const unsigned int len = 4; // size of system
16     vector< vector <double> > A(len, vector<double>(len,0.0));
17     vector< double > b(len, 1.0);
18
19     A[0][0] = 1.0;    // 1 0 0 0
20     A[1][1] = 1.0;    // 0 1 0 0
21     A[2][2] = 1.0;    // 0 0 1 0
22     A[3][3] = 1.0;    // 1 0 0 1
23     A[3][0] = 1.0;
24
25     vector< double > x;
26     lowerTriangularSolve(A, x, b);
27
28     for(unsigned int i = 0; i < x.size(); i = i + 1)
29       {
30         cout << x[i] << endl;
31       }
32
33     return 0;
34   }
```

Running this, we receive the glad report that the solution vector is $\mathbf{x} = \{1, 1, 1, 0\}$, which is correct.

The code in **lowerTriangularSolve.cpp** provides us with the means to solve the inverse tomography problem that I set up in the last section. The following code does so. It reads the masses of slices through a set of square rings from a file and writes the density of the rings into an output file.

inverseTomography.cpp

```cpp
// ==============================================================
// inverseTomography.cpp
// Solves the square ring tomography problem
// ==============================================================
#include <iostream>
#include <fstream>
#include <vector>
#include <cstdlib>
#include <string>
using namespace std;

// Procedures defined elsewhere
void lowerTriangularSolve(const vector< vector< double > > & A,
                                vector< double > & x,
                             const vector< double > & b);
void sliceMassMat(unsigned int numRings,
                  vector< vector< double > > & A);

// Procedures defined here
void getMasses(string inputFile, vector< double > & masses);
void writeDensity(string outputFile, const vector< double > & rho);

// ======>> main <<=========================================
int main()
{
  cout << "Input file name :> ";
  string inputFile;
  cin >> inputFile;
  cout << "Output file name :> ";
  string outputFile;
  cin >> outputFile;

  vector<double> masses;
  getMasses(inputFile, masses);

  vector< vector< double > > A;
  sliceMassMat(masses.size(), A);

  vector<double> rho;
  lowerTriangularSolve(A, rho, masses);

  writeDensity(outputFile, rho);
```

```
43
44      return EXIT_SUCCESS;
45    }
46
47
48    // ====>> getMasses <<============================================
49    // Read mass data from file
50    // Arguments
51    //   inputFile -- the name of the input file
52    //   masses -- reference into which mass data is stored
53    // ================================================================
54    void getMasses(string inputFile, vector< double > & masses)
55    {
56      ifstream in(inputFile.c_str());
57      if(in.fail())
58        {
59          cerr << inputFile << "did_not_open\n";
60          exit(EXIT_FAILURE);
61        }
62
63      double m;
64      in >> m;
65      while(not in.fail())
66        {
67          masses.push_back(m);
68          in >> m;
69        }
70      in.close();
71    }
72
73    // ====>> writeDensity <<==========================================
74    // Write density data to file
75    // Arguments
76    //   outputFile -- the name of the output file
77    //   rho        -- density values to write
78    // ================================================================
79    void writeDensity(string outputFile, const vector< double > & rho)
80    {
81      ofstream out(outputFile.c_str());
82      if(out.fail())
83        {
84          cerr << outputFile << "did_not_open\n";
85          exit(EXIT_FAILURE);
86        }
87
88      for(unsigned int i = 0; i < rho.size(); i = i + 1)
89        {
```

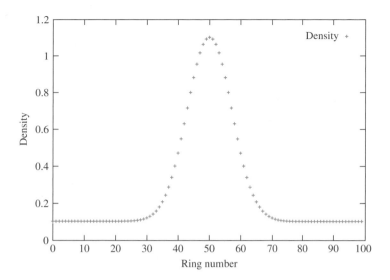

FIGURE 6.15 The density of the rings, reconstructed using the data shown in Fig. 6.14.

```
90        out << rho[i] << endl;
91     }
92   out.close();
93 }
```

Figure 6.15 shows the densities reconstructed by taking the masses from Fig. 6.14 as the measured mass data. The reconstructed densities match those of Fig. 6.13 quite closely.

I must, sadly, report that this approach has limited utility in most real tomography problems. The approach that we have developed here is very sensitive to errors in the measured masses, and even sensitive to the computer's errors in arithmetic. I have been somewhat careful to develop a simplified tomography problem that is not too fragile, so our results look pretty good. But in more realistic tomography problems we must be more careful. The algebraic reconstruction technique developed in Project 11 contains the heart of one of the many more robust techniques for solving tomography problems.

6.8.1 General Systems of Equations

The matrix that arose in the simplified tomography problem had a lower-triangular structure—it had only zero elements above the diagonal. It also had only nonzero elements on the diagonal, and this allowed us to easily solve a system of linear equations based on that matrix, using the algorithm implemented in **lowerTriangularSolve.cpp**. This ease of solution arises because of the triangular structure, which allows us to solve successively for each unknown, using the previously revealed unknowns to find each next unknown in turn.

The same would be true of an upper-triangular system of equations. An upper-triangular system is one in which there are only zeros below the diagonal of the system

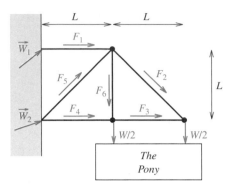

FIGURE 6.16 A weight held up by a cantilever. The length L does not matter.

matrix. If none of the diagonal elements in such a matrix is zero, then it is easy to solve for the unknowns. I will leave writing an algorithm to do so as an exercise.

Unfortunately, most systems of equations are not so nicely organized. A system of equations is usually neither upper-triangular nor lower-triangular. Consider, for example, the cantilever shown in Fig. 6.16, of the sort that has held aloft many an inn sign. Each rigid rod in this truss carries a force, and additionally the wall exerts forces at the attachment points. We should like to know these forces, under the assumption that the cantilever holds its shape independent of the weight of the sign. We don't know the forces F_i, although we know the direction along which each acts, and we don't know the forces $\vec{W}_1$ and $\vec{W}_2$ exerted by the wall. But we do know that these forces all balance at each joint and at the wall, and we know the force that the weight exerts. Writing the balance of forces, in both the horizontal and vertical directions, at each joint, we have

$$F_3 + F_2/\sqrt{2} = 0, \qquad\qquad F_2/\sqrt{2} = W/2 \qquad (6.20)$$

$$F_4 - F_3 = 0, \qquad\qquad F_6 = W/2 \qquad (6.21)$$

$$F_1 - F_2/\sqrt{2} + F_5/\sqrt{2} = 0, \qquad F_5/\sqrt{2} - F_6 - F_2/\sqrt{2} = 0 \qquad (6.22)$$

$$W_{1x} - F_1 = 0, \qquad\qquad W_{1y} = 0 \qquad (6.23)$$

$$W_{2x} - F_4 - F_5/\sqrt{2} = 0, \qquad W_{2y} - F_5/\sqrt{2} = 0. \qquad (6.24)$$

This system of linear equations can be written as

$$
\begin{bmatrix}
0 & 1/\sqrt{2} & 1 & 0 & 0 & 0 & 0 & 0 & 0 & 0 \\
0 & 1/\sqrt{2} & 0 & 0 & 0 & 0 & 0 & 0 & 0 & 0 \\
0 & 0 & -1 & 1 & 0 & 0 & 0 & 0 & 0 & 0 \\
0 & 0 & 0 & 0 & 0 & 1 & 0 & 0 & 0 & 0 \\
1 & -1/\sqrt{2} & 0 & 0 & 1/\sqrt{2} & 0 & 0 & 0 & 0 & 0 \\
0 & -1/\sqrt{2} & 0 & 0 & 1/\sqrt{2} & -1 & 0 & 0 & 0 & 0 \\
-1 & 0 & 0 & 0 & 0 & 0 & 1 & 0 & 0 & 0 \\
0 & 0 & 0 & 0 & 0 & 0 & 0 & 1 & 0 & 0 \\
0 & 0 & 0 & -1 & -1/\sqrt{2} & 0 & 0 & 0 & 1 & 0 \\
0 & 0 & 0 & 0 & -1/\sqrt{2} & 0 & 0 & 0 & 0 & 1
\end{bmatrix}
\begin{bmatrix}
F_1 \\ F_2 \\ F_3 \\ F_4 \\ F_5 \\ F_6 \\ W_{1x} \\ W_{1y} \\ W_{2x} \\ W_{2y}
\end{bmatrix}
=
\begin{bmatrix}
0 \\ W/2 \\ 0 \\ W/2 \\ 0 \\ 0 \\ 0 \\ 0 \\ 0 \\ 0
\end{bmatrix}.
$$

$$(6.25)$$

How shall we create an algorithm to solve such a general system of equations? We know how to solve some special systems of equations; for example, we know how to solve an upper-triangular system. Let's therefore seek to use our solution of this special problem to solve the general problem. What we need to do is transform a general system of equations into an equivalent upper-triangular system. If we can do this, without it affecting the solution, then we can use our ability to solve upper-triangular systems to solve the general linear system. Gaussian elimination provides a means to effect just such a transformation.

6.8.2 Gaussian Elimination

The solution of a lower-triangular system proved quite straightforward, at least so long as there were no zero elements on the diagonal of the matrix. The solution of an upper-triangular system—one in which the matrix has only zeros below the diagonal—is equally simple (see Project 9 at the end of this chapter), again provided there are no zeros on the diagonal. Therefore, if we can transform a general system of linear equations into an equivalent upper-triangular form, we will have the means to solve any such system of equations.

Gaussian elimination allows us to do just this. The basic idea is to develop a set of simple operations that we can apply to a system of equations to rearrange them algebraically, and then to use these transformations over and over to reduce the equations to an upper-triangular form. Two operations will suffice for us but three are traditionally presented. Given a system of equations $\mathbf{Ax} = \mathbf{b}$, we can:

1. Multiply any one of the equations $\sum_{j=0}^{N-1} A_{ij} x_j = b_i$ by any nonzero number α without changing the solution $\mathbf{x}$. This transforms that one equation to

$$\sum_{j=0}^{N-1} (\alpha A_{ij}) \, x_j = (\alpha b_i).$$

In other words, we can multiply row i of the matrix $\mathbf{A}$ by any nonzero number, provided we also multiply row i of the right-hand side $\mathbf{b}$ by that same number.

2. Multiply any one equation $\sum_{j=0}^{N-1} A_{kj} x_j = b_k$ by a number α and add it to one of the other equations $\sum_{j=0}^{N-1} A_{ij} x_j = b_i$, yielding

$$\sum_{j=0}^{N-1} (A_{ij} + \alpha A_{kj}) \, x_j = (b_i + \alpha b_k).$$

Thus, we can add α times row k to row i of the matrix without changing $\mathbf{x}$, provided we also add α times row k of $\mathbf{b}$ to row i of $\mathbf{b}$.

3. Interchange any two equations, so take the equation $\sum_{j=0}^{N-1} A_{kj} x_j = b_k$ in row k and swap it with the equation $\sum_{j=0}^{N-1} A_{ij} x_j = b_i$ in row i. This requires simply swapping rows i and k of $\mathbf{A}$ and $\mathbf{b}$.

Let's write a couple of small routines that apply these transformations to a matrix A and vector b:

equationTransforms.cpp

```
1    // ==============================================================
2    // equationTransforms.cpp
3    // Basic operations on systems of equations
4    // ==============================================================
5    #include <vector>
6    using namespace std;
7
8    // ====>> scaleRow <<=====================================
9    // Scales one row of a system of equations
10   // Arguments
11   //   A    -- matrix to scale
12   //   b    -- right-hand side to scale
13   //   row -- index of row to scale
14   //   s    -- number to scale by
15   // ==============================================================
16   void scaleRow(vector< vector< double > > & A,
17                 vector< double > & b, unsigned int row, double s)
18   {
19     assert(A.size() > row);          // valid row?
20     assert(A.size() == b.size());
21     for(unsigned int j = 0; j < A[row].size(); j = j + 1)
22       {
23         A[row][j] = A[row][j] * s;
24       }
25     b[row] = b[row] * s;
26   }
27
28   // ====>> addToRow <<=====================================
29   // Adds a scaled version of one row of a system of equations
30   // to another row
31   // Arguments
32   //   A    -- system matrix
33   //   b    -- right-hand side vector
34   //   targetRow -- row to add to
35   //   sourceRow -- row to add to it
36   //   s    -- number to scale by
37   // ==============================================================
38   void addToRow(vector< vector< double > > & A,
39                 vector< double > & b,
40                 unsigned int targetRow,
41                 unsigned int sourceRow,
42                 double s)
43   {
```

```
44    assert(A.size() > targetRow && A.size() > sourceRow);
45    assert(A.size() == b.size());
46    assert(A[targetRow].size() == A[sourceRow].size());
47
48    for(unsigned int j = 0; j < A[targetRow].size(); j = j + 1)
49      {
50        A[targetRow][j] = A[targetRow][j] + s * A[sourceRow][j];
51      }
52    b[targetRow] = b[targetRow] + s * b[sourceRow];
53  }
54
55  // ====>> swapRows <<==========================================
56  // Swap two rows of a system of equations
57  // Arguments
58  //    A    -- system matrix
59  //    b    -- right-hand side vector
60  //    rowA, rowB -- rows to swap
61  // ============================================================
62  void swapRows(vector< vector< double > > & A,
63                vector< double > & b,
64                unsigned int rowA,
65                unsigned int rowB)
66  {
67    assert(A.size() > rowA && A.size() > rowB); // valid rows?
68    assert(A.size() == b.size());
69    assert(A[rowA].size() == A[rowB].size()); // same size?
70
71    for(unsigned int j = 0; j < A[rowA].size(); j = j + 1)
72      {
73        double tmp = A[rowA][j]; // save for swap
74        A[rowA][j] = A[rowB][j];
75        A[rowB][j] = tmp;
76      }
77    double tmp = b[rowA];
78    b[rowA] = b[rowB];
79    b[rowB] = tmp;
80  }
```

Using these, we can try to transform equations into simpler forms. Consider the problem of transforming a general system of linear equations into an upper-triangular form, assuming that the diagonal elements of **A** are all nonzero. Then we can use the first row of **A** to eliminate every element of the first column of **A** below the diagonal by adding an appropriate multiple of the first row to all subsequent rows. For example, consider the equations

$$
\begin{bmatrix} 2 & -4 & 6 & -8 \\ 6 & 2 & 3 & 5 \\ 2 & 1 & -1 & 1 \\ -3 & 3 & -3 & 2 \end{bmatrix} \begin{bmatrix} x_0 \\ x_1 \\ x_2 \\ x_3 \end{bmatrix} = \begin{bmatrix} 1 \\ 0 \\ 0 \\ 1 \end{bmatrix}.
\tag{6.26}
$$

Let me first scale the first row by multiplying it by 1/2, yielding

$$
\begin{bmatrix} 1 & -2 & 3 & -4 \\ 6 & 2 & 3 & 5 \\ 2 & 1 & -1 & 1 \\ -3 & 3 & -3 & 2 \end{bmatrix} \begin{bmatrix} x_0 \\ x_1 \\ x_2 \\ x_3 \end{bmatrix} = \begin{bmatrix} 1/2 \\ 0 \\ 0 \\ 1 \end{bmatrix}.
\tag{6.27}
$$

Now, adding -6 times the first row to the second row yields

$$
\begin{bmatrix} 1 & -2 & 3 & -4 \\ 0 & 14 & -15 & 29 \\ 2 & 1 & -1 & 1 \\ -3 & 3 & -3 & 2 \end{bmatrix} \begin{bmatrix} x_0 \\ x_1 \\ x_2 \\ x_3 \end{bmatrix} = \begin{bmatrix} 1/2 \\ -3 \\ 0 \\ 1 \end{bmatrix}.
\tag{6.28}
$$

Thus, by applying our basic transformations to this system of equations, we have introduced a zero into the second row, first column, without changing the solution of the system. Proceeding, by adding -2 times the first row to the third row, and 3 times the first row to the last row, we obtain

$$
\begin{bmatrix} 1 & -2 & 3 & -4 \\ 0 & 14 & -15 & 29 \\ 0 & 5 & -7 & 9 \\ 0 & -3 & 6 & -10 \end{bmatrix} \begin{bmatrix} x_0 \\ x_1 \\ x_2 \\ x_3 \end{bmatrix} = \begin{bmatrix} 1/2 \\ -3 \\ -1 \\ 5/2 \end{bmatrix}.
\tag{6.29}
$$

We can continue this process of introducing zeros below the diagonal by now using the second row to zero out elements of **A** in the second column, below the diagonal, then using the third row to zero out elements from the third column, and so on until there are only zeros below the diagonal. This process is called Gaussian elimination.

gaussianElimination.cpp

```
1   // ==============================================================
2   // gaussianElimination.cpp
3   // Reduces a system of equations to upper-triangular form
4   // by Gaussian elimination.  All elements on the diagonal will
5   // be made equal to 1.0
6   // ==============================================================
7   #include <vector>
8   using namespace std;
9
10  // Declare the needed basic transformations
11  void scaleRow(vector< vector< double > > & A,
12                vector< double > & b, unsigned int row, double s);
```

```
13   void addToRow(vector< vector< double > > & A,
14                 vector< double > & b,
15                 unsigned int targetRow,
16                 unsigned int sourceRow,
17                 double s);
18
19
20   // ===>> gaussianElimination <<=================================
21   // Arguments
22   //    A -- matrix of system of equations
23   //    b -- right-hand side of system of equations
24   // ============================================================
25   void gaussianElimination(vector< vector< double > > & A,
26                            vector< double > & b)
27   {
28     assert(A.size() == b.size());
29     for(unsigned int i = 0; i < A.size(); i = i + 1)
30       {
31         assert(A.size() == A[i].size());  // square matrix?
32         scaleRow(A, b, i, 1.0/A[i][i]);
33         for(unsigned int j = i+1; j < A.size(); j = j + 1)
34           {
35             addToRow(A, b, j, i, -A[j][i]);
36           }
37       }
38   }
```

This routine reduces a system of linear equations, in place, to an equivalent upper-triangular form. Solving such an upper triangular system is easy, and I will leave to you the creation of a routine to do so.

I have tested this Gaussian elimination routine. Have you?

Questions

Question 27 Write a code to solve Eqs. (6.25).

Question 28 Rewrite the gaussianElimination so that it does not call scaleRow and addToRow, but rather performs those operations within the gaussianElimination routine itself.

Question 29 Create a gaussianElimination that transforms a matrix into lower-triangular form, rather than upper-triangular form.

6.9 NATIVE ARRAYS, POINTERS, AND THE COMMAND LINE

Although the vector class is a complex data object that is defined using C++ code constructs, C++ also supports a simpler, more basic, less flexible, and more error-prone native array data type. Does not sound very attractive, does it? In fact, I rarely use these native arrays, except for rather low-level programming. But they are sometimes worth knowing about. They have less overhead than the `vector` class, and sometimes they are handed to us by others, so we should know about them.[13]

C++ Principle

A declaration of the form

```
T x[constantInt];
```

where x is an identifier, declares a native array x that can contain `constantInt` elements of type T. The expression `constantInt` must evaluate to a positive integer *at compile time*.

Such a native array cannot be resized and supports none of the operations of Table 6.2, save indexing [ ]. Native arrays also cannot be returned from functions, and are passed into functions in a special way (which, unlike passing a `vector`, does not involve copying the array). Note also that a native array must be sized using an integer constant that the compiler can evaluate when the code is compiled.[14] Here are a couple of valid, and one invalid, array declarations:

```
1   int a[10];    // a is a native array of 10 ints
2   double b[5];   // b is a native array of 5 doubles
3   int i = 6;
4   double c[i];   // can't do this -- i is not a constant
```

Native arrays can also be initialized when they are created by using a special syntax, one form of which allows the array to be automatically sized at compile time.

C++ Principle

A declaration of the form

```
T x[] = { initializer_list } ;
```

where x is an identifier, declares a native array x whose elements are of the specified simple type T. The `initializer_list` must be a list of literal data values separated by commas, and the array will be sized to hold them.

This can be very useful to hold a common set of numbers. Consider the following version of our old friend **daysThisMonth** from Chapter 4:

---

[13] What I am calling native arrays are usually called "arrays." I'm calling them native arrays so as to maintain a distinction between the abstract notion of an array that supports certain operations, and various realizations of this abstract data type, such as `vector` and C/C++ native arrays.

[14] Some compilers have, in fact, dispensed with this requirement, but such an extension is not part of the standard C++ language.

daysThisMonth4.cpp

```
1   #include <cassert>
2   using namespace std;
3
4   // =================>> daysThisMonth <<========================
5   int daysThisMonth(int month, int year)
6   {
7     assert(0 < month and month <= 12);   // valid month?
8     assert(0 < year);                    // valid year?
9
10    // store the normal number of days in each month
11    const unsigned int days[] =
12                  {31, 28, 31, 30, 31, 30, 31, 31, 30, 31, 30, 31};
13
14    if( month == 2 and
15      (year % 4 == 0 and ( year % 100 != 0 or year % 400 == 0 )))
16      {
17        return 29; // a leap year
18      }
19
20    return days[month - 1];  // do the usual case
21  }
```

This version is much shorter than the originals from Chapter 4, which relied on careful construction of multiple selection statements and their controlling conditions. The case of a leap year is still managed using a selection statement, but the general case is replaced by array indexing.

6.9.1 Pointers

There is a close connection between these native arrays and a group of data types in C++ called pointers. Pointers are very powerful and important tools for managing data in C++, but they are sometimes confusing and error-prone. And for many applications the data classes of the Standard Template Library (such as `vector`'s) are more appropriate. However, the implementation of the Standard Template Library is just packed with pointers, so when we use this library, we are exploiting pointers without having to deal with them explicitly. Because of their importance in implementing data structures in C++, it is worth taking a bit of time to briefly introduce the basic ideas of pointers.

The C++ language imposes a model of memory in which all data is stored in a contiguous sequence of bytes, and each byte is uniquely identified by an *address*, as shown in Fig. 6.17. A pointer is a data type that can store such an address. The name "pointer" is a nicely descriptive one: A pointer *points* to something else. Although, as humans, you and I are probably more comfortable naming our data with meaningful identifiers, pointers provide a less intuitive but more dynamic means to identify data by using an address that can actually be manipulated by our algorithm. A pointer is thus rather

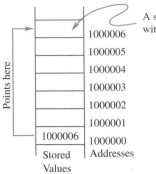

FIGURE 6.17 The C++ model of memory as a large number of contiguous storage locations, each with its own address. An address, 1000006, has been stored as a pointer; this address refers to another storage location.

like a reference, in that it refers to data other than itself. But unlike a reference, a pointer does actually store a value: A pointer stores an address of some object in memory. While a reference has to be initialized when it is declared and can never change—it always refers to the same thing—a pointer does not have to be thus initialized, and the address value that a pointer stores can be changed. This makes pointers both flexible and dangerous; a pointer might not contain a meaningful address value, so it might not point to a valid data object, or it might not point to the data object that we think it does.

C++ Principle

A declaration of the form

```
T * identifier;
```

declares a pointer that can hold the address of an object of type T.

Note that a pointer points to a specific *type*. If I declare a pointer to hold the address of a `double`, then I cannot hope to usefully store the address of an `int` in it. A pointer, once declared, is married to a specific data type.[15]

A pointer can contain the address of an object, but where do such addresses come from? Here are four sources:

- The address of an object can be determined by applying the *address of* operator to it. This operator is denoted & (and so is annoyingly confused with the notation used to declare a reference). If x is a `double`, then

```
double * p = &x;
```

stores the address of x in p.

- The name of a native array evaluates (in most contexts) to a pointer to the first element of the array. Thus, given the declaration `int a[10];`, the statement

```
int * q = a;
```

stores the address of a[0] in q.

---

[15]C++ provides a type called a void pointer that can hold the address of any type of object, but we will not discuss it here.

- The operator new can be called to get a brand new, unused address, which can be either the address of a single object or the address of the start of an array of objects. We will see an example of this in Section 6.9.3.
- Pass a native array "by value" into a function or procedure. A native array, when passed by value, evaluates to the address of its first element, and it is this address that is actually passed by value into the routine.

But what good is a pointer? Pointers are most usefully employed with the *dereference operator*, and with array indexing. The dereference operator is a unary operator using the symbol *, so if p is a pointer that stores a valid address of an object, then *p refers to the object at the address stored in p. For example,

```
1   double r = 1.0;
2   double * p = &r;    // p points at r
3   *p = 2.0;           // r is 2.0
4   cout << "r␣=␣" <<   r << endl;  // writes 2.0 to standard output
5   cout << "r␣=␣" << *p << endl;   // writes 2.0 to standard output
```

We say in *p that * dereferences the pointer p.

However, there is no real need for this new syntax using *. A pointer that stores a valid address can always be conceptually considered to point at an object in an array of at least one element, and pointers support the array indexing operator.

C++ Principle

> If p is declared as T * p, so p is a pointer to an object of type T, and if p has actually been assigned the address of an object of type T, then p[0] refers to the object at that address.

So the previous example can be written equivalently as

```
1   double r = 1.0;
2   double * p = &r;    // p points at r
3   p[0] = 2.0;         // r is 2.0
4   cout << "r␣=␣" <<     r << endl;  // writes 2.0 to standard output
5   cout << "r␣=␣" << p[0] << endl;   // writes 2.0 to standard output
```

I generally prefer this syntax over *p, first because [ ] can't be confused with a stray multiplication, but also because there seems little need to introduce new syntax when existing syntax already does the job.

More generally,

C++ Principle

> If p is declared as T * p; and has actually been given the address of the first object in a native array of T's, then p[i] refers to the element at index i of that array.

Naturally, only valid index values are meaningfully allowed. To illustrate

```
1  string names[3];              // An array of 3 strings
2  string * nameAddress = names; // points at names[0]
3  nameAddress[0] = "Emmylou";   // Same as names[0] = "Emmylou";
4  namesAddress[1] = "B._B.";    // OK
5  namesAddress[2] = "Tricia";   // OK
6  namesAddress[3] = "Aaron";    // error -- invalid index
```

Unfortunately, C++ will not prevent us from using an invalid array index with a pointer, and it is therefore easy to generate memory protection errors or to destroy our own data using pointers. This is especially easy if we should try to dereference an uninitialized pointer.

Neither of these uses of pointers is particularly convincing. We could have achieved the same effects using reference variables. Indeed, pointers are not fundamentally required to implement algorithms, and most programming languages do without them. But in C++ pointers are tightly integrated into the language in order to provide direct access to memory. This allows C++ to be used to write code, such as computer operating systems, that must manipulate computer hardware directly. C++ is an especially interesting language because it allows this kind of low-level access to hardware while simultaneously allowing higher-level abstract data classes such as vector and string to be created. For most applications, these higher-level constructs are more convenient.

One place where pointers are forced on us in C++ is when passing native arrays into routines. A native array is never passed into a routine; instead, a pointer to its first element is passed. For example, consider the following function:

```
1  double sumUp(double * x, unsigned int n)
2  {
3    double sum = 0.0;
4    for(unsigned int i = 0; i < n; i = i + 1)
5      {
6        sum = sum + x[i];
7      }
8    return sum;
9  }
```

which could be used like this:

```
1  double a[] = {1.0, 1.0, 2.0, 2.0, 3.0, 3.0};
2  cout << "Sum is " << sumUp(a, 6) << endl;
```

When the native array `a` is passed into the function `sumUp`, what is actually passed is the address of `a[0]`. The `sumUp` routine really applies array indexing to the pointer `x`. Although we could have declared `sumUp` equivalently as `double sumUp(double x[], unsigned int n)`, this would, in fact, make no difference to the true semantics; the first argument is still passed as a pointer. This silent conversion of native arrays into pointers to their first element pervades much of C++. Or rather, it pervades much of what C++ has unfortunately inherited from C.

C strings, including string literals like `"We are a string"`, are stored as native arrays of `char` values, and are therefore often treated as pointers to `char`. So an array used to refer to 10 C strings could be declared as

```
char * names[10];
```

This does not declare an array *of* 10 C strings; it declares an array of 10 pointers, each of which could potentially point to a C string. But as of yet those pointers do not have meaningful values—they have not been initialized. We must still somehow get addresses to put into this array of pointers. This can be contrasted with

```
string names[10];
```

which does create a native array of 10 string objects, ready for immediate use.

6.9.2 The Command Line

So far in this book we have written `main` as

```
int main()
```

But the C++ standard allows another version of `main` to be written. This alternate can be declared as

```
int main(int argc, char * argv[])
```

and allows our code access to the command line that was used to start it. This variant declaration says that `main` can actually take two arguments, an `int` and an array of pointers to `char`. The latter is, in fact, a native array of C strings. The first argument, `argc`, is the number of "words" that were typed on the command line when the code was started. So if I start a code by typing

```
1  [hagar@localhost TeX]$ ls book.tex data.tex
```

then argc will be 3, because there were three words typed: ls, book.tex, and data.tex. These three words are then available as C strings in the array argv. In particular, argv[0] is "ls", argv[1] is "book.tex", and argv[2] is "data.tex". Note that no attempt is made to interpret these words. If a human types in

```
1   [hagar@localhost TeX]$ ls 10 3.14159
```

there are still three C strings available in argv, not a string and some numbers. If we want to treat the word "3.14159" as a number, we will have to do it ourselves.

A common use of such command line arguments is to provide filenames and other data to our code without having to engage in a conversation. For example, the following code copies the files named on its command line to standard output: it prints the contents of the files, one after another, on the screen. The heart of the code is a simple traversal of the argv array, taking each C string from this array and treating it as the name of a file to copy to the standard output.

myCat.cpp

```
1   // ================================================================
2   // myCat.cpp
3   // Copies all the files named on its command line to cout
4   // ================================================================
5   #include <iostream>
6   #include <fstream>
7   #include <string>
8   #include <cstdlib>
9   using namespace std;
10
11  // declare functions
12  void outputFile(string name);
13
14  // ================>> main <<================================
15  int main(int argc, char * argv[])
16  {
17    if(argc == 0)
18      {
19        cerr << "Command line arguments not supported.  Sorry\n";
20        return EXIT_FAILURE;
21      }
22    if(argc < 2)
23      {
24        cerr << "Usage: " << argv[0] << " file_names\n";
25        return EXIT_FAILURE;
26      }
```

```
27
28    // Copy each file to standard output
29    for(int i = 1; i < argc; i = i + 1)
30      {
31        outputFile(argv[i]);
32      }
33    return EXIT_SUCCESS;
34  }
35
36  // ==============>> outputFile <<===============================
37  // Copies the named file to standard output
38  // =============================================================
39  void outputFile(string name)
40  {
41    ifstream out;
42    out.open(name.c_str());
43    if( out.fail() )
44      {
45        cerr << "File " << name << " did not open\n";
46        return;
47      }
48
49    string line;
50    while( not out.fail() )
51      {
52        getline(out, line);
53        cout << line << endl;
54      }
55    out.close();
56  }
```

I could have declared outputFile as

```
void outputFile(char * name)
```

and simply passed the character pointer name into out.open. But I prefer to minimize the regions of code into which pointers are allowed to spread. By declaring outputFile to take a string and then passing it a character pointer, we allow the code to convert the C string into the safer and more flexible string object.

6.9.3 The New Operator

The new operator is yet another means to obtain a valid pointer. The purpose of new is to find a contiguous section of memory in which a specified number of objects, all of the same type, can be stored.

C++ Principle

> A statement of the form
>
> ```
> T * identifier = new T[integer_expression];
> ```
>
> where `integer_expression` evaluates to a nonnegative integer, allocates space for a native array of objects of type `T`. The length of the array will be the value of the `integer_expression`, and the address of its first element will be stored in `identifier`. The compiler must know how to construct an object of type `T`.

The `new` operator generally asks the operating system for additional memory space to be provided to the executing code, and if that space cannot be provided, the code will terminate. For each element of the newly allocated array, the compiler will arrange to construct a default object of type `T`. It can do this for any of the simple numeric types (like `double`, `int`, or `char`), and also for more complicated types such as `string`. Indeed, it can do so for any of the types that appear in this text, but it is possible to create data types in C++ that the compiler cannot figure out how to construct.[16]

With `new` we can create arrays whose size is determined dynamically at run time, and gain access to these through pointers to their first element. For example, here is a bit of code to prompt for an array of numbers to be entered on standard input:

```
1  unsigned int n;
2  cout << "Size_of_array_:>_";
3  cin >> n;
4  double * numbers = new double[n];  // allocate space for n doubles
5  cout << "Enter_" << n << "_values_:>_";
6  for(unsigned int i = 0; i < n; i = i + 1)
7    {
8      cin >> numbers[i];
9    }
```

But as a native array, such a dynamically allocated array does not provide any conveniences. We cannot say `numbers.size()`, for example, and we must therefore keep track of the number of elements in the array. These dynamically allocated arrays are very useful for the construction of data management utilities such as the `vector` class, but when implementing algorithms for higher-level problems in engineering, we are better served by building on top of such utilities.

Because memory is a finite resource, we must release memory when we are done with it. C++ provides the `delete` operator to do this.

---

[16] In order to automatically construct an object of some class, the compiler requires that the class possess a "default constructor," but some classes defy default construction!

C++ Principle

If pointer p contains an address that was provided by new, then

```
delete [] p;
```

will free the memory that new allocated.

The empty pair of [] is important. This reminds the C++ compiler to release resources associated with all of the elements of the array, so don't leave it out! For example, when we are done with the numbers pointer above, we should execute the code

```
delete [] numbers;
```

to free up the memory to which numbers pointed. Also, delete can only free memory that was allocated with new. If delete is given an address that was not provided by new, then something bad, and undefined, will happen. If you are lucky, the operating system will notice a memory protection error and kill your program; if you are unlucky, your code will just silently do wrong things and generate incorrect results.

An inexcusably common problem is to allocate memory, and then lose track of it, so that it can never be freed. For example,

```
 1  unsigned int n;
 2  cout << "Size_of_array_:>_";
 3  cin >> n;
 4  double * numbers = new double[n];
 5  cout << "Enter_" << n "_values_:>_";
 6  for(unsigned int i = 0; i < n; i = i + 1)
 7    {
 8      cin >> numbers[i];
 9    }
10
11  double x;
12  numbers = &x;      // The previous value of numbers is lost!
13                     // Now we can never free the memory
14                     // allocated by new
```

By assigning a new address to numbers before deleting the allocated memory, we have lost our chance to ever release that memory. The memory allocated on line 4 cannot be freed until our code terminates its execution. This is known as a memory leak. Unfortunately, too many codes leak memory, and these often lead to problems for their users as they consume and lose the available memory of the computer on which they run. Although a modern operating system can sort this all out once the execution terminates, until that time the memory is lost.

Because there is much that can go wrong, it is best not to dynamically allocate memory with new, or even to use pointers, unless you are implementing a data management class that needs such immediate access to memory. The purpose of the vector class, and the many other data management classes of the C++ standard libraries, is to provide robust data management facilities. The purpose of pointers and dynamically allocated memory is to implement such facilities.

Questions

Question 30 Suppose I want to read a list of numbers from an `istream` and store it in an array. Comment on any problems with the following routine to do so:

```
unsigned int getData(double x[],
                        istream &in)
{
  unsigned int i = 0;
  double datum;
  in >> datum;
  while( not in.fail() )
    {
        x[i] = datum;
        i = i + 1;
        in >> datum;
    }
  return i;
}
```

Question 31 Rewrite the routine from the previous question as a procedure that stores the list of data in a `vector< double >`. Declare it as `void getData(vector< double > &x, istream &in)` and avoid any problems you identified in the native-array-based version.

Question 32 Write a short code that will echo whatever the user types in on the command line back to standard output.

Question 33 Write a routine

```
void getStringMem(unsigned int n,
                     string * & mem)
```

that will dynamically allocate space for n `string`'s, fill all of the space with empty strings, and return a pointer to that space through the reference `mem`. *Note:* `string * & mem` says that `mem` is a reference to a pointer to a `string`!

Projects

Here is a range of exercises that involve array semantics. You should always consider testing such codes with small data sets where you can be sure of the results, and then later test them with large data sets too.

PROJECT 1

The palindrome functions given earlier in this chapter can all be fooled by strings of mixed case, whitespace, and punctuation. Write, and test, a palindrome function that ignores the case of letters, whitespace, and punctuation.

PROJECT 2

Write a code that will search for a pattern, as defined below, in a text file. The code should print out the line number and line on which each match occurs.

A pattern is to be either a literal string, possibly containing whitespace, or else a string that contains the wildcard character '.' which is to match one occur-

rence of any character. Thus, the pattern `"thus"` does not match the line

```
Thus the pattern
```

while `".hus_t.e"` does match it. Finally, in order to match a '.' in a line, we escape the period with a back slash, so that `"\."` matches a single period.

PROJECT 3

Web browsers do not display C++ source text in a very pretty way. Write a program that will read a C++ source text and write an html file that presents the source text in a pleasing way. This should include the handling of characters that are special in html (&, <, and >), showing literal strings in a different color than other text, showing literal characters in another color, and showing source code comments in yet another color. Additional bells and whistles are welcome.

PROJECT 4

A polynomial $P_n(x) = a_0 + a_1 x + a_2 x^2 + a_3 x^3 + \cdots + a_n x^n$ of order n can be stored as an array of the coefficients $(a_0, a_1, a_2, a_3, \ldots, a_n)$. The *derivative* of the polynomial P_n is a polynomial Q_{n-1} of order $n - 1$:

$$Q_{n-1} = a_1 + 2a_2x + 3a_3x^2 + \cdots + na_nx^{n-1}.$$

Write a procedure that replaces a polynomial, represented by a vector of coefficients, with its derivative.

PROJECT 5

A polynomial $P_n(x) = a_0 + a_1x + a_2x^2 + a_3x^3 + \cdots + a_nx^n$ of order n can be stored as an array of the coefficients $(a_0, a_1, a_2, a_3, \ldots, a_n)$. The *indefinite integral* of the polynomial P_n is a polynomial O_{n+1} of order $n + 1$:

$$O_{n+1} = 0 + a_0x + a_1x^2/2 + a_2x^3/3 + a_3x^4/4$$
$$+ \cdots + a_nx^{n+1}/(n + 1).$$

Write a procedure that replaces a polynomial, represented by a vector of coefficients, with its indefinite integral.

PROJECT 6

Write an algorithm that will find the largest contiguous partial sum within a vector<double>. That is, we want to sum up any number of neighboring elements from the array, starting from anywhere, and find the largest possible sum. For example, if the array contains

```
-3 4 2 1 -4 6 -10 0 -4 3
```

then the algorithm should report 9, because $4 + 2 + 1 + (-4) + 6 = 9$ is the largest sum of contiguous elements from that array of numbers. The routine you create in C++ should also provide the starting and ending indices of the summed elements back to its caller (indices 1 and 5 in the example).

PROJECT 7

Consider the electric circuit shown here:

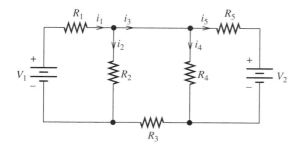

Using Ohm's law, the fact that the voltage drop around any closed loop is zero (conservation of energy), and the

fact that the sum of all currents entering any junction is equal to the sum of all currents exiting the junction (conservation of charge), develop a system of five linear equations that can be solved for the five indicated currents. Write a routine that takes as input a vector of resistance values, and the two indicated voltages, and provides as output a vector containing the five current values.

PROJECT 8

In this chapter I asserted that a vector of data $\mathbf{x}$ could be filtered by multiplying it by a matrix whose rows summed to 1.

Here is one way to create such filter matrices: Select an even function $f(s)$ and a *filter width* w, which is any real number. From these compute the matrix of coefficients $f_{ij} = f((j - i)/w)$. For each row of this matrix, compute the row sum $F_i = \sum_{j=0}^{N-1} f_{ij}$ and then define $A_{ij} = f_{ij}/F_i$ (this process is called normalization). This matrix $\mathbf{A}$ is then a filter matrix, and it can filter a signal $\mathbf{x}$ by matrix-vector multiplication.

Here are three interesting and common choices for $f(s)$, all of which yield low-pass filters—meaning that they tend to kill high frequencies and leave low frequencies alone:

$$f(s) = e^{-s^2} \qquad \text{Gaussian filter}$$
$$f(s) = \text{sinc}(s) \qquad \text{Sinc filter}$$
$$f(s) = \begin{cases} 1 & |s| \leq 1/2 \\ 0 & |s| > 1/2 \end{cases} \qquad \text{Moving average}$$

where

$$\text{sinc}(s) = \begin{cases} 1 & s = 0 \\ \sin(s)/s & s \neq 0 \end{cases}.$$

Write a procedure that will build a filter matrix from any function of the form double f(double). The procedure should also take the filter width w as a parameter. Write a code that will apply a Gaussian, sinc, and moving-average filter, all of the same width, to data read from a file, and write all three filtered signals to a single output file. Write a code to generate a noisy signal, for example, of the form $\cos(i\Delta x) + \sin(40i\Delta x)$ for $\Delta x = 0.01$ and $i = 0, 1, \ldots, 3{,}000$. Plot the results to compare the effectiveness of the filters for various filter widths w.

PROJECT 9

Suppose you have a matrix $\mathbf{A}$ with zeros below the diagonal and no zeros on the diagonal. Such a matrix is called upper-triangular. Write a procedure, analogous to **lowerTriangularSolve**, that solves the system of linear equations $\mathbf{Ax} = \mathbf{b}$.

PROJECT 10

Suppose you have a two-dimensional data set, a rectangular table of numbers, stored in a `vector< vector< double > >`. Such a data set may represent an image, for example, but may contain noise or static. A simple filter to reduce the effect of such noise is based on replacing each element of the array with the average of itself and all of its immediate neighbors. The neighbors of a few typical data cells are shown in the figure below:

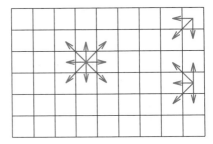

Note that the number of neighbors of an element of the array depends on where the element is: most elements have eight neighbors, most edge elements have five neighbors, and corner elements have only three neighbors. Write a routine that will perform such a filtering operation. Can you perform this smoothing operation in place, using only the storage that holds the original data, or do you have to create a second `vector< vector< double > >` in which to place the filtered data?

PROJECT 11

Imagine that a thin ore layer of variable density lies a distance h below the surface. The surface, and the ore layer below, are divided into a uniform grid of $N \times M$ *pixels,* and the acceleration due to gravity a_{ij} is measured at each pixel i, j on the surface.[17] Because of the $1/r^2$ law of gravity, the contribution to a_{ij} due to the mass m_{op} of ore at location o, p is

$$\frac{m_{op}}{(i-o)^2 + (j-p)^2 + h^2},$$

where the units have been chosen to absorb all physical constants. Adding up all the contributions to a_{ij} from all the ore masses yields

$$a_{ij} = \sum_{o=1}^{N} \sum_{p=1}^{M} \frac{m_{op}}{(i-o)^2 + (j-p)^2 + h^2},$$
$$i = 1, \ldots, N \text{ and } j = 1, \ldots, M.$$

The determination of the acceleration when the masses are given is known as the forward problem. The inverse problem is to determine the masses from the measured accelerations.

Note that the acceleration values can be organized into a matrix, and the mass values may be similarly organized. I have selected units so that the matrix indices also represent distances in real space. You will solve the inverse problem, so the acceleration values are given, and your task is to find the mass values that correspond to them.

The inverse problem can be solved, approximately, by iteration. We will progress from one guess of the mass distribution, $\mathbf{m}^{old}$, to the next, $\mathbf{m}^{new}$. This updating must be performed over and over, either until the mass matrix is considered to be converged, or we weary of the effort. Each complete iteration (also called *cycling through the data*) consists of:

- For every pixel i, j, adjust the masses everywhere, as described below, so that the acceleration a_{ij} produced by that new mass distribution is exactly correct for just that one specific pixel:
  Note that there are $N \times M$ substeps, one for each pixel, in each such cycle through the data.

  Each substep produces a new mass distribution, and that new mass distribution is used for the next substep.

  In general, each substep will partially upset the work from the previous step.

- To adjust the masses to exactly reproduce the acceleration a_{ij} at i, j, we compute a new mass m_{op}^{new} at every point o, p according to

$$m_{op}^{new} = m_{op}^{old} + \frac{r_{ij}}{n_{ij}} \frac{1.0}{(i-o)^2 + (j-p)^2 + h^2},$$
$$o = 1, \ldots, N$$
$$p = 1, \ldots, M$$

---

[17] Actually, it's the change in the acceleration due to the presence of the ore, but no matter.

where

$$r_{ij} = a_{ij} - \sum_{s=1}^{N} \sum_{t=1}^{M} \frac{m_{st}^{\text{old}}}{(i-s)^2 + (j-t)^2 + h^2}$$

and

$$n_{ij} = \sum_{s=1}^{N} \sum_{t=1}^{M} \left[\frac{1.0}{(i-s)^2 + (j-t)^2 + h^2} \right]^2.$$

This method is called the algebraic reconstruction technique, or ART. Write a code that reads a file of acceleration data and uses ART to reconstruct the density of the ore layer, and writes this density data to an output file. The first line of the input file will contain the depth of the ore layer, a relative convergence tolerance, and a maximum number of cycles to use. The rest of the file will contain acceleration values, one row of data per line of the file.

CHAPTER 7

AGGREGATE SEMANTICS

ARRAYS ARE all very well. But they are not the only means that we might use to manage a collection of data. Indeed, there are cases when arrays are not particularly appropriate, or in which they are error-prone. For example, suppose I need to manage data related to the probability of various faults in a chemical process plant. A fault might have a name (a string), a subsystem number in which the fault can occur (a positive integer), and a probability of occurrence. So "valve 6 sticks open with a probability of 0.001" might be encoded as {"valve stuck open", 6, 0.001}. Although these data are all connected, and should logically be treated as a unit, they cannot be stored in an array of three elements because they are all of different types. We need some way to manage such a heterogeneous collection.

Even when all the data to be managed are of the same type, an array may not be appropriate. An array forces us to refer to data via an index, and while indices can be very convenient and useful, they are not particularly transparent. Consider storing the resistance, capacitance, and inductance of a single electronic circuit element; each of these three quantities can be stored as a double, but they each have different physical units and their meanings are quite different. Although we could store them in an array of three elements, it would be somewhat artificial to do so. It would be sensible to package them together, since they all describe the same circuit, but it's not clear that an array is the right container for them. It is sometimes desirable to treat even such homogeneous aggregates of data in a more structured way, and in this chapter we will explore a means to do just that.

7.1 PACKAGES OF RELATED DATA

Imagine that we have a large number of particles, interacting via their mutual gravitational attraction. Each particle has a mass m, a position x, y, z, and a velocity v_x, v_y, v_z. That's seven numbers to describe each particle. To describe N particles, we would have to store $7N$ numbers. How shall we organize these? We could organize them into a two-dimensional table of numbers with seven columns and N rows. We could give this table some useful name like `particles`, and then write code like

```
1   double rsq = pow((particles[i][1] - particles[j][1]),2) +
2               pow((particles[i][2] - particles[j][2]),2) +
3               pow((particles[i][3] - particles[j][3]),2);
4
5   double F = G * particles[i][0] * particles[j][0] / rsq;
```

But this code is not very transparent, and is very likely to contain an error. This sort of code requires the author, and her readers, to mentally recall all sorts of conventions, like "column 0 contains the mass, and columns 1–3 contain the spatial coordinates x, y and z, and columns 4–6 store the velocity components v_x, v_y, and v_z." I can't speak for you, but my brain is too busy to engage in such calculating trivia.

Claim

> We should oppose obscure conventions for managing data. We should map our data into the structures supported by a programming language in a maximally transparent way.

Let's examine a few other ways to manage this particle data using arrays, before coming to the correct answer.

A more structured approach is provided with *parallel arrays*. In this technique, we would introduce not one two-dimensional table, but rather seven one-dimensional arrays, one for the mass, one for each spatial coordinate, and one for each velocity component. Then we could write the previous code as

```
1   double rsq = pow((x[i] - x[j]),2) +
2               pow((y[i] - y[j]),2) +
3               pow((z[i] - z[j]),2);
4
5   double F = G * mass[i] * mass[j] / rsq;
```

This is better—the code is easier to grasp, and it is easier to recognize the mathematical and physical computation that is being developed.

Definition

> *Parallel arrays* are arrays in which each separate array represents a different characteristic of a compound object, and in which a single index is used with each of the different arrays to provide access to all of the characteristics of a single object.

Parallel arrays often provide a better structure than arrays of arrays for managing a collection of complex objects, and are certainly more flexible. But they still present a danger to code quality. In our particle example, we now have seven beastly arrays to manage, and they must be cared for in a carefully coordinated way so that they remain consistent. Their use presents many occasions for error. Can you quickly tell if the procedure call

```
moveParticles(mass, x, y, z, vx, vy, vz, dt);
```

passes all seven arrays in the proper order? Of course not; you would have to check the documentation for moveParticles carefully, and then you might discover that the author of the procedure arranged for the mass vector to be the seventh argument, not the first. Or perhaps he ordained that the velocity components were to be passed before the position coordinates. OK, but what if in the call

```
totalEnergy(vx, vy, vz, x, y, z, mass, dt);
```

the code author had assumed, in contradiction to the previous routine, that the mass should be the first argument, and for position data to be passed before the velocity data? Ugh. We again must rely on a convention. These errors of augment order cannot be caught by the compiler, so the code would compile and would be wrong. Well, maybe somebody will catch the problem in testing . . . .

Claim

> An error caught by the compiler is a good error. An error caught in testing is a bad error.

If we are going to make errors (and we all are), it is far better for our errors to be noisy, so that we notice them. Errors caught by the compiler will not result in our using a broken code. Errors that are not caught by the compiler can be missed in testing, and result in a code that silently gives wrong answers.

A dirty trick that combines the array-of-arrays approach with the parallel array approach is to store the data in an array that has seven rows and N columns. If myParticles is such an array, we can then use tricky code like

```
1   vector<double> & x = myParticles[1];   // row 1
2   vector<double> & y = myParticles[2];   // row 2
3   vector<double> & z = myParticles[3];   // row 3
4   double rsq = pow((x[i] - x[j]),2) +
5                pow((y[i] - y[j]),2) +
6                pow((z[i] - z[j]),2);
7
8   vector<double> & mass = myParticles[0]; // row 0
9   double F = G * mass[i] * mass[j] / rsq;
```

Here the data is managed as one package, as an array of arrays, but that package is easily broken apart into parallel arrays to make expressions appear more transparent.[1] But this

---

[1]Doing so is efficient because we simply use references to each of the rows to define an alias for the row, but with a meaningful name.

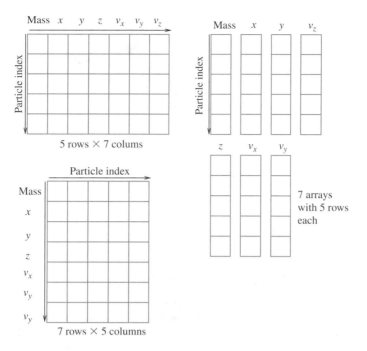

FIGURE 7.1   Three annoying ways to deal with five particles, each having a mass, velocity (v_x, v_y, v_z), and position (x, y, z). Only in one of the three cases can we transparently refer to these attributes by name, and in that case we must manage seven different arrays and keep them consistent.

still requires the memorization of a set of conventions about which row is which, and a mistake of recall will result in code that is defective but compiles, resulting in an executable that runs and joyfully gives wrong answers. Figure 7.1 cartoons the logical structure that we are using in each of the three data management strategies just outlined.

What we really need is a way to package together seven pieces of data as an aggregate unit, but still give each datum its own name. Let's imagine such a package, and call it `particleData`. Then we could have an array of `particleData` packages to manage the totality of particles. If the member selection syntax, `object.member`, would allow it, we could then write relatively transparent code like

```
1   double rsq = pow((particle[i].x - particle[j].x),2) +
2                pow((particle[i].y - particle[j].y),2) +
3                pow((particle[i].z - particle[j].z),2);
4
5   double F = G * particle[i].mass * particle[j].mass / rsq;
```

This more closely mirrors the actual situation: We have an array of particles, each of which is referred to by an index, but each particle has various attributes like `x`, `y`, or `mass`. This chapter is concerned with creating such data packages.

Questions

Question 1   Many code authors would choose to use the array of arrays to manage the data for a collection of particles, simply to make the interfaces to routines simpler. Write a procedure that reverses the sign of each of the components x, y, z, v_x, v_y, and v_z in the particle population; write the procedure twice, once using an array of arrays, and once using seven parallel arrays. Which do you prefer?

Question 2   You have to manage a database of various materials' properties. Each material is described by numerical properties: density, thermal expansion coefficient, yield stress, and Young's modulus. In addition, each material has a name. Declare `vector`'s to manage these data in C++ using a parallel array approach. Can you manage these data using a `vector` of `vectors` in C++?

Question 3   Suppose I have an array of strings that are supposed to represent names of people. Which do you consider a better name for this array: `name` or `names`? Support your answer with some rational discussion.

7.2   STRUCTURES AND CLASSES

A class, as it was already defined in Chapter 5, is a collection of data and algorithmic routines packaged together. C++ actually provides two keywords to define a new class: `struct` and `class`. These differ in their default behavior, but anything that can be done with the one can be done with the other. Both allow us to create a package of named data, as well as attach method routines to this data. But in a `class` everything is hidden and unusable by default, and special permission must be granted to access the data or use the methods. In a `struct`, in contrast, everything is accessible by default, and special steps must be taken to restrict access to the data or methods.[2] In this text I will only use the `struct` keyword, and avoid the very interesting and important access control issues that arise with using `class`[3]

I will focus first on defining aggregates of only data, without methods attached. Such methodless classes are often called *structures*, since their semantics are identical to the structures of the C language on which C++ was built.

C++ Principle

A declaration of the form

        struct name { simple_declarations };

declares `name` to be a *structure*, all of whose data members are publically accessible. Here `simple_declarations` is any number of simple declaration statements.

---

[2]Historically, the C language had the notion of a structure, denoted with `struct`. When C++ was built on top of C, it first introduced a new notion called `class`, but the first C++ compilers actually translated these classes to C structures. Eventually, as the C++ language was standardized, the two notions merged. The current C++ standard uses the word *class* to refer to objects declared with the key word `struct`.

[3]These access control issues are very important in the style of algorithm organization known as *object-oriented programming*. Object oriented programming takes a view of algorithm construction that is rather different from the imperative approach that I have used in this text.

For example,

```
    struct pairInts{ int first; int second; };
```

declares a structure called `pairInts`, whose two data members are called `first` and `second`. Such a declaration introduces a new data object that we can then use in our own code, like:

```
1  struct pairInts
2  {
3    int first;
4    int second;
5  };  // note this semicolon
6
7  int main()
8  {
9    pairInts a;  // declare an object of type pairInts
10   a.first = 23;  // refer to first in pairInts a
11   a.second = 56;  // refer to second in pairInts b
12   cout << a.second << "_" << a.first << endl;
13   return 0;
14 }
```

There is no need for the types stored within a structure to be the same. We can gather as many types of data together as we want. So we can put `string`'s and an `int` together in a structure, as in the following example:

```
1  #include <iostream>
2  #include <vector>
3  using namespace std;
4
5  struct studentData
6  {
7    string name;           // student name
8    string grade;          // A+, A, A- ...
9    unsigned int score;    // 0 -- 100
10 }
11
12 void getData(vector< studentData > & student);  // get student data
13 void putData(const vector< studentData > & student); // save data
14 void determineGrade(studentData & student);
15
16 int main()
```

```
17   {
18     vector< studentData > student;
19     getData(student);
20     for(unsigned int i = 0; i < student.size(); i = i + 1)
21       {
22         determineGrade(student[i]);
23         cout << student[i].name << "_earned_" << student[i].grade;
24       }
25     putData(student);
26     return 0;
27   }
28
29   void determineGrade(studentData & student)
30   {
31     assert(student.score <= 100);  // Or should I allow extra credit?
32
33     if( student.score < 60 ) student.grade = "E";
34     else if( student.score < 70 ) student.grade = "D";
35     else if( student.score < 80 ) student.grade = "C";
36     else if( student.score < 90 ) student.grade = "B";
37     else student.grade = "A";   // nice default, eh?
38   }
```

Traditionally, structures are declared outside of `main` or any other function, and thus made available throughout the scope of the file in which they are declared, from their point of declaration to the end of the file. In fact, they are often declared in header files and brought into a source text using the `#include` directive. This allows the structure to be defined in only one place in the source text, namely in the header file, and that same declaration can then be included where and when it is needed. Following an old convention, and one not always followed anymore, I will give such header files names that end with "`.h`".

So, to deal with the particle problem introduced in Section 7.1, we could write

particleData.h

```
1    // ============================================================
2    // particleData.h
3    // Declare a structure to manage particle data using Cartesian
4    // coordinates for position and velocity.
5    // ============================================================
6    struct particleData
7    {
8      double mass;   // particle mass
9      double x;      // position in Cartesian coordinates
10     double y;
11     double z;
```

```
12    double vx;       // Cartesian components of velocity
13    double vy;
14    double vz;
15  };
```

and then to manage a large number of particles, we can create an array

```
vector< particleData > particle(N);
```

of such particle data structures. We can then populate the data in that array with code like this:

```
1   vector< particleData > particle(100);
2   for(unsigned int i = 0; i < particle.size(); i = i + 1)
3   {
4     particle[i].mass = 1.0;  // all particles have same mass
5     particle[i].x = static_cast<double>(rand())/RAND_MAX;
6     particle[i].y = static_cast<double>(rand())/RAND_MAX;
7     particle[i].z = 0.0;
8     particle[i].vx = 0.0;
9     particle[i].vy = 0.0;
10    particle[i].vz = 1.0;  // particles moving up!
11  }
```

Questions

Question 4 Suppose that parts for the Space Shuttle have a descriptive name, an integer part number, an inspector's name, and a mass. Create a structure that can hold this data. Be sure to name everything well.

Question 5 Using your structure from Question 4, write a scrap of code that will, when provided with an array of part data structures, compute the total mass of parts, and will also describe the most massive part.

Question 6 A triangle in the plane is described by three points (x_i, y_i), $i = 1, 2, 3$. Define a C++ struc-

ture called `triangle` that manages a collection of three points.

Question 7 A circular cylinder is described by a radius r and height h. What's wrong with the following definition of a structure to describe a cylinder?

```
structure cylinder;
{
  double radius;   int height };
```

7.3 METHODS

Suppose that we want to keep track of the momentum (the product of mass and velocity) of a particle, as well as its velocity, position, and mass. Using a `particleData` object named p, we can easily compute the three components of momentum using statements like

```
1  px = p.vx * p.mass;
2  py = p.vy * p.mass;
3  pz = p.vz * p.mass;
```

But if we often need to perform this computation, then we should prefer to package even this simple code in a function or procedure. We could certainly do so with a procedure like the following:

```
1  void compMomentum(particleData p,
2                     double & px, double & py, double & pz)
3  {
4    px = p.vx * p.mass;
5    py = p.vy * p.mass;
6    pz = p.vz * p.mass;
7  }
```

But this is a bit awkward. We must compute all three momentum components even if we only want one of them. Worse, we must set up a function call with four arguments, recalling the correct order, every time we need to use this procedure. Further, it's somewhat artificial: We have a property of the particle, its momentum, that has not been captured in the particleData structure. Ideally, particleData should capture all the needed properties of a particle.

Fortunately, C++ offers a way to attach a routine directly to a class, so that the function or routine thus attached is really a logical part of the class. We have seen this in the example cin.fail(), in which the fail function is, in fact, a part of cin. In the case of the particle, we could define a class like this

```
1  struct particleData
2  {
3    double mass;   // particle mass
4    double x;      // position in Cartesian coordinates
5    double y;
6    double z;
7    double vx;     // Cartesian components of velocity
8    double vy;
9    double vz;
10
11   double px()
12     {
13       return vx * mass;
14     }
15
```

```
16      double py()
17        {
18          return vy * mass;
19        }
20
21      double pz()
22        {
23          return vz * mass;
24        }
25    };
```

Now the structure contains not only simple declarations of data, but also declarations and definitions of three functions, px, py, and pz, beginning on lines 11, 16, and 21, respectively. Because it contains these method functions, I will call this aggregate a class, rather than a structure. Now when we have a particleData object wreckingBall, we can get the *y* component of momentum simply through the expression wreckingBall.py().

Note that the function definitions, which appear within the compound statement that defines the class, refer directly to other members of the class. For example, in the boxed line, line 18, the identifiers vy and mass appear. The semantics of classes in C++ allows a function or procedure defined as part of the class to have access to the class data members without any explicit passing of those data into the routine. Indeed, these semantics allow reference to any members of the class, data or routines, from within the class text. So in the call to wreckingBall.py(), it is understood that in the function py the identifiers vy and mass refer to the data members of wreckingBall.

C++ Principle

A declaration of the form

```
struct name
{
  simple_declarations;
  routine_definitions
};
```

declares name to be a *class*, all of whose data members and methods are publically accessible. Here simple_declarations is any number of simple declaration statements, and routine_definitions is a collection of function and/or procedure definitions.

Within the text of a method routine, the members of the class are in scope, so they can be referred to without any qualification.[4]

---

[4]I must admit that this is certainly not a complete description of the class definition syntax. It is not necessary to define its full complexity here.

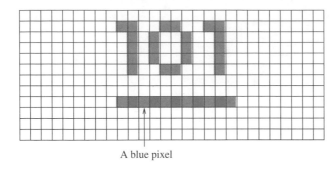

A blue pixel

FIGURE 7.2   An image as a table of pixels—patches of color.

7.3.1   Images

Let's examine the heart of computer graphics systems. Logically, an image is a rectangular table of *pixels*, as shown in Fig. 7.2. Each pixel is logically a single cell of color—black, white, or red, blue, or green, or something in between. To show an image on the screen—the text of a document or the rendering of a scene from a movie—we must therefore specify what color to make each pixel. Thus in order to manipulate an image within the computer, we need some way to represent each pixel as an encoded color, and then to manage a whole image of many pixels, we need to store an array of pixels.

Representing color in a computer requires mapping the physical phenomena to a discrete representation that a computer can manipulate. The colors that we see are mixtures of many wavelengths of light, and perfectly specifying most colors would require a tremendous amount of wavelength data. Fortunately, the human visual system is less precise than a spectrometer, and we can usually get away with rather simple color models. One of the simplest is the RGB color model. In this model we specify only three nonnegative integers to describe any color. These three values represent the amount of red (R), green (G), and blue (B) light needed to mix together to make the final color.[5] Each integer can range from a minimum of zero, representing no light of that color, up to some maximum value, representing that color at its full intensity. The maximum allowed intensity value is therefore an important part of the model, because RGB values are really relative to the assigned maximum.

For example, if we select a maximum value of 128, then the triple of integers (128, 128, 64) represents a color with red at full intensity, green at full intensity, and blue at 64/128 = 50% of full intensity; this color is a slightly pale yellow. On the other hand, the triple (500, 128, 64) is invalid, because 500 is larger than the agreed to maximum intensity of 128. This maximum intensity value is somewhat arbitrary; we could agree to a maximum of 8, 32, 512, or any other positive number that is convenient. But we do need to keep a record of this allowed maximum, because all the other intensity values are relative to it. For example, the color white is an equal mix of red, green, and blue *at their full intensities*. In general, an equal mix of red, green, and blue values is a gray,

---

[5]This can be contrasted with the print-oriented CMYK color model, in which four numbers are used to represent the amount of cyan (C), magenta (M), yellow (Y), and black (K) ink to mix together on a white page.

sliding from black to white as the three equal values range from zero to the maximum intensity. Thus, without specifying a maximum intensity, there is no way to distinguish white from gray. Indeed, in an image *all* pixels need to be relative to the same maximum value, so that white for one pixel is white for another, or so that fully intense red for one is not a pale red for another. So although we need to manage individual pixels, these are all connected as part of the same image and must be constrained to have the same allowed maximum intensity.

So let's create a pixel as a structure of the form

```
struct pixelData
{
  unsigned int red;
  unsigned int green;
  unsigned int blue;
};
```

and define an image as a structure of the form

```
struct image
{
  vector< vector< pixelData > > pixels;
  unsigned int max; // maximum value for any color value
};
```

If `picture` is an `image` object, we can then refer an individual pixel with code like

```
picture.pixels[i][j]
```

and because vectors keep track of their own size we can determine the width of the image with a wonderful statement like

```
width = picture.pixels[0].size();
```

Well, maybe this statement is not so wonderful. Let's add some functions to the `image` class to make size determination easier by wrapping this code into a method function:

```
1  struct image
2  {
3    vector< vector< pixelData > > pixels;
4    unsigned int max; // maximum value for any color value
5    unsigned int width()  // return width of image
6      {
7        return pixels[0].size();
8      }
9    unsigned int height()  // return height of image
10     {
11       return pixels.size();
12     }
13 };
```

Now we can obtain the width of an image with a simple and more expressive expression like `picture.height()`.

Once you start adding methods to a class and start using them, you often begin to lust for other functionality.[6] For example, it can be inconvenient and error-prone to create `pixel` objects by hand, because the RGB values are relative to the maximum value for the entire image. A utility function like

```
1   pixelData makePixel(float R, float G, float B)
2   {
3     assert(0.0 <= R and R <= 1.0);
4     assert(0.0 <= G and G <= 1.0);
5     assert(0.0 <= B and B <= 1.0);
6
7     pixelData p;
8     p.red = static_cast<unsigned int>(R * max);
9     p.green = static_cast<unsigned int>(G * max);
10    p.blue = static_cast<unsigned int>(B * max);
11
12    return p;
13  }
```

can be very useful for creating pixels "by hand." It takes relative RGB color values as floating point numbers between zero and 1.0, and scales those values to the maximum integer color value for the image. The resulting pixel is returned so that it can be easily used to set pixel values in the image. For example, to set a pixel in the image, we can now write

```
picture.pixels[row][col] = picture.makePixel(1.0, 0.5, 0.5);
```

As another convenience procedure, here is a procedure that wipes an image clean, resizes it, and fills it with a solid background color:

```
1   void reset(unsigned int newWidth, unsigned int newHeight,
2              unsigned int newMax, float R, float G, float B)
3   {
4     // set max and build background pixel
5     max = newMax;
6     pixelData background = makePixel(R, G, B);
7
8     // resize
9     pixels.resize(newHeight);
10    for(unsigned int i = 0; i < height(); i = i + 1)
```

---

[6]Often the trick is to not give in and add too much functionality!

```
11      {
12        pixels[i].clear();  // clear out whatever is there
13        pixels[i].resize(newWidth, background);
14      }
15    }
```

Note the sequencing of these statements; we must set max to the new value (on line 5) *before* computing the new background pixel. Otherwise, the new background would be based on the old, and hence wrong, maximum RGB intensity value. Similarly, the height must be reset before we can usefully start resizing the rows of the pixels array.

It is convenient to pull all these declarations and definitions together into a single header file:

image.h

```
1   #include <vector>
2   using namespace std;
3
4   struct pixelData
5   {
6     unsigned int red;
7     unsigned int green;
8     unsigned int blue;
9   };
10
11  struct image
12  {
13    vector< vector< pixelData > > pixels;
14    unsigned int max; // maximum value for any color value
15
16    unsigned int width()  // return width of image
17      {
18        if( height() == 0 ) return 0;
19        return pixels[0].size();
20      }
21
22    unsigned int height()  // return height of image
23      {
24        return pixels.size();
25      }
26
27    // makePixel method =====================================
28    // Arguments
29    //   R, G, B  -- RGB values between 0 and 1.0
30    // Returns a pixel based on current max color value
31    pixelData makePixel(float R, float G, float B)
```

```
32      {
33        assert(0.0 <= R and R <= 1.0);
34        assert(0.0 <= G and G <= 1.0);
35        assert(0.0 <= B and B <= 1.0);
36
37        pixelData p;
38        p.red = static_cast<unsigned int>(R * max);
39        p.green = static_cast<unsigned int>(G * max);
40        p.blue = static_cast<unsigned int>(B * max);
41
42        return p;
43      }
44
45      // reset method ===================================
46      // Arguments
47      //  newWidth, newHeight -- new size information
48      //  newMax             -- new maximum integer RGB value
49      //  R, G, B            -- RGB values between 0 and 1.0
50      void reset(unsigned int newWidth, unsigned int newHeight,
51                 unsigned int newMax, float R, float G, float B)
52      {
53        // set max and build background pixel
54        max = newMax;
55        pixelData background = makePixel(R, G, B);
56
57        // resize
58        pixels.resize(newHeight);
59        for(unsigned int i = 0; i < height(); i = i + 1)
60          {
61            pixels[i].clear();  // clear out whatever is there
62            pixels[i].resize(newWidth, background);
63          }
64      }
65
66    };
```

7.3.2 Image Files

This is all very well and good, but how do we get to see such an image? I can offer
no definitive answer to this question. There are many (even hundreds) of ways to have
an image displayed on a computer screen, depending on the operating system, display
system, and available graphics libraries. But I'd like you to be able to see the images
that we create here, so I will pursue a means that provides the greatest portability and
trivial ease of creation. I will lay out a routine to store images in a file using a format
called portable pixmap (PPM). It is a very inefficient and weak format, but it is very

easy to create and manipulate plain PPM files, and there are graphics programs for most every computer platform that can display them.[7]

A plain PPM is a text file. It contains a series of data values separated by whitespace. Except for the first two characters, all of the data are nonnegative integers. The data are, in order:

1. The two characters "P3"
2. An integer w representing the width in pixels of the image
3. Another integer h representing the height in pixels of the image
4. The maximum color value (must be less than 65,536)
5. $w \times h$ lines of text, each containing three integers that represent the red, green, and blue color values of each pixel[8]

The pixels are ordered by their row in the image, meaning that all of the data for a particular row of the image are written together, before moving on to the next row.

But there is one wrinkle in this: By long convention those who develop computer graphics have come to consider the upper left corner of an image to be the pixel in row zero, column zero. This makes some sense from a hardware perspective, because the upper left corner is the first pixel to be displayed by most hardware. But it is somewhat upside down to those of us who tend to see a rectangular data set as representing a discretization of the x, y plane, as we think of the row index as increasing up the y axis. From this perspective, it's more natural to consider the lower left corner to be row zero and column zero of an image. I will use this convention explicitly from now on: Row zero, column zero is the lower left corner of my images. OK, very natural. But when we write a PPM file, we must account for the standard ordering used in a PPM file, in which row zero is the top of the image, not the bottom. So when we write an image, we shall write the rows from last to first.

Here is a procedure that will write a PPM file:

writePPM.cpp

```
1   // =================================================================
2   // writePPM.cpp
3   // Writes a text ppm image file
4   // =================================================================
5   #include <string>
6   #include <fstream>
7   #include "image.h"
8   using namespace std;
9
10  // ====>> writePPM <<===============================================
11  // Arguments:
12  //    p          -- image to be saved
```

[7]The Gnu Image Manipulation Program, known as GIMP, is one freely available program for Unix, Linux, Windows, and Mac OS/X that can read PPM files and display the encoded image.

[8]Actually, the data do not have to be organized into lines in just this way, but they do have to be organized into lines, and this is the simplest valid arrangement.

```
13    //    filename -- name of file to write
14    // ================================================================
15    void writePPM(image p, string filename)
16    {
17      assert(p.height() > 0 and p.width() > 0);
18
19      ofstream imageFile(filename.c_str());
20      assert(not imageFile.fail());
21
22      imageFile << "P3_";
23      imageFile << p.width() << "_" << p.height()
24                << " " << p.max << endl;
25      for(int i = p.height() - 1; i >= 0; i = i - 1)
26        {
27          // Require: all rows same size
28          assert(p.width() == p.pixels[i].size());
29          for(unsigned int j = 0; j < p.width(); j = j + 1)
30            {
31               imageFile << p.pixels[i][j].red    << " "
32                         << p.pixels[i][j].green << " "
33                         << p.pixels[i][j].blue  << endl;
34            }
35        }
36
37      imageFile.close();
38    }
```

There is one subtle issue in this code. In the boxed line of code you will see that I have used an int, rather than an unsigned int, to control the loop. This is because the continuation condition for the loop i >= 0 would always be true for an unsigned int. With an unsigned int i = 0 the expression i - 1 is not negative. This is often a problem: Subtraction and unsigned int do not always play together well.

So let's use the routines we now have to create an image file:

pixelPlay.cpp

```
1    // ================================================================
2    // pixelPlay.cpp
3    // Writes a PPM image file that contains a solid background color
4    // and a rectangle of white
5    // ================================================================
6    #include "image.h"
7    #include <string>
8    #include <cstdlib>
9    using namespace std;
10
11    // Procedures defined elsewhere
```

```
12   void writePPM(image p, string filename);
13
14   // procedure declared in this file
15   void printUsage(string name);
16   void drawWhiteBox(image & p);
17
18   // ====>> main <<=================================================
19   int main(int argc, char * argv[])
20   {
21     if(argc != 8)
22       {
23         printUsage(argv[0]);
24       }
25
26     // Get image size
27     int width = atoi(argv[1]);
28     int height = atoi(argv[2]);
29
30     // get maximum color value
31     int max = atoi(argv[3]);
32
33     // get background color as fraction of max
34     float R = atoi(argv[4])/static_cast<float>(max);
35     float G = atoi(argv[5])/static_cast<float>(max);
36     float B = atoi(argv[6])/static_cast<float>(max);
37
38     // create image of solid color
39     image picture;
40     picture.reset(width, height, max, R, G, B);
41
42     // add a white box
43     drawWhiteBox(picture);
44
45     // write image file
46     string fileName(argv[7]);
47     writePPM(picture, fileName);
48
49     return EXIT_SUCCESS;
50   }
51
52   // ====>> printUsage <<==========================================
53   void printUsage(string name)
54   {
55     cerr << name << "_width_height_max_R_G_B_filename" << endl;
56     exit(EXIT_FAILURE);
57   }
58
```

```
59  // ====>> drawWhiteBox <<=====================================
60  // Draws white box on the image p
61  // ==========================================================
62  void drawWhiteBox(image & p)
63  {
64    unsigned int lowerLeftRow = p.height()/4;
65    unsigned int lowerLeftCol = p.width()/4;
66    unsigned int upperRightRow = (3*p.height())/4;
67    unsigned int upperRightCol = (3*p.width())/4;
68    pixelData white = p.makePixel(1.0, 1.0, 1.0);
69    for(unsigned int row = lowerLeftRow;
70                        row <= upperRightRow;
71                        row = row + 1)
72      {
73        p.pixels[row][lowerLeftCol] = white;
74        p.pixels[row][upperRightCol] = white;
75      }
76    for(unsigned int col = lowerLeftCol;
77                        col <= upperRightCol;
78                        col = col + 1)
79      {
80        p.pixels[lowerLeftRow][col] = white;
81        p.pixels[upperRightRow][col] = white;
82      }
83  }
```

This code takes seven arguments from the command line: the image size (width and height); the maximum color value; a red, green, and blue (RGB) triple; and a filename. It can be run like

```
1  [hagar@localhost Code]$ ./pixelPlay 200 100 255 0 0 255 blue.ppm
2  [hagar@localhost Code]$
```

and hey, presto, an image is created in a solid blue background with a white box on it! And there it is, Fig. 7.3. I'd show you some other colors, but this book is printed only with black and blue ink.

FIGURE 7.3 An image created by **pixelPlay**.

Questions

Question 8 You are given a pixel with RGB triple (100, 100, 23) along with the information that the maximum allowed color intensity is 512. You must scale this pixel's RGB values so that the maximum intensity is 255. What is the value of the RGB triple in this new scale?

Question 9 Discuss the promise and problems with attaching the maximum allowed color intensity to each pixel, instead of to the image as a whole.

Question 10 Have a look at line 18 in the declaration of the image class method width in **image.h**. Why is that line necessary? Provide some arguments for or against making that check an assertion.

Question 11 Modify the reset method of the image class so that it fills the image with the background color everywhere except for a two-pixel-wide strip around the edge of the image, which is made black.

Question 12 Modify the image class by adding the writePPM routine to it as a class method.

Question 13 Modify the image class by adding a routine

```
setPixel(int row, int col,
         float R, float B, float G)
```

which will set row and col of the image to the color specified by the relative RBG triple (floating point values between zero and 1), provided that row and col represent valid indices, and which does nothing if row and col do not represent valid indices.

7.4 LINES AND PLOTTING

Let's use our ability to create images to plot some data. Suppose, for example, that we want to plot sin(x) for $0 \leq x \leq 4\pi$. We can discretize this problem by selecting a discrete grid of x values, $x_i = i\Delta x, i = 0, 1, 2, \ldots, N-1$, for some fixed mesh spacing $\Delta x = 4\pi/(N-1)$ and then computing sin(x_i) for each of those discrete values. This gives us a set of discrete points, and we could then color corresponding pixels to show the data visually.

So the problem is to map a general point (x, y) to a row and column index in the image. This is easily done with a linear mapping. Let y_{max} and y_{min} represent the maximum and minimum values of y to be represented by the image. Also let h represent the (integer) height of the image. Then we can map any y to a row index j as

$$j = \text{round}\left((h-1)\frac{y - y_{min}}{y_{max} - y_{min}}\right), \tag{7.1}$$

where "round" rounds its argument to the nearest integer. Similarly, we can map any x value to a column index i as

$$i = \text{round}\left((w-1)\frac{x - x_{min}}{x_{max} - x_{min}}\right), \tag{7.2}$$

where w is the (integer) width of the image.

Here is a code that uses this sort of mapping on both x and y to plot a set of data in an image:

plot.cpp

```
1  #include <vector>
2  #include "image.h"
3  using namespace std;
4
```

```
5    // Declare a point structure to hold x, y pairs
6    struct point
7    {
8      double x;
9      double y;
10   };
11
12   // Declare functions whose definitions are in this file
13   void findRange(const vector< point > & data,
14                  point & lowerLeft, point & upperRight);
15   unsigned int scale(double x, double xmin, double xmax, unsigned int w);
16
17   // ====>> plot <<=================================================
18   // Plots the x, y data on the image
19   // Arguments
20   //   p     -- image to plot on
21   //   data  -- array of points
22   //   pixel -- pixel (color) to use for plotting data
23   // ================================================================
24   void plot(image & p, const vector< point > & data, pixelData pixel)
25   {
26     point lowerLeft;
27     point upperRight;
28     findRange(data, lowerLeft, upperRight);
29
30     for(unsigned int i = 0; i < data.size(); i = i + 1)
31       {
32         unsigned int col =
33                 scale(data[i].x, lowerLeft.x, upperRight.x, p.width());
34         unsigned int row =
35                 scale(data[i].y, lowerLeft.y, upperRight.y, p.height());
36         p.pixels[row][col] = pixel;
37       }
38   }
39
40   // ====>> findRange <<=============================================
41   // Computes maximum and minimum values in vector
42   // Arguments
43   //   data -- data whose min and max we desire
44   //   lowerLeft, upperRight -- min and max values returned through these
45   // ================================================================
46   void findRange(const vector< point > & data,
47                  point & lowerLeft, point & upperRight)
48   {
49     assert(data.size() > 0);
50     lowerLeft.x = data[0].x;
51     lowerLeft.y = data[0].y;
```

```
52    upperRight.x = data[0].x;
53    upperRight.y = data[0].y;
54
55    for(unsigned int i = 0; i < data.size(); i = i + 1)
56      {
57        if(data[i].x > upperRight.x) upperRight.x = data[i].x;
58        if(data[i].y > upperRight.y) upperRight.y = data[i].y;
59        if(data[i].x < lowerLeft.x) lowerLeft.x = data[i].x;
60        if(data[i].y < lowerLeft.y) lowerLeft.y = data[i].y;
61      }
62 }
63
64 // =====>> scale <<===========================================
65 // Scales x value to image width w
66 // Arguments
67 //    x            -- data value
68 //    xmin, xmax -- min and max of x to use for scaling
69 //    w            -- image width
70 // =============================================================
71 unsigned int scale(double x, double xmin, double xmax, unsigned int w)
72 {
73   assert(x >= xmin and x <= xmax);
74   return static_cast<unsigned int>((w - 1)*(x - xmin)/(xmax - xmin)
75                                      + 0.5);
76 }
```

And here is a code that uses this to plot the values of the function $\sin(x)$ for $0 \le x \le 4\pi$:

plotSin.cpp

```
1  // =============================================================
2  // plotSin.cpp
3  // Plots sin(x)
4  // =============================================================
5  #include <string>
6  #include <cstdlib>
7  #include <cmath>
8  #include "image.h"
9  using namespace std;
10
11 // Declare a point structure to hold x, y pairs
12 struct point
13 {
14   double x;
15   double y;
16 };
17
```

```
18   // Procedures defined elsewhere
19   void writePPM(image p, string filename);
20   void plot(image & p, const vector< point > & data, pixelData pixel);
21
22   // Procedures defined below
23   void printUsage(string name);
24   void compValues(vector< point > & data);
25
26   // ====>> main <<=============================================
27   // Arguments
28   //   argv[1]  -- width of image
29   //   argv[2]  -- height of image
30   //   argv[3]  -- number of x values to sample
31   //   argv[4]  -- file name for PPM file
32   // ===========================================================
33   int main(int argc, char * argv[])
34   {
35     if(argc != 5)
36       {
37         printUsage(argv[0]);
38       }
39
40     unsigned int w = atoi(argv[1]);
41     unsigned int h = atoi(argv[2]);
42
43     unsigned int N = atoi(argv[3]);
44     vector< point > data(N);
45     compValues(data);  // compute x and sin(x) values
46
47     unsigned int max = 255;  // max color intensity
48     image p;
49     p.reset(w, h, max, 1.0, 1.0, 1.0);  // make p white
50
51     pixelData blue = p.makePixel(0.0, 0.0, 1.0);  // a blue pixel
52     plot(p, data, blue);
53
54     string fileName(argv[4]);
55     writePPM(p, fileName);
56
57     return EXIT_SUCCESS;
58   }
59
60   // ====>> printUsage <<==================================
61   void printUsage(string name)
62   {
63     cerr << name << " width height gridPts filename" << endl;
64     exit(EXIT_FAILURE);
```

```
65  }
66
67  // =====>> compValues <<================================
68  // Computes vectors x and y = sin(x) values
69  // ========================================================
70  void compValues(vector< point > & data)
71  {
72    double h = 2 * (atan2(1.0, 0.0) * 4.0) / (data.size() - 1);
73    for(unsigned int i = 0; i < data.size(); i = i + 1)
74      {
75        data[i].x = i * h;
76        data[i].y = sin(i * h);
77      }
78  }
```

This code now uses several of the pieces that were defined in this chapter. Compiling and running this code

```
1  [hagar@localhost]$ g++ writePPM.cpp plotSin.cpp plot.cpp -o plotSin
2  [hagar@localhost]$ ./plotSin 200 200 200 sine.ppm
```

yields Fig. 7.4. This is certainly not meant to be a graph of publication quality. But it does begin to give you some idea of what a plotting program does.

An unfortunate feature of the sine plot just produced is that it has holes. Even though, in Fig. 7.4, every *x* value corresponds to one pixel column, the changes of the sine function are too rapid, so there are gaps between the data pixels. This is a discretization problem. We could address this by using lots more *x* values than there are pixels in the horizontal direction, something like

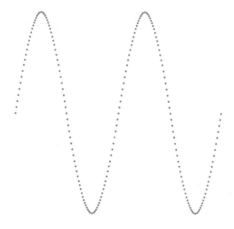

FIGURE 7.4   The sine function plotted as an image.

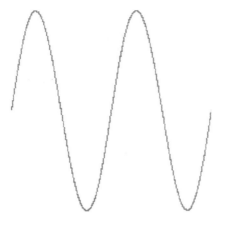

FIGURE 7.5 The sine function plotted as an image, using 200 pixels along the horizontal but with the sine function sampled at 2,000 points between zero and 4π.

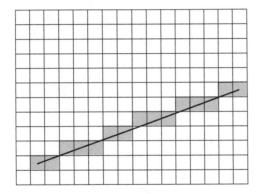

FIGURE 7.6 A line drawn on a grid of pixels. $(c_0, r_0) = (1, 1)$, $\Delta r = 14$, and $\Delta c = 5$.

```
1    [hagar@localhost]$ ./plotSin 200 200 2000 sineFine.ppm
```

producing Fig. 7.5. But this is overkill—we do not need 2,000 values of the sine function to make a good plot of it. What we need to do is to draw lines between the sampled points (x_i, y_i), rather than just plotting the points themselves.

7.4.1 Line Drawing

Let's develop an algorithm to draw a line between two pixels. Because an image is inherently discrete, we cannot draw a true line in the sense of Euclid. Instead, we must draw an approximation to a line. But in doing so, we must make the line as faithful to a true line as possible, as suggested in Fig. 7.6.

Imagine that we have two points in an image, and wish to connect them by a line segment. To organize the discussion, suppose that the line starts at column c_0 and row r_0, and that it extends to column $c_0 + \Delta c$, Δc an integer, and to row $r_0 + \Delta r$, Δr an integer. Then ideally, the line is represented by the set of row, column coordinates (c, r)

TABLE 7.1   Row Values as a Function of Column

c	$r_0 + (\Delta r/\Delta c)(c-c_0)$	Nearest integer
1	1	1
2	1.357	1
3	1.714	2
4	2.071	2
5	2.429	2
6	2.786	3
7	3.143	3
8	3.5	4
9	3.857	4
10	4.214	4
11	4.571	5
12	4.929	5
13	5.286	5
14	5.643	6
15	6.000	6

The values $r_0 + (\Delta r/\Delta c)(c - \Delta c_0)$ for $(c_0, r_0) = (1, 1)$, $\Delta c = 14$, and $\Delta r = 5$, along with these row values rounded to the nearest integer

satisfying

$$r_{\text{ideal}} = r_0 + \frac{\Delta r}{\Delta c}(c - c_0) \tag{7.3}$$

but in general, for an integer c, the value r_{ideal} will not be an integer. Assume now that $|\Delta c| \geq |\Delta r|$, so the slope of the line is between -1 and 1. We can then pick each integer value of c between c_0 and $c_0 + \Delta c$ and round $r_0 + (\Delta r/\Delta c)(c - c_0)$ to the nearest row integer. Thus we use

$$r(c) = \text{round}\left(r_0 + \frac{\Delta r}{\Delta c}(c - c_0)\right) \tag{7.4}$$

to provide a row index for each column index. Because I assumed $|\Delta c| \geq |\Delta r|$, the slope of the line is less than or equal to 1 in magnitude, and there will be no gaps in the row values—every r between r_0 and $r_0 + \Delta r$ will be used. Table 7.1 shows the values of $r_0 + (\Delta r/\Delta c)(c - c_0)$, and the integer value closest to each of these, for the line in Fig. 7.6.

This algorithm, restricted to $|\Delta r/\Delta c| \leq 1$, is then relatively straightforward to implement in C++, as in plotLineByCols below. It is also then easy to deal with $|\Delta c/\Delta r| < 1$ by swapping the roles of rows and columns, as is done in plotLineByRows.

plotLine.cpp

```
1  #include "image.h"
2  #include <cmath>
3  using namespace std;
4
5  // ===>> round <<===============================================
```

```cpp
6    // Rounds its argument to the nearest unsigned int
7    unsigned int round(float v)
8    {
9      assert(v >= -0.5);  // slightly negative numbers are OK
10     return static_cast<unsigned int>(v + 0.5);
11   }
12
13   // ====>> swapPoints <<=======================================
14   // Swaps (colA, rowA) with (colB, rowB) in caller
15   void swapPoints(int & colA, int & rowA, int & colB, int & rowB)
16   {
17       unsigned int tmp = colB;
18       colB = colA;
19       colA = tmp;
20       tmp = rowB;
21       rowB = rowA;
22       rowA = tmp;
23   }
24
25   // ===>> plotLineByCols <<===================================
26   // Plot a line of pixels on an image, with |slope| <= 1
27   // Arguments
28   //   colLeft, rowLeft  -- the left end of the line
29   //   colRight, rowRight   -- the right end of the line
30   //   pixel -- pixel to use for the line
31   //   p      -- the image on which to plot
32   // =========================================================
33   void plotLineByCols(int colLeft, int rowLeft,
34                       int colRight, int rowRight,
35                       pixelData pixel, image & p)
36   {
37    // make sure start has the lower column value
38    if( colRight < colLeft)
39      swapPoints(colLeft, rowLeft, colRight, rowRight);
40
41    float deltaRow = (rowRight - rowLeft);  // this will force calcs
42    float deltaCol = (colRight - colLeft);  // in floating pt math
43    float slope = deltaRow / deltaCol;
44    assert(fabs(slope) <= 1.0);
45
46    for(unsigned int c = colLeft; c <= colRight; c = c + 1)
47     {
48       unsigned int r = round(rowLeft + slope * (c - colLeft));
49       p.pixels[r][c] = pixel;
50     }
51   }
```

```
52
53   // ===>> plotLineByRows <<=====================================
54   // Plot a line of pixels on an image, with |slope| >= 1
55   // Arguments
56   //   colLeft, rowLeft  -- the left end of the line
57   //   colRight, rowRight   -- the right end of the line
58   //   pixel -- pixel to use for the line
59   //   p      -- the image on which to plot
60   // ===========================================================
61   void plotLineByRows(int colLeft, int rowLeft,
62                       int colRight, int rowRight,
63                       pixelData pixel, image & p)
64   {
65    // make sure start has the lower row value
66    if( rowRight < rowLeft)
67      swapPoints(colLeft, rowLeft, colRight, rowRight);
68
69    float deltaRow = (rowRight - rowLeft);
70    float deltaCol = (colRight - colLeft);
71    float slope = deltaCol / deltaRow;
72    assert(fabs(slope) <= 1.0);
73
74    for(unsigned int r = rowLeft; r <= rowRight; r = r + 1)
75      {
76        unsigned int c = round(colLeft + slope * (r - rowLeft));
77        p.pixels[r][c] = pixel;
78      }
79   }
80
81   // ===>> plotLine <<=========================================
82   // Plot a line of pixels on an image
83   // Arguments
84   //   colStart, rowStart  -- one end of the line segment
85   //   colFinal, rowFinal  -- other end of the line segment
86   //   pixel -- pixel to use for the line
87   //   p      -- the image on which to plot
88   // ===========================================================
89   void plotLine(int colStart, int rowStart,
90                 int colFinal, int rowFinal,
91                 pixelData pixel, image & p)
92   {
93     assert(colStart < p.width() and colFinal < p.width());
94     assert(rowStart < p.height() and rowFinal < p.height());
95
96     if( abs(rowFinal - rowStart) <= abs(colFinal - colStart) )
97       {
```

```
98        plotLineByCols(colStart, rowStart, colFinal, rowFinal,
99                        pixel, p);
100   }
101   else
102   {
103     plotLineByRows(colStart, rowStart, colFinal, rowFinal,
104                      pixel, p);
105   }
106 }
```

Note that the column and row indices are passed as int, rather than unsigned int. This is because the code must contain expressions like rowFinal - rowStart, but when applied to unsigned int operands, the subtraction operator can produce unexpected results. In C++, the subtraction of unsigned int's can't compute a negative number. The alternative would be to have a set of selection statements to sort out all four possible orderings of the starting and ending points on the line segment; to keep this first code uncluttered, I have elected to use int's instead.

With an ability to draw lines, we can rewrite **plot** to connect the dots of data:

plot2.cpp

```
1  #include <vector>
2  #include "image.h"
3  using namespace std;
4
5  //Procedure defined elsewhere
6  void plotLine(int colStart, int rowStart,
7               int colFinal, int rowFinal,
8               pixelData pixel, image & p);
9
10 // Declare a point structure to hold x, y pairs
11 struct point
12 {
13   double x;
14   double y;
15 };
16
17 // Declare functions whose definitions are in this file
18 void findRange(const vector< point > & data,
19               point & lowerLeft, point & upperRight);
20 unsigned int scale(double x, double xmin, double xmax,
21                    unsigned int w);
22
23 // ====>> plot <<=================================================
24 // Plots the x, y data on the image
25 // Arguments
26 //   p     -- image to plot on
```

```
27   //   data  -- array of points
28   //   pixel -- pixel (color) to use for plotting data
29   // ================================================================
30   void plot(image & p, const vector< point > & data, pixelData pixel)
31   {
32     point lowerLeft;
33     point upperRight;
34     findRange(data, lowerLeft, upperRight);
35
36     for(unsigned int i = 0; i < data.size() - 1; i = i + 1)
37       {
38         unsigned int colStart =
39           scale(data[i].x, lowerLeft.x, upperRight.x, p.width());
40         unsigned int rowStart =
41           scale(data[i].y, lowerLeft.y, upperRight.y, p.height());
42
43         unsigned int colFinish =
44           scale(data[i+1].x, lowerLeft.x, upperRight.x, p.width());
45         unsigned int rowFinish =
46           scale(data[i+1].y, lowerLeft.y, upperRight.y, p.height());
47
48
49         plotLine(colStart, rowStart, colFinish, rowFinish, pixel, p);
50       }
51   }
52
53   // ====>> findRange <<=============================================
54   // Computes maximum and minimum values in vector
55   // Arguments
56   //   data -- data whose min and max we desire
57   //   lowerLeft, upperRight -- min and max values returned by these
58   // ================================================================
59   void findRange(const vector< point > & data,
60                  point & lowerLeft, point & upperRight)
61   {
62     assert(data.size() > 0);
63     lowerLeft.x = data[0].x;
64     lowerLeft.y = data[0].y;
65     upperRight.x = data[0].x;
66     upperRight.y = data[0].y;
67
68     for(unsigned int i = 0; i < data.size(); i = i + 1)
69       {
70         if(data[i].x > upperRight.x) upperRight.x = data[i].x;
71         if(data[i].y > upperRight.y) upperRight.y = data[i].y;
72         if(data[i].x < lowerLeft.x) lowerLeft.x = data[i].x;
```

```
73          if(data[i].y < lowerLeft.y) lowerLeft.y = data[i].y;
74      }
75  }
76
77  // =====>> scale <<=============================================
78  // Scales x value to image width w
79  // Arguments
80  //    x          -- data value
81  //    xmin, xmax -- min and max of x to use for scaling
82  //    w          -- image width
83  // =============================================================
84  unsigned int scale(double x, double xmin, double xmax,
85                     unsigned int w)
86  {
87    assert(x >= xmin and x <= xmax);
88    return static_cast<unsigned int>((w - 1)*(x - xmin)/(xmax - xmin)
89                                     + 0.5);
90  }
```

Compiling and running **plotSin** using this improved plotting routine and only 30 discrete values of *x* produce the image shown in Fig. 7.7.

7.4.2   Bresenham's Algorithm

The line-drawing algorithm presented in the previous subsection is a pretty good one, but its implementation is slower than it needs to be. Line drawing is a common need in graphics creation, so it may certainly be worthwhile to make it fast. In plotLineByRows I convert int's to float's, and then perform various computations using floating point values. These floating point computations might be slower than integer operations, although in modern multipipelined CPUs this is not necessarily the case. But the conversion of integers to floating point values is often a remarkably

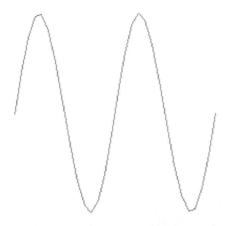

FIGURE 7.7   A plot of the sine function with 30 data points connected by straight lines.

expensive operation.[9] Furthermore, the algorithm uses division, and division is also a very slow operation. However, we can actually eliminate all floating point operations and all division from the line-drawing algorithm, and stick to adding, subtracting, and multiplying integers. This is an interesting exercise; it will take us through the process of morphing an algorithm into a very different but equivalent form. In the end we will have an algorithm that is at first glance not recognizable, but which is faster.

To eliminate the floating point operations, let us ask ourselves "why were they needed?" After all, we want to get an integer row value for a number of integer column values, or vice versa. Why is it necessary to work with real numbers rather than integers? The rounding operation is the essential task. If we could predict when it would round up, and when it would round down, we could eliminate all of the floating point operations.

Let's consider the case of $|\Delta r/\Delta c| \leq 1$, and write the row $r(c)$ selected for each column c using Eq. (7.4). This can be written in the, perhaps obscure, form

$$r(c) = \overbrace{r_0 + \frac{\Delta r}{\Delta c}(c - c_0)}^{\text{truth}} + \underbrace{\left[\text{round}\left(r_0 + \frac{\Delta r}{\Delta c}(c - c_0)\right) - \left(r_0 + \frac{\Delta r}{\Delta c}(c - c_0)\right)\right]}_{\text{error}(c)}. \quad (7.5)$$

The first term is the exact line, which we cannot plot on the discrete image, and the difference in braces is the error due to rounding the true line to the nearest row index. We can develop a different, and in the end more useful, equation for the error from the observation

$$\text{error}(c + 1) = \text{round}\left(r_0 + \frac{\Delta r}{\Delta c}(c + 1 - c_0)\right) - \left(r_0 + \frac{\Delta r}{\Delta c}(c + 1 - c_0)\right) \quad (7.6)$$

$$= r(c + 1) - \left(r_0 + \frac{\Delta r}{\Delta c}(c - c_0)\right) - \frac{\Delta r}{\Delta c}. \quad (7.7)$$

Assume, for the moment, that $0 \leq \Delta r/\Delta c \leq 1$. There are only two possibilities: Either $r(c)$ increased by 1 in going from column c to $c + 1$, or else it stayed the same. These possibilities present two potential changes to the error between our pixelated line and the true line, namely

$$\text{error}(c + 1) = \begin{cases} \text{error}(c) - \dfrac{\Delta r}{\Delta c} & \text{row index unchanged, } r(c + 1) = r(c) \\ \text{error}(c) + 1 - \dfrac{\Delta r}{\Delta c} & \text{row index changes by 1, } r(c + 1) = r(c) + 1. \end{cases}$$
$$(7.8)$$

So we can link the change in the error from one column to the next to the change in the row index. Now, the rounding of a fractional row value to the nearest integer row value ensures that $|\text{error}(c)|$ is as small as possible within the constraint of discrete pixels. So when going from column c to column $c + 1$, we must act to keep the magnitude of

---

[9]This is because of the very different representations used for integers and floating point data. We will discuss these differences in Chapter 8.

the error as close to zero as possible, and this gives us the hook we need to altogether eliminate the rounding operation.

If $\text{error}(c) - \Delta r/\Delta c \geq -1/2$, we can afford to leave the row index unchanged, $r(c + 1) = r(c)$, and go to $\text{error}(c + 1) = \text{error}(c) - \Delta r/\Delta c$. This choice gives us an error that is smaller in magnitude than the alternative of $\text{error}(c) - \Delta r/\Delta c + 1$. On the other hand, if $\text{error}(c) - \Delta r/\Delta c < -1/2$, then we should increase the row index by 1, $r(c + 1) = r(c) + 1$, and go to $\text{error}(c + 1) = \text{error}(c) - \Delta r/\Delta c + 1$, since this error is smaller in magnitude than the alternative error of $\text{error}(c) - \Delta r/\Delta c$.

The same considerations would apply for $0 > \Delta r/\Delta c \geq -1$, except we must consider reducing the row index, instead of increasing it, because the line is sloping down. This gives

$$
\text{error}(c+1) = \begin{cases} \text{error}(c) - \dfrac{\Delta r}{\Delta c} & \text{row index unchanged, } r(c + 1) = r(c) \\ \text{error}(c) - 1 - \dfrac{\Delta r}{\Delta c} & \text{row index changes by } -1, r(c + 1) = r(c) - 1. \end{cases}
$$
(7.9)

And now if $\text{error}(c) - \Delta r/\Delta c \geq 1/2$, then we should reduce the row index, $r(c + 1) = r(c) - 1$; otherwise, we should leave the row index unchanged, $r(c + 1) = r(c) - 1$.

In implementing this idea, we can eliminate all division and floating point operations by keeping track not of $\text{error}(c)$, but instead of $2\Delta c \times \text{error}(c)$. We simply have to multiply, for example, Eq. (7.8) through by $2\Delta c$, and all factors of $1/2$ and $1/\Delta c$ will be gone,

$$
\text{delta}(c + 1) = \begin{cases} \text{delta}(c) - \Delta r & r(c + 1) = r(c) \\ \text{delta}(c) + 2\Delta c - \Delta r & r(c + 1) = r(c) + 1, \end{cases}
$$
(7.10)

where $\text{delta}(c) = 2\Delta c\, \text{error}(c)$.

The resulting algorithm is known as Bresenham's algorithm for line drawing, and here is a version of it:

plotLineByCols.cpp

```
1   void plotLineByCols(int colLeft, int rowLeft,
2                       int colRight, int rowRight,
3                       pixelData pixel, image & p)
4   {
5     // make sure start has the lower column value
6     if( colRight < colLeft)
7       swapPoints(colLeft, rowLeft, colRight, rowRight);
8
9     int deltaRow = (rowRight - rowLeft);
10    int deltaCol = (colRight - colLeft);
11
12    int rowIncrement = 1;
13    if(deltaRow < 0)
14      {
15        rowIncrement = -1;    // we will decrease row values
```

```
16        deltaRow = -deltaRow;
17      }
18    assert(deltaRow <= deltaCol);
19
20    int r = rowLeft;
21    int c = colLeft;
22    int delta = 0;
23    while(c <= colRight)
24      {
25        // Invariant: (c, r) is the next pixel in the line
26        p.pixels[r][c] = pixel;
27
28        if(delta - 2 * deltaRow >= -deltaCol)
29          {
30            delta = delta - 2 * deltaRow;
31          }
32        else
33          {
34            r = r + rowIncrement;
35            delta = delta - 2 * (deltaRow - deltaCol);
36          }
37        c = c + 1;  // (c, r) is the next pixel to set
38      }
39  }
```

A version of `plotLineByRows`, suitable for lines with a slope greater than 1 in magnitude, can be constructed by switching the roles of the rows and columns.

Questions

Question 14   Suppose I had translated Eq. (7.2) into C++ as

```
(w - 1) * static_cast<unsigned int>
((x - xmin)/(xmax - xmin) + 0.5)
```

What would be the problem with this?

Question 15   By hand, determine and plot the line of pixels that connects column 6, row 2 to column 1, row 8.

Question 16   Write a version of `plotLineByRows` based on Bresenham's algorithm.

7.5   GRAVITY AT WORK

As a final application in this chapter, let's create a simulation of a number of particles interacting via gravity, and plot their trajectories as they dance under their mutual attraction. To simplify the simulation, let's restrict the particle motion to the $x - y$ plane. We will need some means, based on physics, to move the particles from place to place, and to accelerate or decelerate them based on their mutual gravitational attraction. This is a challenging problem, and the method that I will prescribe is not necessarily optimal, especially for large numbers of particles. But it is fairly intuitive and understandable using only basic physics, yet is simultaneously sophisticated in its treatment.

We will introduce a time grid with time step Δt, and then only consider time values of the form $t_n = n \times \Delta t$. If, at discrete time t_n, particle i is located at x_i^n, y_i^n and has velocity v_{xi}^n, v_{yi}^n, then our goal for one time step is to compute x_i^{n+1}, y_i^{n+1} and v_{xi}^{n+1}, v_{yi}^{n+1}, the position and velocity of particle i at time t_{n+1}. Only we must do this simultaneously for every particle, $i = 0, 1, \ldots, N - 1$ because they all influence each other through their mutual gravitational attraction.

If we ignore the effect of gravity for a moment, then we can assert that at time $t_i + \Delta t/2$, particle i will be located at

$$\tilde{x}_i = x_i^n + v_{xi}^n \Delta t/2 \tag{7.11}$$

$$\tilde{y}_i = y_i^n + v_{yi}^n \Delta t/2. \tag{7.12}$$

We have simply moved the particle for half of a time step, without accounting for acceleration. At this point we can compute the force, and hence the acceleration, on every particle. Let m_j denote the mass of any particle j, and let

$$r_{ij} = \sqrt{(\tilde{x}_j - \tilde{x}_i)^2 + (\tilde{y}_j - \tilde{y}_i)^2} \tag{7.13}$$

denote the distance from particle i to particle j. Every particle $j \neq i$ attracts particle i toward itself with an acceleration that is proportional to its mass m_j and inversely proportional to the distance r_{ij} squared. This is the $1/r^2$ force of gravity. The total acceleration on particle i is the sum of all the accelerations from all the other particles $j \neq i$. In $x - y$ Cartesian coordinates, this gives the acceleration components

$$a_{xi} = G \sum_{\substack{j \neq i \\ j=0}}^{N-1} m_j \frac{\tilde{x}_j - \tilde{x}_i}{r_{ij}} \frac{1}{r_{ij}^2} \tag{7.14}$$

$$a_{yi} = G \sum_{\substack{j \neq i \\ j=0}}^{N-1} m_j \frac{\tilde{y}_j - \tilde{y}_i}{r_{ij}} \frac{1}{r_{ij}^2}, \tag{7.15}$$

where G is the universal gravitational constant, whose value depends on the units we use.[10] The factors $(\tilde{x}_j - \tilde{x}_i)/r_{ij}$ and $(\tilde{y}_j - \tilde{y}_i)/r_{ij}$ are simply the cosine and sine, respectively, of the angle θ_{ij} made by the line from particle i to particle j and the x axis, as shown in Fig. 7.8.

With these accelerations we can change the velocity of the particles by accelerating them across the whole time step:

$$v_{xi}^{n+1} = v_{xi}^n + a_{xi}\Delta t \tag{7.16}$$

$$v_{yi}^{n+1} = v_{yi}^n + a_{yi}\Delta t. \tag{7.17}$$

Finally, we can move the particles spatially for the rest of their time step as

$$x_i^{n+1} = \tilde{x}_i + v_{xi}^{n+1} \Delta t/2 \tag{7.18}$$

$$y_i^{n+1} = \tilde{y}_i + v_{yi}^{n+1} \Delta t/2. \tag{7.19}$$

---

[10]In SI units, $G = 6.6726 \times 10^{-11}$ N m^2/kg^2.

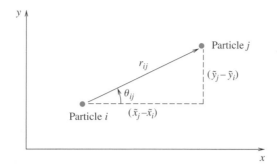

FIGURE 7.8   The acceleration on particle i due to particle j points along the line between them.

Note the use of the new velocity components v_{xi}^{n+1} and v_{yi}^{n+1} in these last two equations. Physically, we have allowed the particles to move without any acceleration except for a sudden sharp impulse of force applied at the midpoint of the time step. This particular way of moving particles actually has many merits. One of the most important is that it exactly conserves the total momentum of all the particles.[11]

Let's turn to the implementation. To store particle data, we can use the structure `particleData` that is declared in **particleData.h** from Section 7.2. We won't need to use all of the structure, because the particles are restricted to the $x - y$ plane, but allow me this excess for the moment, and you can better me in an exercise. The key implementation issue involves the treatment of particle position at the half-time step. I called these positions $\tilde{x}_i$ and $\tilde{y}_i$ in Eqs. (7.11) and (7.12), and we need these mid-time step position values for all particles in order to compute the acceleration on any. A quick and thoughtless transcription of the mathematics in Eqs. (7.11) and (7.12) into code will lead us toward something like this:

```
1  vector< double > tildex(particle.size());
2  vector< double > tildey(particle.size());
3  for(unsigned int i = 0; i = i + 1; i < particle.size())
4    {
5      tildex[i] = particle[i].x + 0.5 * dt * particle[i].vx;
6      tildey[i] = particle[i].y + 0.5 * dt * particle[i].vy;
7    }
```

Here I am again using parallel arrays to keep track of some of the particle data. Perhaps this is not so horrible, since it will be well localized in a single routine where the chance of error is not very great—it would be of greater concern if we were going to pass those parallel arrays around to a large number of other routines. And if the parallel arrays were really so offensive, we could allocate a single array of structures to hold these "tilde" data. But either way, it does seem to require the allocation of a large chunk of memory to store all these extra velocity data.

[11]It also captures a subtle feature known in mechanics as the symplectic property. But to appreciate this, you will have to conquer Hamiltonian mechanics in your senior-level physics class.

In fact, a bit of thought will lead you to realize that we don't need to store all these values at all. We could instead algebraically eliminate from Eqs. (7.14–7.19) all quantities that are decorated with a tilde. This would result in somewhat more complicated expressions to implement in C++, but these are easily organized, and no extra storage would be required.

However, instead of eliminating the tilde quantities algebraically, observe that after $\tilde{x}_i$ is computed, we no longer need to know x_i^n at all; the original x_i^n and y_i^n values do not appear in any equations after Eqs. (7.11) and (7.12). So we can simply write the $\tilde{x}_i$ and $\tilde{y}_i$ values into the same storage that we use for the x_i^n and y_i^n values. Thereby, we simply update the spatial coordinates in place. Here is an implementation with all particle data updated in place. The updates are shown in the boxed lines of code:

moveParticles.cpp

```
1    // ======================================================================
2    // moveParticles.cpp
3    // Moves particles subject to their own gravitational interaction
4    // ======================================================================
5    #include <cmath>
6    #include <vector>
7    #include "particleData.h"
8    using namespace std;
9
10   // ====>> moveParticles <<===============================================
11   // Arguments:
12   //    particle -- array of particleData structures that describe the
13   //                particles
14   //    G    -- Gravitational constant Normally G = 6.6726e-11 Nm^2/kg^2
15   //    dt   -- time step size
16   // ======================================================================
17   void moveParticles(vector< particleData > & particle,
18                      double G, double dt)
19   {
20     // change particle positions for half a time step
21     for(unsigned int i = 0; i < particle.size(); i = i + 1)
22       {
23         particle[i].x = particle[i].x + 0.5 * dt * particle[i].vx;
24         particle[i].y = particle[i].y + 0.5 * dt * particle[i].vy;
25       }
26
27     // change particle velocities without changing position
28     for(unsigned int i = 0; i < particle.size(); i = i + 1)
29       {
30         double ax = 0.0; // acceleration on particle i
31         double ay = 0.0; // acceleration on particle i
32         for(unsigned int j = 0; j < particle.size(); j = j + 1)
```

```
33             {
34               if(i != j) // don't count self
35                 {
36                   double dx = particle[j].x - particle[i].x;
37                   double dy = particle[j].y - particle[i].y;
38                   double rsq = dx * dx + dy * dy;
39                   double r = sqrt(rsq);
40
41                   ax = ax + particle[j].mass * dx/(r * rsq);
42                   ay = ay + particle[j].mass * dy/(r * rsq);
43                 }
44             }
45
46         particle[i].vx = particle[i].vx + dt * G * ax;
47         particle[i].vy = particle[i].vy + dt * G * ay;
48     }
49
50   // change particle positions for half a time step
51   for(unsigned int i = 0; i < particle.size(); i = i + 1)
52     {
53         particle[i].x = particle[i].x + 0.5 * dt * particle[i].vx;
54         particle[i].y = particle[i].y + 0.5 * dt * particle[i].vy;
55     }
56 }
```

Let's put this routine together with a driver that runs the overall simulation and plots the particles on an image, so that we can visualize their motion.

gravity.cpp

```
1  // ================================================================
2  // gravity.cpp
3  // ================================================================
4  #include <cstdlib>
5  #include <fstream>
6  #include <iostream>
7  #include <string>
8  #include <vector>
9  #include "image.h"
10 #include "particleData.h"
11 using namespace std;
12
13 // Declare procedures defined elsewhere
14 void moveParticles(vector< particleData > & particle,
15                    double G, double dt);
16 void writePPM(image p, string fileName);
17
```

```
18    // Declare procedures
19    void printUsage(string name);
20    void getInitialData(string inName,
21                        vector< particleData > & particle);
22    void runSimulation(double dt, double T,
23                       vector< particleData > & particle,
24                       double xmin, double ymin,
25                       double xmax, double ymax,
26                       image & p);
27    void plotParticles(const vector< particleData > & particle,
28                       double xmin, double ymin,
29                       double xmax, double ymax,
30                       image & p);
31    void writeFinalData(const vector< particleData > & particle,
32                        string outName);
33    void frameImage(image & p);
34
35    // ===>> main <<=================================================
36    int main(int argc, char * argv[])
37    {
38      if(argc != 12)
39        {
40          printUsage(argv[0]);
41          exit(EXIT_FAILURE);
42        }
43
44      double dt = atof(argv[1]);
45      double T  = atof(argv[2]);
46      vector< particleData > particle;
47      getInitialData(argv[3], particle);
48      double xmin = atof(argv[4]);
49      double ymin = atof(argv[5]);
50      double xmax = atof(argv[6]);
51      double ymax = atof(argv[7]);
52      unsigned int width = atoi(argv[8]);
53      unsigned int height = atoi(argv[9]);
54      string imageName(argv[10]);
55      string outName(argv[11]);
56
57      image p;
58      p.reset(width, height, 255, 1.0, 1.0, 1.0); // white image
59      runSimulation(dt, T, particle, xmin, ymin, xmax, ymax, p);
60
61      frameImage(p);
62      writePPM(p, imageName);
63      writeFinalData(particle, outName);
64
```

```
65    return EXIT_SUCCESS;
66  }
67
68  // ===>> printUsage <<=========================================
69  void printUsage(string name)
70  {
71    cerr << "Usage:_" << name <<
72              "_dt_T_inputFile "
73              "_xmin_ymin_xmax_ymax_width_height_imageFile"
74              "_outputFile\n";
75  }
76
77  // ===>> getInitialData <<=====================================
78  // Gets initial particle data from input file inName
79  // ===========================================================
80  void getInitialData(string inName,
81                       vector< particleData > & particle)
82  {
83    ifstream in(inName.c_str());
84    if(in.fail())
85      {
86        cerr << "File_" << inName << "_did_not_open\n";
87        exit(EXIT_FAILURE);
88      }
89    particleData p;
90    in >> p.mass >> p.x >> p.y >> p.vx >> p.vy;
91    while(not in.fail())
92      {
93        particle.push_back(p);
94        in >> p.mass >> p.x >> p.y >> p.vx >> p.vy;
95      }
96
97    in.close();
98  }
99
100 // ===>> runSimulation <<======================================
101 // Simulate the motion of a number of particles under the influence
102 // of their own gravity.
103 // Arguments
104 //   dt -- time step
105 //   T  -- duration of simulation
106 //   particle -- vector of particle data (initial data on entry,
107 //                                        final data on exit)
108 //   xmin, ymin -- minimum x, y coordinate for image plot
109 //   xmax, ymax -- maximum x, y coordinate for image plot
110 //   p          -- image on which to plot trajectories
111 // ===========================================================
```

```
112   void runSimulation(double dt, double T,
113                      vector< particleData > & particle,
114                      double xmin, double ymin,
115                      double xmax, double ymax,
116                      image & p)
117   {
118     const double G = 6.6726e-11;
119     double t = 0.0;
120     while(t <= T)
121       {
122         moveParticles(particle, G, dt);
123         plotParticles(particle, xmin, ymin, xmax, ymax, p);
124         t = t + dt;
125       }
126   }
127
128   // ===>> plotParticles <<=======================================
129   // Plots current location of particles in image in black or blue
130   // Arguments
131   //    particle   -- vector of particle data to plot
132   //    xmin, ymin -- minimum x, y coordinate for image plot
133   //    xmax, ymax -- maximum x, y coordinate for image plot
134   //    p          -- image on which to plot trajectories
135   // =================================================================
136   void plotParticles(const vector< particleData > & particle,
137                      double xmin, double ymin,
138                      double xmax, double ymax,
139                      image & p)
140   {
141     for(unsigned int i = 0; i < particle.size(); i = i + 1)
142       {
143         double x = particle[i].x;
144         double y = particle[i].y;
145         if(x >= xmin and x <= xmax and y >= ymin and y <= ymax)
146           {
147             unsigned int col = static_cast<unsigned int>(
148               (p.width()-1) * ((particle[i].x - xmin)/(xmax -xmin)));
149             unsigned int row = static_cast<unsigned int>(
150               (p.height()-1) * ((particle[i].y - ymin)/(ymax -ymin)));
151             p.pixels[row][col] = p.makePixel(0.0, 0.0, (i%2) * 1.0);
152           }
153       }
154   }
155
156   // ===>> writeFinalData <<=================================
157   // Write particle data to output file
158   // Arguments
```

```
159   //    particle -- particle data
160   //    outName  -- name of file into which to place data
161   // ================================================================
162   void writeFinalData(const vector< particleData > & particle,
163                       string outName)
164   {
165     ofstream out(outName.c_str());
166     if(out.fail())
167       {
168         cerr << "File " << outName << " did not open\n";
169         exit(EXIT_FAILURE);
170       }
171     for(unsigned int i = 0; i < particle.size(); i = i + 1)
172       {
173         out << particle[i].mass << " "
174             << particle[i].x << " " << particle[i].y << " "
175             << particle[i].vx << " " << particle[i].vy << endl;
176       }
177
178     out.close();
179   }
180
181   // =====>> frameImage <<====================================
182   // Puts a black frame around image p
183   // ================================================================
184   void frameImage(image & p)
185   {
186     pixelData black = p.makePixel(0.0, 0.0, 0.0);
187     for(unsigned int i = 0; i < p.width(); i = i + 1)
188       {
189         p.pixels.front()[i] = black;
190         p.pixels.back()[i] = black;
191       }
192     for(unsigned int i = 0; i < p.height(); i = i + 1)
193       {
194         p.pixels[i].front() = black;
195         p.pixels[i].back() = black;
196       }
197   }
```

This code has been organized to accept 11 arguments from its command line:

1. The time step Δt.
2. The final time at which to stop the simulation.
3. An input filename. This file will contain lines of particle data, with each line consisting of mass, position x, y, and velocity v_x, v_y. These will be the initial position and velocity of the particle.

4. The minimum x value to use for plotting.

5. The minimum y value to use for plotting.

6. The maximum x value to use for plotting.

7. The maximum y value to use for plotting.

8. The width, in pixels, of the image.

9. The height, in pixels, of the image.

10. An image filename. This image will be created to show the trajectories of the particles.

11. An output filename. This file will be written to show the final particle positions and velocities. It will be in the same format as the input file.

All physical units are assumed to be SI.

Navigating a space probe from the Earth to Jupiter is a rather difficult engineering feat, yet it is one that we can accomplish. The trajectory of a probe through a complex gravitational system—one sun, nine planets, numerous other objects—can be quite complex. Passing close to a large orbiting body can transfer orbital angular momentum from the large body to the space probe, shooting the probe off in a wild new direction with greater speed than with which it entered the encounter. This can be a problem, or it can be exploited to fling a probe farther than its own chemical rocket could carry it.

Imagine then the distant future when we send a 1,000,000-ton probe to a distant binary star system. Figures 7.9 and 7.10 show two images generated by the gravity code, modeling such an encounter. The two black circles are the trajectories of the two stars, each about 1/10 the mass of our sun. I've arranged the stars rather carefully to give nice simple trajectories, and the simulation starts with the stars as far apart as possible. The blue trajectory is the path of the probe during its encounter with the binary system. The probe enters the picture from the center-left with a velocity of $v_x = 100$ m/s at a distance of 5×10^{11}m from the center of the system. It careens around and eventually, after about 300 years, escapes the system, traveling up and back to the left. Figure 7.9 shows the encounter on a large scale, illustrating the long slow loop to the right, while Fig. 7.10 shows the same encounter, but zoomed in on a smaller region near the stars.

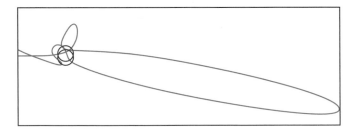

FIGURE 7.9 The trajectories of the suns in a binary star system along with the exciting path of a spacecraft through that system. The figure is 3.3×10^{12} m long. The time step has been made rather small (1,000 s), and the entire simulation lasts 10^9 s.

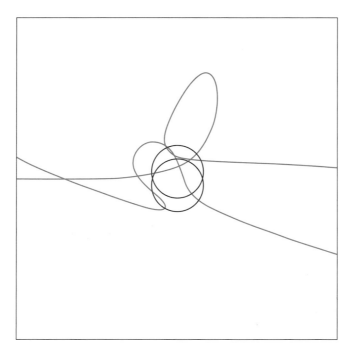

FIGURE 7.10   The same simulation, but zoomed in on the center of the system. The image is 10^{12} m on a side.

Questions

Question 17   In writing moveParticles, I have used the particleData structures introduced earlier in the chapter, but I never accessed the data members z or vz. Declare a new structure called particleData2D that stores only the data needed to describe particles moving in the x, y plane.

Question 18   Algebraically eliminate $\tilde{x}_i$ and $\tilde{y}_i$ from Eqs. (7.16–7.19), and from Eqs. (7.14) and (7.15), and rewrite moveParticles so that particle[i].x and particle[i].y are only changed once.

Question 19   The nested loops in shiftVelocity do about twice as much work as they need to because, for example, once the distance from particle 6 to particle 10 is computed, there is no need to compute the distance from particle 10 to particle 6. Find a way to eliminate this excess work without storing any extra information.

7.6 CONSTRUCTORS, DESTRUCTORS, AND A MATRIX CLASS

Classes often contain data that should be initialized before their first use. They therefore allow special methods called constructors, whose purpose is to initialize the data of the class whenever an object of that class is created. In C++ a constructor is identified by defining a class method whose name is the same as that of the class itself. A constructor can have arguments, but cannot have a return type (not even void).

C++ Principle

> In the text defining a class C, a statement of the form
>
>   C(formal_parameter_list) compound_statement
>
> defines a constructor for the class C. If the formal_parameter_list is empty, the constructor is the default constructor.

A class can have more than one constructor. For example,

```
1   struct RGBpixel
2   {
3     unsigned int red;
4     unsigned int green;
5     unsigned int blue;
6
7     RGBpixel()    // default constructor
8     {
9       red = 0;
10      green = 0;
11      blue = 0;
12    }
13
14    RGBpixel(int r, int g, int b)  // constructor with arguments
15    {
16      red = r;
17      green = g;
18      blue = b;
19    }
20
21  };
```

The purpose of a class' constructors is to provide a group of routines that can be called whenever an object of that class is created.

C++ Principle

> If T is a class, then a declaration of an object x of the form
>
>   T x;
>
> causes the object x to be created and its default constructor to be called. Similarly, a declaration of the form
>
>   T x(argument_list);
>
> causes the object x to be created and the constructor whose argument types match the argument_list to be called on the object.

So the compiler can call a default constructor itself, and for the RGBpixel class would do so whenever an RGBpixel is created without any integer arguments. This ensures that RGBpixel structures have been initialized (to a black pixel) as soon as they are created. In contrast, the RGBpixel constructor that requires arguments needs to be called explicitly, because the compiler can't know what integer values to provide. Either of these constructors may be used when an object of type RGBpixel is declared, as in

```
1  RGBpixel b;   // Compiler calls default constructor
2              // pixel is black
3  RGBpixel r(10, 0, 0);   // Constructor with 3 int arguments
4                      // called --- pixel is red
```

We have, of course, seen both of these declaration forms before, as in

```
1  string e;   // Compiler calls default constructor
2  string name("Landau");   // Compiler calls constructor that builds
3                        // string from a C string literal
```

Because a class might allocate resources, for example, open a file or acquire memory using new, it is also useful to have a routine that will be called whenever an object reaches the end of its life. For this C++ provides the notion of a destructor. The destructor is a class method that takes no arguments and has no return type, and whose name is that of the class prefixed by a tilde (~).

C++ Principle

In the text defining a class C, a definition of the form

    ~C() compound_statement

defines a destructor for the class C.

The compiler arranges to call an object's destructor whenever that object reaches the end of its lifetime during execution. For example, when we leave a routine in which an object was defined, that object's destructor is called. In the following routine, the string's destructor is called when the return statement is reached:

```
1  void fun()
2  {
3    string message("Are we having fun yet?");
4    cout << message;
5    return;   // message's destructor is called.
6  }
```

A very common use for a destructor is to call `delete` to release memory that was previously allocated by the object. That is almost certainly happening here, as the `string` allocated memory to store the characters of my message on line 3. When the `fun` routine returns, we are done with the string `message`, and the memory that it allocated needs to be released. This will happen when the destructor is called as part of finishing up the procedure call.

As an example of a class with constructors and a destructor, let's define a simple matrix class. We have previously used `vector< vector<double> >` to store matrices, but it can certainly be argued that this is overkill. We do not really need the full flexibility of `vector`'s to manage a simple rectangular table of numbers. Further, a `vector< vector<double> >` cannot enforce the rectangular shape of the matrix; each row in a matrix should be the same length, but this is not necessarily true of a `vector< vector<double> >`.

A matrix class needs:

1. A constructor so that it can obtain space to store the elements of the matrix.
2. A way to set element values. I will call this method `setElement`.
3. A way to get the value of each element. I will call this method `element`.
4. A destructor to clean up when the matrix is no longer needed.

I will go a bit further and make sure that all elements are initialized to the value `0.0`, and arrange so that any use of invalid indices will cause a noisy error message. I will also provide a way for users of the `matrix` class to check how many rows and columns a `matrix` object has.

The general strategy for storing the elements of an $N \times M$ matrix is to store $N \times M$ numbers in a single, one-dimensional array, and to translate row and column indices into a single index. The question then is how to use a row and column index, say, r and c, to compute a corresponding index i into the one-dimensional array. Figure 7.11 shows how the elements of a matrix can be stored in a single array. Given the row index r, we know that we need to skip over r entire rows in order to find an element in row r. That requires skipping rM elements, because there are M elements in each row of an $N \times M$ matrix. We must then skip another c elements to reach the desired element in row r. So the index i in the one-dimensional matrix is given by

$$i = rM + c. \tag{7.20}$$

Now it's simply a matter of organizing a class that manages this transformation for us.

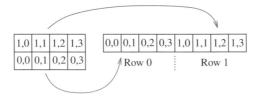

FIGURE 7.11 A matrix with two rows and four columns, indexed using offsets in the C style, can be mapped to a single one-dimensional array by placing each row in a segment of the one-dimensional array.

matrix.h

```
1   // ================================================================
2   // matrix.h
3   // A matrix class
4   // ================================================================
5   #include <cassert>
6   using namespace std;
7
8   struct matrix
9   {
10    // queries -----------------------------------------------------
11
12    // get element value at row and col --------------
13    double element(unsigned int row, unsigned int col)
14    {
15      assert(row < rows() and col < cols());
16      return _data[row * cols() + col];
17    }
18
19    // number of rows
20    unsigned int rows()
21    {
22      return _rows;
23    }
24
25    // number of columns
26    unsigned int cols()
27    {
28      return _cols;
29    }
30
31    // set element value ----------------------------------------
32    void setElement(unsigned int row, unsigned int col, double value)
33    {
34      assert(row < rows() and col < cols());
35      _data[row * cols() + col] = value;
36    }
37
38    // constructor ----------------------------------------------
39    matrix(unsigned int numRows, unsigned int numCols)
40    {
41      _data = new double[numCols * numRows];
42      _cols = numCols;
43      _rows = numRows;
44
```

```
45      // initialize all elements with zero
46      for(unsigned int i = 0; i < rows(); i = i + 1)
47        {
48          for(unsigned int j = 0; j < cols(); j = j + 1)
49            {
50              setElement(i, j, 0.0);
51            }
52        }
53    }
54
55    // destructor -------------------------------------------------
56    ~matrix()
57      {
58        delete [] _data;  // free space allocated with new
59      }
60
61    // data -------------------------------------------------------
62    unsigned int _cols;
63    unsigned int _rows;
64    double * _data;        // where data is stored
65  };
```

I have chosen to give the data elements unpleasant names that begin with an underscore, like _cols. This is to discourage the direct use of these class data members. Class methods, such as cols(), have been provided to query the values stored in the class, and there is no reason to access the data members directly.[12] This class has no default constructor because the compiler cannot determine how big a matrix will be desired at execution time; this must be specified by providing the required number of rows and columns as integer arguments to the constructor. This matrix class does not support indexing via the [ ] operator. Instead, I have provided the methods setElement and element that can set and query elements of the matrix, respectively.[13]

Here is a sample use of this matrix class:

matrixUse.cpp

```
1  // =============================================================
2  // matrixUse.cpp
3  // =============================================================
4  #include <iostream>
5  #include "matrix.h"
6  using namespace std;
```

[12]There is some significant object-oriented philosophy behind this attempt to discourage direct access to the data members of a class, but this text is not the place to discuss such ideas.

[13]It is possible, but outside the scope of our discussion here, to define [ ] for our matrix class, but in fact it does not naturally provide the appropriate index-pair semantics needed for a matrix.

```
7
8   int main()
9   {
10    matrix m(5, 5);  // create matrix, filled with zeros
11
12    // put 1.0 on the diagonal
13    for(unsigned int i = 0; i < m.rows(); i = i + 1)
14      {
15        m.setElement(i,i, 1.0);
16      }
17
18    // display matrix on standard output
19    for(unsigned int i = 0; i < m.rows(); i = i + 1)
20      {
21        for(unsigned int j = 0; j < m.cols(); j = j + 1)
22          {
23            cout << m.element(i, j) << "␣";
24          }
25        cout << endl;
26      }
27
28    return 0;    // Note: m's destructor will be called here
29  }
```

You can't see it, but when `main` returns the variable, `m` goes out of scope, so the compiler arranges for its destructor to be called. Thus, the memory that was allocated to store the data for the matrix elements is freed as soon as it is no longer relevant.

Questions

Question 20 Reimplement the `matrix` class using a `vector<double>` to provide the required storage. In this case, there is nothing for the destructor to do, because the `vector`'s destructor will take care of cleaning up after itself.

Question 21 Reimplement the `matrix` class using a

`vector< vector<double> >`

to provide the required storage.

Question 22 I chose to write the `setElement` and `element` methods to take `unsigned int` arguments for element indices. State at least one reason to support this choice over `int` indices. Indicate at least one reason to use `int` instead.

Question 23 The `matrix` class above stores a matrix in a one-dimensional array by keeping rows together, and laying each row in turn in the array. This is called *storage by row*. Rewrite the matrix class to use storage by column.

Projects

PROJECT 1

A rational number is one that can be represented as n/m, where n and m are both integers. Write a C++ structure that stores rational numbers and write functions to add, subtract, multiply, and divide them.

PROJECT 2

Self-scan checkout systems are all the rage. One problem faced in designing such systems is determining the optimal organization of change based on a purchase price and the available change in the machine. Let money be measured in integer numbers of cents. Possible types of change include bills (in units of 2,000, 1,000, 500, and 100 cents) and coins (in units of 100, 50, 25, 10, 5, and 1 cents). Organize the machine's store of change using a class called `changeStore`, and include a method called `makeChange` that will take the purchase price and money paid and return a structure reporting the number of each type of change paid out (how many 2,000 cent bills, how many 1,000 cent bills, and so on). The `makeChange` method should also decrement the store of change according to the change paid out. In determining change, large denominations are preferred over smaller denominations, and bills are preferred over coins.

PROJECT 3

Create a class called `date` that represents a date (year, month, day). Give this class a method called `nextDate` that returns a `date` representing the next day's date in the Gregorian calendar. Next write a function

    int daysBetween(date initial, date final)

that will return the number of days from the `initial` date to the `final` date. Finally, write a test code for your class and function that asks the user for two dates and reports the following days and the number of days between them. Don't forget those pesky leap years.

PROJECT 4

Write a procedure to draw a closed polygon on an image, using data from a vector of the pixel coordinates of the polygon's corners.

PROJECT 5

Modify the `image` class by adding to it a member procedure that will smooth the image by replacing each pixel's RGB values by the average of itself and all its immediate neighbors (see Project 10 in Chapter 6).

PROJECT 6

Write a procedure to plot a circle of a given radius and center, with all quantities measured in pixels, on an image. Allow both an edge color and a fill color to be specified, so that the central region of the circle can be colored.

PROJECT 7

Suppose that you have an image with a connected region of one color, and wish to change that color to another (in other words, you want to flood a region with color). The floodfill4 algorithm does this recursively by starting with a pixel in the region, changing that pixel to the new color, and then recursively repeating this process for each of its four immediate neighbors (to the north, east, south, and west), provided that those pixels are of the original color. Write a C++ procedure

    floodfill4(image & p, pixelData original,
               pixelData new)

that implements this algorithm. Note that you will need a means to compare two pixels for equality of color.

PROJECT 8

Often, we need to manage huge arrays of `double`'s that contain mostly zero values. These are called sparse arrays, and we can save storage and time by not actually storing the zeros, but instead only storing the nonzero values and somehow encoding information about where the zeros are. We should then provide arraylike indexing for such an object and make the storage details invisible to the user of the object.

Write a C++ class called `sparseArray` that supports the following methods:

1. A constructor that initializes the `sparseArray` to an array of size zero.

2. `unsigned int size()` returns the length of the array.

3. `void resize(unsigned int newsize)` changes the size of the array—the number of elements it contains—to `newsize`. Removes elements from the end of the array, or appends `0.0` values to the array, as needed.

4. `double at(unsigned int offset)` returns the value stored at the specified `offset`. Should check `offset` against the size of the array and violate an `assert` if it's too large.

5. `void set(unsigned int offset, double value)` sets the value stored at `offset` to `value`. The array should automatically expand if `offset` is larger than `size()-1`.

6. Optionally, a destructor if it is needed.

Your `sparseArray` should make the following scrap of code work:

```
const unsigned int twoBillion
                     = 2000000000;
sparseArray x;
sparseArray y;

// Resize by explicit call
x.resize(twoBillion);

// Resize by setting an element
y.set(twoBillion, 2.0);

for(unsigned int i = 0;
    i < 2000;
    i = i + 1)
  {
    x.set(i, i * 5.0);  // set a bunch
                        // of elements
  }

x.resize(10);  // x now stores only
               // 10 elements
```

The precise means by which you store the data of the array is up to you, but you should not store most of the zero values (indeed, on most computers available today you can't store an array of 2 billion double's).

One strategy to store a sparse array is to maintain two vectors, one storing the nonzero elements of the array and the other storing the indices at which those elements are logically located. Another approach is to store a *run-length encoded* array in which neighboring repeated zero values are stored as a single zero and a repeat count, so 3.0 0.0 200000 4.0 can represent an array of size 200,002, whose first element is 3.0 and last element is 4.0, and which has 200,000 zero elements between them. Each of these strategies has its merits, and there are several ways to implement the details of each.

CHAPTER 8

FINITE SPACE AND TIME

COMPUTERS ARE finite. They are finite in space, and so limited in the quantity of information they can store. They are finite in speed, and thus limited in the number of operations they can perform. This finiteness has implications for what computers can practically accomplish. Because the storage available is finite, a computer cannot store the full range of real numbers, but rather must work approximately with only a subset. The limited amount of time available to us mandates that many of our algorithms must solve a problem only approximately.

In this chapter we will explore some of these issues, especially as they impact computations in engineering. We will explore the encoding of integers and floating point numbers in computers and touch on the limitations that these finite representations impose. We shall also look again at some of the issues surrounding discretization—replacing a continuous variable with a set of discrete values. Finally, we will look at the speed of algorithms, and see how a well-selected algorithm can be much faster than a carelessly chosen one, or how we can sometimes trade speed against generality.

8.1 ENCODING INTEGERS

We must represent the information that we wish to manipulate in a form that is efficient for our computing machine to store and manipulate. That is, we must encode the abstract idea of information in a simple form that can be mapped directly to a physical computer system. The computer then provides us with simple operations to manipulate this encoded information, and our task is to combine these simple, basic operations into more complex algorithms that solve problems of import.

The basic underlying physical representation that has so far proved to be the most effective is binary. In binary, all information is encoded as a series of zeros and 1's. Each such digit is called a bit.

Definition

Bits are commonly organized into groups of four called *nybbles*, and into pairs of nybbles called *bytes*.

TABLE 8.1   The Numbers 0–15 in Binary, Decimal, and Hexadecimal Form

Binary	0000	0001	0010	0011	0100	0101	0110	0111
Decimal	0	1	2	3	4	5	6	7
Hexadecimal	0	1	2	3	4	5	6	7
Binary	1000	1001	1010	1011	1100	1101	1110	1111
Decimal	8	9	10	11	12	13	14	15
Hexadecimal	8	9	A	B	C	D	E	F

Organizing bits into 8-bit bytes is a reflection of computer hardware organization; most computers now have memory in which data can be directly addressed 1 byte at a time. The organization into nybbles is convenient largely because there are only 16 unique patterns of 4 bits, and each such pattern can therefore be represented using a single base 16, or hexadecimal, digit. These digits are shown in Table 8.1.

So information, be it the strain on a rivet in an airplane wing, the number of megawatts of electricity used by Chicago, or my son's name, will all, somehow, be encoded into a bit pattern, like 0010 1100 0000 1100, or in equivalent hexadecimal, 2C 0C.

Now certainly any bit pattern can always be interpreted as a nonnegative integer by using base 2 place value notation, and this gives us our first, and simplest, scheme for encoding information.

8.1.1 Nonnegative Integers

Consider the 4 bits 1101. Let's interpret this as an unsigned integer value using base 2 place value notation. In place value notation, as you know, each digit contributes to a number its value times a magnitude that is determined by (1) where the digit sits in the number, and (2) the base being used in the representation of the number. Together these two attributes, place and base, determine the place value in which a digit sits. So

$$1101 \longrightarrow 1 \times 2^3 + 1 \times 2^2 + 0 \times 2^1 + 1 \times 2^0 = 13. \tag{8.1}$$

In general, any pattern of N bits, $b_{N-1}b_{N-2}\ldots b_1 b_0$, can be interpreted as the nonnegative number:

$$b_{N-1}b_{N-2}\ldots b_1 b_0 \longrightarrow \sum_{i=0}^{N-1} b_i 2^i. \tag{8.2}$$

Note that for convenience the bits were labeled from zero to $N-1$, and that the most significant bits were written on the left, as is traditional in the base 10 encoding that you use every day.

Consider now the 32 bits

11101010 00101100 00001100 10000000

or equivalently, the hex EA 2C 0C 80. What is this, when interpreted as an unsigned integer? It looks pretty painful to work out by hand, so let's write a code to do it:

doBits.cpp

```cpp
1   // ============================================================
2   // doBits.cpp
3   // Reads binary digits (as '0' and '1') from the command
4   // line and interprets them as an unsigned integer.
5   // Spaces, within a single command line argument, can be
6   // used to separate bits.  The code can only deal with the
7   // number of bits used for an unsigned int.  Bits after that
8   // will be ignored.
9   // ============================================================
10  #include <iostream>
11  #include <cstdlib>
12  #include <limits>
13  using namespace std;
14
15  int main(int argc, char * argv[])
16  {
17    if(argc != 2)
18      {
19        cerr << "Usage:_" << argv[0] << "_bbbbb...\n";
20        return EXIT_FAILURE;
21      }
22    numeric_limits<unsigned int> uintLimits;
23
24    unsigned int num = 0;
25    unsigned int i = 0;
26    while(argv[1][i] == '0' or
27          argv[1][i] == '1' or
28          argv[1][i] == ' ' and
29          num < uintLimits.max())
30      {
31        if(argv[1][i] != ' ')
32          {
33            num = num * 2;   // got new digit - make room
34          }
35        if(argv[1][i] == '1')
36          {
37            num = num + 1; // new digit contributed
38          }
39        i = i + 1;
40      }
41
42    cout << "That's_" << num << endl;
43    return EXIT_SUCCESS;
44  }
```

Running this code reveals that the 32 bits above can be interpreted as the integer 3928755328:

```
1  [hagar@localhost]$ ./doBits "11101010 00101100 00001100 10000000"
2  That's 3928755328
```

For a hand calculation, the hex representation EA 2C 0C 80 is more convenient, simply because there are fewer digits to deal with. Using Table 8.1 to look up the value of each hex digit, we can write EA 2C 0C 80:

$$14 \times 16^7 + 10 \times 16^6 + 2 \times 16^5 + 12 \times 16^4 + 12 \times 16^2 + 8 \times 16^1 = 3928755328. \quad (8.3)$$

This was easier than the binary, but still fairly painful. Such manipulations are best left to the computer.

8.1.2 Integer Addition

The addition of binary numbers is a trivial exercise—it's exactly like adding base 10 numbers, but generally you have to carry more often because there are only two digits. The basic algorithm of such place value addition is based on the representation of the two numbers as sums:

$$\sum_{i=0}^{N-1} b_i 2^i + \sum_{i=0}^{N-1} d_i 2^i = \sum_{i=0}^{N-1} (b_i + d_i) 2^i, \quad (8.4)$$

where b_i and d_i are the binary digits of the two numbers. Consider adding two bits that are in the 2^ith place in a binary number. Table 8.2 covers all possible cases of adding two such digits. The rules are then easy: If both bits are zero, then the bit in the sum is zero; if one bit is 1 and the other zero, the bit in the sum is 1; if both bits are 1, the bit in the sum is zero and there is a 1 carried to the next higher place. So, for example, we can add

Binary	Decimal
01001100	76
00101110	46
01111010	122

TABLE 8.2 Adding Binary Bits. There are only three possibilities.

Digits to add	Means	Result	Carry
0 + 0	$0 \times 2^i + 0 \times 2^i = 0 \times 2^i$	0	0
0 + 1	$0 \times 2^i + 1 \times 2^i = 1 \times 2^i$	1	0
1 + 1	$1 \times 2^i + 1 \times 2^i = 1 \times 2^{i+1}$	0	1

This is all very well, but what happens when we limit ourselves to a fixed number of bits? In exact arithmetic it is possible that the sum of two N bit numbers might require a carry into the 2^Nth place—the $N + 1$st bit. Consider the addition of the two 8-bit numbers:

	Binary	Decimal
Overflow bit	11001100	204
	10101110	174
	(1)01111010	378

But an $N + 1$ bit number cannot be stored in N bits, so something has to give. When an arithmetic operation generates a number whose magnitude is too big to be represented in the fixed number of bits being used, we say that an *overflow* has occurred.

The use of fixed-size data types is critical in a computer. Without a fixed limit, the number of bits required to store the results of a computation could grow and grow and grow until the entire available memory space in the machine is exhausted in just storing the digits of one number. This is seldom useful.[1] Furthermore, by selecting a fixed number of bits to represent a number, we can develop very efficient hardware that will operate on just numbers of that fixed size. This is one reason for having data types: Hardware that works with 32-bit integers can be very efficient; hardware that must deal with numbers of arbitrary size is much more difficult to design. Therefore, when a bit must be carried over to the $N + 1$st bit of an N bit unsigned integer, that bit is simply discarded. There's no place to put it, so it goes nowhere.

This treatment of overflow in the addition of binary integers is rather like having a binary odometer. We set the odometer to one of the addends and then step the odometer forward by the number of times specified by the second addend. When a digit on the odometer reads 1, and subsequently is advanced, it will roll over to zero, and the next higher digit will advance, just as happens when a 9 rolls over on a standard automobile odometer. But when a mechanical automobile odometer reads 99999, and 1 more mile is added, the odometer runs out of digits. There's no higher wheel to advance, and the whole thing rolls over to read 00000. So it is with nonnegative integers in a computer. When we reach the largest possible integer, and add 1 to it, the carry will have no place to go. It will simply be discarded, and the number will wrap around to zero.[2] Figure 8.1 shows an 8-bit binary odometer advancing toward 255 and beyond that to zero.

The following code demonstrates this:

overflow.cpp

```
1  // =================================================================
2  // overflow.cpp
3  // =================================================================
```

---

[1] Sometimes useful, but seldom.

[2] The C++standard actually requires unsigned integers to wrap around. That is, arithmetic on unsigned integers is performed modulo 2^N, where N is the number of bits used to store an `unsigned int`.

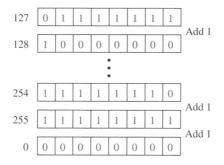

FIGURE 8.1 A binary odometer being advanced one place at a time up to 255 and beyond that to zero. The decimal value of each binary number is shown to the left.

```
4  #include <iostream>
5  using namespace std;
6
7  int main()
8  {
9  unsigned int overflow = 1;  // will overflow
10 unsigned int count = 0; // will reach max unsigned int
11
12 while(overflow != 0)
13   {
14     overflow = overflow + 1;
15     count = count + 1;
16   }
17   cout << "overflow_is_zero_at_count_=_" << count << endl;
18
19   return 0;
20 }
```

At first sight, this code looks crazy—it keeps adding 1 to overflow, but the loop will not stop until overflow equals zero. Surely the code will run forever, stuck in an endless loop. But when compiled and run on a computer using 32-bit unsigned integers, this code produces the output

```
1  [hagar@localhost Code]$ ./overflow
2  overflow is zero at count = 4294967295
3  [hagar@localhost Code]$
```

In other words, according to my computer, $1 + 4294967295 = 0$. The number 4294967295 is a magic one. It is equal to $2^{32} - 1$, and is the largest unsigned int that can be represented using place value notation with 32 bits.

So the largest possible integer on a 32-bit computer is about 4 billion. Not really very big; 4 billion is a number not even large enough to count all the people on

Earth.[3] And if I want to keep count of the number of atoms in a piece of matter, on the order of 10^{22}, I am really out of luck with `unsigned int`'s on my 32-bit computer. We certainly need other data types for storing numbers that might be very large, even when they have integer values.

8.1.3 Signed Integers

Marking an integer as positive or negative will take up 1 bit. If I store an integer in 32 bits, that leaves only 31 bits to determine the magnitude of the integer, which will therefore be limited to about $2^{31} \approx 2$ billion.

But how shall we encode a signed integer? The obvious way is to use base 2 place value notation to store the magnitude of the number, and store 1 more bit to denote the sign—say, zero for a positive number, and 1 for a negative number. This scheme is called *sign plus magnitude*. In such a scheme, the 8 bits 1100 0011 are understood as a negative number, because the first bit is 1. The magnitude of the number is determined by the remaining 7 bits 100 0011, and the number is thus -67. In contrast, 0100 0011 is 67.

However, most computer designers today prefer to follow the odometer analogy. Suppose we have an 8-wheel binary odometer. Starting at 0000 0000, we roll it forward by 1, and the odometer reads 0000 0001, which we of course interpret as 1. But if we again start at 0000 0000 and roll the odometer backward by 1, the odometer then reads 1111 1111, and we interpret this as -1. Why? Because if we add 1 to -1, by rolling the odometer forward, we correctly get zero. By following this odometer analogy, we obtain a representation of negative numbers for which addition works just like it does for unsigned integer values. So the hardware that deals with unsigned integers can also deal with signed integers.

The resulting encoding scheme is called *twos complement*. To get the twos-complement representation of an integer, we proceed as follows

ALGORITHM   *Twos-Complement Representation*

Determines the bit pattern to represent integer i in N bit twos complement
Require: ($i \geq 0$ and $i \leq 2^{N-1} - 1$) or ($i < 0$ and $|i| \leq 2^{N-1}$)
1:   **if** $i \geq 0$, **then**
2:       use the N bit base 2 representation r
3:   **else**
4:       replace i by $-i$ (so i is now positive)
5:       determine the N bit base 2 representation r of i
6:       reverse every bit of r (switch zero to 1 and vice versa)
7:       treating r as an unsigned integer, add 1 to it to produce the twos-complement representation r
8:   **end if**
9:   return r to caller

---

[3]In 2000 the world's population was estimated to be slightly over 6,000,000,000.

Let's look at this with $N = 8$ bits. The number 6 is positive, and so is represented as 0000 0110. But to represent -6, we start with 0000 0110, reverse every bit to get 1111 1001, and then add 1 to this, yielding 1111 1010 as the twos-complement representation of -6. Adding this, in binary, to 6 suggests why it works:

Overflow	Binary	Decimal
	0000 0110	6
	1111 1010	-6
1	0000 0000	0

A cascading chain of carries overflows into the nonexistent ninth bit, where it is lost, leaving zero as the proper result of $6 + (-6)$.

The effect of adding 1 to the largest positive integer is rather interesting. Suppose we use 8-bit integers. Then 0111 1111 is the largest positive integer (and equals 127). Adding 1 to this yields 1000 0000, which is the smallest number that can be represented, -128. In other words, in 8-bit twos complement

$$127 + 1 = -128. \tag{8.5}$$

So beware that the computer's concept of arithmetic is not exactly in tune with the arithmetic you and I use in casual conversation.

Questions

Question 1   Add together the two binary numbers 0101 0101 and 1000 0001. Is there any overflow beyond the eighth bit? Do the same for 0101 0101 and 1100 0001.

Question 2   Write 13 and -13 in 8-bit twos-complement representation.

Question 3   What precisely is the largest number that can be represented in 32-bit twos complement? the smallest?

Question 4   Suppose that integers are represented using a simple sign-plus-magnitude encoding. How many ways can you write zero?

Question 5   Confirm that in twos-complement representation there is only one way to represent zero.

8.2   IEEE FLOATING POINT

Although sign plus magnitude encoding is seldom now used to represent signed integers on our computers, it is often used in the representation of floating point numbers.

IEEE binary floating point encoding is a standard (IEEE 754) developed by the Institute for Electrical and Electronics Engineers for the encoding of numbers with fractional parts, and with large and small magnitudes. It is basically a base 2 version of scientific notation, with a few twists, and has become a very common encoding of floating point numbers in today's computers. I will focus here on IEEE double-precision encoding, but will later briefly describe some of the other IEEE encodings.

Sign

Exponent   Significand

FIGURE 8.2   The 64 stored bits of an IEEE double precision floating point number.

IEEE double precision uses 64 bits (8 bytes) to store a number: The number is represented by a sign bit (1 bit), an exponent (11 bits), and a 53-bit mantissa, more commonly called the significand. If you counted carefully, you will note that this is $1 + 11 + 53 = 65$ bits, which is 1 bit too big for 8 bytes. Interestingly, only 52 bits of the significand are actually stored, because the 53rd can be inferred from the other bits, as we shall see. Figure 8.2 shows the layout of the 64 stored bits of an IEEE double.

The sign bit is used to determine the overall sign of the number; a 0 sign bit indicates a positive number, and a 1 sign bit a negative number. The rest of the bits are used to encode the magnitude of the number, or to indicate that the number is either infinite, or else is not a number. The exponent is decoded as a standard unsigned integer; since it uses 11 bits, the exponent bits can represent any integer from zero to $2^{11} - 1 = 2047$. This 11-bit integer is interpreted as the actual exponent of the encoded number, but with 1023 added to it. So, denoting the 11 bits of the exponent as $e_{10}e_9e_8 \ldots, e_1e_0$, let

$$E = \sum_{i=0}^{10} e_i 2^i - 1023. \tag{8.6}$$

This number satisfies $-1023 \leq E \leq 1024$, and is used to determine how the significand bits should be interpreted. There are three cases:

- A normalized number: $-1022 \leq E \leq 1023$
- A denormalized number or zero: $E = -1023$
- A special representation: $E = 1024$

Let's consider the special representations $E = 1024$ first: There are, broadly speaking, two cases here. If all the significand bits are zero, then the encoded number is infinity, with the sign of infinity determined by the sign bit. Such an infinity would arise, for example, from evaluating the expression $1.0/0.0$. On the other hand, if any of the significand bits is nonzero, then the 64 bits of data are said to be a NAN, or not a number. Such nonnumbers result from computations that can be given no useful meaning, like $0.0/0.0$ or $(1.0/0.0) * 0.0$.

Consider next the case of a denormalized number, $E = -1023$. Let $m_1m_2m_3 \ldots m_{51}m_{52}$ represent the 52 stored significand bits. We compute the significand f as

$$f = m_1 2^{-1} + m_2 2^{-2} + \cdots + m_{51} 2^{-51} + m_{52} 2^{-52} = \sum_{i=1}^{52} m_i 2^{-i}. \tag{8.7}$$

Note that $0 \leq f < 1$. The number $\tilde{x}$ represented by the bit pattern is then

$$\tilde{x} = (-1)^s \times f \times 2^{-1022}, \tag{8.8}$$

where s is the sign bit. Note that this case includes $\tilde{x} = 0$, and allows only numbers of rather small magnitude, $|\tilde{x}| < 2^{-1022} \approx 2.2 \times 10^{-308}$.

Finally, we are left with the case of a normalized number, arising when $-1022 \leq E \leq 1023$. These numbers are known as normalized because the unstored 53rd significand bit is understood to be 1, and the significand f is computed as

$$f = 1 + \sum_{i=1}^{52} m_i 2^{-i}. \tag{8.9}$$

The leading 1 is the 53rd digit of precision; it does not need to actually be stored because it is always understood to be 1 when $-1022 \leq E \leq 1023$. This significand satisfies $1 \leq f < 2$, and the number $\tilde{x}$ represented by the bit pattern is

$$\tilde{x} = (-1)^s \times f \times 2^E. \tag{8.10}$$

Normalized numbers can be as big as 1.7×10^{308} and as small in magnitude as 2.2×10^{-308}; for smaller numbers, to partially fill in the gap from 2.2×10^{-308} down to zero, we have the denormalized numbers of Eq. (8.8). The difference is that the normalized numbers always have 53 binary digits of precision; a normalized number never wastes bits to store leading zeros. In contrast, the denormalized numbers do store leading zeros, and so can have as many as 52 digits of precision or as few as one.

8.2.1 Error in Floating Point Representation

Because floating point numbers are interpreted as binary, even so innocent a number as 0.1 is problematic. This number cannot be exactly represented using the IEEE double-precision floating point encoding. Instead, 0.1 must be rounded to the nearest value that *can* be represented by an IEEE double. How bad can this rounding be? Suppose that a positive real number x is written exactly as

$$x = \left(1 + \sum_{i=1}^{\infty} d_i 2^{-i}\right) 2^E, \tag{8.11}$$

where $d_i = 0$ or 1 is a binary digit. This representation can be exact because the sum is infinite. If $d_{53} = 0$, then we can round down to find the floating point approximation to x, but if $d_{53} = 1$, we will almost always round up.

Suppose first that $d_{53} = 0$, so we will round down. Then we choose $m_i = d_i$ for $i = 1, 2, \ldots, 52$ in Eq. (8.9) and the corresponding normalized floating point number is, from Eq. (8.10),

$$\tilde{x} = \left(1 + \sum_{i=1}^{52} d_i 2^{-i}\right) 2^E. \tag{8.12}$$

The relative error in the floating point representation of x is then

$$\frac{x - \tilde{x}}{x} = \frac{\sum_{i=53}^{\infty} d_i 2^{-i}}{1 + \sum_{i=1}^{\infty} d_i 2^{-i}}. \tag{8.13}$$

But the denominator is always 1 or bigger, and $d_{53} = 0$ by assumption, so

$$\frac{x - \tilde{x}}{x} \leq \sum_{i=54}^{\infty} d_i 2^{-i} \tag{8.14}$$

$$\leq 2^{-53}. \tag{8.15}$$

The floating point approximation to x has a relative error of no more than $2^{-53} \approx 1.11 \times 10^{-16}$.

On the other hand, suppose $d_{53} = 1$. There are two possibilities here. First, it could be that $d_{53} = 1$ and $d_i = 0$ for all $i > 53$, in which case x is half-way between its rounded up value and its rounded down value (like 10.5 is half-way between the rounded up value of 11 and the rounded down value of 10). Second, it could be that $d_{53} = 1$ and $d_i \neq 0$ for some $i > 53$. This latter case is easy: We must round up. But the former case is more subtle, because we could round up or down. Let's consider for the moment only the case of rounding up. When we round up, we are using

$$\tilde{x} = x - 2^E \sum_{i=53}^{\infty} d_i 2^{-i} + 2^E 2^{-52}, \tag{8.16}$$

where the subtraction removes the higher digits d_i, $i \geq 53$, and adding 2^{-52} rounds up to partially compensate for the neglect of those higher digits. So we have $\tilde{x} \geq x$ and

$$\frac{\tilde{x} - x}{x} = \frac{2^{-52} - \sum_{i=53}^{\infty} d_i 2^{-i}}{1 + \sum_{i=1}^{\infty} d_i 2^{-i}} \tag{8.17}$$

$$\leq 2^{-52} - \sum_{i=53}^{\infty} d_i 2^{-i}. \tag{8.18}$$

Since we are considering the case $d_{53} = 1$, $2^{-53} \leq \sum_{i=53}^{\infty} d_i 2^{-i} \leq 2^{-52}$, and so

$$\frac{\tilde{x} - x}{x} \leq 2^{-52} - 2^{-53} = 2^{-53}. \tag{8.19}$$

Once again, the floating point approximation has a relative error of no more than $2^{-53} \approx 1.11 \times 10^{-16}$.

Now let's revisit the annoying case in which we might round up or down with equal error. This awkward choice occurs only when $d_{53} = 1$ and $d_i = 0$ for $i > 53$. Whichever way we round for a normalized number, we make a relative error of 2^{-53}.

Thus, in all cases with IEEE double-precision floating point, the relative error in a normalized number is less than or equal to 2^{-53}. In general, if p binary digits are used to represent the significand, we can bound the relative error in representing any number by a normalized floating point number as

$$\left| \frac{\tilde{x} - x}{x} \right| \leq 2^{-p}. \tag{8.20}$$

Definition

> The maximum relative error $|\tilde{x} - x|/|x|$ incurred in representing a real number x as a correctly rounded and normalized floating point value $\tilde{x}$ is called the *unit roundoff u*.

As we have seen, for IEEE encodings $u = 2^{-p}$, where p is the total number of bits of the significand. I remind you that the most significant of these p digits is always 1 for a normalized number, and so does not need to be stored, but it still contributes to the precision and hence helps decrease the relative error.

8.2.2 Floating Point Operations and the Machine Epsilon

Because floating point encodings cannot represent all real numbers, the basic operations of addition, subtraction, multiplication, and division cannot operate exactly. When trying to emphasize the distinction between correct operations such as addition and the result of the corresponding floating point operation, it is standard to write floating point operations using symbols surrounded with a circle, like $\oplus$, $\ominus$, $\otimes$, and $\oslash$.

Ponder then the addition $1 \oplus 2^{-54}$ using IEEE double precision. There is no place for the 2^{-54} to go, because there are only 52 bits after the decimal place, so we round down and the result must be $1 \oplus 2^{-54} = 1$. The addition is only *approximately* correct.

The IEEE floating point standard requires that the four basic operations $\oplus$, $\ominus$, $\otimes$, and $\oslash$ should operate as though the result was computed exactly and *then* rounded to the nearest floating point value. Further, this rounding should use round-to-even to deal with the annoying case of a tie between rounding up and rounding down.

Round-to-even is a rounding technique many of us learned in secondary school, and quickly forgot; in base 10 round-to-even asserts that 23.5 should be rounded up to 24, while 22.5 should be rounded down to 22. In either case, we round so that the least significant digit retained is even. This avoids the tendency for a sum of rounded numbers to creep upward, as could happen if we always round up for numbers like 22.5.

In base 2 the number $1 + 2^{-53}$ faces the same challenge: It is half-way between the rounded up value of $1 + 2^{-52}$ and the rounded down value of 1. Round-to-even asserts that it should be rounded down to 1, since the last digit retained, zero, is then even. In consequence for IEEE floating point operations, we have $1 \oplus 2^{-53} = 1$. In general, if $u = 2^p$ is the unit roundoff, then $1 \oplus u = 1$, and indeed if we take any number δ with $0 \leq \delta < u$, then $1 \oplus \delta = 1$.

The unit roundoff u is closely related to a quantity called the machine epsilon.[4]

Definition

> The *machine epsilon* of a floating point system is the smallest positive number ϵ such that $1.0 \oplus \epsilon > 1.0$.

---

[4]In some literature, you will find the machine epsilon defined as 2^{-p}, which is more often called the unit roundoff. The definition given here for the machine epsilon seems to be the most common today.

TABLE 8.3 IEEE Binary Floating Point Number Formats

	Single	Single-extended	Double	Double-extended
Digits precision	24	32	53	64
Maximum exponent	127	1,023	1,023	16,383
Minimum exponent	-126	$-1,022$	$-1,022$	$-16,382$
Exponent bits	8	11	11	15
Unit roundoff	2^{-24}	2^{-32}	2^{-53}	2^{-64}
Machine epsilon	2^{-23}	2^{-31}	2^{-52}	2^{-63}

In real arithmetic ϵ would have to be zero, but in the inexact world of floating point math there is indeed a positive number ϵ such that $1.0 \oplus \epsilon > 1.0$ but $1.0 \oplus \delta = 1.0$ for every positive $\delta < \epsilon$.

It is easy to compute the value of ϵ for IEEE floating point. We already know that $1 \oplus u = 1$, so let's consider then $1 \oplus (2u)$. The number $1 + 2^{p-1}$ is exactly representable in the floating point encoding as a normalized number; it simply has a 1 bit in the last place (bit $p - 1$ of the significand), so using $u = 2^{-p}$, we have $1 \oplus (2 \times 2^{-p}) > 1$. Thus, the machine epsilon $\epsilon = 2u$ is simply twice the unit roundoff.

8.2.3 The IEEE Floating Point Formats

There are actually four different floating point number formats specified in the IEEE binary floating point standard: single precision, single-extended, double precision, and double-extended. These are described in Table 8.3.[5]

On many current 32-bit computers using IEEE floating point encodings, C++ compilers use IEEE single precision to represent a `float` and the 64-bit double precision is used to encode a `double`. However, this correspondence often relates only to the storage format for the numbers, and not to the format used when actually operating on them. Some CPUs natively operate on the 80-bit double-extended format, no matter whether the number is stored as a single- or double-precision IEEE floating point number. This complicates our thinking about "machine" epsilon, since on such a machine there is a machine epsilon associated with the storage format, and a smaller machine epsilon associated with numbers being manipulated in the CPU itself.

Here is a code that determines the machine epsilon using the operational definition that ϵ is the smallest positive number such that $1.0 \oplus \epsilon > 1.0$:

epsilon.cpp

```
1  // ========================================================
2  // epsilon.cpp
3  // ========================================================
```

---

[5] Actually, the IEEE standard specifies the extended formats in terms of upper and lower bounds; the table shows the "best" single-extended and the minimal double-extended. This minimal double-extended is usually encoded in 80 bits by explicitly storing the redundant bit of the significand. The 80-bit double-extended is used internally in the Intel Pentium line of CPUs.

```
4   #include <iostream>
5   #include <fstream>
6   #include <cmath>
7   using namespace std;
8
9   int main()
10  {
11    cout.precision(20);
12
13    double epsIEEE = pow(2.0, -52);
14    double epsIEEEextend = pow(2.0, -63);
15    cout << "IEEE double machine epsilon = " << epsIEEE << endl;
16    cout << "IEEE double-extended machine epsilon = "
17         << epsIEEEextend << endl;
18
19    unsigned int bits = 0;
20    double eps = 1.0;
21    while(eps + 1.0 > 1.0)
22      {
23        eps = eps / 2.0;
24        bits = bits + 1;
25      }
26    eps = 2.0 * eps;
27    cout << "Computed Machine epsilon = " << eps << endl;
28    cout << "Bits of precision = " << bits << endl;
29
30    return 0;
31  }
```

When run on a CPU with recent Intel architecture, this code reports

```
1   [hagar@localhost Code]$ ./epsilon
2   IEEE double machine epsilon = 2.2204460492503130808e-16
3   IEEE double-extended machine epsilon = 1.084202172485504434e-19
4   Computed Machine epsilon = 1.084202172485504434e-19
5   Bits of precision = 64
6   [hagar@localhost Code]$
```

So the machine is using double-extended precision for floating point computations. However, this same machine stores double values using IEEE double precision, so the relative error in storing a number as a double will be about 2.22×10^{-16}, even though more precision is available when carrying out floating point operations.

Here is the output of the same code on a machine with Sun Sparc architecture:

```
1  bash-2.04$ ./a.out
2  IEEE double machine epsilon = 2.2204460492503130808e-16
3  IEEE double-extended machine epsilon = 1.084202172485504434e-19
4  Computed Machine epsilon = 2.2204460492503130808e-16
5  Bits of precision = 53
6  bash-2.04$
```

This machine uses IEEE double precision both for the storage of `double`'s and within the CPU to perform floating point computations.[6]

Note that the standard numeric limits library, declared in the header `limits`, provides some information about machine epsilon values, although the `limits` library generally provides information about storage formats, and not information about the CPU's use of extended precision encodings. The call

$$\text{numeric\_limits<double>::epsilon()}$$

will report the machine epsilon for a `double`, and there's an obvious parallel call for `float`.

8.2.4   Errors in Floating Point Operations

Because floating point operations act on floating point numbers, and floating point numbers are only a subset of the real numbers, it is not possible for the basic arithmetic operations of addition, subtraction, multiplication, and division to be carried out exactly. I have already said that the IEEE standard demands that these operations act as though they were carried out exactly, and the result then rounded (using round-to-even) to the nearest representable floating point number. Such rounding introduces the possibility of error in every floating point operation. Even if we start our computations with exact inputs (a rare case indeed), after a few floating point operations we will have accumulated some error from rounding, and as more and more operations are carried out, we may collect more and more rounding error. This continual accumulation of rounding error can be a concern.

Consider the innocent computation

$$x = 1 \oplus 10^{-15} \ominus 1. \tag{8.21}$$

In exact arithmetic the result is $x = 10^{-15}$. But using IEEE 64-bit double-precision numbers and floating point operations, the result is about $x \approx 1.11 \times 10^{-15}$. Although the magnitude is correct, the relative error in the numerical result is more than 11%. This error is perhaps surprising. After all, each floating point operation can introduce a relative error of no more than u. But this is the error introduced by assuming that the operands are exact. In this example the result of the first addition, $1 \oplus 10^{-15}$, is in error

---

[6]It is interesting to note that Sun's Java language specification demands that IEEE double-precision encoding (and not double-extended) be used for the storage and manipulation of `double` values in Java.

by less than $u = 2^{-53}$, but the second operation $\ominus$ acts on this slightly erroneous data; $\ominus$ produces a result that is fairly accurate, with an error less than 2^{-53}, but it does so using an operand that is already slightly in error. The result of this relatively accurate computation on relatively accurate operands is then a shocking 11% off of the mathematically correct answer.

This error is due to the inability of the IEEE-based double-precision floating point to exactly represent the sum $1 + 10^{-15}$. The number 10^{-15} can be represented with high precision, with a full 53 binary digits of precision. But the sum $1 + 10^{-15} \approx 1 + 2^{-50} + 2^{-52} \approx 1 + 1.110 \times 10^{-15}$ contains only the three most significant binary digits from 10^{-15}. This sum *is* being represented with great precision, with a relative error less than the unit roundoff of 2^{-53}. But subtracting 1 from $1 + 2^{-50} + 2^{-52}$ yields $2^{-50} + 2^{-52} = 1.110 \times 10^{-15}$, which contains only three significant binary digits. So in a sequence of two floating point operations, we have gone from three numbers with 53 binary digits of precision to a result with only three correct binary digits, corresponding in this case to only one correct decimal digit, and a relative error of about 10% compared to the correct mathematical result. This dramatic loss of precision is loosely called a catastrophic cancellation error.

If the operands of a floating point operand are exact, then the error in the result is bounded by the unit roundoff u. If $\tilde{x}$ and $\tilde{y}$ are floating point numbers, then it is true that

$$\left| \frac{(\tilde{x} \ominus \tilde{y}) - (\tilde{x} - \tilde{y})}{\tilde{x} - \tilde{y}} \right| < u. \tag{8.22}$$

But if the operands are only approximations to real numbers x and y, we are really interested in the true relative error

$$\left| \frac{(\tilde{x} \ominus \tilde{y}) - (x - y)}{x - y} \right|, \tag{8.23}$$

in which we compare the floating point result $\tilde{x} \ominus \tilde{y}$ to truth $x - y$. Unfortunately, this true relative error does not have to be small. The most dramatic error is the catastrophic cancellation error that arises when subtracting two nearly equal floating point numbers $a \approx b$; the floating point result $a \ominus b$ can then have very few digits of precision, because the subtraction cancels many of the significant figures. However, even absent such dramatic cancellation, it is easy for rounding error to insidiously build up as more and more floating point operations are undertaken.

Catastrophic cancellation error can be very impressive; here is another example. Suppose we want to solve the two equations in two unknowns:

$$ax + by = 1 \tag{8.24}$$
$$x + y = 1 \tag{8.25}$$

with

$$a = 1 + 2 \times 10^{-15} \tag{8.26}$$
$$b = 1 + 1 \times 10^{-15}. \tag{8.27}$$

Doing a bit of algebra, we get the expression

$$x = (1 - b)/(a - b). \tag{8.28}$$

Evaluating this expression on a computer using IEEE double-precision arithmetic yields the rather embarrassing result x = -1.25. The correct answer is -1, so the computer has produced a result that is in error by an impressive 25%. Think about it: Only three floating point operations, $\ominus$, $\ominus$, and $\oslash$, and the relative error has grown to 25%. That's a cautionary tale indeed.

Of course, in these examples I picked the numbers carefully in order to trip up the floating point operations in a dramatic way. But significant roundoff often occurs in practice, although usually it results from the slow accumulation of error over very many operations. Algorithms can often be designed to suppress the buildup of rounding error, and simply using double precision helps immensely, but we must be always cautious. Roundoff errors occur silently and so often go unmarked. Significant catastrophic cancellation might occur only for special certain input data, and so you can easily miss it when you test your code.

Because arithmetic is not exact, theorems of arithmetic that you know as true, like

$$a + (b - c) = (a - c) + b, \tag{8.29}$$

cease to be true when applied to floating point numbers using floating point operations. For example, $(10^{30} \ominus 10^{30}) \oplus 1 = 1$, and this is not the same as $10^{30} \oplus (1 \ominus 10^{30}) = 0$; in other words,

$$a \oplus (b \ominus c) \neq (a \ominus c) \oplus b. \tag{8.30}$$

This is scary stuff.

Imagine the following innocent-looking loop intended to evaluate $\sin(x)$ on a very fine mesh of 1,001 points of the form $i \times 0.001$ for $i = 0, 1, \ldots, 1000$:

```
1   for(double x = 0.0; x <= 1.0; x = x + 0.001)
2     {
3       cout << x << " " << sin(x) << endl;
4     }
```

When x exceeds 1.0, the loop will terminate. Unfortunately, the last trip through the loop will be the trip number 1000, not trip number 1001, and on this last trip x = 0.99900000000000077. There will be no 1001st trip to compute sin(1). So if I was counting on 1001 values of sine, I will be disappointed. The problem here is that, once again, floating point operations do not obey the rules of arithmetic that you know and love. It is not the case that

$$1 = \sum_{i=1}^{N} \frac{1}{N} \tag{8.31}$$

when the addition is floating point addition. Therefore, we arrive at the following:

Claim

> Never use floating point numbers to control counting loops.

There is too much about floating point arithmetic that is unfamiliar; when we use floating point numbers to control counting loops, we can't be sure of how many times
the loop will, in fact, be executed. A better way to write the sine evaluation loop is
this:

```
1  double h = 1.0/1000.0;
2  for(unsigned int i = 0; i <= 1000; i = i + 1)
3    {
4      double x = i * h;
5      cout << x << "_" << sin(x) << endl;
6    }
```

This version is guaranteed to produce 1001 values of sine. Furthermore, each
value of x is the result of only two floating point operations (one $\otimes$ and one $\oslash$) rather
than a large number of floating point additions. There is therefore far less opportunity
for the rounding of the floating point operations to contaminate the more significant
binary digits of x.

8.2.5 Comparison of Floating Point Numbers

There are some facts about real numbers that do apply to IEEE floating point numbers.
One is that $x = y$ if and only if $x \ominus y = 0$. This is true because of the presence of
the denormalized numbers. The denormalized numbers guarantee that if two different
floating point numbers are subtracted, the result will have some place to be rounded
to other than zero. Consider the numbers $\tilde{x} = 2^{-1022}$ and $\tilde{y} = 2^{-1022} + 2^{-1074}$, both
of which are exactly representable as normalized numbers in IEEE double precision.
But their difference, 2^{-1074}, can only be represented as a denormalized number (with a
single nonzero bit in the last place). If the denormalized numbers were not available, we
would have to round $\tilde{x} - \tilde{y} \approx 0$, and the difference of two different numbers would be
zero. Yuck. Fortunately, the denormalized numbers are part of the encoding, so although
they lack the full 53 bits of precision, they do have an important role to play in relating
differences to inequality.

You will often see it commanded that "thou shalt not compare floating point numbers for equality." This is well-intentioned advice, but a bit too absolute for the real
world. After all, if we don't compare two numbers for equality, how should we compare them? for mere closeness? How close is close? Demanding absolute avoidance of
exact comparison introduces as many problems as it solves. Nevertheless, I'll give the
same advice, just rather less absolutely.

Claim

> Compare floating point numbers for equality only after much thought and soul searching. And then reconsider, because there's almost certainly no point.

The IEEE floating point formats *have* been designed to allow comparison. But frankly, it seldom makes sense to compare numbers for equality. Consider the code to compute square roots using Newton's method, given in Section 3.6; when checking for convergence, we needed to test that some quantity was small, but we could not claim that it would ever be zero even in exact arithmetic. It would take an infinite number of steps before the Newton iteration made the residual zero. Hence, there was no reasonable need to test for the residual to be exactly zero. In general, if we are making a comparison between numbers that were arrived at by *approximation*, it seems senseless to check for *exact* agreement. To do so would be optimism of the most opulent sort!

But often we are concerned about division by zero. Consider, for example, the linear system of equations

$$\begin{pmatrix} a_{11} & a_{12} \\ a_{21} & a_{22} \end{pmatrix}\begin{pmatrix} x_1 \\ x_2 \end{pmatrix} = \begin{pmatrix} b_1 \\ b_2 \end{pmatrix}. \tag{8.32}$$

The solution for x_1 is algebraically

$$x_1 = \frac{a_{22}b_1 - a_{12}b_2}{a_{11}a_{22} - a_{12}a_{21}}, \tag{8.33}$$

and if $a_{11}a_{22} - a_{12}a_{21} = 0$, then the equations do not have a solution for arbitrary b_1 and b_2. When implementing Eq. (8.33) in a code, we clearly don't want to divide by zero, so we might be tempted to check this with something like

```
if( (a11 * a22 - a12 * a21) != 0.0 )
```

This does little harm, but it's not clear that it does much good either. Such a check leaves us with two questions:

1. What shall we do if `a11 * a22 - a12 * a21` does evaluate to zero? Given the computer's inexact arithmetic, such an event does *not* mean that $a_{11}a_{22} - a_{12}a_{21}$ *is* zero, and even if it is, this does not mean that Eq. (8.32) has *no* solutions. It could have many.

2. Since the computer's arithmetic is not exact, shouldn't we be concerned if `a11 * a22 - a12 * a21` is simply very small, even if not strictly zero? And if so, how small is small?

The answers to these questions really depend on *context*: What do these linear equations represent? What does it mean if they don't have a solution? Do the equations have any special properties that allow for a solution even if `a11 * a22 - a12 * a21` evaluates to a small number, or even to zero? For example,

$$\begin{pmatrix} 1 & 1-u \\ 1 & 1 \end{pmatrix} \begin{pmatrix} x_1 \\ x_2 \end{pmatrix} = \begin{pmatrix} 1 \\ 1 \end{pmatrix},\tag{8.34}$$

where u is the unit roundoff, has $a_{11}a_{22} - a_{12}a_{21} = u$ and the unique solution $x_1 = 1$ and $x_2 = 0$. However, in our friendly but inexact floating point arithmetic `a11 * a22 - a12 * a21 == 0.0` certainly is true. Even in the more problematic case

$$\begin{pmatrix} 1 & 1 \\ 1 & 1 \end{pmatrix} \begin{pmatrix} x_1 \\ x_2 \end{pmatrix} = \begin{pmatrix} 1 \\ 1 \end{pmatrix}\tag{8.35}$$

we have the (nonunique) solution $x_1 = 1$ and $x_2 = 0$, although $a_{11}a_{22} - a_{12}a_{21} = 0$ exactly.

A certain concern is this. If $|x \ominus y| \le \epsilon|x|$, then the difference $x \ominus y$ has at most one digit of precision. That is, subtracting numbers down to near a relative difference of the machine epsilon leaves us with very little accuracy in the difference. Using such a difference in further computation is likely to generate a garbage result. Let `epsilon` store the machine epsilon for a double, hopefully determined using

```
const double epsilon = numeric_limits<double>::epsilon();
```

A comparison like

```
abs(a11 * a22 - a12 * a21) <= epsilon * abs(a11 * a22)
```

may therefore be more appropriate than checking for zero, because if this test evaluates true, then `a11 * a22 - a12 * a21` will not be accurately computed. But even this test is not without ambiguity. Perhaps we should test

```
abs(a11 * a22 - a12 * a21) <= 8 * epsilon * abs(a11 * a22)
```

in order to ensure *more* than one digit of precision. But why `8 * epsilon`? Why not, say, `128 * epsilon`? There's no completely objective resolution to this issue of how to ensure that a small difference is meaningful. A judgment must be made, in context.

When comparing floating point values then, it is best to understand your application, to understand that the computer does arithmetic inexactly, and then to judge the best course of action within that context. Then be properly cautious and skeptical about the results.

Questions

Question 6 Consider the following pattern of 64 bits:

```
1100 0111   1001 1010 ... followed by 48
zero bits
```

Interpret this as an IEEE double-precision floating point value and determine its value in base 10.

Question 7 Can the number 10 be written exactly using an IEEE double-precision floating point? Write the bit pattern that represents this number (but there's no need to write lots of trailing zeros).

Question 8 Suppose we use 32 bits to represent an `unsigned int`, and 64-bit IEEE double precision to store `double`'s. What's the largest *integer* that can be represented by each of these formats? Is there any loss of information in converting an `unsigned int` into a `double`? Explain.

Question 9 We have noted that in IEEE double precision with $u = 2^{-53}$, the floating point addition $1 \oplus u = 1$. What's the value of $1 \ominus u$?

8.3 TRUNCATION AND DISCRETIZATION ERRORS

Many of the methods that we have used to simulate physical processes using computation have been based on approximations. We have truncated infinite series expansions at a finite number of terms. We have replaced the continuous independent variables that describe a phenomenon by a discrete set of values. Indeed, because floating point numbers are finitely represented, we always, in the end, use a discrete set of values for all quantities in a problem.

This replacement of infinite and continuous processes by discrete and finite approximations is necessary for most successful engineering computations, but this forced finiteness does introduce awkward questions. Did we retain sufficient terms from an infinite sum to well approximate it with a finite one? Did we use a fine enough mesh to capture the essential features of the continuous problem? In most cases, it takes experience and intuition to select sufficient terms or to develop a grid good enough to represent some real problem, but this is an experience that you must seek to develop as you use computation to model and analyze the real world.

Consider the problem of computing the cosine of an angle. In Project 11, in Chapter 3, I provided the infinite series

$$\cos(x) = \sum_{n=0}^{\infty} (-1)^n \frac{x^{2n}}{(2n)!} \tag{8.36}$$

and asked you to write a code that summed the terms of this series up to $n = N$. But suppose I want to know the $\cos(x)$ with a specified accuracy. How many terms must I retain in the series? It would be dangerous to simply guess, "Oh, I think $N = 100$ will do the trick." This choice is foolish from an implementation viewpoint, since I seem intent on computing 200 factorial, which is way too large to be represented using even a double-extended floating point value. But worse, I have no quantitative idea what the error in my cosine value will be when using $N = 100$ terms; it might be OK, but I can't tell without some actual analysis.

There is no universal trick to determine how many terms should be retained in a series, or how fine a mesh needs to be to capture the desired physics. Each problem must be carefully examined and its own peculiar features exploited. In the present case of the cosine, we can exploit the trigonometric identities; in particular, the periodicity of the cosine function, $\cos(\theta + 2\pi) = \cos(\theta)$, and the half-angle formula $\cos(2\theta) = 2\cos^2(\theta) - 1$ in order to compute the cosine of any angle from a knowledge of the cosine for angles smaller than $\pi/4 \approx 0.78$. This reduces the problem to determining how many terms should be used from the sum in Eq. (8.36) in order to estimate the cosine of angles that are less than $\pi/4$.

Without much work I can then overestimate the neglected terms in the sum of Eq. (8.36), assuming $|x| < 1$, as

$$\left| \sum_{n=N+1}^{\infty} (-1)^n \frac{x^{2n}}{(2n)!} \right| \leq \frac{x^{2(N+1)}}{[2(N+1)]!} \sum_{n=0}^{\infty} (x^2)^n \tag{8.37}$$

$$\leq \frac{x^{2(N+1)}}{[2(N+1)]!} \frac{1}{1 - x^2}, \tag{8.38}$$

and so for $|x| < \pi/4$ we can be sure that

$$\left| \cos(x) - \sum_{n=0}^{N} (-1)^n \frac{x^{2i}}{(2n)!} \right| \leq \frac{(\pi^2)^{(N+1)}}{16^{(N+1)}[2(N+1)]!(1 - \pi^2/16)} . \tag{8.39}$$

This error we can make as small as we like by selecting a sufficiently large N. For $N = 7$ the error is less than 2.7×10^{-15}, and for $N = 8$ it is less than 6×10^{-18}, which is plenty accurate for IEEE double precision. Similar estimates can be developed for the error in approximating $\sin(x)$ by a truncated series. So, in general, we can determine how large to make N in order to achieve a desired maximum error, at least for angles that are not too large, and larger angles can be dealt with by using trigonometric identities.

As another illustration of error in numerical approximations, consider the radioactive transformation of Bromine-87 to Rubidium-87. In this process, Bromine-87, with a half-life of 55.9 s, turns into Krypton-87, which itself decays with a half-life of 1.27 hours, into Rubidium-87:

$$^{87}\text{Br} \xrightarrow{55.9 \text{ s}} {}^{87}\text{Kr} \xrightarrow{1.27 \text{ h}} {}^{87}\text{Rb}.$$

These half-lives imply 1.24×10^{-2} decays/s per Bromine-87 nucleus and 1.52×10^{-4}/s per Krypton-87 nucleus. To develop a very simple time-stepping algorithm to describe this radioactive decay process, let B_n represent the number of Bromine-87 nuclei at time step n, and similarly let K_n and R_n represent the number of Krypton-87 and Rubidium-87 nuclei. The number of Bromine-87 nuclei lost during the time step Δt from t_n to t_{n+1} is then

$$1.24 \times 10^{-2} B_n \Delta t \tag{8.40}$$

and the number of Krypton-87 lost in time Δt is

$$1.52 \times 10^{-4} K_n \Delta t. \tag{8.41}$$

So we can compute B_{n+1}, K_{n+1}, and R_{n+1}, the numbers of Bromine-87, Krypton-87, and Rubidium-87, from a simple accounting as

$$B_{n+1} = B_n - \underbrace{1.24 \times 10^{-2} \Delta t B_n}_{\text{Number of Br-87 lost in } \Delta t} \tag{8.42}$$

$$K_{n+1} = K_n + \underbrace{1.24 \times 10^{-2} \Delta t B_n}_{\text{Number of Kr-87 produced in } \Delta t} - \underbrace{1.52 \times 10^{-4} \Delta t K_n}_{\text{Number of Kr-87 lost in } \Delta t} \tag{8.43}$$

$$R_{n+1} = R_{n+1} + \underbrace{1.52 \times 10^{-4} \Delta t K_n}_{\text{Number of Rb-87 produced in } \Delta t} . \tag{8.44}$$

Here's a quick code to simulate this decay process:

BrDecay.cpp

```
1  // =================================================================
2  // BrDecay.cpp
3  // Simulates the decay of a Bromine-87 into Rubidium-87.
4  // Results are reported as fractions of the initial number of
```

```cpp
// Bromine-87 nuclei.
// ================================================================
#include <iostream>
#include <string>
#include <cstdlib>
using namespace std;

int main(int argc, char * argv[])
{
  if(argc != 3)
    {
      cerr << "Usage: " << argv[0] << " dt T\n";
      return 1;
    }

  const double dt = atof(argv[1]);
  const double T = atof(argv[2]);

  assert(dt > 0.0 and T > 0.0);

  const double BrLambda = 1.24e-2;  // Bromine decay constant
  const double KrLambda = 1.52e-4;  // Krypton decay constant

  double B = 1.0;  // All Bromine-87 to start
  double K = 0.0;
  double R = 0.0;

  double t = 0.0;
  while(t <= T)
    {
      // Invariant: B, K and R contain estimates for time t
      cout << t << " " << B << " " << K << " " << R << endl;

      double Bn = B * (1.0 - dt * BrLambda);
      double Kn = K * (1.0 - dt * KrLambda) + B * dt * BrLambda;
      double Rn = R + K * dt * KrLambda;

      // copy new values into B, K and R
      B = Bn;
      K = Kn;
      R = Rn;
      t = t + dt;
    }

  return 0;
}
```

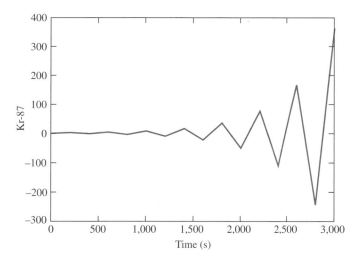

FIGURE 8.3 The fraction of Krypton-87 nuclei estimated using simple time stepping with time step Δt = 200 s. The huge oscillations, growing with time, are evidence of a numerical problem.

Imagine that I am particularly interested in the amount of Krypton-87, whose half-life is 1.27 hours, or 4,570 s. So I choose to run this code with a time step dt = 200 (in seconds), which seems sufficiently short compared to 4,570 s to give me a good picture of the creation and loss of the Krypton. The unhappy results for the fraction of Krypton are shown in Fig. 8.3. These numbers are more than merely wrong: They are disastrous! The simulation shows that the amount of Krypton oscillates, even becoming negative. These strange oscillations are actually growing with time, so that at 3,000 s there are more Krypton atoms than there were Bromine atoms at the start. This is physically ridiculous, although the computer can't tell me so and I must judge this for myself. The machine just computes away, generating nonsense.

The problem is that I make a small *truncation error* at each time step—Eqs. (8.43) and (8.44) are not exact. For example, the number of Bromine-87 nuclei lost during the time step Δt from t_n to t_{n+1} is not *exactly*

$$1.24 \times 10^{-2} B_n \Delta t \qquad (8.45)$$

because, in reality, during the time step the number of Bromine-87 nuclei is not constant. Taylor's theorem and a bit of differential equations will tell us that I am making a small error of size Δt^2 at every time step.

This small error is not a problem if the time step is small enough to resolve all of the timescales in the problem, but if the time step Δt is too large, then the errors accumulate and ruin the approximate solution. The smallest timescale in the problem is the 60-s half-life of Bromine-87. So if the time step is larger than about 60 s, there will be some accumulation of error. But if the time step is smaller than this, the approximation might be decent.[7] Figure 8.4 shows two simulations, one using a time

[7]This can, in fact, be proven, but I will not show you the proof here.

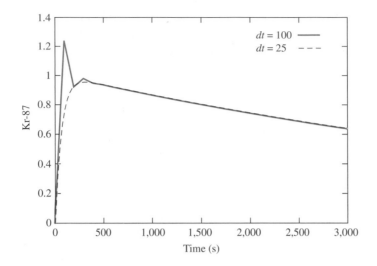

FIGURE 8.4 The fraction of Krypton-87 nuclei estimated using simple time stepping with $\Delta t = 100$ s (solid line) and $\Delta t = 25$ s (dashed line).

step of $\Delta t = 100$ s, which is a bit too big, and one using a time step of $\Delta t = 25$ s, which is small enough to prevent a catastrophic accumulation of error in following the decay of Bromine-87. The simulation with $\Delta t = 25$ is free of strange nonphysical oscillations, and in fact is reasonably accurate.

We are often forced to discretely approximate the continuous mathematics of the real world in order to exploit computation for engineering, and so we must therefore carefully examine the effect of any discretization or truncation on the results that we compute.

Claim

> No computed result to model a continuous problem is meaningful unless the effects of discretization and truncation on the result are well understood.

Too seldom do we take the time to explore the effect of artificial parameters, introduced in a problem simply to make it amenable to computation. For example, in the radioactive decay computation just illustrated, it is easy to compare the results computed using $\Delta t = 25$ with those computed using $\Delta t = 12.5$, and thereby confirm that the results for the amount of Krypton are well converged in Δt, and hence probably reliable. Figure 8.5 shows such a comparison.

As you continue your use of computation to solve problems in engineering and science, you should always be asking yourself, "How do I know these results are right?" We must understand how the error in our approximations behaves as we refine computational grids or increase the number of terms in some sum. This is the field of numerical analysis—the analysis of algorithms designed for numerical computation. Such analyses require calculus and differential equations, as well as a good dose of physical insight.

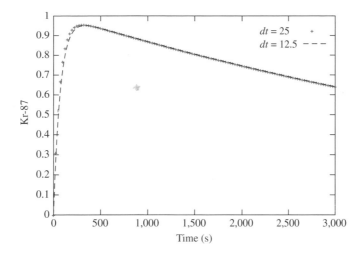

FIGURE 8.5 The fraction of Krypton-87 nuclei estimated with $\Delta t = 25$ s (blue crosses) and $\Delta t = 12.5$ s (dashed line). The results agree quite closely.

Questions

Question 10 Using the simple time-stepping scheme above, compute the fraction of Br-87 as a function of time from 0–200 s using time steps of 20, 10, and 5 s. Can you have faith in the results?

Question 11 Using the time-stepping method in **BrDecay.cpp**, evaluate the number of Bromine, Krypton, and Rubidium at time $t = 200$ s as a function of the time step Δt. Observe the convergence of these values as $\Delta t \to 0$ by making plots of these final values as a function of Δt.

Question 12 Return to Newton's method for computing the square root, and estimate the number of iterations required to get the root $r \approx \sqrt{f}$ to within an error 10^{-15} of the correct value for $1 \leq f < 2$. Describe how you could use this with a knowledge of the floating point representation $x = f \times 2^E$ to compute square roots of normalized numbers to within a relative accuracy of 10^{-15}.

8.4 SPEED

So far in this text I have largely ignored speed. But computations take time, and if a computation takes too much time, it is of little value. In this section let us therefore briefly revisit some of the algorithms we met earlier and make some estimates of the numbers of operations or the amount of work they require. To measure the amount of work that an algorithm requires, we generally make a rough count of the number of basic operations—such as addition, multiplication, or even accesses of a variable—and try to determine how this count of operations scales with the size of the problem.

So in a simple running sum of N numbers, roughly like

```
1   const unsigned int N = x.size();
2   double sum = 0.0;
```

```
3   for(unsigned int i = 0; i < N; i = i + 1)
4   {
5     sum = sum + x[i];
6   }
```

we require one addition and perhaps three variable accesses (look up value of sum, look up value of x[i], and write new value into sum) in each trip through the loop. In total then we require N additions and $3N$ accesses, so the amount of work required is roughly $4N$ operations. We say that this is order N work, and write this symbolically as $O(N)$. In this we are noting that if we double the size of the problem, the amount of work is doubled, but we do not worry too much about the exact coefficient of the scaling. We say that $2N = O(N)$, and that $100N = O(N)$ too, because the interesting observation is the scaling with N, not the precise coefficient.

Unless we are dealing with the very aggressive optimization of a piece of code, this rough order estimate is enough. We can't actually say that the work required for an addition is the same as that required to access a variable, and a compiler may be able to arrange the generated machine code in such a way that some variable accesses are eliminated entirely. So it's generally the scaling with problem size that we are interested in, and not the system and compiler-influenced coefficient.

Definition

> We say that functions $f(N)$ and $g(N)$ are of the same order as $N \to \infty$, $f(N) = O(g(N))$, if
>
> $$\lim_{N \to \infty} \left| \frac{f(N)}{g(N)} \right| = C$$
>
> for some finite constant $C > 0$.

Note that C must be greater than zero. If C is zero, then $g(N)$ must be going to infinity with N more quickly than $f(N)$ is, and so $f(N)$ is of a lower order than $g(N)$.

Consider the matrix-vector multiplication code of Section 6.7. In particular, examine Eq. (6.9) and its implementation in **matvecDouble.cpp**. When the matrix is $M \times N$, the body of the outer loop must be executed M times, and for each such execution N multiplications and N additions must be performed by the inner loop. The entire matrix-vector multiply operation therefore takes $2\,NM$ floating point operations and NM assignments, and a matrix-vector multiply therefore requires $O(NM)$ work. It scales as the product of the number of rows and the number of columns. If the matrix is square, say, $N \times N$, then matrix multiplication requires $O(N^2)$ work. This scaling captures the notion that if we double the number of rows and columns of the matrix, the amount of work required for a matrix-vector product increases by four times.

It should be no surprise that in the case of a general square matrix, the matrix-vector product requires $O(N^2)$ work. This is the optimal scaling; it's not possible *in general* to do less work than this. However, it is possible *in special cases* to perform a matrix-vector multiply in less than $O(N^2)$ work. This occurs if the matrix has a special structure that can be exploited when doing the multiplication. For example, if I know that the matrix has nonzero elements only on the diagonal, then I can do a matrix-vector multiplication in $O(N)$ steps. This is a case in which the matrix is sparse, meaning that it has mostly zero entries. There are many cases when such a special structure arises in matrices. Another and most important special case is the discrete Fourier transform, which is a matrix-vector multiply that allows signals to be decomposed into their sine and cosine components. In certain cases, this matrix-vector multiply can be accomplished in only $O(N \log(N))$ operations by using an algorithm named the fast Fourier transform (or FFT); this algorithm is the heart of many signal processing codes and electronic devices.

The appearance of a logarithm may seem peculiar to you. Let us consider how such a strange scaling for computational work might arise by examining a simpler algorithm that we have ourselves developed: the recursive merge sort from Section 6.5. Let $W(N)$ be the work required to merge sort an array of size N. Each step of the merge sort requires sorting two arrays of roughly size $N/2$, and then merging those two sorted arrays back together into a fully sorted array. The merge process itself takes αN units of work, where α is simply some constant that I won't care about in the end. Therefore,

$$W(N) = 2W(N/2) + \alpha N. \tag{8.46}$$

We need to use this recursion relation to evaluate $W(N)$ more explicitly in terms of N. Let's write Eq. (8.46) with $N/2$ replacing N, yielding

$$W(N/2) = 2W(N/4) + \alpha N/2. \tag{8.47}$$

But I can use this in Eq. (8.46) itself; hence,

$$W(N) = 2[2W(N/4) + \alpha N/2] + \alpha N = 4W(N/4) + \alpha 2N. \tag{8.48}$$

Now using Eq. (8.46) with $N/4$ replacing N, we discover that

$$W(N/4) = 2W(N/8) + \alpha N/4 \tag{8.49}$$

and so Eq. (8.48) can be written as

$$W(N) = 4[2W(N/8) + \alpha N/4] + \alpha 2N = 8W(N/8) + \alpha 3N. \tag{8.50}$$

Continuing in this way, we discover that

$$W(N) = 2^m W(N/2^m) + \alpha mN \tag{8.51}$$

for integer m. Suppose that $N = 2^m$ for some $m = \log(N)/\log(2)$; then we have

$$W(N) = 2^m W(1) + \alpha mN = NW(1) + \alpha N \frac{\log(N)}{\log(2)}. \tag{8.52}$$

The work $W(1)$ to merge sort an array of size 1 is about one unit, so we have

$$W(N) = N + \alpha N \frac{\log(N)}{\log(2)} = N\left[1 + \frac{\alpha}{\log(2)} \log(N)\right]. \tag{8.53}$$

For large N we have that $1 \ll [\alpha/\log(2)]\log(N)$, so we have the scaling

$$W(N) = O(N\log(N)). \tag{8.54}$$

This $N\log(N)$ scaling is typical of algorithms that work by splitting the subject of their work into two parts of equal size and then proceed by recursively applying themselves to each half.

Strictly speaking, the development just given for the scaling $W(N) = O(N\log(N))$ is true only if $N = 2^m$, which is certainly a special case. But in a more general case, we can easily see that the scaling is still correct: Suppose that $2^{m-1} < N \leq 2^m$ for some m, and let $\beta = 2^m/N < 2$. We could then, conceptually at least, increase the length of the array being sorted to length 2^m by appending to it $2^m - N$ elements that are larger than any element in the list. The work required for this extension is no worse than $O(N)$. These extra elements are already in place (for sorting into ascending order), so they never actually have to be sorted; they are just imagined as part of a thought experiment. But because they don't have to be sorted, the work to sort the original array is less than that to build and sort this imagined augmented array. That latter amount of work is

$$O(2^m\log(2^m)) = O(\beta N\log(\beta N)) = \beta N(\log(N) + \log(\beta)). \tag{8.55}$$

For large N we certainly have $\log(\beta) < \log(2) \ll \log(N)$, so it is still the case that the work to merge sort an array of arbitrary length N is

$$W(N) = O(N\log(N)), \tag{8.56}$$

even when N is not a power of 2.

Having an estimate of the order of work of an algorithm can be very helpful in establishing its utility for a particular problem. If an algorithm requires $O(N^3)$ work, and needed 1 day to solve a problem of size $N = 1000$, it will take over a week to solve a problem of size $N = 2000$, and over a month to solve a problem of size $N = 4000$. But if the algorithm was $O(N)$, then the problem of size $N = 2000$ would take only 2 days, and the problem of size $N = 4000$ would take only 4 days. This can easily be the difference between irrelevancy and practicality.

Let's consider a different recursive algorithm, namely the recursive algorithm to evaluate Legendre polynomials from **legendre1.cpp** in Chapter 4. This analysis will show the impracticality of that particular implementation. Let $W(n)$ represent the amount of work, roughly measured by the number of arithmetic comparison and assignment operations, required to execute `legendre(n, mu)`. An examination of the algorithm shows that $W(1) \approx W(0) \approx 1$, while more generally,

$$W(n) = W(n-1) + W(n-2) + k, \tag{8.57}$$

where k is a constant, independent of n, that represents the incremental work required to combine the Legendre polynomials P_{n-1} and P_{n-2} into P_n. This recursion for $W(N)$ may look familiar to you. If $k = 0$, then the recursion relation looks like

$$F(n) = F(n-1) + F(n-2) \tag{8.58}$$

and the sequence of $F(n)$ values are $1, 1, 2, 3, 5, 8, 13, \ldots$. These are called the Fibonacci numbers. Since $k > 0$, we can easily see that $W(n) \geq F(n)$. This is clearly true for $n = 0$ and $n = 1$, and if it's true for $m < n$, then $W(n) = W(n-1)+W(n-2)+k > F(n-1)+F(n-2) = F(n)$, so it's true in general. Thus, the Fibonacci numbers provide a lower bound for the work required of the recursive Legendre evaluation algorithm.

This connection between Fibonacci numbers and the work $W(n)$ is useful because it is straightforward to show that $F(n) > g^n/\sqrt{5}$, where $g = (1 + \sqrt{5})/2$. To see this, note that $g \approx 1.6$ and $\sqrt{5} \approx 2.2$, so $F(0) = 1 > g^0/\sqrt{5}$ and $F(1) = 1 > g^1/\sqrt{5}$. Suppose now that $F(m) > g^m/\sqrt{5}$ for all $m < n$. Then

$$F(n) = F(n-1) + F(n-2) > g^{n-1}/\sqrt{5} + g^{n-2}/\sqrt{5} \tag{8.59}$$

$$> \frac{g^n}{\sqrt{5}}\left(\frac{1}{g} + \frac{1}{g^2}\right) \tag{8.60}$$

$$> g^n/\sqrt{5} \tag{8.61}$$

because $1/g + 1/g^2 = 1$. So indeed $F(n) > g^n/\sqrt{5}$ for all n. Thus, the Fibonacci numbers grow (at least) exponentially fast,[8] and so the work in computing Legendre polynomial values using a recursive implementation is at least $O(g^n)$. This exponential growth in work, $W(n) \geq O(g^n)$, is much too rapid to be practically useful as n becomes large.

On the other hand, the nonrecursive implementation of legendre in **legendre2.cpp** requires only n trips through a single loop, with each trip requiring perhaps 15 arithmetic, comparison, and assignment operations. So the nonrecursive implementation of the recursion relation for Legendre polynomials requires only $O(n)$ work, and is much, much faster than the recursive implementation that requires exponential work.

Thus, recursive algorithms can be very efficient, as in merge sort, and they can be very inefficient, as in the recursive implementation to evaluate Legendre polynomials. There is a powerful temptation in these days of fast computers to ignore the speed of algorithms. Correctness is certainly more important than speed, but a slow correct algorithm is less useful than a fast correct algorithm. Some estimate of the amount of work required to execute an algorithm is worth having, and in selecting among different algorithms to solve a problem, their relative speed is certainly a factor.

Questions

Question 13 To appreciate the advantage of an $N \log(N)$ algorithm over an N^2 algorithm, make a plot of each of these functions for $1 \leq N \leq 100$.

Question 14 Estimate the amount of work required in **movingAverage.cpp** from Chapter 6 when applied to a signal of size N, and compre this to the matrix-vector multiply version **movingAverage2.cpp**.

Question 15 Estimate the amount of work required in Gaussian elimination and in solving an upper-triangular system of equations of size $N \times N$.

Question 16 Show by considering the limit $N \to \infty$ that $N + N \log(N) = O(N \log(N))$. Demonstrate that $N \log(N)$ is *not* $O(N^2)$.

---

[8] In fact, it can be shown that F_n is the integer closest to $g^{n+1}/\sqrt{5}$, so $F(n) = O(g^n)$.

8.5   COMPUTERS IN ENGINEERING

Computers are a marvelous tool for engineering analysis. Therefore, I encourage you to distrust them, and view the results they yield with a skeptical eye.

Computation provides us with the means to simulate the physical world, and it thereby provides us with the means to analyze an engineering design without actually building it. We can use computational models to predict the wind force on a skyscraper or the pressure on an artificial heart valve. We can use computers to predict the radiation fields created by a medical accelerator or to describe what neutrons do in a nuclear reactor. With optimization algorithms we can even use computers to help us select the best among a range of designs. These computational tools are wonderfully useful in helping us do our work as engineers.

But computers cannot, by themselves, design. It is still up to the human intellect and imagination to recognize a problem, to ask the right questions, to formulate these questions in a useful way, and to design a creative solution. The computer can only compute answers; it cannot ask the right questions.

The algorithms that we create, to allow us to model physical reality or to otherwise help us in various engineering analyses, are seldom perfect. First they are creations of our own flawed intellect. Then they must execute within the finite limits of the computer. Any code that attempts to model reality always does so in an approximate way. Every model may neglect some key bit of important physics that did not seem so important to its creator, or was not important in an old class of problems, but is important in the new problem that you want to solve. Many phenomena, even everyday phenomena such as the boiling of water, are so difficult to understand that there are no really first-rate computational models of them, and only rough, technology-specific approximations abound. Many codes do contain wonderful physics and are amazingly accurate, but even the best has its limits, beyond which it may silently fail.

You have by now written a few codes, and you know that it can be strangely difficult to get them right. So you should not be surprised that the codes sold to you to perform engineering analyses often have defects, although these are seldom advertised on the shrink-wrap. The engineers and programmers who create commercial modeling codes are not superhuman, and they make mistakes too.

So as you move on in your engineering career, you will, and should, use computational models. But you should do so carefully, with doubt in your mind. You must have some independent intuition as to what the answer to your question is, so that you can judge what a code predicts. You must explore the range of answers that a code may give as its input parameters are varied, so you develop some further confidence in its results. It is easy in the press of deadlines to simply run and trust a code, but such a path of blind acceptance is not a wise one.

You always have to wonder, "How do I *know* that this is right?"

Projects

Well, this is the end. You are probably anxious to move on, so I've given you only a few projects here. But this is the culmination of the text, so some of them are pretty difficult.

PROJECT 1

Suppose we represent an unsigned integer as a vector of bool values. Write a routine that will accept two such vectors and return a vector of bool that represents their sum.

PROJECT 2

Suppose we represent an unsigned integer as a vector of bool values. Write a routine that will accept two such vectors and return a vector of bool that represents the integer part of their quotient.

PROJECT 3

Using 32-bit unsigned integers, we cannot even compute 13 factorial. So let's create a code to carry out exact integer arithmetic without the annoyance of overflow. One way to do this is to create our own class that will manage an integer using place value notation in a resizable array of digits, so that we can grow the number of stored digits as necessary.

Write a set of routines that will perform exact arithmetic on nonnegative integers with the integers represented as arrays of base 10 digits. Use a vector<char> to save space, but treat the char as integers, so that, for example, the array containing the integer values {1, 3, 5, 5} represents 1,355.

Create these facilities as a class called Integer and provide methods that create an Integer from an unsigned int, add one to the Integer, add another Integer in to an Integer, multiply the Integer by another Integer, and return a representation of an Integer as a human readable string. Note that some of these operations will require you to increase the number of digits stored in the Integer. Use these facilities to create a factorial function that returns the factorial of its Integer argument as an Integer.

PROJECT 4

You are given a table of integers, containing 0 and 1 only. Develop and implement an algorithm that will find the largest, by area, rectangular subset of this table that is filled only with 1's. Here's an example of such a table. In this example, the largest rectangular subset has an area of 10, and is shown by the blue 1's

1	1	0	0	1	1
1	1	1	1	0	1
0	1	1	1	1	1
0	1	1	1	1	1
1	0	0	0	1	0
1	0	1	1	1	0
0	1	1	1	0	0
0	0	1	1	0	1

The obvious algorithm is an exhaustive search that looks at every possible rectangular subset of the table; this algorithm would require an unacceptable $O(M^3 \times N^3)$ operations, where M is the number of rows and N is the number of columns in the table. Make your algorithm faster than $O(M^3 \times N^3)$, and for a real challenge make it function in $O(M \times N^2)$ operations.

C++ CONSTRUCTS IN BRIEF

IN **THIS** appendix I will provide a brief overview of the C++ language, with a particular focus on the elements of the language used in this book. In most areas this appendix provides only an outline of language constructs that were described in greater detail throughout the text, although in a few sections additional language details are provided. But you must realize that C++ is a large programming language, and this appendix barely scratches the surface. Those wishing a complete reference will find no more precise and complete a source than the ANSI/ISO standard document (ISO/IEC 14882).

A.1 SOURCE TEXT ORGANIZATION

A C++ program is a written text. So like other such texts, it is made up of letters, punctuation, and other symbols; in other words, a source text is composed of characters. This written text is organized into *source files*. Each source file provided to the compiler is separately translated, in several phases of processing, into corresponding machine code. Those multiple streams of machine code are linked together along with machine code for standard library functions, into a functioning program, ready for execution.

A source text file containing function and procedure definitions is often organized as follows:

```
1   // comments to introduce the file
2
3   // include standard declarations ===============================
4   #include <iostream>
5   #include <strings>
6
7   // put standard facilities in the global namespace
8   using namespace std;
9
```

```
10   // declare fundamental constants ===============================
11   const double massElectron = 0.5110034 // MeV
12
13   // declare routines ============================================
14   int wineFull();
15
16   // ==============>> main <<======================================
17   int main()
18   {
19      // main body
20   }
21
22   // ==============>> wineFull <<=================================
23   int wineFull()
24   {
25      // wineFull body
26   }
```

In an early phase of translation, source code text between // and the end of the line on which it appears is replaced by a single space, so the compiler effectively does not see text in comments.[1] After this any files listed in #include directives are similarly stripped of comments, and the remainder of the included text is merged into the source text.

Include directives in a source text file can have one of two forms:

```
1   #include <special_name>
2   #include "a_source_file_name"
```

How the compiler treats these is not completely specified in the C++ language standard, but both forms cause the inclusion of another source text file into the source text stream being processed. In the first the special_name is intended to be one of the standard "header" files such as iostream, cmath, or string that declare identifiers used in the standard libraries.

In most implementations #include <special_name> causes the compiler to search for a file named special_name in a special repository of such header files,[2] while #include "a_source_file_name" causes the compiler system to search for the file a_source_file_name in the current working directory. The C++ standard does say that if this file cannot be found or included, then the compiler should retry the #include as though the directive had been written as #include <a_source_file_name>.

---

[1] The compiler similarly replaces text from any /* to any */ with a single space, providing a second form of comment.

[2] For example, /usr/include on a Linux or Mac OS/X system.

The source text is next broken up into a stream of tokens. Tokens come in five flavors: identifiers, keywords, literal data values, operators, and punctuation. Note that once the input has been parsed into tokens, whitespace characters—spaces, tabs, and newlines—have no significance, except for whitespace appearing in string literals. This means that whitespace has *almost* no meaning in the original source text. The only exception arises when whitespace is required to remove an ambiguity in the text; this is the case in a construct like `vector< vector<double> >`. It would be incorrectly parsed if written as `vector<vector<double>>`, because many compilers can't tell if `>>` closes the two template parameters, or is an `>>` operator.

A.1.1 Identifiers

Identifiers are used to name objects, including variables and functions, within a C++ source text. Identifiers consist of sequences of certain allowed characters, of arbitrary length. Here are the rules for forming a valid identifier:

1. An identifier can begin with any of the following characters: _ (an underscore), a through z or A through Z. Note that uppercase letters are different from lowercase letters.

2. An identifier may continue with any number of additional characters: _, 0 through 9, a through z or A through Z, and note that uppercase letters are still different from lowercase letters.

Although the C++ language standard says identifiers can be of any length, many C++ compiler implementations do not comply with the standard in this respect and instead have a maximum identifier length. In most compilers this length limit is several hundred characters. Such a long identifier would be of questionable style, so this limitation is often of no significance.[3]

There are many schools of thought[4] about what constitutes a good identifier. It is quite clear that an identifier should be meaningful in the context of the algorithm being expressed, so an identifier like `averageArea` looks promising, while `aa` is rather questionable. I have used a style in this text in which most identifiers are combinations of a few English words, with the first word written in all lowercase characters, and subsequent words capitalized. The purpose of the capitalization is to make the start of the later words obvious. The alternative `averagearea` is rather harder to read. A different, and reasonable, scheme is to use the underscore as a word separator, as in `average_area`.

A.1.2 Keywords

The following keywords cannot be used as identifiers because they are used as part of the syntax of the C++ language:

---

[3]However, some powerful automatic code-generation techniques do generate identifiers that are hundreds of characters long, intended for compiler consumption but not for humans.

[4]Meaning, many pointless debates.

asm	do	if	return	typedef
auto	double	inline	short	typeid
bool	dynamic_cast	int	signed	typename
break	else	long	sizeof	union
case	enum	mutable	static	unsigned
catch	explicit	namespace	static_cast	using
char	export	new	struct	virtual
class	extern	operator	switch	void
const	false	private	template	volatile
const_cast	float	protected	this	wchar_t
continue	for	public	throw	while
default	friend	register	true	
delete	goto	reinterpret_cast	try	

Nor can the following be used as identifiers because they are alternative representations of certain operators:

and	and_eq	bitand	bitor	compl	not
not_eq	or	or_eq	xor	xor_eq	

Older Logical Operators I have used the keywords and, or, and not to represent the logical operators throughout this text. My view is that they are much more readable than their strange symbolic counterparts &&, ||, and !. However, these older symbolic forms were inherited directly from C, and are recognized by all C++ compilers, while the forms and, or, and not were introduced only more recently when C++ was standardized. A few older compilers therefore do not yet recognize the logical operators and, or, and not.

A.1.3   Literal Data

When writing a C++ source text, we often want to represent literal data values. Here are some rules for writing literal int's, unsigned int's, char's, bool's, doubles's, floats's, and C strings.

Literal int A literal int can be written as a sequence of base 10 digits, 0 through 9, that *does not start* with a 0. So 123 is a literal int written in base 10, 123. is not, and neither is 0123. The former case contains a decimal point, and so is not an int; the latter case starts with a 0, and this is used to indicate that the number is being written in base 8.

It is amusing to note that the C++ standard does not specify any way to write a negative integer literal! This is not really an issue, as -123 is the negation operator - applied to the literal integer 123.

Literal unsigned int An unsigned int literal can often be written just like an int, but this actually causes a type conversion. In the statement unsigned int i = 1;

the compiler (logically at least) constructs an `int` with value of 1 and converts it to an `unsigned int`. This is seldom a problem unless we want to write an `unsigned int` that is too large to be an `int`. A literal `unsigned int` can be written just like an `int` but with a suffix of U. So 4000000000U is a literal `unsigned int`.

***Literal* char**   Most literal `char` values can be written as a single character placed between single quotes (or apostrophes), like `'Z'`. Three characters that definitely cannot be written this way are the backslash (\), newline, and single quote. These are written instead as `'\\'`, `'\n'`, and `'\''`, respectively. These are called *escape sequences*. The double quote can also be written as an escape sequence `'\"'`, as can several other special characters. In addition, a `char` may also be written as a number in hexadecimal (base 16) in the form `'\xhh'`, where the x is literal, and h's are hexadecimal digits. So `'\x41'` is a character. But what character it may be is not specified by the C++ standard (in ASCII it would be a `'B'`).

The special `char` null, written as `'\0'`, is used to denote a paradoxical noncharacter. The null character is guaranteed never to be used as any real character; its purpose is to mark the end of a C string in memory. When a C string is stored in memory, it is stored as a native array of `char`'s, with the null `char` appended to the end of it. Because this null character is there to mark the end of the string, the length of the string does not need to be stored; we can always walk down the list of characters in the C string until we find the null.

***Literal* bool**   A literal value of true can be written as `true`, and a value of false can be written as `false`. We can also use the integer value 0 to mean false, and any nonzero integer, such as 1, to mean true. Generally, it is better to use the forms `true` and `false`; they are easier to read and quickly understood.

***Literal* double**   Literal `double` values can be written in two ways. The first is as a base 10 representation *including* a decimal point, much the way we learned to write such numbers in elementary school. So 3.14159 is a literal `double` value, and so is 2.0 or even 2. But the decimal point *must be there*; 2 is not a `double`.

This method of writing floating point values is fine for numbers whose magnitude is not too big or too small, but becomes unworkable for a number like 1.6×10^{-19}. Therefore, an optional part of a floating point number is allowed to signify multiplication by powers of 10; in this form, we write e (or E) followed by an integer power of 10. For example, we can write 1.6e-19 or 1.6E-19 to mean 1.6×10^{-19}.

***Literal* float**   Literal `float` values are written like `double` values, but with the suffix F attached to them. So 3.14159F is a float, as is 1.6E-19F. I seldom bother to do this, and freely write code like `float x = 2.0;`. The compiler will convert the `double` value 2.0 to the `float` value 2.0F.

***Literal* C Strings**   The C string is a simple means to represent a collection of characters in a C++ code. It has largely been replaced by the `string` class, but is sometimes useful, and occasionally required. Literal C strings can be written by enclosing a list of characters in double quotes, as in `"The quick brown fox"`. Such a string must be contained on a single line.

In order to place a double quote or a backslash within a string we must use the escaped character sequences described above under the literal `char`'s. For example,

```
"Here is a \"quote\", and here is a backslash \\"
```

represents the list of characters

```
Here is a "quote", and here is a backslash \
```

Similarly, if we want to put a newline character into a string, we must use `'\n'`, as in `"Start a \nnew line"`. Finally, two literal C strings can be combined by writing them separated only by whitespace, as in

```
"The quick brown " "fox "
"jumped over the lazy dog"
```

This represents the single list of characters

```
The quick brown fox jumped over the lazy dog
```

A.1.4 Operators, Associativity, and Precedence

You cannot accuse C++ of providing a paucity of operators. Here is a partial list of unary and binary operators in C++, showing their associativity—R for right to left and L for left to right—and precedence level:

17L	`::`	Scope resolution
16L	`., ->`	Member selection
16L	`[]`	Array index
16L	`()`	Function call
15R	`not, !`	Logical not
15R	`*, &`	Dereference and address of
15R	`-, +`	Unary minus and plus
15R	`new, delete`	Allocate and free memory
13L	`*, /, %`	Multiplicative operators
12L	`+, -`	Additive operators
10L	`<, <=, >=, >`	Relational operators
9L	`==, !=`	Relational operators
5L	`and, &&`	Logical and
5L	`or, ||`	Logical or
2R	`=`	Assignment

Note that the C++ language defines many more operators than these, but this list will serve our needs.

A.1.5 Numeric-type Conversions and Static Casts

It is sometimes necessary to convert one numeric type into another. Such a conversion is performed automatically by the compiler when an arithmetic operation (such as +, -, *, /) is applied to two different numeric types. The basic philosophy of these conversions is to convert the type of one operand to the same type as the other. The conversions occur by moving one operand up this list:

1. double
2. float
3. unsigned int
4. int
5. char

So an int added to a double is first converted to a double. The most surprising conversion is from int to unsigned int. This sometimes results in semantic errors, as in the following code:

```
1  int j = -1;
2  unsigned int i = 0;
3  cout << i + j << endl;   // prints 4294967295 on a 32-bit computer
```

Here the value of j is converted to an unsigned int before the addition in i + j takes place, and the result is an unsigned int.

We force the conversion of a numeric type to another numeric type using static_cast. The expression

```
static_cast<T>(expression)
```

will cause expression to be evaluated, and this value to be converted to type T.

A.2 EXPRESSIONS

An expression is a sequence of language constructs that *evaluates*, that is, has a value when the code is executed. An expression is built out of literal data values, variable names, operators, and function calls (but not, conceptually at least, procedure calls, because a procedure does not return a value). Here is an expression:

```
x = f(x, y) * 2.0 + z
```

In contrast, this selection statement is *not* an expression:

```
if( x < y ) cout << "x_is_small";
```

Because it does not evaluate, it does not have a value. But it does contain two expressions, namely, x < y and cout << "x_is_small".

The evaluation of an expression is sequenced by the precedence and associativity of the operators that are used to construct it.

A.3 STATEMENTS

Statements in C++ include:

1. Simple declaration statements, which might include an initialization, such as `double weight = 0.0;`
2. Compound statements, which are simply groups of statements between { and }
3. Expression statements, which are expressions followed by a semicolon (;), for example, `x = sin(y) * p;`
4. Jump statements
5. Iteration statements, including `for` and `while` loops
6. Selection statements such as `if` and `if-else` statements

A.3.1 Jump Statements

A `return` statement is known as a jump statement, because it causes the thread of execution to jump from the enclosing routine back to the routine's caller.

There are also two jump statements that can control the execution of iteration and selection constructs. A `break` statement can occur inside any iteration statement or inside the `switch` selection statement. It causes the thread of execution to jump out of the enclosing iteration or `switch`.

The following code controls the loading of a cargo container by creating a list of items to put into the container, but only up to a certain mass limit. If the next candidate item for the container has too large a mass, the `break` statement comes into play and causes the thread of execution to jump out of the loop. Execution then continues with line 16.

```
1   vector<unsigned int> itemsAccepted; // items to go in container
2   unsigned double totalMass = 0.0;    // total mass of container
3   unsigned int itemID;                // id of current item
4   double mass;                        // mass of current item
5   cargofile >> itemID >> mass;
6   while(not cargofile.fail())
7     {
8       if(totalMass + mass > maximumMass)
9         {
10          break;  // too much mass -- declare container full
11        }
12      itemsAccepted.push_back(itemID);
13      totalMass = totalMass + mass;
14      cargofile >> itemID >> mass;
```

```
15    }
16    cout << "Cargo_container_complete_with_mass_of:_"
17        << totalMass << endl;
```

The `continue` statement can appear only within an iteration statement. It causes the thread of execution to jump to the bottom of the enclosing iteration, but *not* out of it, so the loop continues. The `continue` statement thereby provides a means to skip a collection of statements in the body of a loop, but to allow the loop to continue on. For example,

```
1     vector<unsigned int> itemsAccepted; // items to go in container
2     unsigned double totalMass = 0.0;    // total mass of container
3     unsigned int itemID;                // id of current item
4     double mass;                        // mass of current item
5     cargofile >> itemID >> mass;
6     while(not cargofile.fail())
7       {
8         if(totalMass + mass > maximumMass)
9           {
10            // that doesn't fit, try something else
11            cargofile >> itemID >> mass;
12            continue;  // skip rest of loop body
13          }
14        itemsAccepted.push_back(itemID);
15        totalMass = totalMass + mass;
16        cargofile >> itemID >> mass;
17      }
18    cout << "Cargo_container_complete_with_mass_of:_"
19        << totalMass << endl;
```

In this version of the cargo-loading loop, an item that is too heavy for the container is skipped and another item is considered. The loop continues until the `cargofile` `istream` fails, presumably meaning that there are no more items to consider.

Neither `break` nor `continue` is *ever* needed. The equivalent control can always be accomplished with selection statements and, sometimes, changes to loop control statements. Neither should `break` nor `continue` be used lightly. They make the flow of control much harder to see in the source text. But sometimes they can be useful in escaping from inside a set of deeply nested selection statements inside a loop body.

Here is the cargo-loading code, written without any jump statements:

```
1     vector<unsigned int> itemsAccepted; // items to go in container
2     unsigned double totalMass = 0.0;    // total mass of container
3     unsigned int itemID;                // id of current item
4     double mass;                        // mass of current item
```

```
5   cargofile >> itemID >> mass;
6   while(not cargofile.fail())
7     {
8       if(totalMass + mass <= maximumMass)
9         {
10          itemsAccepted.push_back(itemID);
11          totalMass = totalMass + mass;
12        }
13      cargofile >> itemID >> mass;
14    }
15  cout << "Cargo␣container␣complete␣with␣mass␣of:␣"
16       << totalMass << endl;
```

A.3.2   Iteration

C++ provides three iteration statements: while, for, and do-while. I have not used do-while in this text, but it is briefly presented here.

While Statement   A while loop is expressed with the statement

```
while (condition) loop_body
```

where condition is an expression with a bool value and loop_body is a statement. When the loop is executed, condition is first evaluated, and if true, loop_body is executed, and then the loop begins again. If condition is false, then the loop is complete and execution continues with the statement following the loop.

For Statement   The for loop is expressed with a statement of the form

```
for( initialization ; condition ; iteration_statement )
loop_body
```

where initialization is an expression, condition evaluates to a bool, iteration_statement is an expression, and loop_body is a statement. The semantics of a for loop are identical to

```
initialization;
while (condition)
  {
     loop_body;
     iteration_statement;
  }
```

Do Statement   The do statement, more often called the do-while loop, is written in the form

```
do loop_body while( condition )
```

where `loop_body` is a statement and `condition` is an expression with a `bool` value. The semantics of this loop are equivalent to

```
loop_body
while (condition)
  {
     loop_body;
  }
```

In other words, it always executes the `loop_body` once, and then checks the `condition` and continues onward like a while loop from then on. Here's an example use of a `do-while` loop:

```
1   int sum = 0;
2   int i = 1;
3   do
4     {
5        sum = sum + i;
6        i = i + 1;
7     } while (sum < 100)
8   cout << "The_sum_exceeds_100_when_the_first_"
9          << (i-1) << "_integers_have_been_used." << endl;
```

I must admit that I never use `do` statements.

A.3.3 Selection

C++ provides two forms of selection statement: the `if-else` statement, and the `switch` statement. We used the `if-else` statement endlessly in the text. It has two variants, namely,

```
if( condition ) statement1
```

and

```
if( condition ) statement1 else statement2
```

where `statement1` and `statement2` are C++ language statements, including possibly other `if-else` statements. In either case, `statement1` will be evaluated only if `condition` evaluates to `true`, and `statement2` will be evaluated only if `condition` evaluates to false.

The `switch` statement was rarely used in this text.[5] It is designed to allow the thread of execution to jump to a number of distinct possibilities based on an integer value. The form of the switch statement is

```
switch( integer_expression ) compound_statement
```

---

[5] This statement offers no functionality not already available in `if-else`, and the default idiom for its use is rather peculiar and error-prone. Many newer languages do not include such a statement.

The `integer_expression` must evaluate to an integer. The value of this integer will be used to jump the thread of execution into the middle of the `compound_statement`. The `compound_statement` can contain multiple `case` labels of the form

```
case constant_expression:
```

or additionally one label of the form

```
default:
```

In these `case` labels, the `constant_expression` is an expression that might involve literal data values or `const` identifiers that can be evaluated to an integer when the code is compiled (rather than when it executes). The semantics of the `switch` statement are then the following:

1. The `integer_expression` is evaluated.
2. The thread of execution will immediately jump to the `case` label whose `constant_expression` matches that value.
3. If none of the `case` labels match, then the thread will jump to the `default` label.
4. If there is no `default` label, then the thread of execution will jump past the `switch` statement and continue on.

Note that the labels have no impact on the thread of execution other than as targets of a jump. They do not themselves break the flow of control.

This means that the `switch` does not directly provide for multiple *alternatives*, but rather it allows us to jump into the middle of some statements and continue from there. Consider the following code:

countup1.cpp

```
1   // ================================================================
2   // countup1.cpp
3   // ================================================================
4   #include <iostream>
5   using namespace std;
6
7   int main()
8   {
9     int i = 2;
10
11    switch(i)
12      {
13        case 1:
14          cout << "one\n";
15        case 2:
16          cout << "two\n";
17        case 3:
18          cout << "three\n";
19        default:
```

```
20        cout << "many\n";
21     }
22
23    return 0;
24  }
```

This will write

```
1  two
2  three
3  many
```

to standard output. After the flow of control jumps to `case 2:`, it continues from there on down, executing every statement. The other `case` statements do not hinder it.

You will seldom see `switch` used in this way in introductory texts. Instead, each `case` label is usually paired with a `break;` statement. A `break;` statement causes the thread of execution to immediately jump out of the enclosing `switch` statement.

countup2.cpp

```
1  // ============================================================
2  // countup2.cpp
3  // ============================================================
4  #include <iostream>
5  using namespace std;
6
7  int main()
8  {
9    int i = 2;
10
11   switch(i)
12     {
13       case 1:
14         cout << "one\n";
15         break;
16       case 2:
17         cout << "two\n";
18         break;
19       case 3:
20         cout << "three\n";
21         break;
22       default:
23         cout << "many\n";
24         break;
25     }
```

```
26
27      return 0;
28    }
```

In this code, after `cout << "two\n";` the `break;` statement on line 18 is executed and the thread of execution immediately jumps to line 27. When used in this way, the `switch` statement is a replacement for an `if-else` ladder of the form

```
1    if( i == 1 )
2      {
3        cout << "one\n";
4      }
5    else if( i == 2 )
6      {
7        cout << "two\n";
8      }
9    else if( i == 3 )
10     {
11       cout << "three\n";
12     }
13   else
14     {
15       cout << "many\n";
16     }
```

The `if-else` ladder requires more typing, but it is less prone to error. It is all too common for someone to forget a `break` statement in a `switch`, and such an error is semantic, not syntactic, so the compiler can't catch it. Furthermore, the `if-else` ladder is more flexible.

A.4 FUNCTIONS AND PROCEDURES

The C++ standard, and the standard C++ language literature, make no distinction between "function" and "procedure." However, in this text I have used these terms to describe the abstract concepts, rather than the language construct. A function is a routine that returns a value, and is thus intended to be used in an expression. But a function does not otherwise affect its execution environment. In contrast a procedure does not return a value, but rather affects its execution environment through some side effect. These side effects are often achieved through the use of reference variables, or by exchanging data with external resources.

All routines (functions and procedures) must be either declared or defined before they can be used in a source text. A function definition looks like

```
T identifier( formal_parameter_list ) compound_statement
```

where T is the return type of the function (the function *evaluates* to this type). When the function is to be evaluated, the compound_statement provides the algorithm to do so. The formal_parameter_list is a comma-separated list of type–identifier pairs. As an example of a function definition, consider:

```
1  int g(int i, int p, string q)
2  {
3    int y = i * p + q.size();
4    return y
5  }
```

This defines a function that evaluates to (returns) an int, and takes three parameters, two int's and one string.

In contrast, a definition of the form

```
void identifier( formal_parameter_list ) compound_statement
```

defines a procedure. This routine does not return a value, but must instead affect its environment through some side effect.

In any routine, the formal_parameter_list can contain reference variables, as in void f(double & x, string q). This affects the semantics of the caller. The caller of a routine must provide a variable in the position corresponding to any reference variable, so the following is valid f(y, "hello"), assuming that y has previously been declared as a double, but f(2.0, "hello") is not, and neither is f(x + y, "hello").

Often, it is useful to declare a routine in some piece of source text, but to define it elsewhere in the source text, or even to define it in a different source text file altogether. A function or procedure declaration looks like its definition, but the compound_statement that defines the algorithm for the routine is replaced by a semicolon (;). So a function declaration looks like

```
T identifier( formal_parameter_list );
```

and a procedure declaration looks like

```
void identifier( formal_parameter_list );
```

A routine can be declared as many times as you like, but it can only be defined once.

A.5 POINTERS AND NATIVE ARRAYS

A pointer variable is a type that can store the address of some other object within a computer. A pointer is declared with a declaration of the form

```
T * identifier;
```

where T is any type. The address of a variable can be assigned to a pointer, and such addresses can be found using the address of operator &. So the following code stores the address of sum in the pointer p:

```
1  double sum = 10.0;
2  double * p = &sum;   // store address of sum in p
```

Pointers support array semantics using the indexing operator [ ], but array indexing is only meaningful if the pointer points to the start of a region of storage that was specifically allocated as an array of data. The new operator is provided for this purpose, with semantics so that T* identifier = new T[integer_expression]; will allocate an array of objects of type T, with space for a number of objects specified by the integer_expression. This space can be freed with delete [ ] identifier;.

A native array is a primitive array construct built into the C++ language. It supports array semantics, but the size of the array must be determined at compile time, and cannot be changed. A native array is declared as

    T a[SIZE]

where T is any valid type and SIZE is an integer constant that must be calculable at compile time. The name of an array is evaluated as a pointer to its first element. So the following code assigns the address of the first element of the array x to the pointer variables p and q:

```
1  double x[100];     // x is a native array of 100 doubles
2  double * p;        // p is a pointer to double
3  double * q;        // q is a pointer to double
4  p = x;             // p points to x[0]
5  q = &x[0];         // q points to x[0]
6  x[0] = 0.0;        // use array indexing to put a number into x
7  p[2] = 1.67e-27;   // use array indexing to put a number into x
8  cout << q[2];      // writes 1.67e-27 to standard output
```

A.6 CLASSES

A class is a collection of named data and methods (functions and procedures) that can act on that data. A class introduces a user-defined data type into the source text. A class can be introduced with the keyword class or struct. In a struct all data and methods are publicly accessible by default.

A class can be defined with a definition of the form

```
struct identifier
{
    simple_declarations
    method_definitions
};
```

In general, the method_definitions can be replaced with only method declarations, and the methods actually defined outside of the structure definition but using the scope resolution operator : : to tell the compiler to what class the method defintions belong. As an example,

```
1   struct nuclideData
2   {
3     unsigned int A;  // mass number
4     unsigned int Z;  // atomic number
5     double atomicMass;
6
7     unsigned int N()  // neutron number
8     {
9       return A - Z;
10    }
11
12    double massExcess();  // only a declaration
13  };
14
15  double nuclideData::massExcess()
16  {
17    return atomicMass - A * 931.5;
18  }
```

The definition of massExcess defines a function that is identified as part of the class nuclideData by giving its full name: nuclideData::massExcess.

Data and member routines in a class can be made private, preventing outside use, with a private clause, as in

```
1   struct nuclideData
2   {
3   public:
4     // queries =============================================
5     unsigned int A() { return _A; }  // mass number
6     unsigned int Z() { return _Z; }  // atomic number
7     double atomicMass() { return _atomicMass; }
8
9     int N()  // neutron number
10    {
11      return _A - _Z;   // class method can access private data
12    }
13
14    double massExcess() { };  // only a declaration
15
16    // set values =========================================
17    void setAZ(unsigned int A, unsigned int Z);
18    void setAtomicMass(double atomicMass);
```

```
19
20   private:
21     // data values -- not for direct public consumption =======
22     unsigned int _A;
23     unsigned int _Z;
24     double _atomic_mass;
25   };
26
27   double nuclideData::massExcess()
28   {
29     return _atomicMass - _A * 931.5;
30   }
31
32   void nuclideData::setAZ(unsigned int A, unsigned int Z)
33   {
34     assert(A >= Z);  // validate data before allowing it in
35     _A = A;
36     _Z = Z;
37   }
38
39   void nuclideData::setAtomicMass(double atomicMass)
40   {
41     assert(atomicMass > 0.0);  // we can validate data
42     _atomicMass = atomicMass;
43   }
```

The data marked `private` cannot be accessed from outside the member routines of the class, so lines 2 and 3 in the following code will be invalid:

```
1   nuclideData Al;
2   Al._A = 27;        // ERROR - can't touch _A
3   Al._Z = 13'        // ERROR - can't touch _Z
4   Al.setAZ(27, 13);  // OK
```

The advantage of making some data private like this is that it allows the designer of the class to control access, so that appropriate checks can be made and so that the structure can be changed more easily, independently of those who use it. This begins to touch on the principles of object-oriented class design, which I have not attempted to reveal in this text. C++ is the wrong language in which to learn those principles anyway, because of its complex syntax and multiparadigm support—to really learn object-oriented programming, I suggest studying Eiffel, or perhaps Java.

C++ also allows the keyword `class` in place of the keyword `struct`. The difference between a `class` and a `struct` in C++ is that in a `class` everything is `private` by default, but in a `struct` everything is `public` by default. I have used "structure" to describe a class that contains only data members, and the word "class" to describe a class that contains both data members and member routines. In both cases, I have used only the keyword `struct` to define classes and structures so that all members would be public by default.

Classes allow a special method called a constructor to allow data to be initialized when an object of the class is declared. A constructor is declared as a class method whose name is the same as that of the class itself. A constructor can have arguments, but cannot have a return type (not even `void`). A default constructor is a constructor that takes no arguments. The compiler can call such a default constructor itself, and will do so whenever an object is declared, if no other constructor is called explicitly. A class can have more than one constructor.

A class can also have one special method called a destructor. Its destructor will be called whenever an object of that class reaches the end of its life, as it does when it goes out of scope. The destructor is a class method that takes no arguments and has no return type, and whose name is that of the class prefixed by a tilde (~). So for a class named C the destructor has the declaration ~C();.

Here, for example, is a class that provides very simple array semantics with index checking and array resizing. This class provides two constructors and a destructor.

simpleArray.h

```
1   // ============================================================
2   // simpleArray.cpp -- a very simple array class
3   // ============================================================
4   #include <cassert>
5   using namespace std;
6
7   struct simpleArray
8   {
9     // query size
10    unsigned int size()
11    {
12      return _size;
13    }
14
15    // access an element
16    double item(unsigned int index)
17    {
18      assert(index < size());
19      return _data[index];
20    }
21
22    // set an element
23    void put(unsigned int index, double value)
24    {
25      assert(index < size());
26      _data[index] = value;
27    }
```

```
28
29    // resize
30    void resize(unsigned int newSize)
31    {
32      double * newData = new double[newSize];
33
34      // work out how many existing elements to copy
35      unsigned int max = newSize;
36      if(max > size())  // we have increased the size
37       {
38         max = size();
39       }
40
41      // copy existing data to new location
42      for(unsigned int i = 0; i < max; i = i + 1)
43       {
44         newData[i] = item(i);
45       }
46      delete [] _data;  // release the old storage
47      _data = newData;  // remember the new storage
48      _size = newSize;  // remember the new size
49    }
50
51    // default constructor
52    simpleArray()
53    {
54      _size = 0;   // No space for anything
55    }
56    // constructor
57    simpleArray(unsigned int s)
58    {
59      _data = new double[s];  // get storage
60      _size = s;              // remember size
61    }
62
63    // destructor
64    ~simpleArray()
65     {
66       delete [] _data;       // release memory
67     }
68
69    private:
70      double * _data;         // points to storage for data
71      unsigned int _size;     // size of storage area
72
73  }; // Don't forget the semicolon!
```

SOME ELEMENTS OF THE
C++ STANDARD LIBRARY

THIS APPENDIX touches on some of the many useful functions from the standard C++ library. It is organized roughly around the header files required for each part of the library. Functions and procedures declared in each header file are listed with their argument and return types. The listing is certainly not comprehensive or definitive.

B.1   MATH LIBRARY

The standard math library, declared in the header file `cmath`, contains functions to estimate the value of any of a number of important algebraic and transcendental functions. Several of these functions are described here. All of the arguments shown as `double` can also be `float`, but not `int`. Also, all angles are measured in radians. Degrees are for ancient Babylonians, not twenty-first-century engineers.

`double abs(double x)` Returns the absolute value of *x* (this is really a synonym for `fabs`).

`double acos(double x)` Returns the $\arccos(x)$, an angle between zero and π whose cosine is *x*.

`double asin(double x)` Returns the $\arcsin(x)$, an angle between $-\pi/2$ and $\pi/2$ whose sine is *x*.

`double atan(double x)` Returns the $\arctan(x)$, an angle between $-\pi/2$ and $\pi/2$ whose tangent is *x*.

`double atan2(double y,double x)` Returns the $\arctan(y/x)$; specifically, this function yields the angle between the *x* axis and line $(0, 0) - (x, y)$. The result will be between $-\pi$ and π. A picture may be of some value here:

`double ceil(double x)` Returns a floating point value that is the smallest integer larger than or equal to x. That is, `ceil` rounds toward $+\infty$, so, for example, `ceil(3.14) == 4.0`, while `ceil(-3.14) == -3.0`.

`double cos(double t)` Returns the cosine of the angle t.

`double cosh(double t)` Returns the hyperbolic cosine of the t, $\cosh(t) = (e^t + e^{-t})/2$.

`double exp(double x)` Returns e^x, the Euler number (the base of the natural logarithm e) raised to the power x.

`double fabs(double x)` Returns the absolute value of x.

`double floor(double x)` Returns a floating point value equal to the largest integer that is smaller than or equal to x. That is, `floor` rounds toward $-\infty$, for example, `floor(3.14) == 3.0`, while `floor(-3.14) == -4.0`.

`double fmod(double x, double y)` Returns the remainder of x divided by y.

`double log(double x)` Returns the natural logarithm $\ln(x)$ of its positive argument x.

`double log10(double x)` Returns the logarithm base 10 $\log(x)$ of its positive argument x.

`double pow(double x, double p)` Returns x^p, x to the power of p.

`double pow(double x, int p)` Returns x^p, x to the power of p, with p an integer.

`double sin(double t)` Returns the sine of the angle t.

`double sinh(double t)` Returns the hyperbolic sine of the t, $\sinh(t) = (e^t - e^{-t})/2$.

`double tan(double t)` Returns the tangent of the angle t.

`double tanh(double t)` Returns the hyperbolic tangent of the argument t, $\tanh(t) = \sinh(t)/\cosh(t)$.

`double sqrt(double x)` Returns the square root of its nonnegative argument x.

A piece of advice: Use the specialized functions `sqrt` and `exp` in preference to pow. Compute $\sqrt{x}$ with `sqrt(x)`, not `pow(x, 0.5)`. The `sqrt` function is optimized for taking square roots, and pow is not. Similarly, use `exp(x)` to compute e^x, rather than `pow(exp(1.0), x)`, or, egads, `pow(2.718, x)`:

Here is a sample use of the math library.

mathExamples.cpp

```
1  // ================================================================
2  // mathExamples.cpp
3  // Some brief illustrations of standard math library functions
4  // ================================================================
5  #include <iostream>
6  #include <cmath>
7  using namespace std;
```

```
8
9   int main()
10  {
11    const double pi = 2.0 * atan2(1.0,0.0);
12    const double e = exp(1.0);
13
14    cout << "sin(" << 0.25 * pi << ") = " << sin(0.25 * pi)
15         << endl;
16    cout << "exp(" << -10.0 << ")␣=␣" << exp(-10.0)
17         << endl;
18    cout << "log(e)␣=␣" << log(e) << endl;
19
20    return 0;
21  }
```

With the exception of the function `double pow(double x, int p)`, all of these functions take and return values of type `double`. They can also take and return values of type `float`. Thus, both `sin(4.0)` and `sin(4.0F)` will work. However, `sin(4)` is ambiguous in the C++ standard. Some compilers will allow it, but some will complain that they are not sure what version of `sin` to use.

B.2   RANDOM NUMBERS

It is often very useful to produce a sequence of "random" numbers within a program. The precise definition of this is somewhat technical, and the entire issue is complicated by the the fact that we don't *really* want random numbers, but just numbers that appear random—we want *pseudorandom* numbers. But let's not worry about these subtle details. The basic idea of a random number generator is that it hides some internal state information from which it can generate an apparently random sequence of numbers. But the numbers are not really random, and if the random number generator's internal state is reset to a fixed value, the generator will always produce an identical sequence of numbers.

The header file `cstdlib` declares two interesting functions and an interesting constant:

`srand(unsigned int seed)`   Initializes the random number generator's internal state using the value `seed`.

`int rand()`   Every time `rand()` is called, it returns the next number in the pseudorandom sequence generated by the random number generator. The number returned is between 0 and `RAND_MAX`, inclusive.

`RAND_MAX`   The largest random number that the generator will return. You *cannot change this*.

The seeding of the random number generator is a delicate issue. If it's not done, the random number generator will always return the same sequence of random numbers. If it's done carelessly more than once, the sequence of "random" numbers might not be so random. Codes that use the random number generator sometimes ask their users to provide an integer to seed the generator, and some others, especially games, include a strange statement like srand(time(0)). This seeds the random number generator based on the computer's current notion of time. For example,

randTest.cpp

```cpp
1   // ===========================================================
2   // randTest.cpp
3   // Print a bunch of random numbers on standard output
4   // ===========================================================
5   #include <iostream>
6   #include <cstdlib>  // needed for rand and srand
7   #include <ctime>    // needed for time
8   using namespace std;
9
10  int main()
11  {
12     cout << "How many numbers do you want? > ";
13     unsigned int count = 1;
14     cin >> count;  // count == 1 if input fails
15
16     // seed the generator
17     srand(time(0));
18
19     // report largest possible
20     cout << "Maximum random number = " << RAND_MAX << endl;
21
22     for(int counter = 0; counter < count; counter = counter + 1)
23       {
24         cout << rand() << endl;  // different number every time
25       }
26
27     return 0;
28  }
```

If you want random numbers between zero and some other upper limit, you must scale the numbers returned by rand(). You may want to do this by first converting the int returned by rand() to a double using

```cpp
static_cast<double>(rand())
```

We need to do this because integer division would not usefully scale the integer values to a different range. (Why not?) You can always statically cast the resultant double values back to int if need be. The code

```cpp
static_cast<double>(rand())/RAND_MAX
```

will generate pseudorandom double values between 0.0 and 1.0, inclusive.

Note that rand() is not referentially transparent. It returns a different value every time it is called, even though its argument (it has none) does not change. Note also that rand() does not necessarily provide a *good* random number generator.

B.3   FUNCTIONS WITH CHARACTER

The header file cctype (C character types) declares a collection of useful functions, some of which are outlined here:

int isalnum(char c) Returns 1 (true) if c is either a letter or a digit; otherwise, it returns zero (false).

int isalpha(char c) Returns 1 (true) if c is a letter; otherwise, it returns zero (false).

int isdigit(char c) Returns 1 (true) if c is a base 10 digit (i.e., one of '0' through '9'); otherwise, it returns zero (false).

int islower(char c) Returns 1 (true) if c is a lowercase letter; otherwise, it returns zero (false).

int isspace(char c) Returns 1 (true) if c is a whitespace character; otherwise, it returns zero (false).

int isupper(char c) Returns 1 (true) if c is an uppercase letter; otherwise, it returns zero (false).

int isxdigit(char c) Returns 1 (true) if c is a base 16 digit (i.e., one of '0' through '9', 'A' through 'F' or 'a' through 'f'); otherwise, it returns zero (false).

int tolower(char c) Converts its argument c to lowercase (if c is a letter), and returns this as an int.

int toupper(char c) Converts its argument c to uppercase (if c is a letter), and returns this as an int.

Note that the functions that test the truth or falsity of some preposition return an int value; these functions were created long before the bool type existed. However, no special action is needed to deal with this because bool is compatible with the notion that true is 1 and false is 0. Also note that the functions tolower and toupper, which should return a char, actually return int values. Since a char is an integer type, this usually requires no special consideration, but occasionally it does. Consider the following code:

```
1   char c = 'X';
2
3   // convert it to lowercase
4   char cLower = tolower(c);  // cLower = 'x' -- ok
5
6   // but this is no good
```

```
7   cout << c << "␣in␣lower␣case␣is␣"
8        << tolower(c) << endl;   // goes awry
9
10  // this fixes the problem
11  cout << c << "␣in␣lower␣case␣is␣"
12       << static_cast<char>(tolower(c)) << endl;   // ok
```

When we assign an int to a char, as in line 4, there is no problem; a char is an integer type and the conversion occurs without a problem. But when we throw an int to standard output using cout, as on line 8, an integer value is presented to us in standard output. If we want to see it as a character, we need to cast it to a char before it is pitched to cout, as is done on line 12.

B.4 STANDARD I/O

C++ provides a set of data objects for writing data to standard output, getting data from standard input, and writing data to standard error. These I/O (input/output) channels are specific cases of the general C++ text stream objects, in which data into or out of a code is seen as a stream of characters, organized into "lines" separated by a special newline character '\n'. There are four standard text streams provided to every C++ program by including the iostream header file:

cin Access to standard input. Tied to cout, so that data written to cout will appear to the user before cin attempts its next data read.

cout Buffered access to standard output. Tied to cin, so that data written to cout will appear to the user before cin attempts its next data read.

cerr Unbuffered output to standard error. Data written to cerr appears to the user as quickly as possible.

clog Buffered access to standard error.

All of these I/O text streams are declared and initialized by including the header file iostream. They are placed in the std namespace, and so you must either refer to them using the fully qualified name, like std::cin, or else you must write the statement using namespace std; in your code to include the facilities from std into the global namespace.

Data written to the buffered output streams, using statements like

```
cout << "hello";
```

is placed into storage (a buffer) and only later, when convenient, actually presented to the user. Buffering is generally a performance enhancement. Writing any quantity of data requires turning control over to the operating system, and also involves the operating system directly accessing hardware devices; this imposes some amount of overhead for writing any data. It is much more efficient to amortize this overhead over a large quantity of data. Buffering allows this, since a large quantity of data can be accumulated in a buffer and sent to the operating system in one burp.

Input Issues   The numeric data types can all be read and written from text streams using the extraction (>>) and insertion (<<) operators. char and string data types can also be read and written using these operators, but these operators ignore whitespace (spaces, tabs, and newlines) on input, so

```
char c;
string s;

std::cin >> c; // will not read a space, tab or newline
std::cin >> s; // will not read a string containing spaces,
               // tabs or newlines.
```

It should be realized that the standard I/O text streams are not really designed for complex interaction with human users; more complicated mechanisms are required for that.

Here are some methods attached to the standard input stream cin, which you may find useful:

cin.fail() Returns true if the last operation on cin failed. All subsequent operations on cin will do nothing, until the stream is reset (e.g., with cin.clear()).

cin.clear() Resets cin so that it will again attempt input operations.

cin.get() Reads one char from cin; does *not* ignore whitespace.

cin.unsetf(ios::skipws) Tells cin to stop skipping whitespace, so that, for example, cin >> c; would be able to read a space character.

cin.setf(ios::skipws) Tells cin to start skipping whitespace.

Note that if you write a statement like cin >> i;, where i is an integer, and the user types in something that can't be an integer, like abcd, then the input operation will fail (cin.fail() == true). But worse, the characters 'a', 'b', 'c', and 'd' that the user typed are still in the input stream. So the following code will loop forever if the user fails to type in an integer *on the first try*:

```
int i;
cout << "Please type an integer: ";
cin >> i;
while( cin.fail() )
  {
     cin.clear();  // cin will read again
                   // but bad data is still in there

     cout << "That was not an integer. Try again: ";
     cin >> i;  // gets the same bad data all over again
  }
```

The problem is that in the stream model of input the user enters data on one end, and your code extracts that data from the other end. If `cin >> i;` fails because the available data does not look like an `int`, then the bad data remains at the front of the stream, unhandled. We must write code to consume this junk data ourselves. Here is one simple approach, that although imperfect, may be adequate:

getInt.cpp

```
1   // =================================================================
2   // getInt.cpp
3   // Trys to read a single integer, interactively, from standard
4   // input
5   // =================================================================
6   #include <iostream>
7   #include <string>
8   using namespace std;
9
10  int getInt()
11  {
12    int i;
13    string junk_line;
14
15    cout << "Please type an integer: ";
16    cin >> i;
17    while( cin.fail() )
18      {
19        cin.clear();  // cin will read again
20                      // but bad data is still in there
21        getline(cin, junk_line);  // read to end of line
22                                  // this removes characters
23                                  // from the stream
24
25        cout << "That was not an integer. Try again: ";
26        cin >> i;
27      }
28    return i;
29  }
```

This function could be improved by imposing a maximum number of tries before it gives up on the user. Other improvements are also possible, but interactive interaction with humans is always a difficult problem.

Note also that a statement like `cin >> i;` will read as much from the input stream as makes sense for an integer, and then leave the rest. So if the user types in 123.3, the integer read will be 123, and the input stream will be left with the characters '.' and '3' sitting in it. If the next input operation tries to obtain an integer, it will fail, because it will see that '.' at the front of the stream.

Output issues   The output streams also provide some useful formatting facilities. I will describe these for cout, but they apply to all output streams, including clog and cerr:

cout << endl; The identifier endl can be thrown into an output stream. The effect is to place a newline in the output stream, and to flush its buffer and thus cause the buffered data to be pushed out to the operating system and presented to the user.

cout.setf(ios::scientific) Show floating point numbers in scientific notation.

cout.unsetf(ios::scientific) Show floating point numbers in either scientific or fixed-point format, as seems appropriate (unless ios::fixed is set).

cout.setf(ios::fixed) Show floating point numbers in floating point notation.

cout.unsetf(ios::fixed) Show floating point numbers in either scientific or fixed-point format, as seems appropriate (unless ios::scientific is set).

streamsize cout.precision(streamsize p) Sets the number of digits displayed after the decimal point to p. Returns the old value of precision, so you can save it and reset it if you need to. streamsize is an integer type. (*Note:* Some library implementations require the precision to be set before every output operation, or else a default precision of 6 is used.)

streamsize cout.width(streamsize w) Sets the minimum width of the field (number of characters) used to display an output value to w. Returns the previous width, so you can save it to reset the width to a previous value. Unneeded space is padded with the fill character. streamsize is an integer type. (*Note:* Some library implementations require the width to be set before every output operation, or else a default width is used.)

char cout.fill(char c) Sets the character used to pad a display field to c. The old fill character is returned, so you can save it for later reuse, if desired.

cout.fail() Returns true if the last operation on cout failed.

This last method, cout.fail(), is worth considering. Why could writing data to cout fail? If standard output is connected to a file, and if there is no more space to write data to that file, then writing to cout could fail. A concern for the possibility of failure is always worthwhile, especially when some external resource is being manipulated.

B.5 FILE STREAMS

I will consider only text file streams. These behave nearly identically to the four standard text streams, but they are directly attached to files. Two data types are of interest, ifstream and ofstream, both of which are declared in the fstream header and placed in the std namespace. ifstream is used for data being read from a file (input file stream), and ofstream is used for data being written to a file (output file stream).

File streams can be connected to a file using the open method. So if ifstream in; is used to declare the object in to be an ifstream, then the statement in.open(name.

c_str()); can be used to attach the stream to a file whose name is stored in string name. Note that many C++ libraries require the string to be converted to a C-style string before being passed to open, as I have done here. The C++ standard allows either a string or a C-style string to be used. The close() method for ifstream and ofstream objects will detach the external file from the stream.

Here is a long example using input and output file streams:

longWords.cpp

```cpp
1   // ================================================================
2   // longWords.cpp
3   // Counts and records long words from a dictionary
4   // ================================================================
5   #include <iostream>
6   #include <fstream>
7   #include <string>
8   #include <cstdlib>
9   using namespace std;
10
11  void openFiles(ifstream & in, ofstream & out);
12  unsigned int getUInt();
13  void findLongWords(ifstream & in, ofstream & out,
14                     unsigned int & count, unsigned int length);
15
16  // =====================>> main <<=========================
17  int main()
18  {
19
20    // open files
21    ifstream infile;
22    ofstream outfile;
23    openFiles(infile, outfile);
24
25    // get word length
26    cout << "Input_minimal_length_of_long_words:>_";
27    unsigned int length;
28    length = getUInt();
29
30    // find long words
31    unsigned int count = 0;
32    findLongWords(infile, outfile, count, length);
33
34    // report
35    cout << "Found_" << count << "_long_words\n";
36
37    infile.close();
38    outfile.close();
```

```
39
40     return EXIT_SUCCESS;
41   }
42
43
44   // ======================>> openFiles <<======================
45   void openFiles(ifstream & in, ofstream & out)
46   {
47     // Attempts to open the in and out streams
48
49     cout << "Dictionary_to_check:> ";
50     string input_name;
51     getline(cin, input_name);   // whole line
52
53     cout << "File_for_list_of_long_words:>_";
54     string output_name;
55     getline(cin, output_name);   // whole line
56
57
58     in.open(input_name.c_str());
59     if( in.fail() )
60       {
61         cerr << input_name << "_did_not_open" << endl;
62         exit(EXIT_FAILURE);
63       }
64
65     out.open(output_name.c_str());
66     if( out.fail() )
67       {
68         cerr << output_name << "_did_not_open" << endl;
69         exit(EXIT_FAILURE);
70       }
71
72   }
73
74
75   // ======================>> getUInt <<======================
76   unsigned int getUInt()
77   {
78     const unsigned int maxTrys = 10;
79     unsigned int i;
80     unsigned int trys = 0;
81     string junk_line;
82
83     cin >> i;
84     trys = trys + 1;
```

```
85      while( cin.fail() && trys < maxTrys)
86        {
87          cin.clear();
88          getline(cin, junk_line);  // read junk to end of line
89
90          cout << "That was not an integer. Try again:> ";
91          cin >> i;
92          trys = trys + 1;
93        }
94
95      if( trys >= maxTrys )
96        {
97          cerr << "Giving up...\n";
98          exit(EXIT_FAILURE);
99        }
100
101     return i;
102   }
103
104   // =====================>> findLongWords <<==================
105   void findLongWords(ifstream & in, ofstream & out,
106                      unsigned int & count, unsigned int length)
107   {
108     count = 0;
109     string word;
110
111     while( not in.fail() )
112        {
113          in >> word;  // get whitespace delimited word
114          if( word.size() >= length )
115            {
116              // we found a long word!
117              count = count + 1;
118              out << word << endl;
119              if( out.fail() )
120                {
121                  // something wrong!
122                  cerr << "Can't write " << word
123                       << " to output file.\n";
124                  cerr << "Giving up...\n";
125                  exit(EXIT_FAILURE);
126                }
127            }
128        }
129   }
```

Here is a sample run of this code, checking my system dictionary for words 20 characters in length, or longer:

```
1  [hagar@localhost Code]$ ./longWords
2  Dictionary to check:> /usr/share/dict/words
3  File for list of long words:> impressiveWords
4  Input minimal length of long words:> 20
5  Found 7 long words
6  [hagar@localhost Code]$
```

Here is the list of words that were written into the file **impressiveWords**:

impressiveWords

```
1  antidisestablishmentarianism
2  electroencephalogram
3  electroencephalograph
4  electroencephalography
5  Mediterraneanization
6  Mediterraneanizations
7  nondeterministically
```

B.6 STRINGS

The string class is defined in the standard header string. A string object can be declared and initialized in a number of ways, including:

string s; Declares empty string.

string s(char * cstr); Creates a string and initialize it from a C string.

string s = s2; Used when s2 is a preexisting string or a C string. This really creates an empty string and copies the string s2 into it.

Here are some examples of these string creation patterns:

```
1  string s;  // zero length empty string
2  string str("Hi_there"); // initialize from C string
3  string greet(str);      // copy
4  string welcome = str;   // assign copy
```

Table B.1 lists a number of operators that are defined for string's. In addition, strings support a number of method routines. In this list s and s1 are assumed to be of string

TABLE B.1 **A Collection of Operators Defined for Strings. Both** s **and** s2 **are of the** string **type.**

Operator	Semantics
s[i]	Array indexing of a string with integer index i
s = s2	Assigns copy of s2 to s
s < s2	Evaluates true if s is less than s2, else false
s > s2	Evaluates true if s is greater than s2, else false
s == s2	Evaluates true if s is equal to s2, else false
s != s2	Evaluates false if s is equal to s2, else true
s <= s2	Evaluates true if s is less than or equal to s2, else false
s >= s2	Evaluates true if s is greater than or equal to s2, else false
s + s2	Evaluates to a new string that contains s concatenated with s2

type. size_type is an integral type defined by the C++ library implementor; it is likely either an int or an unsigned int, but its precise type is of little concern. We can place either an int or an unsigned int where a parameter of type size_type is called for. Here are some noteworthy string methods:

s.append(string s2) Appends string s2 to string s.

s.erase(size_type offset, size_type len) Removes len characters from s, starting at offset.

s.find(string s2) Searches for s2 within s and returns the index of the first character of the first match. Returns s.npos if no match is found.

s.insert(size_type offset, string s2) Inserts string s2 into s starting at offset.

size_type s.npos An integer value that is never a valid index into the string s.

s.push_back(char c) Appends char c to string s.

s.replace(size_type offset, size_type num, string s2) Replaces num characters in string s with the whole string s2, starting at offset in string s.

s.resize(size_type len) Resizes the string to length len, truncating it or padding it with null characters as needed.

size_type s.size() Returns number of char's in string s.

s.substr(size_type offset, size_type len) Returns a new string identical to s[offset]...s[offset + len].

The ordering of strings is lexicographical (as in a dictionary) but is case-sensitive and with all characters being significant. The ordering is not totally specified in the C++ standard, since different languages and cultures have different natural orderings for such things. You can expect that in English-speaking locales the ordering of the letters will be much as you expect it, from 'a' to 'z'.

One additional and very useful procedure defined in the string header is istream & getline(istream & is, string & s). This procedure reads an entire line, up to the newline, from the input stream is and stores the line in s. The new-line character itself is discarded. Note that this "procedure" actually returns the same `istream` reference that is passed into it. There is no need to exploit this. The following loop will read all the lines from an input stream until it is exhausted:

```
1  string s;
2  getline(is, s);
3  while( not is.fail() )
4    {
5      // do something useful with line in s
6
7      // try to get another line
8      getline(is, s);
9    }
```

B.7   VECTOR

The `vector` type is declared in the standard header file `vector` and provides a very full-featured data management system with array semantics. Vectors can be declared and initialized using these patterns:

vector< T > v; Declares an empty vector holding objects of type T.

vector< T > v(len); Declares a vector holding len (an integer type) objects of type T. The values of the elements of the vector will be initialized in a type-dependent way (and the compiler must be able to determine how to build an object of type T).

vector< T > v(len, e); Declares a vector holding len (an integer type) objects of type T. The values of the elements of the vector will be initialized using copies of e (and the compiler must be able to copy objects of type T).

Here are a couple examples of `vector` creation:

```
1  vector< double > v;          // empty vector of doubles
2  vector< double > v(100, 0.0); // vector of 100 zeros
```

Here is a list of basic methods and operators on the vector class; v is assumed to have been declared as vector< T >, and similarly for v2.

v2 = v Assigns *a copy* of v to v2.

v.assign(size_type num, T e) Replaces the contents of v with num copies of e.

T & v.at(size_type i) Returns a reference to the element at offset i.

T & v[i] Refers to the element at offset i (with no check on i).

T & v.back() Returns a reference to the last element of the vector.

`void v.clear()` Empties the vector.

`bool v.empty()` Returns `true` if the vector is empty.

`T & v.front()` Returns a reference to the first element of the vector.

`void v.pop_back()` Removes the last element of the vector.

`void v.push_back(T e)` Appends the element e to the vector.

`void v.resize(size_type newSize)` Changes the vector to be of size `newSize`.

`void v.resize(size_type newSize, T e)` Changes the vector to be of size `newSize` and puts e into any newly created elements.

`size_type v.size()` Returns number of elements in vector v.

There is some question about the efficiency of the `vector` class for the sort of numerically intensive computation that is the heart of much of engineering analysis, but an introductory text is not the place to concern ourselves with such things. A good implementation of the `vector` class is probably fast enough for all but the most intensive applications, and the ease with which `vector`'s can be managed makes them very worthwhile for routine use.[1]

---

[1]The C++ standard library also includes the `valarray`, which is another class supporting array semantics but intended to be more highly tuned for managing arrays of numbers. Implementations of `valarray` have varied greatly in their quality, but do seem to be improving. Many nonstandard arraylike classes are also available, and some of these (notably the Blitz library) can be wickedly fast (but Blitz can bring all but the best compilers to their knees).

INDEX